HITCHCOCK'S FILMS REVISITED

ROBIN WOOD

HITCHCOCK'S FILMS REVISITED

REVISED EDITION

COLUMBIA UNIVERSITY PRESS   NEW YORK

COLUMBIA UNIVERSITY PRESS
Publishers Since 1893
New York   Chichester, West Sussex
Copyright © 2002, 1989 Columbia University Press
Frontispiece: Copyright © 1960 Shamley Productions, Inc.
All rights reserved
Printed in the United States of America

LIBRARY OF CONGRESS CATALOGING-IN-PUBLICATION DATA
Wood, Robin, 1931–
    Hitchcock's films revisited / Robin Wood. – Rev. ed.
        p. cm.
    The revised 1989 edition includes a new preface and a new chapter on "Marnie."
    Includes bibliographical references and index.
    ISBN 978-0-231-12695-3 (paper: alk. paper)
        1. Hitchcock, Alfred, 1899—Criticism and interpretation. I. Title.
    PN1998.3.H58 W66 2002
    791.43'0233'092–dc 21   2002067257

p 20 19 18 17 16 15 14 13 12 11

Book design by Ken Venezio

For Takeo-san with love

CONTENTS

BOOK TWO
HITCHCOCK'S FILMS REVISITED

Photos follow pages 98, 194, and 290.

PREFACE TO THE REVISED EDITION: THE EVOLUTION OF A FILM CRITIC; OR, THE PERSONAL IS POLITICAL

For Thom Loree

An invitation from my editor to write a new preface (to a book that already contains two lengthy introductions!) has given me the opportunity to develop a concern that has been on my mind for some time: an examination (and exposure) of the various factors (historical, cultural, personal) that underlie and determine the *kind* of criticism that one writes. This book has been written over a period of more than forty years: the chapter on *Psycho* (the earliest piece of film criticism I ever attempted, with the exception of an essay on Ingmar Bergman's *The Virgin Spring*, cowritten in Sweden with Göran Persson) was written in 1960 and first published in *Cahiers du Cinéma* in a French translation; a sketch for the new chapter on *Marnie* in the present volume first appeared in *CineAction 50* for the Hitchcock centenary of 1999. The various writings that have accumulated in this book cover, in fact, four distinct periods of my life: the original *Hitchcock's Films* (1965) was written during the four years preceding publication; the somewhat jaundiced and ungenerous revisionist view expressed in the addendum to it—which I cannot entirely retract, its sense of Hitchcock's limitations having I think a certain validity—was produced in the early 1970s, during the most difficult and painful period of my life; the fundamentally different approach of the new (and in my opinion vastly superior) essays in *Hitchcock's Films Revisited* (1990) owes that difference to a different environment (Canada), a different life, and a different cultural-historical period (the aftermath of

1960s/1970s radicalism, when one could still cling to more hope for the future of our civilization than seems possible today); I am writing the present preface in a time when optimism is becoming, almost daily, a commodity that evaporates whenever one tries to grasp it. I should add that I am now in my seventies and have recently gone through a near-death experience and a month in hospital, a valuable *memento mori*. I may last another twenty years (to write yet another preface?); on the other hand, it seems an appropriate moment to take stock and try to account for myself.

I must reiterate here my disbelief in the possibility of so-called objective or scientific criticism. There are of course degrees, which are partly degrees of concealment. I have never attempted to conceal the personal nature of my own work, even to the extent of calling one of my books (defiantly, at the height of the semiotics movement) *Personal Views*, in which I exposed (I believe definitively) the highly personal animus behind Peter Wollen's "structuralist" reading of Howard Hawks in his generally brilliant and stimulating *Signs and Meaning in the Cinema*. A personal voice is always present in the work of the semiotician whose work I most admire, Stephen Heath. It is true that semiotics made possible a whole slew of academic articles and analyses in which the personal voice is drowned out by the methodology, but they are strictly "painting by numbers," always unreadable and now forgotten. I don't expect every critic to tell his life story (as I am selectively doing here), but I think it is only honest to make clear to readers: "Here I am. *I* am writing this. I am not infallible. I am just a human being like yourself. What I have to say and the way in which I say it was determined by my own background, my own experience, my own understanding (or lack thereof). I make no pretense to Absolute Truth."

HITCHCOCK'S FILMS (1965): 1960–1969 *

Critical   I think I can claim for the original *Hitchcock's Films* at least the distinction of oddity. Its critical background consisted, really, of two powerful influences which happen to be completely incompatible: the criticism of F. R. Leavis, whose lectures I attended at Cambridge and

---

*Each period of my development is identified by a book (with its date of publication), followed by the time frame.

whose intransigence and integrity remain a model I struggle and fail to live up to, and *Cahiers du Cinéma* in its "Nouvelle Vague" heyday. Had Leavis's influence not been so overwhelming, and had I had more confidence in my own voice, I might well have written literary rather than film criticism; as it was, I was fully aware that anything I wrote about literature would be merely a pale imitation. I had been in thrall to cinema (especially Hollywood cinema) since I saw *Top Hat* at the age of five, and the Astaire/Rogers movies meant to me, during a deeply disturbed childhood, rather what the songs of Grace Chang mean to Tsai Ming-Liang in one of my favorite films of recent years, *The Hole*: they helped make life bearable. My Cambridge days (1949–1953) had their own oddity, attending Leavis's lectures in the mornings, then sneaking off (when my intellectual friends, to whom I stood in awe, weren't looking) to see *Red River*, *The Thing from Another World*, *Monkey Business*, and *Gentlemen Prefer Blondes* in the afternoon. (My level of cinematic awareness can be estimated from the fact that I didn't realize they were all by the same director until about ten years later, although I already loved them.) Around the same time, I was discovering the foreign "art" movies, mainly French (Marcel Carné, Marcel Pagnol, René Clair, Julien Duvivier, the *auteurs* of the period, who are today greatly in need of reassessment, or were we *entirely* wrong?) and diligently reading *Sight and Sound*. After Cambridge I taught in a variety of schools, and it was a visiting French student of extraordinary brilliance, Philippe Lefournier, who introduced me to *Cahiers*. Its influence on me is difficult to explain, seeing that my French was poor and I could understand very little of the magazine's often abstruse and fanciful prose. I suppose what was crucial was simply that, with its "Politique des Auteurs," it licensed me to love openly the films I had always loved in secret. It opened the way to my sudden urge to write the article on *Psycho* (which struck me like a thunderbolt; I came out of the theater in a complete daze and could barely speak). When the article was rejected by *Sight and Sound* I sent it to *Cahiers* "on the rebound," never having the least thought that it would be accepted (or, for that matter, that they would even read it). I had to read the letter of acceptance (from Eric Rohmer, no less, with a promise of sixty francs) about six times before I began to believe it. The money never reached me, and I was much too shy to write and complain. But I realize now that my career as a film critic dates from that moment. The British film scene (too long dominated by *Sight and Sound*, which was far beyond its early and short-lived prime) was just opening up, all the younger critics were under *Cahiers*'s influence, and here was someone not only published in that totally awesome journal but featured as the lead article.

So much depends on chance. If Rohmer had not accepted the article, if it had been rejected or (as I had expected) simply ignored, would I have gone on writing film criticism (I had certainly not thought of myself as a critic)? Would I have been taken up by *Oxford Opinion*, and subsequently *Movie*, founded by the Oxford magazine's critics? Would I have been invited to write a book on Hitchcock (it would never have occurred to me to propose such a thing)? I doubt it. I would probably now be a (retired) British schoolteacher, looking back on a much less hectic, confusing, and unconventional life than mine has proved, for better or worse, to be.

Political/Cultural/Personal   The political can be dealt with summarily: when I wrote *Hitchcock's Films* I was still totally apolitical. I can't even remember if I voted (though if I did, it would probably have been for the quasi-socialist Labor party, but without any real conviction or even interest, just out of a very vague and generalized sense of human decency). The cultural and the personal go together, inseparably.

Because of my lack of any political interest, of any awareness of my own position within the culture—because, in short, I was completely trapped within what we would later come to call "the dominant ideology," incapable of seeing it as such, accepting it unthinkingly as "truth"— the major determining factor on my critical thinking was my personal life and its underpinning psychology. When I wrote *Hitchcock's Films* I was living (a part of me now wants to say "masquerading," though a part of me then believed in the masquerade quite passionately) as a happily married bourgeois family man, with a wife, a little suburban home complete with garden, and (by the date of publication) three children. No one in the world (I think), except my wife, knew or even guessed that I was gay, and that beneath the apparent happiness and security lurked Bergmanesque demons and a fairly pervasive despair. If anyone guessed, it was from my writings, not from my behavior (I preserved strict monogamy throughout the ten years of the marriage): an article in *Movie* on *Advise and Consent*, and parts of my book on Bergman (which Peter Harcourt once described as my "autobiography"—perhaps, at that time, it was). I tended to gravitate rather obviously to gay references or aspects, always treating gayness (I'm glad to say) sympathetically.

I know people (especially *young* people) today, when gay liberation has taken such strides, find it difficult to understand, let alone empathize with, the situation I have described. They didn't grow up in middle-class Britain in the 1930s and 1940s. I have traced my homosexual responses back to the age of six, but (such was the secrecy and horror of it) I didn't even discover the word *homosexual* until I read a biography of Tchaikovsky around the age of fifteen. That, at least, made me aware that there were other people like me, that I wasn't just some appalling freak. On the other hand, the book emphasized (and I think rather relished) the composer's shame and misery, and the fact that he tried to commit suicide. This was at a time when the word *sex* was never used in polite society, except to differentiate between males and females ("the gentle sex," etc.). Sex (in the sense of "having sex") was still, in D. H. Lawrence's famous phrase, "the dirty little secret." I was in my twenties when I first confessed (in a letter to my best friend) that I was gay, and (although his response was very kind) I never felt at ease with him again. There were of course gay bars, meeting places . . . but I never heard of them and would have been much too terrified to frequent them: gay sex, even between consenting adults in the privacy of their own homes, was legally punishable by up to ten years' imprisonment. Is it so very surprising that so many gay men deluded themselves into thinking that, with a little practice, they could become heterosexual, hence got married? In my case, I explained everything to the wholly admirable woman I asked to marry me, and whose life I subsequently ruined (temporarily, at least). My error was that I asked her to "save" me, a plea to which she, being a beautiful and noble person, responded. I should of course have realized that a gay man who has never been anything else cannot be "saved" and certainly, today, shouldn't want to be. Like so much else, the social taboo on homosexuality did irreparable harm to so many human lives; outside the major urban areas of the West, it still does.

We were, in most respects, the ideal bourgeois family, according to the traditional ideological model: husband as breadwinner, wife as household manager and mother—a model that, in those days, neither of us questioned, although my wife (I think she would prefer not to be named) had a university degree and could have been developing a career as well as I. She was even envied by certain of her friends because I took an active part in the home, cooking sometimes, bathing and tending to the children, the first two of whom had been born at home, in my presence, a wonderful experience I was denied with the third, when we had moved to a more urban and "enlightened" location. The only problem was sex, which I could just about manage but never (at that time) really enjoyed. I find it somewhat extraordinary that my feeble, brief attempts at intercourse produced three children. My wife always seemed satisfied, something I could never understand and couldn't bring myself to ask about; I suppose it's possible that, like so many women back in those days, it was as much as she'd been taught to expect, but that never occurred to me at the time, women's liberation being still in its infancy. I used to agonize for hours over my inadequacy, and fantasize about men, which made me feel even guiltier. I was Bergman's perfect victim, ready for total identification with, for example, Max von Sydow in *Hour of the Wolf* or Ingrid Thulin in *The Silence*: they were dramatizations up there on the screen of the "real" me, the secret self hidden beneath the cheerful surface—a surface I could never, of course, have preserved had it not had a degree of authenticity. Much of the time I was happy and satisfied, teaching English in high school, coming home to a family I loved.

Quite early in our marriage I discovered that my wife was homophobic—not in any ranting, religious-Fundamentalist way, but casually, with the ignorance of the ordinary prejudices of that time. And we could never talk about my homosexual desires: the few times I tried she simply shut herself off. I think now the subject terrified her at some level—that she *knew* more than she could bring herself consciously to face. Would it have made any difference? I doubt it. I don't think it would have made it any easier for me to cope. I suppose what I always wanted (without ever daring to formulate such a thought) was for the marriage to continue while I was allowed the occasional "diversion" on the side, on the "Don't ask, don't tell" principle. But she could never have countenanced such an arrangement, and I doubt whether it would have satisfied me, although certain later developments suggest that it might have.

All this is the background to the writing of *Hitchcock's Films*: its very basis is the commitment to what I had been taught to see as "normality," inseparably fused with my knowledge that I would never be "normal." The book lacked any awareness whatever of what we now call "sexual politics" (see, for example, the difference between my treatment of *Vertigo* there and my very different analysis toward the end of this book). It examined the films in terms of a "surface order" and an "underlying chaos." That remains, I think, a viable way of reading them, but it leaves out so much that matters to us today: if that was all there was, would the films still be so resonant? It also has the very unfortunate effect of seeing life in terms of some unchanging and unchangeable "human condition," hence precludes all awareness of social conditioning, implying that radical change is impossible. It makes these very dangerous films "safe": their power to disturb is enclosed within a metaphysic that makes irrelevant the capacity that human beings have to transform their society. From my present viewpoint, then, the original book itself becomes dangerous because it encourages a kind of stoical despair rather than anger and protest. In essentials it points ahead a few years to my book on Bergman, which offers more of the same but much more so, Bergman's films (with their almost total lack of interest in anything beyond some abstract and unanalyzed "human condition") lending themselves far more readily to such treatment than Hitchcock's. Of my early books, the one that most successfully evaded conscription into my personal psychology was the one on Hawks, which is perhaps why today it seems to me the best of them, the least in need of "revisionist" thinking. Hawks's films stubbornly opposed any such attempts at assimilation, neither of their complementary worlds (action/adventure, screwball comedy) having much affinity with my own. Indeed, they are built upon an uncompromising repudiation of it, which doubtless accounts both for my attraction to them back then and my continuing delight in them today. They are the films to which I most often return; just recently I have been quite astounded by the contemporary relevance of *Only Angels Have Wings* and *Monkey Business*.

There was another reason why I moved into film criticism, which had nothing to do with Dr. Leavis. From a very early age I had written stories; at the age of twelve I wrote what at that time I believed to be a novel (it might have covered twenty pages of print). During my years at Cambridge I wrote stories for a student magazine (one of which, about the sexual abuse of a child, was considered very shocking and had to be bowdlerized by the editor as it used the "f" word). By the time of my marriage I had written longer pieces, long stories, short novels. I continued to do so during the first years of married life, and proudly showed these to my wife. They were received with total silence. I would wait a week, two weeks, for her reaction, and eventually have to ask. She was not encouraging, just saying something like "Yes, it's quite good," but in a tone that seemed to add "I hated it." I realized that she was disturbed by the sexual content, though I had been careful to exclude any explicit gay content. I began writing film criticism; it would be thirty years before I again attempted fiction.

What amazes me, looking back at those ten years, is how prolific I was: a full-time schoolteacher (with a family) who produced books on Hitchcock, Hawks, Bergman, and Arthur Penn along with substantial articles and essays on Godard, Makavejev, Antonioni, Preminger, and other Hollywood directors, and began a book on Chabrol (in collaboration with Michael Walker), completed during the following two years in Canada. For all of this I must thank my publishers: Peter Cowie for the original *Hitchcock's Films*, the British Film Institute (and especially Peter Wollen) for *Howard Hawks*, and Ian Cameron, cofounder of *Movie* and editor-publisher of the *Movie Paperbacks* for the rest. I have never again written so much in so short a time, even though my future life was to offer me far more leisure hours.

PERSONAL VIEWS (1974): 1969–1977

Personal   One fateful morning a letter arrived from Peter Harcourt, whom my wife and I had known in England, and who had returned to his native Canada to found a film department (in those days an extremely rare undertaking, one of those newfangled notions that the more conservative academics passionately oppose) at Queen's University. Having taught film single-handed for a couple of years, he had secured the right to a second appointment. Was I interested?

I laughed. It seemed a ridiculous idea. I didn't have a degree above a second-class B.A., and the idea of teaching in a university terrified me. But my wife said "Why not? You could do it," so we went to Canada.

Was it the more permissive atmosphere of North America, or the very different milieu of university life, with its love affairs, its marital breakups (in one of which we became deeply entangled, as confidants of all four participants), its pervasive sense of "Who's sleeping with whom?" Or was it quite simply my own newfound sense of greater freedom, greater authority, responsibility and adventure, teaching what was then an entirely new discipline to university students after the years of high school English? I know I suddenly felt a new freedom, my fantasies began to seem more practicable, more *possible*. After about a year, at the age of thirty-nine and after ten years of strict monogamy (my wife being the only person with whom I had ever had sex), I floundered blindly into my first homosexual experience, during a weekend away from home in Toronto, with a man probably fifteen years or more younger than myself.

Through no fault of his (he took it for granted that I was thoroughly experienced in one-night stands), it was a truly horrible, near-traumatic experience, physically painful, emotionally and psychologically devastating. After he left I lay for hours on the bed in my hotel room, bleeding, trembling violently from head to foot. But when I woke up the next morning, I think I already sensed that there would be no turning back: what I had spent my whole life longing for and dreading had happened, the taboo had been broken, and abruptly anything was possible.

The immediate consequence, however, was quite unpredictable; I'm not sure I understand it even now. I returned home on the train in a complete daze, I remember nothing. I walked into our rented home and found my wife in the kitchen. I know others were there (our children? a friend dropped in to visit?), but I ran to her, took her in my arms, suddenly loving her as I never had before. It was as if I had been released from some spell: I had done it and it *didn't matter*; what had been a guilty obsession from around the age of twelve was just an action, something millions of men did every day. There followed an extraordinary six months, the only period in my life when I had a real sexual relationship with a woman. My wife was as surprised as I was, and for that six months I believe we were authentically happy. But I continued to want men, and I began experimenting in secret, feeling a kind of excitement, not taking any of the experiences very seriously though I wanted them to go on: it seemed a very pleasing form of contact.

All this ended abruptly. In the middle of one night, during a trip back to England, in an excess of happiness and confidence, I told my wife everything that had happened. The reaction was immediate, and that night (I see in retrospect) ended the marriage: she turned away from me in hurt and repugnance, and the new relationship I thought we had formed was over. I was plunged back into my Bergmanesque world of guilt and self-disgust. Then, a few months later, I fell in love with the man I was to live with for the next seven years.

I have never (I hope it goes without saying) blamed my wife. I took—and still take—complete responsibility. She had her own moral code, her own passionate and instinctual revulsion. Moreover, she had behind her that massive, virtually omnipotent, force, of the very existence of which I was still unaware, "the dominant ideology."

The two years from the fall of 1971 to the summer of '73 were the most troubled of my life; I cannot imagine how I would have got through them without the support of my lover John, whose strength, intelligence, and readiness to make sacrifices still amaze me. I had a year to go on my three-year contract at Queen's. My wife took our three children back to England, leaving me with an implicit ultimatum: either live with John or renounce all future sexual contact with men and come home to the family. It seems disturbingly typical of me that I became quite incapable of doing either: the choice seemed absolutely impossible. Sexually, with my wife, I had moved virtually overnight from ecstasy to total impotence: I felt that I disgusted her so much that I could scarcely bring myself to touch her. I moved out of our now empty house, spent every weekend with John in Toronto, slept on the floor of my office during the week (most of my salary went to England). I can dredge up only one vivid memory of that Canadian winter: standing on a street corner at night ankle-deep in snow trying to convince myself to throw myself under a car. I got as far as moving forward to the curb as a car approached and preparing for the leap, but the car pulled over and the driver offered me a lift (he was a family friend, a teacher in the university). Eventually I told my wife I was coming "home" (the traditional Hollywood happy ending?). John was quietly sympathetic, never protesting for a moment. My wife came over from England and we had a couple of days together in New York before flying back. In a restaurant, in the middle of lunch, I made the excuse of going to the washroom and phoned John hysterically, saying I couldn't go through with it but I couldn't leave my children. He calmed me down and said he would follow me to England. The worst thing of all is that I couldn't bring myself to tell my wife this. I suppose, somewhere, I was still hoping that some compromise could be reached, but it was too unrealistic a notion to think consciously.

So John (still in his twenties, with a position many fifty-year-olds would dream of, in sole charge of the 16mm division of Universal in Toronto), gave up his job, drew out all his savings, and came to England with all the belongings he didn't sell, on a tourist passport. I've never quite made out John, or done him justice: he is so made up of apparent contradictions, so quiet, so reticent, so practical, so impractical, so "clas-

sical" in his restraint, so "romantic" in his actions, so (apparently) coldly rational in his speech, yet so precipitate in his actions. He was not the
easiest person to live with, in many ways my opposite (or complement?),
with all the willpower that I totally lack and a very highly developed (if
unconventional) personal ethic. In the weeks before his arrival I had
rented a single-room London flat in which we lived (or at least existed)
for the next nine months. It was insufficiently heated, and the truly horrible landlady's reaction to complaints was along the lines of, "Most
people wouldn't let people like you into their houses at all." To which
there was, at that time, no answer. I was allowed to see my children (the
only reason for my return to England) once a week.

Political It is at this point in my life that the critical, the political, and
the personal become inseparable, one blending into the other. But in fact
they always are, if in less obvious ways: in my early life, while unaware
of holding any definable political position, I had been an unquestioning
conservative, "within the ideology," my imbibed conservatism constantly
troubled and threatened by my inner disturbance, my critical writings
reflecting this duality.

Queen's is thought of as a conservative university, its embracing of
Film Studies therefore quite surprising but due largely to Peter Harcourt's
initiative; Peter and I were the only two teachers during my tenure. As far
as I can recall, I had not even heard the word *semiotics* during my three
years' stay there, in those crucial years beginning in May 1969.

When I returned to England, I rapidly discovered that the critical climate had changed completely and radically. Before I left, my early work
(though often criticized by the Establishment for my absurd overvalua-
tions of Hollywood directors) had been treated with a certain respect;
now, to my bewilderment, I was suddenly The Enemy, my books dismissed as outmoded and hopelessly conservative. "Serious" criticism
meant now, and exclusively, semiotics, and its writings were dominated
by names I had not even heard of: Althusser, Barthes, Lacan . . . (not to
mention a whole new vocabulary as foreign to me as Greek). It took
some time for me to figure out what was happening. As a result, I found
it extremely difficult to find work in London. I managed to land a night
school class in Film Study and a daytime class teaching the Romantic
poets (I greatly enjoyed the opportunity to return to literature), plus a
few guest spots. One of these was especially humiliating and I believe

was set up specifically for that purpose: a lecture on Mizoguchi's *Sansho Dayu* (*Sansho the Bailiff*) at the Slade School of Art. I delivered my long-gestated and loving lecture on what was and is still among my favorite films (it later became an essay in *Personal Views*), only to be told roundly by the carefully prepared students that Nöel Burch (a name then new to me) had decreed that all Mizoguchi's late works fell "within the Hollywood codes" and were consequently unworthy of discussion. The resident lecturer who invited me was an old friend and colleague of mine, previously associated (like myself) with *Movie* and now presumably ashamed of it, a recent convert to Burch's strict formalism. He was also a friend of my wife's, and I like to think he set me up as punishment for my conjugal delinquency (a reaction I could respect) rather than from any more petty motivation. The happy result was that I later read Burch's books and learned a great deal from them: they brilliantly illuminated aspects of film I had neglected. He and I, though we have never met, have recently enjoyed a lengthy correspondence on e-mail, acknowledging a mutual, and mutually beneficial, influence. He has now repudiated his early narrow formalism.

The leaders of the British semiotics movement never attempted contact with me, and I was far too terrified to approach (let alone challenge) them. Their view of me and my work was generally reported secondhand and may be inaccurate: I was told that Ben Brewster (one of the editors of *Screen*, the major stronghold of British semiotics) described me as an "unreconstructed humanist," a title I really didn't mind and subsequently used as the title of one of the essays in *Personal Views*, and that Sam Rohdie described me as an "anti-intellectual." When I mentioned the latter to Stephen Heath at one of our all too rare and brief meetings, he expressed surprise and indignation, and I wonder now if he realized how much such a response, coming from him, a critic and thinker of undeniable brilliance, meant to me at the time.

But my lack of communication with them was certainly as much my fault as theirs. I realize now that my instinctual response was to retreat into my childhood sense of total powerlessness and inferiority: I somehow *knew* that they must be right and therefore I must be wrong. I not only didn't speak their language, I didn't fully grasp the political basis of their largely unintelligible writings. I was afraid to speak to them and literally trembled in their presence. It was only later that I realized that they too saw themselves as a group under siege: the major universities, with their habitual conservative dread of the "newfangled," were at that time closed to them on principle. (The semioticians were associated either with the British Film Institute or with London University, regarded as a notoriously "progressive" site of subversive activity.) (I was delighted, subsequently, to learn of Heath's appointment at my own university, Cambridge, and within my own college, Jesus, but that was much later.)

What angered them was my salvation, and I am not proud of this: when, in the middle of that terrible year 1972, Warwick University declared its readiness to appoint its first lecturer in Film Studies, I applied and, to my own astonishment, got the position. My sense of relief was already mixed with guilt: I couldn't help thinking that the post *should* have gone to a semiotician, since they were obviously right and I was obviously wrong. Or to another candidate . . . While I sat waiting for my interview, a young man was seated in another corner. I took him for a student and wondered why he was there. He proved to be Richard Dyer, my chief competitor for the post. We subsequently had a slightly uneasy friendship, and he has long been among my favorite writers on cinema. The anecdote has a happy ending: since my departure, Richard now teaches at Warwick University, along with Victor Perkins, friend and colleague from my *Movie* days, and *another* of my favorite film critics.

My appointment at Warwick saved me. I don't think I can quite say it saved my life but, inspired by my favorite novel, I had several times during that year in London stood right at the edge of a subway platform, in emulation of Anna Karenina. I don't think I could ever have brought myself to jump, of course. Indeed, I rather wonder whether people who think often about suicide are, perhaps, the least likely to do it, and that most actual suicides are spontaneous acts of desperation. I *have* made suicide threats and gestures at various times of my life (they began, I think, when I was about ten years old and was not allowed to see *Suspicion*, the latest film by my then favorite director, on the grounds that it was unsuitable), but they have always been pleas for help rather than true wishes to be dead. I've never really wanted to die, but I have often wished that I had never been born: it would have saved a number of good people so much pain.

I described "the dominant ideology" earlier as virtually omnipotent, but now—thanks partly to what I understood of *Screen* and, especially, Roland Barthes—I began to develop the only weapons with which it can be challenged: awareness, and perpetual vigilance. My later writings will show the degrees of my success and failure, and I leave readers to judge. I had always (like, I find, so many of my students) taken the term *ideology* to refer merely to specific political ideologies, but now I took the leap into seeing it as all-pervasive. Being, it seems, congenitally incapable of abstract thought (I have never been able to read philosophy, always requiring concrete examples before I can understand what exactly is being said), I clarified this new concept for myself as a concrete image, which I have often used subsequently in explaining it in class: an iceberg. Only one-eighth is above the surface (one's consciously held beliefs, opinions, etc.). The other seven-eighths is hidden below: all those assumptions (about life, about morality, about relationships . . .) that one has imbibed from the culture since the moment of birth ("Blue for a boy, pink for a girl . . .") and never questioned. One's task, then, is to uncover as much of the iceberg as possible, subjecting these assumptions to critical scrutiny. This is likely to be a very painful and dangerous process: if all one's most cherished notions—the assumptions by which one has lived life so far—are suddenly no longer "truth" but simply "ideology," one is released from one's shackles but then may abruptly find one's life in ruins. For myself, of course, there was no choice: my life as it had been lived before 1971 was already a wreck. This new conceptualization of ideology merely freed me from despair, and to some extent from my sense of guilt: was it entirely my fault I had lived the way my unexamined assumptions had told me I should?

This account, of course, oversimplifies: ideological awareness is not some kind of instant cure for all one's problems. One can start to recognize cultural determinants, gradually deciding rationally what to accept and what to reject or modify; there remain the problematic dark areas of the Freudian unconscious. I so often do things for what seems a good, sound reason, only to discover, perhaps years later, that that wasn't the reason I did them at all, that the *real* reason was quite other and far less admirable. I have hurt so many people without the least intention of doing so: especially, people I have loved. It sometimes seems to me that I have rushed through life mindlessly, leaving behind a trail of damaged lives. I also tell myself that they were intelligent people who made their own choices, as I made mine, that the responsibility is not exclusively my own. But telling yourself such things doesn't always help. Yeats's haunting, unforgettable phrase summing up human existence, "A blind man battering blind men," continues to linger as a definition of what remains of "the human condition" after "ideology" has been stripped away. Yet Yeats's phrase is, of course, also a part of ideology, and I am not suggesting that the Freudian unconscious somehow exists apart from ideological determination; only that it represents depths of the iceberg that are extremely difficult to reach.

When we moved to Coventry (the nearest city to Warwick University, though most lecturers prefer to live in the more genteel Leamington Spa), John invested all his savings in the down payment on a house at the end of a cul-de-sac in a working-class district; he now had no legal status in the country, hence little hope of finding work, and I had agreed to do my best with the mortgage while continuing my monthly payments to my wife (we became officially divorced during this period). Having my summers largely free, I bolstered our income by teaching summer courses in literature for Britain's Open University (which offered correspondence courses throughout the year). *Anna Karenina* was one of the required texts, and teaching it gave me great pleasure and satisfaction, not only because it is a very great work but also because it gave me practice in unmasking ideology. The experience led to what is perhaps the best essay in *Personal Views*, my only book during this seven-year period. Or perhaps it is merely the essay that meant the most to me personally, its production opening up new critical landscapes. Roughly, I came to see the novel in terms of a battleground between Tolstoy's conscious beliefs (which demanded Anna's—or my?—suicide) and his passionate instinctual commitment to her, which is surely the source of the novel's true greatness and why so many of us return to it, perhaps even forgetting that her suicide is not the end of the book. In short, by rethinking Tolstoy I rethought my own life, and the future opened up before me.

The process was enormously advanced by the entry into my life of Andrew Britton, the major influence on all my subsequent work. Andrew came to me as Warwick University's second graduate student in film; though he was always humble, never making me aware of my inadequacies (of which *he* must have been thoroughly aware), I soon realized that our roles had become reversed: I was the student, he the teacher. (You do not presume to "supervise" a mind like Andrew's.) Andrew died of AIDS many years ago; with his relatively small body of published work (which includes the most devastating assaults on mainstream academic film theory ever written), he remains for me the best film critic in the English language. The failure of university presses to publish his collected writings posthumously is a major component in my contempt for contemporary academia. How would what we call "Film Studies" have been transformed (and entirely for the better) if Andrew had been invited to play a role in it? I still sometimes sense him looking over my shoulder as I write, encouraging me, pushing me a bit further, increasing above all my grasp of ideology and its workings in movies. I still occasionally "dream him alive" again.

Personal Views (never published outside England and long out of print) is a curious work for which I continue to have great affection. Some of it (essays attempting to defend my position against the semioticians) has dated badly and is probably now of no more than historical interest, but much of the remainder (studies of films by Ophuls, Welles, Mizoguchi, etc., which had their origins in my lectures at Queen's) seems to me worth rescuing. I was grateful to the British editor for allowing me a chapter largely on a Russian novel in a book supposedly about movies, just as I am grateful to my present editor for allowing me a lengthy section on a Mozart opera in *Sexual Politics and Narrative Film*. But on a level with the Tolstoy essay in its personal importance to me was my much-reprinted little piece (not in the book), "Responsibilities of a Gay Film Critic." It originated as a lecture at London's National Film Theatre, and was scheduled to be given (I was pleased to learn) during a far more ambitious and groundbreaking season of gay-themed movies and seminars organized by Richard Dyer: I began to feel (however marginal my contribution) a *part* of something. It was, in fact, my official "coming out" moment (though I had already "come out" somewhat surreptitiously in, of all places, the *Times Educational Supplement*, thanks to another progressive editor), which I had delayed as long as I decently could in the interests of my children: in particular, I didn't want my son, the youngest, to get teased in school if it got out that he had a gay father. The politics of "coming out" went hand in hand with the discovery of ideology: to move from being a respectable bourgeois family man to becoming a member of (at that time) a generally despised and vilified minority group was inevitably to become political.

I also wrote essays for *Film Comment* during this period. These included the piece that became (in revised form) the "Afterword" to *Hitchcock's Films*, published in the edition of 1977 though the original was written much earlier. This piece, published as "Lost in the Wood" and attributed to George Kaplan (a name my editor and I thought should be familiar to any Hitchcockian), masqueraded as an attack on myself and my own excesses. This joke resulted, however, in one of my most embarrassing moments. I was invited, shortly after its publication, to give a talk on Hitchcock to the film society of Swansea University in Wales. The organizer, a young man of tremendous enthusiasm and a passionate admirer of my work, met my train. In the ride to the university he turned to me suddenly, very earnest and serious, and said "I have to tell you how much I *hated* that *dreadful* attack on you in *Film Comment.*" I know I should just have kept my mouth shut, but I'm afraid, caught like that, I acknowledged authorship. To this day I feel I was very cruel, but I suppose he would have found out anyway.

I think today that the "Afterword" has a certain validity, and is perhaps more important now than it was back then, when the question "Should we take Hitchcock seriously?" was still open. Today, Hitchcock seems in danger of being elevated to a height where he is beyond criticism, a sure way of turning a great artist into a museum exhibit. If the films are to remain alive for us, they must always be subject to adverse criticism, and their limitations continuously exposed.

I have wonderful memories of life in Coventry with John. A small group of friends collected around us: Andrew, of course, was a constant visitor; and Deborah Thomas, from America, who wrote her thesis on Ingmar Bergman's color films under my nonsupervision; also Tom Ryan, from Australia, who came to study with me, the first graduate student in Film Studies, preceding Andrew by one year, and became our lodger. Deborah remained in England and is now married, a university teacher and author of distinguished articles in addition to two fine books, *Teaching Hollywood* and *Beyond Genre*; Tom returned to Australia, married, and is now (together with his wife) a successful film critic. I recall wonderful summer parties in our intractable, frequently waterlogged back garden. I also recall our splendid salt-of-the-earth neighbors, a working-class family totally unperturbed by having a gay couple move in next door; we left our semiwild cat McCabe with them, confident of his continued well-being. Yet, inevitably, it all fell apart.

There were two main causes. One was John's precarious legal position and the difficulty of getting legitimate work (he did some film programming for the university), leading to his uneasiness with new acquaintances and constantly dreading that favorite party opener, "So, what do *you* do?" But our relationship was also developing severe internal cracks, and here the responsibility was all mine. My abrupt entry into gay life, after twenty-nine years of total abstinence and ten years of heterosexual monogamy, had provoked an extreme, perhaps hysterical reaction: I became obsessed with the notion of total sexual freedom, which translated itself into a compulsive promiscuity, sex with any man available, like a kind of delirium. Through it all, my commitment to John never faltered. I kept a lot of this from him, or thought I did: somehow he always *knew*. I was never sure just how upset he was, his calm exterior being so difficult to probe. He wasn't exactly judgmental, but I know he was deeply hurt. By 1977 the relationship had developed an almost insupportable tension. Coincidentally, it was Peter Harcourt who again changed my life. I received a letter from Toronto: he was teaching at York University and there was a vacancy. Did I want to apply?

Aside from our circle of friends, there was by now little reason to stay in England. I still saw my children once a week at weekends (sometimes I went to London, occasionally they came to Coventry), but we could never seem to relax together, more because of my guilt than their resentment I think.

Knowing how much happier John would be in Canada, I imagined that the move would restore our relationship; we would "start over," as they say in movies. I flew to Toronto, got the job, then we sold the house in Coventry and headed back to Toronto, where I rented a two-bedroom apartment. Our relationship as lovers ended only a few weeks later.

HOLLYWOOD FROM VIETNAM TO REAGAN (1986): 1977–1990

I find it difficult to describe my feelings or account for my reactions once the move to Toronto was accomplished. I was separated from my children by an ocean, cast adrift in a city I had previously known only as a visitor, and what I believed to be the central relationship of my life was apparently over. Certainly I experienced a sense of loss, yet I also felt strangely exhilarated: for the first time in my life I was completely free— no ties, no responsibilities outside my work at York. I could invent my life all over again. I continued in my reckless course of promiscuity, but it soon began to evolve into something rather different from the enjoyable evanescence of the one-night stand. I began to want not just sexual encounters but free and open relationships. Amazingly, it seemed to work, and the possibility of a whole new system of relationships remote from any models available in the West opened up. For a few months I had four lovers. I was completely frank with all of them, introduced them to each other, made it clear (I hope) that it was not a matter of choice, of anyone having to make up his mind. Nothing had to be permanent; there was to be no possessiveness and, more importantly, no restrictions. It all seemed to come together in one night of solidarity when Anita Bryant came to Toronto on one of her crusades and—in the middle of winter, in deep snow and freezing temperatures—the five of us as one joined a protest outside the church where she was "preaching."

Of course it couldn't last. But it did leave me with a new, if somewhat incoherent, model of what relationships might be in a truly liberated society—the corollary being that it was impossible within our own. One of the four was Richard Lippe, an American, whom I had met many years earlier when lecturing at Madison, Wisconsin, and with whom I had maintained contact ever since. He came up several times to visit when I was settled in, then decided to move here permanently. I invited him to stay in my apartment until he found his own; the other three men tactfully withdrew, making the obvious assumption. Happening more or less by accident, it proved to be the start of the longest relationship of my life: Richard and I celebrated our twenty-sixth anniversary last spring (2001).

Once again, as with life in Coventry, a kind of *ad hoc* group began to collect around us, independent people living their own lives yet coming together in a loose solidarity. John has gradually become our closest friend; Andrew Britton visited from England then emigrated here; my son Simon, similarly, visited then (with his mother's approval) came over permanently, set up a vintage clothing business (becoming a nonexploitive capitalist, insofar as such an apparent contradiction is possible), and married.

I seem to be describing a kind of perfection, but nothing in our civilization is, or can be, perfect. Looking back, I know I have never understood the concept of monogamy, even when I was monogamous: *why*, in a supposedly liberated age (but perhaps every age believes itself to be liberated?) should so much importance be attached to sex, so that it becomes the test of fidelity? Within my own concept of the term, I have always been faithful to Richard, having never at any point wanted to break off our relationship, as, earlier, I never wanted to break off my relationship with John. Yet I continued to want to experiment with my notions of sexual freedom, which *has* caused us some (happily resolvable) problems.

I think all of the above autobiographical revelations can in fact be found, unrevealed and implicit, by the diligent seeker, in my writings since my residence in Canada (which I now see as permanent). The present account of external events simply brings out their implications. I have produced my three books for Columbia University Press in conditions of absolute freedom, my editor allowing me to say whatever I wanted to say. Behind them is the support of wonderful people like Richard, John, and Andrew, the last always a tangible influence.

There is also, in this period, *CineAction*, and here I must seize the opportunity to set right a common misconception. On several occasions people have referred to *CineAction* as "my" magazine. It never was and isn't now. The original impetus for its founding came from Richard Lippe and Florence Jacobowitz, my erstwhile student, now our close friend; they have developed a permanent partnership, collaborating on university courses, articles, and the editorship of issues. I have never been more than one of the collective, which originally had eight members but has dwindled to five, where it has remained for the past several years. We take turns editing, either individually or in partnership; each editor has full control over (hence full responsibility for) his/her/their issue, the diversity of our positions and interests accounting for the diversity of the magazine. Andrew Britton was for a time a member, and his articles remain (for me, at least) the highest points of our history. The magazine's original subtitle was "A magazine of radical criticism," to which ". . . and theory" was subsequently added. Most of us regarded "radical" and "criticism" as the operative words: we were heartily sick of the domination of theory (frequently so abstruse as to be accessible only to a relatively small academic elite) in writings on cinema. The movement of our cultural/political history since the first issue appeared in 1985 is epitomized, for me, in the dropping of the word "radical," which I opposed while acknowledging its accuracy: in the 1980s we could still feel something of the impetus of '60s/'70s radicalism, but where, today, in our disillusioned world, does one look for enough "radical" film criticism to fill an issue? But I jump ahead . . .

Hollywood from Vietnam to Reagan (*Hitchcock* apart my nearest approach to a bestseller) had behind it the whole charge of the various radical movements that derived, ultimately, from what was sometimes, optimistically, referred to as "the second French Revolution," the events of the late spring and summer of 1969: extreme leftist politics, radical feminism, antiracism, gay rights. Behind it were my adventures into ideology and the influence of Andrew Britton. But the section that seems to have attracted the most attention, on the seventies horror films, derived from a series of seminars Richard Lippe and I organized for the Toronto Film Festival in the days when it still encouraged such enterprises: the screening of over thirty films, and personal appearances by directors such as Brian De Palma, George A. Romero, Stephanie Rothman, Wes Craven, publicly interviewed by Richard and myself. I wore a gay rights T-shirt for most of them, at that time still quite a daring gesture (today it would be taken for granted). It was a wonderful, euphoric moment in our lives, and I think some of the euphoria found its way into the book, as did the invisible, unacknowledged presences of Richard and Andrew. Its pervasive political anger, its demand for radical change, went hand in hand with my increasing personal happiness, my sense that, "With a little help from my friends," I did more than "get by": I had found myself.

HITCHCOCK'S FILMS REVISITED (1990)

So I come at last to the present volume, now reprinted (somewhat amazingly) in paperback. It really belongs to the previous section, but demands some comment in its own right.

I can't remember now whether the idea for a return to the work of one of the cinema's great *auteurs* came from me or my editor; I think it was I who suggested the reprinting of the original *Hitchcock's Films* within it, so that the new book would become not just "yet another book on Hitchcock" but, implicitly, a book about the changes in approaches to film, to theory, criticism, interpretation, that had taken place over a period of almost thirty years. I have, since its publication, been both surprised and depressed by the number of people who have praised me for it and it has then become apparent that what they are praising is the original book. My idea was to show that that kind of writing about Hitchcock was now hopelessly dated. For me, the *new* sections of the book are vastly superior to anything in the original work. But perhaps I am deluding myself. On the other hand, the original book is "safe": it says that Hitchcock's films are about "the human condition," which you can't change. Very nineties: we live (or try to) in an age where the Right has announced itself triumphant, and all those silly radical notions of the sixties and seventies can be forgotten. So I shall just warn you now: if you think the best parts of the book you are reading are the chapters from the original *Hitchcock's Films*, don't tell me, or you will have me standing on the edge of subway platforms thinking about Anna Karenina again.

SEXUAL POLITICS AND NARRATIVE FILM (1998): 1990–2001

My personal life, since Richard and I began living together, though not without the problems that surely, in one way or another, arise in every close relationship, has been built upon a consistent premise: I am committed to Richard but have never relinquished my right to other, more transient and peripheral relationships. But there has been one major deviation, producing one major development.

In 1989, my sabbatical year, I had an invitation to teach for the spring semester at San Francisco State University. Having already taught, much earlier, for a semester at Berkeley, I had fallen in love with San Francisco and jumped at the opportunity to live there for three months. On a bus coming home from a movie (I remember it was *Women on the Verge of a Nervous Breakdown*) I became aware that an Asian teenager was repeatedly making eye contact with me; I thought he was just being friendly, and smiled back. When I got off the bus he followed. This was the prelude to one of the most remarkable relationships of my life. When (after two more apparently coincidental meetings) I invited him to dinner, the first thing I did when he arrived was to demand to see his ID card: I did not want to spend the semester in jail. It showed his age as thirty-one, making him only a little less than thirty years my junior. It was obvious from the start that we were hopelessly mismatched. We came from different worlds, not just geographically, which is perhaps what (given a mutual attraction) fascinated us both. Subsequently, I submitted my resignation at York (taking early retirement, against everyone's warnings about the financial disadvantages) at the age of fifty-nine, completed my final year there, and moved to San Francisco.

Yuichi restored my youth. His appetite for life amazed me, his energy, his interest in virtually every cultural manifestation. We would go to a

Billy Joel concert one night (something that would never have occurred
to me for a moment), a Murray Perahia piano recital the next, a week
later a Rolling Stones concert followed closely by the San Francisco Symphony Orchestra (Beethoven's Seventh: I glanced at Yuichi during the
slow movement and saw tears falling down his cheeks, his expression
totally rapt). His enthusiasms, indeed, appeared inexhaustible: I have
never met anyone, before or since, with such an open-minded appetite
for experience.

The effect of his personality on me was quite remarkable, and I still
don't entirely understand what happened. With a full-time job, he got up
every other morning to exercise at a health club. The only exercise I've
ever enjoyed is swimming, and one day he took me as a guest. But when
we arrived he told me firmly that before I swam I must exercise for an
hour on the various machines. After feeble attempts at protest I obeyed,
and found myself enjoying it. Then he went off to work and I went back
to his apartment. I vividly remember sitting down in an armchair and
thinking, "I want to write a novel. I'll write down the first thing that
comes into my head and go on from there." I did exactly that, and about
nine months later had completed a 500-page (double-spaced) thriller in
which I, Richard, and Yuichi all had leading parts but in which the central character was a woman, an amalgam of several strong, independent,
dynamic women who have been among my friends.

Yuichi, as I said, restored my youth: his vitality and enthusiasm had
somehow steered me back to my beginnings as a writer, a writer of fiction, from which I had been diverted into criticism. That first novel is, I
think, recoupable (though my description of it won't suggest such a possibility!): one day I shall revise it drastically. Since then, however, I have
written two more novels and the first half of a third. One of them captured the attention of a San Francisco agent, who told me it would be a
bestseller and advised me to get an unlisted phone number when it was
published or I would be harassed constantly by religious fundamentalists
and other right-wing groups, but after a dozen refusals from publishers
she lost confidence and asked me to revise it in ways I couldn't possibly
accept. I am currently revising it in my *own* way, and hope to see one
novel published before I die.

I did not, however, "leave" Richard, in the usual sense of that term. I
had already told Yuichi that I had a permanent commitment; Richard
flew down and spent Christmas with us, and he and Yuichi became

almost instant friends. We continue to visit every year. Richard remains an American citizen, and has always (at least until the election of George W. Bush) retained a desire for his origins. The plan (which he, with some hesitation, accepted) was that I would get legal status in America, he would come down, and the three of us would live "together" but in separate apartments, preferably in the same building. But I was uncomfortably aware that this would be the realization of *my* ideal, not Richard's. In any case, the ideal proved unrealizable: I tried everything, but could find no way in which a retired sixty-year-old with no American relations and no desire for employment could get legal status.

Parts of *Sexual Politics and Narrative Film* (the book that contains, in my opinion, most of my best work, and for which—unless for my novels—I would most like to be remembered) was written in San Francisco, in my one-room apartment next to Yuichi's; the rest was written in Toronto; some of the essays first appeared in *CineAction*. My interpretation of Renoir's *La Règle du Jeu* (*The Rules of the Game*) (and of Mozart's *Così fan tutte*), with its defense and celebration of "promiscuity" (slightly glossed as "relating freely"), is the chapter that most obviously grows out of my immediate experiences, but the book as a whole is the one that best speaks for me, and represents me, as I am today. I opened it by announcing that I would write no more books of film criticism, which has been taken to mean that I would stop writing on film altogether, which was never my intention. I have since published regularly in *CineAction* and have written for the British Film Institute what *they* call a book but *I* call an "extended essay" on the film version of James's *The Wings of the Dove*. But mainly, today, I want to write what I have wanted to write since I was eight years old: fiction. Meanwhile, to my astonishment, two Ph.D. dissertations have been written about my work (I feel a bit like Sally Field: "You *like* me, you *like* me"), and I am, as I write this, about to go to Lund, Sweden, as some kind of guest, to attend the ceremony of the author of the more recent thesis, whose work has been published as a book—in Swedish yet, which I can't read (which is probably just as well).

In the Year 2001—and Beyond   So, "Where are you now?"—as the harried hero (?) of *Memento* (like me, struggling to recapture memories with some degree of accuracy) repeatedly asks himself.

The fundamental shift in my position can be judged most clearly in the very different treatments of films to which I have returned: the essay on *Letter from an Unknown Woman* in *Personal Views*, basically a style-and-meaning analysis, and the much later one in *Sexual Politics and Narrative Film*, centrally concerned with examining the film's presentation of the subjugation of women and its disastrous consequences for both genders; or the two attempts to grapple with *Vertigo*, both essays included in the present book. In these separate cases, my sense of the main thrust of the film, its essential meaning, has changed in accordance with my greater ideological awareness. My most recent articles, published in *CineAction* and in the Swedish magazine *Filmhäftet*—on Jasmin Dizdar's *Beautiful People*, on Hou Hsiao Hsien's *Flowers of Shanghai*, on American high school movies of the 1990s—show, I think, that my fascination with form and style has not diminished with the years; what is different is my awareness that form and style do not exist in and for themselves but have always a sociopolitical significance.

I now see the practice of film criticism not only as a means of elucidating films but as a means of encouraging—indeed, *demanding*—political and social change: of insisting on the necessity, today, for the most extreme leftist radicalism short of physical violence. The means to this end is the uncovering of the radicalism contained within the films. Most of those who talk with me about my work appear quite unaware that this is what it says: they prefer to discuss points of interpretation (e.g., do I think Hitchcock really meant this or that?). I sometimes think the only practical function of my rediscovered political radicalism is my own satisfaction, as it seems to have little effect beyond this. I have just run across, while writing this, a passage in *The Strangeness of Beauty*, the wonderful novel by Lydia Minatoya, in which a Japanese war hero (turned pacifist) says of his experiences, "I thought I was committed to social justice but my commitment was all to self-image." I have to ask myself, Is that, perhaps, all my work amounts to?

But consider where, today, we are.

First, we must go back a few years, to the declaration of the end of Communism in the Soviet Union. No one in his senses, I take it, can regret the demise of Stalinism, its repressions, persecutions, and death camps outdoing the monstrousness even of Hitler and Nazism. But in the West, for a long time now, the public has been duped into a state of total mystification: the terms *Stalinism*, *Communism*, and *Socialism* have somehow mysteriously become synonymous. This has been the dominant ideology's method of demonizing *any* form of leftist thinking. Ideally, the collapse of Soviet Communism *should* have led to a thorough rethinking of Marxist/Socialist principles (with special attention to Trotsky, the most progressive of the early Marxist theorists, though one must not look to his work for easy answers to the problems raised by Communism), with a view to their reinstatement as the logical flowering of a true democracy, with built-in safeguards against the possibility of its perversion into another totalitarian police state. The problems of such an undertaking may prove insuperable (I am not exactly an optimist): the attempt to solve them with "free" elections by the Sandinistas in Nicaragua ended abruptly in their electoral defeat, the voters terrified of the consequences if they defied the United States and its Contras. Instead, it was greeted as the triumph of capitalism, globally. In any worst-case scenario, the doom of our planet may have been sealed at that historic moment.

(A brief digression here, as this *is* a book about cinema: There seems, today in the West, a dominant myth that the Russian Revolution ended all possibility of "progressive" art in Russia. The evidence to the contrary is there for all to see, and one is forced to believe that people obstinately refuse to see it. The films of Dziga Vertov—"modernist" masterpieces that still appear "progressive" in the context of today's avant-garde— were made during the twenties with the full endorsement of the revolutionary authorities; the utter exhilaration and energy of these films, their technical, stylistic, and formal inventiveness when added to the sheer excitement of producing thoroughly liberated art in a period of radical change, are there for everyone who has eyes to see.)

Capitalism today no longer can be represented by Jimmy Stewart and *It's a Wonderful Life*; it cannot even be adequately represented by Mr. Potter. Capitalism today means *corporate capitalism*, the global dominance of the huge companies, amalgamations, and corporations that are infiltrating every aspect of our existence; the Free Trade Agreement (if it happens) will simply cement this. The triumph of corporate capitalism also means, of course, the triumph of the United States. In the days of Reagan and his much-touted *Star Wars* program, Russia was the "Evil Empire"; today, not entirely without reason, many people in the world are beginning to view the Evil Empire as the USA itself. (This is, in fact, not at all an indefensible position—considering the huge proportion of the world's resources that redound to that country—nor is it one that advocates "terrorism," the very idea of which appalls me; the slaughter of innocent people, whether carried out by terrorists or on the orders of an American president, is something no one who retains a modicum of human feeling, conscience, or empathy can countenance, even in this dehumanizing age.)

For several years now, concerned scientists have been warning us about the rising levels of pollution, about the dangers of global warming, about the devastation of our planet by the unrestrained "enterprise" of the corporations, masked as a "positive good" in the relentless production of "products" (most of them unnecessary, some actively dangerous), but actually almost exclusively motivated by the corporations' ever-increasing obsession for power and money. The corporations now dominate the media (currently dedicated to "keeping people happy" with "the newest, and therefore best" productions, fashions, rock groups, etc.) as well as most governments, who are in many ways dependent on them (especially the right-wing governments—and all North American governments today are right-wing: there is no truly effective—let alone official—leftist opposition any more).

Aside from the corporate capitalist takeover, the most destructive, backward, and pernicious forces operating in the world at the present time are still what they have always been, from the beginning of recorded civilization: religion and patriotism, both extremely relevant today, unfortunately. Three of the world's most developed and influential religions (Christianity, Judaism, Islam) are built ultimately on the Old Testament, a collection of writings in which tall stories, myths, and superstitions were inscribed thousands of years ago within a cultural situation very different from our own; their relevance to us today is minimal, at best. Over the centuries, these beliefs have clearly been the cause of a very great proportion of the misery and suffering of the human race, resulting in persecutions and wars (known as "Holy," whether originating from the contemptible Imperialist Christian Crusades to the present Taliban monstrousness) as well as in personal and national divisiveness. Will this absurdity never end? I recall vividly the liberating feeling of the moment when, at the age of seventeen, I suddenly realized (ironically in one of those moments of revelation that are traditionally the preserve of religious converts) that the entire paraphernalia of Christianity that I had espoused so passionately (from the age of twelve, when I absolutely insisted—in my belief in a god who would send me to limbo for eternity if a priest didn't splash a bit of water over my head—on being baptized) was (a few useful, quasi-Marxist, quotes from Jesus aside) a meaningless, useless farago of nonsense.

As for patriotism (or "My country, right or wrong," as I was taught to believe in my childhood—and of course the sentiment still persists, although no one would dare say it so blatantly now): insofar as I lay claim to any nationality (beyond the formalities of a passport), I regard myself today as Canadian: Canada seems a relatively decent place to live, as those things go nowadays, and (in Toronto at least) it actually celebrates the ideal of multiculturalism. (An anecdote here, however, that acknowledges the gulf between ideal and actuality, as well as illustrating the persistence of white and moneyed dominance: Richard and I were traveling on the subway one day. I looked around and pointed out, with the pleasure of realization, that there were far more "people of color" in the car than whites. Richard, who is often way ahead of me in such perceptions, replied that rich people don't use the subway.) I cannot, however, become a Canadian citizen, because to do so still requires that I swear an oath of allegiance to the British monarchy. This is, of course, an empty formality: it has by now, presumably, been sworn by many thousands of Italians, Chinese, Iranians, Pakistanis, Africans, West Indians, Vietnamese . . . none of whom can have much personal investment in the British royal family. But they have never lived in Britain, where each year this useless and largely risible monarchy drains millions of dollars from the national budget that could go to nourish the poor, the homeless, the hospitals, the arts . . . even, perhaps, a real university somewhere, if anyone considered the preservation of our (multi)cultural history worth a small expenditure.

As for education (especially relevant here as this book is published by a university press): the term has changed its meaning since I studied at Cambridge in the early 1950s. Then, it meant (to me at least) something like "defining oneself in relation to our cultural history, our living past, and in relation to the world today; developing oneself intellectually, emotionally, culturally; learning to make choices, to discriminate; discovering oneself, developing oneself." Today (to judge from the responses of many students I have encountered) it means, "Will this help me to a career? If not, will I at least get a good grade?" There must have been some defining—and disastrous—moment in the evolution of the modern American university when it was decided to attach the writing of essays and the awarding of grades to lecture courses (the contamination spread, a long time ago, to Britain). At Cambridge we attended a course because we were interested, and for no other reason. That was why, after the first few weeks, certain lecturers' courses retained perhaps half a dozen students, while in Dr. Leavis's courses, in one of the largest lecture halls, students sat on the stairs when all the seats were occupied. Nowadays I have not infrequently been approached by students on the first night of a course who asked, "What must I do to get a B plus?" (The correct answer: "You just failed"—but no one dares give it; I haven't myself. It's not the student's fault, after all.)

I should make it clear that I am not (given the present circumstances of our alleged civilization) opposed to the idea of career-training colleges (people do have to make a living, after all, and I have sometimes found myself, somewhat to my shame, writing articles "for the money"). I only wish that there were still just a few *real* universities, and that there were governments that supported such anomalies. The university as I knew it seems no longer to exist. I spent four years at Cambridge reading the books I wanted to read, watching the films I wanted to see, listening to the music I wanted to hear, entering into endless debates with my friends, attending the lectures I felt were productive in the ways I was then thinking and feeling. Today, if I were still that age, I would probably be approaching the professor after the first lecture and asking, "What must I do to get a B plus in your course?"

One of Freud's most controversial (and today, I think, largely forgotten or ignored) theories is that of the universal death wish, present and potent in the unconscious: the notion that the human race—seen, presumably, as some kind of evolutionary error—has an inbuilt desire to destroy itself. Freud's arguments were challenged, in the not-so-distant past, by Herbert Marcuse and Norman O. Brown, both of whom (as post-Freudians) accepted his basic diagnosis but argued that the death wish was not necessarily irreversible; that, contained within Freud's own theories, there were the weapons with which it might be countered and transformed. Both writers, since the seventies, seem to have dropped completely out of fashion. Should we take this as a sign that the theory of the universal death wish is now implicitly accepted in the collective unconscious? Recent political events, too familiar to be worth enumerating, suggest this strongly.

So, again, "Where am I now?" In my personal life I have never been happier and, looking back, I can see that (certain episodes aside) each of the major periods of my life since childhood has been happier than the one before. Having survived my traditional three-score-years-and-ten, and an illness and operation during which (or so I am told) I almost died three times, I feel a curious, totally unearned, tranquility, within which *Rio Bravo* seems to have established itself definitively as my favorite film. (Some will call this "senility.") Hawks's masterpiece systematically rejects all the obvious, traditional reasons why its heroes fight: comfort, security, glory, prestige, the acquisition of wealth, the future of civilization. Everything is pared down to the ultimate human essential—the preservation of self-respect. Far from finding their situation bleak and desolate, they embrace it with joy, which is primarily the joy of solidarity and community. Of course, they live (or lived) in a world in which the Burdetts could still be defeated; today we face a world in which the forces of repressive conservatism appear to be triumphant, which makes the possibility of inner peace far more difficult to attain. For the present, however, there appears to be nothing else, no recourse. On the other hand, to retain one's self-respect, one is necessarily committed to continuing the struggle: we lose it as soon as we concede victory. One *must* continue the fight, even in a worldwide battle that already seems lost. But then, to go backwards a little through Hawks's films to *To Have and Have Not*, "How little we know . . ."

The one positive sign at present—and I find it very moving—is the growth of protest: today, it seems to me the duty of every artist, every writer—indeed of every thinking person to encourage and promote it. This could lead, conceivably, to the establishment of what our world so disastrously lacks: the rise of a new, organized Left. Yet think what dissent has, now, to contend with: all the governments of what is laughably called the "free" world, which includes all the major powers, most of them "democratically" elected; the vast network of corporations and conglomerates that supports and, effectively, owns them (and which is more or less systematically destroying the environment); the media—the all-influential, all-powerful, all-pervasive media, especially advertising and television—which dictate what one must be interested in, what one should buy, what side one should be on, the news and how it's reported, *and*, not so incidentally, which keep us "entertained" (read: distracted), allowing and incorporating *just so much* dissent and criticism so that we all know the process is "democratic" and that everyone is allowed a voice (so long as it can be drowned out when necessary). In the face of such powerful and oppressive forces, one wonders what protest can achieve or how far it can get. But in a world gone certifiably mad, protest becomes the only sane response.

This brings the history of my criticism and its personal background up to date; there remain a few addenda which seem to me important, the first being the obvious and simple statement that this is only *my* (highly selective) account of my past. You might very well get quite different (and probably even less flattering) accounts from the people who have been close to me and whom I have attempted briefly to evoke. I have done my utmost to be honest, and this honesty is what I want to discuss further.

Some readers (I am acutely aware) will react with some embarrassment to the often highly personal nature of what I have written: this is, after all, a work of film criticism, which is expected to sustain at least a pretense of objectivity and detachment. "Why does he have to tell us these things?" is a possible predictable response. My first answer is that perhaps we all *need* to be embarrassed more often (and less ashamed to embarrass ourselves): it might pave the way to going beyond embarrassment to greater openness. We are all human, and human beings are by definition imperfect; and none of us, in my opinion, can claim to have access to the "truth" about existence (though some *think* they can). Isn't it possible that we would all get on better together if we accepted, acknowledged, and discussed our imperfections, our often terrible mistakes, the cruelties that we inflict on others, the ways in which we discover that we have deceived ourselves—in short, if we were as honest as possible, with ourselves and with each other.

But I find "honesty" a difficult and deeply problematic concept. I was careful to say above that I have done my best to be honest; yet I am not at all sure I have succeeded. The human desire to preserve some kind of positive self-image appears to me (largely from my own introspection) virtually incorrigible, and to preserve it we need the approval or, better still, admiration of others. I have been unable to avoid, as I write, the uneasy feeling that perhaps this assumed "honesty" is yet another way of asking for admiration ("Oh, he's so *honest*!")—yet another subterfuge for inviting people to like me. This is what I had in mind when I referred to Sally Field's celebrated—and frequently parodied—Oscar moment. I feel that my own honesty is rather like that: I *mean* to be sincere, but underneath I know that "having people like me" is something I've wanted all my life.

Which brings me to my own "Rosebud"—the moment in the movie where (frequently in a flashback) everything is suddenly explained. When I was born my parents were well into their forties; they had already produced four children, and there had been a twelve-year gap between me and my nearest sibling. It takes little ingenuity (or even common sense) to read "unwanted accident," and I am sure this was the case (brought up in Victorian days, my parents would never have countenanced birth control or abortions even if they knew about such shocking things). Throughout childhood, then, I was both unwanted and extremely spoiled—the spoiling the result of my mother's guilt feelings, which probably I intuitively exploited. I usually got my way (they eventually did let me see *Suspicion*), but I think I always knew I was felt by everyone to be a constant nuisance, an impediment, a feeling which led in its turn to my constantly *making* myself a nuisance to attract attention—anyone's attention, but especially my two brothers', respectively twelve and fourteen years my seniors. It takes no great imaginative leap to connect my continuous desire to be liked, to gain attention, and to provoke when necessary (as a means of attracting such attention), to childhood experience. But as we all know, "Rosebud" doesn't explain *everything* . . . And because the convolutions are endless, perhaps we shouldn't get into the question of my motivation in being so honest about my honesty . . . ("Oh, he's so *disarming!*").

I want to end by returning to my critical roots in the work and influence of Dr. Leavis, to whose various books I still return at least once every few years (as well as to the poets and novelists on whom he wrote with such brilliance amd integrity), with renewed admiration and not a little guilt, my relation to his work today seeming to me something of a betrayal. Let me say at once that I am fully aware that I do not possess anything comparable to him in intelligence and discipline: my own work, in the comparison, can only appear haphazard and slapdash. It is fortunate indeed that my major area of concentration has been in a subject (film) in which he showed almost no interest whatever, and especially within that branch (modern popular culture) which he tended to dismiss out of hand. I wonder how he would have reacted to the suggestion that the best films of Hawks are distinguished descendants of an American literary tradition (Cooper, Twain, Melville . . .) he greatly admired. I also wonder how he would react to my current political stance. He would never have accepted it during his lifetime, but today the deterioration of our civilization (with the virtual annihilation of the university as Leavis knew it, and which he saw as the necessary center of a living culture) has gone so far that it is difficult to be certain what his position would be. But he wrote, "The life is in us too, and makes it impossible for us to wait inertly for the covert disaster—which is now imminent." That was in 1974, and the "disaster" is no longer "covert."

He remains, for me, the greatest of all critics, and I owe him a debt that can never be repaid. And he is still (though I imagine he would not wish to be associated with most or all of my work) to some extent a role model. When I began writing I was frequently called a "Leavisite," one of those derogatory terms that people use when they are confronted with genius (and I trust the reader will understand that I am not referring to my own). I responded by substituting "Leavisian," the difference being that between unquestioning disciple and humble follower. I was never (or only briefly) a Leavisite; I hope I am still a Leavisian, however far I have strayed from my origins.

Perhaps the one way in which I resemble Leavis is that we were both, always and necessarily, outsiders. Insofar as we worked with groups, they were "outsider groups": if Leavis's books, the magazine *Scrutiny*, his and its influence, were the most important things that emerged from the Cambridge English Department, it was in opposition to the dominant university culture. It was a not uncommon sight to see Leavis walk down a corridor outside the lecture rooms and be conspicuously ignored by other lecturers. This "outsiderness" applies most importantly, I think, to our refusal to connect ourselves to theories, be they theories of philosophy, theories of literature, theories of film. Leavis was a critic and proud of it; insofar as I am proud of anything in my life, I would claim the same. Every new theory gives itself airs; it says to everyone, "This is the truth, it explains everything." I have learned from many theories, but subscribed to none. I recall a wonderful remark, in an interview, by Jean Renoir. Asked if he believed in any theories, he replied that he thought they were probably all true, depending upon their application, but he didn't accept any as absolute. Each theory of film (some are more helpful than others) I have encountered has given me certain insights into certain films. But what I still want to ask are the questions Leavis asked of works of literature: Is this important? What exactly does it do? What does it do for *me*, and for what I believe? How fully achieved is it? What kind of impulse is behind it? Such questions—to me indispensable—are irrelevant to theory.

When I wrote the original *Hitchcock's Films* I mailed a copy to Dr. Leavis, with a letter that (knowing myself at least a little) probably managed to be simultaneously self-abasing and presumptuous. Some time later a friend of mine who knew him personally (as I never did) told me he had seen it prominently displayed on Leavis's bookshelf. I wonder if he ever opened it? I half hope he didn't.

In the ongoing saga of my life (personal and professional) I must here add the name of Thom Loree, dedicatee (and, indeed, "onlie begetter") of this preface, with whom I hope to collaborate on a book in the near future.

ACKNOWLEDGMENTS (1988)

Careers are dependent, in so many cases, not on personal determination and ambition but on more-or-less chance occurrence. The first piece of film criticism that I submitted for publication was an article on *Psycho* that, in a considerably expanded form, was the basis of the chapter in *Hitchcock's Films*. I wrote it purely because I was engaged at that time in fairly automatic (though not actively unpleasant) manual labor (weeding baby fir-trees on a plantation in Scotland) and became so bored that I had to think about *something*, and *Psycho* was what I had just seen. I submitted the article to *Sight and Sound*, and it was rejected by Penelope Houston, who informed me in a very courteous letter that I had failed to grasp that the film was intended as a joke. I wish to thank her now both for the courtesy and the rejection. I then sent the article to *Cahiers du Cinéma* and, to my amazement, it was accepted by Eric Rohmer, then the editor of that illustrious publication. My career as a film critic and teacher really dates from that moment.

It was Peter Cowie who, during a late night party, suggested I write a book on Hitchcock for his publishing company the Tantivy Press. If I had been halfway sober I would certainly have laughed and swept aside such a ridiculous suggestion; as it was, I took the idea home to my then wife Aline, recounting it to her as a joke, and she calmly told me that of course I must do it. I thought she must be crazy, too, but I allowed myself to be talked into it. The original book was, and remains, gratefully dedicated to her. I wish also to thank Peter Cowie for what at the time seemed a hopelessly misguided faith in my abilities and stamina. The "Retrospective" of 1977 belongs to the period when I lived with John Anderson. John is still a loved and valued friend, and I wish to thank him again for the strength and firmness he provided during the most difficult period of my life.

Some of the more recent material in this book has already appeared in periodicals and is reprinted here with the permission of the various editors. "Ideology, Genre, Auteur" (now chapter 14) appeared in *Film Comment* and "Male Desire, Male Anxiety" (now chapter 18) in *American Film;* I have slightly revised and expanded the former and have written a new introduction for the latter. The essay on *Blackmail* and the section of the new introduction on F. R. Leavis were originally published in *CineAction!*. Many of the stills were supplied by the Ontario Film Institute, and I want to thank Gerald Pratley for his generous cooperation.

One name crops up repeatedly in the text, that of Andrew Britton. Andrew is both a dearly loved friend and the major influence on my work over the past decade.

Finally I want to thank Richard Lippe, but there is so much to thank him for that I hardly know where to begin or end. Richard and I have lived together for almost twelve years, and our work as critics and teachers has become increasingly collaborative. Beyond that is the incalculable debt I owe Richard for his emotional support, love, and comradeship.

HITCHCOCK'S FILMS REVISITED

INTRODUCTION (1988)

THE QUESTION OF AUTHORSHIP

The project undertaken in this book has posed a problem to which there is probably no completely satisfying solution. *Hitchcock's Films* was written in the early '6os: it has been through three editions (accruing extra material in its different incarnations) and has been out of print for a number of years. When I wrote it the technology of film study was still in a fairly primitive stage (as was the critical apparatus): with most of the films I worked from memory, or from notes scribbled in movie theaters during public screenings: the most sophisticated machinery I had (occasionally) at my disposal was a standard 16mm. projector. Many Hitchcock films, including "key" works like *Shadow of a Doubt* and *Under Capricorn* were not available at all at that time in England; others were available only in errant formats (the chapter on *Vertigo* was written using a low contrast 16mm. black-and-white print).

More important, however, than the deficiencies of technology and availability is the fact that the book belongs firmly to a certain phase in the evolution of film theory/criticism whose assumptions are no longer acceptable without qualifications so drastic as effectively to transform them: the high point of auteur theory in its original, unmodified form, as developed out of Bazin and the early *Cahiers du Cinéma*. Those assumptions (to a degree new to the criticism of Hollywood movies, though not foreign to many of the forms of traditional aesthetics) can be spelled out quite crudely as follows: The critic's task is to discover great works and explicate their significance, acting as a mediator between the artist and the less educated, less aware public; great works of art are produced by great artists; the interest—degree of success or failure—of any work derives unproblematically from the artist who created it; aspects of the work that cannot be argued to be personal to the artist can be dismissed as insignificant or as unfortunate impediments or irritants; the artist's "great" works must be singled out and pantheonized, the lesser works pushed aside as relatively unimportant, their interest (if any) lying in their relationship to the "great" works; these "great" works are statements about the human condition, about "life," and they are essentially self-contained and self-sufficient. Assumptions such as these will be found to inform *Hitchcock's Films*.

Finding, twenty years later, that I have more to say about Hitchcock, and wishing to discuss some of the films the original book neglected (rectifying, for example, its completely indefensible attitude to the British period), what relationship should I establish between the new work and the old? Two solutions immediately proposed themselves (and were proposed by interested editors and their professional readers). One: to consign *Hitchcock's Films* to oblivion and produce an entirely new book. Two: to revise the original in order to bring it into line with my current critical position, incorporating the new material so that the films would be treated (as in the original) in chronological order. Both these solutions swiftly proved impossible for me; I think they are also undesirable.

First solution: Whatever my own present attitude to *Hitchcock's Films* (it is far from simple), it is clear that many people continue to regard it as important. Some have told me that it is still the best book on Hitchcock; I am frequently asked why it is out of print and whether it is possible to obtain a copy anywhere. And the tone of these remarks and inquiries suggests clearly enough that the book is not regarded as of merely historical interest. Even if I wished to repudiate it altogether, who am I among so many? But the matter is not so simple. If my list of underlying assumptions suggests repudiation, I would have to qualify this by saying that those assumptions, even today, do not seem to me entirely untenable and cannot simply be swept aside contemptuously (they would of course need careful and thorough reformulation). It is also true that a book (like a film) cannot be reduced to its underlying assumptions (though it is very important to be aware of them). The analyses in *Hitchcock's Films* seem to me, by and large, to stand up still (which is not to claim that they are "correct" or exclusive, the only possible readings); and, on the whole, I stand by the evaluations to which the analyses lead (where I now think I was wrong I have indicated my disagreement with myself in endnotes). A difference in critical position may and often does produce radically different insights, but this is not necessarily the case. Raymond Bellour's account of *Psycho*, for example, though the theoretical apparatus he employs is vastly more sophisticated, does not seem to me to differ in its basic apprehensions from the one I offered in *Hitchcock's Films* (both center their argument on the continuity the film establishes between "normal" and "abnormal," neurosis and psychosis); it was simply written from a different ideological position and in another language (I don't just mean French). In general I have no urge to produce new essays on the films covered in the original book (I have made an exception in the case of *Vertigo*, though there too the new reading will be found to recapitulate many of the insights of the old, from a different ideological position).

It is the ideological shift that renders the second solution impossible: I cannot now "revise" *Hitchcock's Films*. If the perceptions and the insights would be broadly similar they would invariably be expressed quite differently, the difference being one of viewpoint and attitude.

The author of *Hitchcock's Films* was totally innocent even of any concept of ideology: he literally didn't know what the term meant. In effect, of course, what this amounted to was that he saw everything through the tunnel vision of bourgeois ideology, its assumptions naturalized into "truth," "reality," "the human condition," "human nature," "common sense." He was also untouched by feminism: the relative positions of men and women in our culture were taken as natural and "given," as a fact of life, and if you had told him that gender roles were culturally constructed he would not have listened. Somewhere around 1970 he received a rude awakening on two fronts simultaneously, personal and professional.

Certain critics have expressed the view that the result of this awakening has been constricting, that my approach to the cinema has become limited by ideological concerns and my adopted political position. I disagree entirely. I believe that I now see far more in films then I used to, because I have allowed myself to become aware of depths, tensions, conflicts that lie beneath the "auteurist" surface, that enter the film through the author from the culture of which both he and his work are products (though never *mere* products).

There is another issue here, that of honesty. It is notorious that W. H.

Auden, when he passed from his Communist period to his Christian period, revised a number of his earlier poems in order to eliminate their Communist references and make them conform to his later position. That this could be achieved relatively easily testifies to the superficiality of his Communism, but it also seems to me deeply dishonest, amounting to a pretense that he didn't say what in fact he said. There are strong moral grounds, then, on which I must decline to "translate" (or disguise) my earlier work. It was written from the viewpoint of a somewhat confused and despairing liberal humanist, at a period when I could still convince myself (with a certain struggle and many suppressions) that such a position was viable amid the conditions of modern capitalism.

Hence the unorthodox (as far as I know unique) structure of the present book. The first half consists of the original *Hitchcock's Films* reprinted "warts and all" as it was written, preceded by an introductory account of some of the basic developments in film criticism/theory since the '60s and the problems they have given rise to, with footnotes that correct its errors and record my own disagreements with its readings. The errors are, I think, worth registering rather than surreptitiously correcting: to draw attention to their existence should help to counter the very common tendency among film students to quote from printed texts uncritically, as if they were assumed to be sacrosanct and infallible. I have also restored to its proper place the "retrospective" that I wrote for the third edition: I always intended it to come at the end of the book, not at the beginning, and it now forms a transition to the book's second part. With the exception of chapter 14 (1976), all the material in book 2 has been written since 1980. If the primary text remains the analysis of Hitchcock's work, this unusual structure provides the book with a sub-text: the shifts in critical perspective (both personal and more-than-personal) over the past three decades. It becomes as much a book about critical practice as a book about Hitchcock.

One major characterizing difference between the two halves of this book will immediately strike the reader: the original text constitutes a coherent whole (or the illusion of such), the essays that make up the book's second half do not. I am not proposing this as a relative *weakness* of the new material, rather the contrary. The coherence of *Hitchcock's Films* was the logical consequence of its commitment to auteur theory; the absence of coherence within its sequel follows from the dissolution of that "theory," at least in its original, unmodified form. *Hitchcock's*

Films had as its premise not only that the films—insofar as they are significant—belong exclusively to Hitchcock, but that every great artist's work follows a logical and progressive development. The book was centered firmly on the notion of Hitchcock-as-artist, and could trace the evolution of his thematic concerns chronologically. No such simple structuring principle operates in the second half of this book. Hitchcock, to be sure, remains a constant reference point (the films could not possibly have come into existence without him and his presence remains their strongest connecting link). But the films do not belong *only* to him: they belong also to commercial cinema (British or American), its conventions and constraints, both what it enables and what it prohibits, its various systems (studio, star, genre); and they belong to the culture, its institutions, its values, its ideology, its internal conflicts and struggles. The essays in book 2 are still arranged, for the most part, chronologically, but here this is largely arbitrary, a matter of convenience and convention rather than necessity. Rather than seeking to build a coherent, step-by-step argument (demonstration of an artist's greatness), they seek to explore individual films from a variety of approaches, retaining an awareness of the complex of influences and determinants operating upon the production of a given work. I certainly do not wish to deny that the dominant approach, within which all others are contained, remains "auteurist" (this is still a book about *Hitchcock's* films); but I have wanted to take into account and make use of the many valuable critical developments of the past two decades—work on generic convention, the principles of classical narrative, the construction of "classical Hollywood films" both overall and from shot to shot, stars and how they signify, the relation of films to our culture's construction of gender. I do not, of course, mean "absence of coherence" to be synonymous with "incoherence": the essays that form the second half belong to each other, but loosely, in a complex and far from comprehensive interdependence, not as steps in a sequential argument.

One thing further has to be said about the relation between the books' two halves: If I am now "some kind of a Marxist" (in the rather dubious sense in which Hank Quinlan was "some kind of a man"), I have reached that position without abandoning my basic humanist assumptions. Indeed, I would argue that a Marxism that finds humanism totally incompatible and rejects any attempt to rethink and incorporate it invalidates itself: there is something very peculiar about a Marxism that finds no place for the recognition of individual human skills, intelligence, and emotion. The ultimate aim must always be a society in which individuals can develop and fulfill themselves to the maximum. The possibility of doing so, however, must be available to all human beings equally, not just to those of a privileged class, color, gender, sexual orientation, etc. The values of capitalism, the cruder, more blatant aspects of its ideology, must also be countered and undermined: the concept of individual fulfillment becomes perverted and ludicrous if it is perceived in terms of money, power, status, "success." There must be the recognition that fulfillment can be achieved only though human cooperation not competition, and that, if there is a final, irreducible component of "human nature," it is precisely the ability to cooperate, to relate. Such, roughly, seem to me the fundamental and constitutive ideals of humanism, and they could only conceivably be realized through a socialist organization of culture—a Marxism informed by feminism and the revelations of psychoanalytic theory.

One of the more obvious continuities between my early and later work is the consistently critical, hostile attitude to the dominant trends of our culture. In the early work the criticism of culture is weakened by various factors, particularly by an unthinking belief in something called "the human condition," a belief that "life is like that," that its basic conditions are universal and unchangeable. Such a belief is clearly an indispensable staple of bourgeois intellectualism: it automatically precludes the necessity of analyzing the actual conditions of life in our culture and the social forces that have constructed those conditions. Ideological blinkers apart, it was impossible for me then on a personal level to challenge (or even imagine the possibility of challenging) the bourgeois concept of the nuclear family (and the gender roles and positions it is built upon and reproduces) as a supreme value. I had a very generalized sense that capitalist civilization had reached an extreme phase of degeneracy and decadence, and the family seemed the only refuge from that outside world, existing somehow apart from it. The only hope for positive change I could see lay in education, especially education in the arts: if people could learn to love works of art (our "storehouse of recorded values," in I. A. Richards' famous and beautiful phrase) they would be transformed as individuals and gradually this would lead to the transformation of our culture. I don't think I was ever really convinced by this belief: I was constantly haunted by a sense of impotence and desperation (my gravitation during this period to the films of Ingmar Bergman and my close identification with them—or at least with the image of them that I constructed—is symptomatic). Now, of course, the sheer absurdity of such a belief is fully evident. Back then, I couldn't allow myself to grasp that the damage and brutalization wrought upon the human sensibility by consumer capitalism had already progressed far beyond hope of any incidental bits of repair work, and I had no concept of base and superstructure and the relationship between them. Neither could I grasp, being myself then a schoolteacher, that the "progressive" work that is possible within our educational system is necessarily extremely limited, that system being itself the product and instrument of bourgeois patriarchal capitalism, hence fundamentally inimical to anything that seriously threatens it.

Many would argue that the logical consequence of such a shift in position would be a commitment to the school of structuralism and semiotics, with its admixture of Lacanian psychoanalytic theory, as offering the most penetrating radical analysis available of our culture, its inhabitants, its artifacts. I have always had a strong inbuilt resistance to such a step, which I now think subsequent developments have justified. The resistance was always partly the result of personal deficiency, my incapacity for abstract theorizing; my mind (such as it is) has always demanded the practical and the concrete, and the only abstract ideas it seems capable of assimilating are those that it can relate directly to experience. Another, less self-denigrating way of putting this would be to say that I am very British, with deep roots in a peculiarly British tradition that my semiological fellow countrymen have rejected (implicitly, on occasion explicitly) with an unreflecting and comprehensive contempt, in favor of a peculiarly French tradition. I am no isolationist, I am opposed to all forms of political nationalism, and I believe firmly that we should expose ourselves to influences from other cultures; but I also think we do ourselves a very substantial injury when we deliberately cut ourselves off from our cultural roots. The British tradition to which I refer (both creative and critical) might be represented by such figures as William Blake, George Eliot, D. H. Lawrence, F. R. Leavis, and Raymond Williams: the range and partial incompatibility of those writers should effectively counter any suggestion that I think any one of them (any more than Freud or Marx) should be accepted unquestioningly.

Indeed, it is precisely the phenomenon of unquestioning acceptance—
the illusory and misguided search for an oracle who reveals "truth"—
that I have always profoundly mistrusted in the semiotic structuralist
tradition: the parade of gods—Barthes, Lacan, Foucault, Derrida—has
become embarrassing. The sense of Divine Revelation is epitomized in
one constantly recurring, peculiarly irritating trait: we are never told
that "Barthes (etc. . . . .) *argues* that . . . ," always that "Barthes *shows*
that . . . ." We must not, *cannot,* argue with something that has been
shown to be so. For myself, I don't dismiss the French tradition, and I
make use of whatever odds and ends of it I can assimilate; but I need
something more concrete, more directly engaged with life as it is lived
and with culture as it practically exists; I have come to find Raymond
Williams more useful than Barthes. The political thrust of the semiotics
movement seems now largely lost: the adoption of Lacan was the decisive step in the process, his idiosyncratic combination of obscurantism,
essentialism, and abstraction leading inevitably away from any practical
and direct political involvement in actual social practices. With Lacan
"the human condition" and its fixed and unchangeable gender roles
come back with a vengeance, and political engagement is abandoned in
favor of the furthering of academic careers through the churning out of
increasingly hermetic learned "papers."

Revisiting Hitchcock twenty-five years later necessarily involves reopen-
ing the issue of authorship. So much has happened in the interim. At the
most extreme, the author as controlling and responsible agent has disappeared altogether: Barthes' celebrated formulation, "The author does
not write, he is written," seems to have gained widespread currency
throughout the semiotic/structuralist school. There have also been numerous attempts to reformulate the notion of the author: Peter Wollen's
suggestion that we distinguish between Hawks (a person) and "Hawks"
(a body of work bearing his signature as director); the *Cahiers du
Cinéma* notion of "inscription" (it is Ford's "inscription" that is held
largely responsible for the ideological rupturing of *Young Mr. Lincoln*);
Raymond Bellour's substitution of the term "enunciator." All of these
seem to me interesting, suggestive, useful up to a point, but finally
unsatisfying—the usefulness being primarily a matter of drawing attention to the problems.

Initially, the assault on the notion of personal authorship was a perfectly justifiable response to the early excesses of auteur theory. Auteurism emphasized the personal signature at the expense of everything else (sometimes valuing a director's work just because it could be demonstrated to have one) and, at the worst, claimed or at least implied that the author was solely and exclusively responsible for the meaning and quality of his texts. Its opponents countered this by pointing out that the author did not invent the language and conventions of his medium, the genre within which the work was located, the ideological assumptions inherent in the culture and necessarily reproduced (with whatever inflections) in the individual text; neither did the author control the conditions of production. However necessary at the time to counterbalance auteurist excess, this scarcely constituted a novel or startling revelation. Anyone with even a casual familiarity with the history of Shakespeare criticism will be aware that critics through all periods have not generally credited Shakespeare with the invention of the English language, blank verse, the iambic pentameter, the forms, genres, and conventions of the Elizabethan drama, or even the plots of his own plays. No sane person, as far as I am aware, has ever sought to claim that a work of art or entertainment has ever been produced by some kind of immaculate conception and virgin birth, or like Minerva springing fully armed from the head of Zeus.

The crux is of course the introduction into criticism of concepts of ideology. If one begins to see a film as the product of multiple determinants—the auteur, other contributors, generic conventions, studio conditions, the prevailing social/political climate, etc.—one quickly sees that all these are contained within something much bigger, all-embracing: the assumptions, values, and ideas available within the culture, which may extend back from this week's latest trend to the dawn of the human race. Behind "the author does not write, he is written" lies the assumption that we are all the slaves or prisoners of ideology, that we have neither control, responsibility, nor the power of decision, that everything we do, say, or write is determined: we are the prisoners of language, and language is ideology made concrete. It seems true that we cannot live outside ideology—if by ideology we mean the human need to formulate ideas about and attitudes to life and relationships, ideas, and attitudes that will inevitably be influenced (positively or negatively) by those already available within the culture, or available from other cultures to which we have access. In this sense, ideology would appear to be one of the major phenomena that distinguish humans from the lower animals. I presume that our cat Max does not have a defined ideological position, although he does have opinions about certain basic needs such as food and cuddles, and at times expresses them quite vociferously. If we cannot live outside ideology, this does not—it seems to me—make us its slaves. Unlike Max, I am able to choose my ideological position: the combined facts that I know I must have a position and that many different positions are available make choice possible. That choice will of course be partly determined by many factors, but the more I become aware of those factors, and aware of the positions that are available to me, the more responsible I shall be for my decision. This constitutes the basic difference between the two halves of this book: the author of *Hitchcock's Films* was not aware that he had an ideological position any more than Max; the author of *Hitchcock's Films Revisited* accepts full responsibility for his, whatever complex forces—personal, psychological, intellectual, political—may have contributed to its formation, because he has consciously and deliberately adopted it.

"The author does not write, he is written": it may have made useful polemics at a certain phase in the evolution of critical theory/practice, but does anyone seriously believe it? It is one thing to acknowledge the myriad influences on one's work (many of which one can never even hope to become aware of), another to abdicate from personal responsibility for what one is saying by subscribing to a total determinism. I am never convinced that proponents of this doctrine really apply it to themselves. When Balzac produced *Sarrasine* he did not write, he was written; presumably, then, Barthes "was written" when he produced his reading of *Sarrasine, S/Z.* Or is a (thoroughly arrogant and presumptuous) distinction being made between critical discourse and creative discourse? Stephen Heath, in his massive and intellectually very impressive tour de force on *Touch of Evil,* clearly follows Barthes in seeing Welles as "written"; does he equally disclaim responsibility for his reading of the film?—was he "written" also, and if so by whom or by what? One could easily list the influences on the article, and Heath was obviously fully aware of them, but it still appears to be the outcome of a personally accepted commitment (the feature, in fact, that gives it its distinction).

The Barthesian pronouncement is in effect merely a variation (though a peculiarly drab and demoralizing one) on a notion of authorship usually associated with the excesses of Romanticism: the notion that the author is "taken over." It exists in many forms: the religious author becomes merely the instrument of the Divine Voice, the pantheist surrenders to the "life force," the Freudian to the subconscious or the unconscious, the novelist is "taken over" by his characters. The reduction of this to the notion that we are simply taken over by ideology is a way of denying life any spiritual dimension, and of denying the possibility that any forces exist within us that are not reducible to "ideology"—forces which might be struggling against ideological determination at some deep level. Personally, I far prefer D. H. Lawrence's formulation "Not I, not I, but the wind that blows through me" to "the author does not write, he is written." The former implies voluntary submission to forces greater than oneself (if one can choose one's ideology one can equally choose one's gods), the latter mere impotence and passivity; a wind is dynamic and transformative, ideology merely much dead weight from the past. The drive to transform culture, for example, and the protest that animates it, must come from somewhere: merely from some alternative ideology that we have in some mysterious way absorbed? (from where?). The "religious" (I don't mean orthodox Christian—or orthodox anything) belief in forces both within and beyond the self seems far more politically usable than the sense of powerless submission to all-pervasive, all-embracing, inescapable "ideology." If we cannot "write" but can only "be written," if any sense of control, self-definition, responsibility, and personal commitment we feel is illusory, then why bother to do anything? I have a very strong desire that our civilization, and the human race, should not be annihilated in a nuclear war. Is this desire reducible to a product of "ideology" (what ideology?)? I have an equally strong desire (indeed, the two are exactly complementary) that we might move forward to some form of authentically liberated community united and motivated by love and cooperation rather than hatred, distrust, and competition. Is this desire merely "ideological"?—which is to say, can such a desire be explained solely in terms of my conditioning?

What is it, then, that lies in the shadowland beyond ideology? One can scarcely define it except in oblique and nebulous ways, since its defining characteristic is to be indefinable. The moment it becomes concrete, takes on flesh, it inevitably becomes ideological, the "flesh" being always culturally specific. I am forced, reluctantly, to have recourse to the phrase "religious experience": reluctantly, not because I am afraid of it myself, but because it will certainly be willfully misunderstood and misrepresented. (I can already read the reviews: "After his shaky conversion to Marxism ten years ago, Wood has now converted even more abruptly to Christianity . . ."). I must, then, step very carefully.

That Marxism dissociated itself rigorously from all forms of orthodox or organized religion was of course an absolute historical necessity. It seems to me now that Marxism's major limitation, which has yet to be seriously confronted, is its lack of interest in religious experience, the religious impulse: its refusal, if you like, of a spiritual dimension. It heedlessly threw out the baby of spiritual regeneration with the bathwater of religious dogma. The terms are, once again, dangerous, simply because, in our culture, rather as the term "sexuality" immediately evokes genital copulation, so words like "religious" or "spiritual" immediately evoke Christianity. The organized religions are, precisely, the ideological flesh, always compromised, always subject (as Marxism has also proved to be) as they become ideologically crystallized, to revisionism and reaction, a hardening into dogma (St. Paul played Stalin to Christ's Lenin). We should note, however, that all the great religions have been in their first, relatively pure phases revolutionary, and were persecuted as such. In other words, the authentic religious impulse has always been intimately associated with drives toward liberation. It is the expression of everything within us that rebels against constraint: of the struggle of the oppressed against the oppressor, of the libido against the superego, of (to borrow a title from Norman O. Brown) "Life Against Death." At bottom it is the instinctual revolt against ideology of everything that ideology seeks to contain or repress. That is why, if we associate it with the spiritual, we must equally associate it (and learn to comprehend the ultimate unity of the two) with the sexual. Without wishing to reduce the manifold delights of erotic experience to the orgasm, I don't think the orgasm has been overrated. All *forms* of the sexual, like all forms of the spiritual, must inevitably be culturally specific, hence ideological. The significance of the orgasm is that it takes us, as we pass the point of no return, beyond choice and control, and beyond ideology, to a place where indeed "Alle Menschen werden Bruder" (one regrets only the inherent sexism of Schiller's language). It should be recognized as corresponding to those moments of *spiritual* exaltation—the momentary intimation of the transcendent—that we commonly describe as religious experience. One must here acknowledge the pervasive tendency of our culture to turn everything, orgasms included, into commodities. Yet—as Pasolini so piercingly perceived (it is the theme of *Teorema*)—it is the fusion of the sexual and the spiritual that, within the debasements of late capitalist culture, provides the surest way to subversion and revolution.

One may glance here at the disparate religious manifestations of our own century. They confirm fully the association of the authentic religious impulse and revolution. There is the great chain of works by Stravinsky, from the *Rite of Spring* and *Les Noces* through the Symphony of Psalms and the Mass to *Threni,* consistently revolutionary on the aesthetic and emotional levels, however orthodox certain of their texts. But it is significant that the most convincing religious statement in twentieth-century music should be the work of a composer dedicated throughout his career to radicalism and protest—and a man who, in his seventies, could still fall passionately in love: Janaček's *Glagolitic Mass,* in which religion and revolution, the spiritual and the sexual, become one within a celebration of struggle and an affirmation of life. (I choose the *Mass* because it has a specifically religious text, in the traditional sense, and because it is arguably the greatest of Janaček's many late masterpieces. From my viewpoint, *The Diary of One Who Disappeared* is equally a religious work.)

The *Glagolitic Mass* at once incomparably dramatizes and transcends the Christian text: its feeling is as much pagan as Christian, the creative impulse it embodies rooted in a commitment to nature and fertility. The Credo, with its repeated, unifying "Veruju" ("I believe"), is above all an affirmation of life itself rather than of a specific creed. Its supreme moment of ecstasy, the tenor soloist's affirmation of belief in "one Catholic and apostolic Church" ("katolicesku i apostolsku crkov")—surely one of the most uplifting moments in twentieth-century music—transcends any actual commitment to a denominational Christianity, both in the work's refusal of the (sanctified) Latin text and in the moment's achieved sense of organic, earned growth out of the musical material. The entire work is set apart simply by being so utterly unlike any of the culturally sanctioned settings of the text: its tone consistently repudiates Christianity's reactionary elements, the emphasis on self-sacrifice, resignation, acceptance of misery in *this* world as a guarantee of beatitude in the next. The Mass conspicuously lacks a "Dona nobis pacem." I am ignorant as to whether this text is lacking from the

Slavonic version of the Mass or whether its omission was Janáček's personal decision. Whichever is the case, the point lies in what Janáček replaces it with: a dark and turbulent organ solo (liturgically, for the exit of the clergy) and a fiery and triumphant orchestral postlude (for the exit of the congregation, on one level enacting the return to sunlight from the darkness of the church), precisely reversing the moods of the opening Introduction and Kyrie. "Give us peace" is replaced by a further development of the work's passionate dark/light dialectic: struggle issuing in triumph that is above all a celebration of energy. In this age when intellectuals are bent on reducing human experience to an arid heap of signifiers, it seems necessary sometimes to exclaim with Janáček, "Veruju!"

At the other end of the scale we find the ultimate debasement of Christianity in the sordid proliferation of "fundamentalist" sects, where the religious experience is systematically perverted and degraded: sexually repressive, spiritually impoverished, politically reactionary. Rock music even at its most debased, perverse, and negative is closer to the religious impulse than fundamentalist Christianity.

Ultimately, the religious impulse might be described as the drive to affirmation: Albert Schweitzer's wonderful phrase "reverence for life" comes to mind. *Pace* Hitchcock's Catholic apologists, I would assert that the major limitation of his work—its *defining* limitation, of which its peculiar force and distinction are the corollary—is the relative weakness within it (in a film like *Frenzy,* the almost total absence) of the religious impulse as I have sought to define it. I threw out above a reference to Pasolini: Hitchcock's achievement seems to me decidedly superior, yet it lacks precisely the quality that gives Pasolini's work its (very intermittent and compromised) distinction, the sense of wonder. This is another way of putting the reservations that I attempted to put forth in the "Retrospective" of 1977.

Closely tied to affirmation, another key word would be creativity: the creative impulse, the drive to create, the pleasure of creating, seems common to all cultures and all levels of culture, manifesting itself, in however stunted a form, even within the most distressingly hostile and brutalizing social conditions such as are dominant in our own culture. The pleasure of creativity—for example, the pleasure I am experiencing at this moment in writing this paragraph—cannot be reduced to ideology even if, as always the form it takes is ideological. (The pleasure, I should add, is in no sense directly proportionate to any "absolute" assessment of value; it is the pleasure of feeling that one has said what one wanted to say, that one has done one's best. I don't think it is reducible to a sense of satisfaction—inevitably weary and relieved—in fulfilling one's duties at the level of the "work ethic".) Like sexuality, like religious experience, creativity will always of necessity take on culturally specific forms: it is obvious that Shakespeare could not have composed Mozart's operas, nor Mozart written Shakespeare's plays. Yet this seems pitifully inadequate grounds on which to deny the creativity —to flaunt another forbidden word, the genius—of Mozart and Shakespeare. But creativity needs wider definition than this: it might be defined simply as the blossoming of the soul. With roots in the impoverished, polluted soil of patriarchal capitalism, few souls can blossom freely, realizing their potential. What is amazing, what amply and daily confirms one's sense of "reverence for life," is that so many blossom at all, in conditions where one would have no right to expect anything beyond the most stunted, blighted growth. The resilience of the creative, the religious human spirit is a source of endless astonishment.

It is in relation to human creativity that one returns to Marxism; if the human soul is to blossom freely, the social soil must be changed, and only Marxist social theory—with all its limitations, blindnesses, repressions, and shortcomings—points the way toward the necessary transformation. A Marxism crossed with feminism, incorporating a rethought humanism, and animated by a religious impulse as I have defined it, could give us the way toward the transfigured civilization envisioned by Janáček in his late music, the valid longing for which motivates all authentic creativity. It might also eliminate, or at least greatly diminish, the fear of death. Aside from the dispensable, imaginary terrors inculcated by guilt-oriented religions, the fear of death seems deeply connected to the sense of nonfulfillment—of energies dissipated in alienated labor, of potential cruelly wasted, of creativity frustrated. If the soul could blossom freely, it would fear death no more than the perfect rose fears the dropping of its petals.

The various reformulations of the notion of "the author" noted above call for brief consideration here. Wollen's distinction between Hawks and "Hawks" seems largely mystificatory: one has to posit such an intimate connection between the two (Hawks the man not only directed but produced many of the films that make up the body of work labeled "Hawks," and also chose the subjects, cooperated on the screenplays, and improvised with the actors), that we are really back where we started. Bellour's "enunciator" is initially tempting. The implication is that the realized material of the film (in the widest, most inclusive sense — "material" here covers subject, plot, thematic content, and the whole mass of ideological assumptions/tensions/contradictions enacted through them) comes from the culture and is "enunciated" by the filmmaker, the process of enunciation covering the entire spectrum of mise-en-scène and editing. But on reflection, this raises more problems than it solves. On the one hand, any account of the "enunciated" (what the film says, what it means) would swiftly make clear that Hitchcock is just as implicated in that as he is in the "enunciation." On the other hand, contrariwise, Hitchcock's enunciation reveals multiple determining influences including German Expressionism and Soviet montage theory (as I argue in the "Retrospective" added for the third edition of *Hitchcock's Films*): the "enunciation" is no more (and no less) his than the "enunciated."

The *Cahiers* notion of "inscription" comes much closer to being usable. Here it seems profitable to compare, briefly, two celebrated and seminal critical texts offered as exemplary readings of Hollywood films: the *Cahiers' Young Mr. Lincoln* article and Stephen Heath's work on *Touch of Evil*. The two are often linked and there are good reasons for this: the methodologies have common sources (Althusser, Barthes, Lacan, Metz); both insist at the outset that they are offering something significantly different from traditional "interpretations"; both offer a reading of a specific film as exemplary—that is to say, the reading is to reveal certain general principles of the working of classical Hollywood narrative, rather than simply heightening the reader's appreciation/understanding of a particular work of art or artifact. Both articles, in fact, patently produce interpretations of the respective films (and highly tendentious and problematic ones at that); one may concede that their claim to reveal general principles is justified (and is what gives both pieces their interest and value), though one must add that this is scarcely a new phenomenon in criticism: an intelligent and firmly "traditional' aesthetician such as E. H. Gombrich is equally concerned with exposing general principles.

The Heath article is dauntingly impressive (I still find sections of it virtually impenetrable) and immensely irritating, notably in its attitude to "interpretations" of Welles' film. Heath is careful to pay these polite lip service ("The question here is *in no sense*—my italics—"to refuse these interpretations, to which systems in the film clearly respond"). At other points a marked animus against traditional approaches obtrudes, as here where, significantly, Heath confronts the notion of the "author";

> The opening of *Touch of Evil* with its "extraordinary" tracking shot has become a famous point of reference in "film culture" and the "breathtaking achievement" it represents is one element among many others which can be systematized in reading as the signature "Orson Welles," the style of the author.

The function of Heath's quotation marks (they do not appear to mark actual quotations, as no source is given) can only be to express sarcasm: a "film culture" that sees the opening shot of *Touch of Evil* as "extraordinary" is clearly beyond the pale (I am perplexed as to the standards by which it could be considered "ordinary," as I can think of nothing closely comparably to it in the whole of Hollywood cinema). I am not and never have been happy with the state of "film culture," and I believe my record is clear on this; I do not think, on the other hand, that traditional aesthetics and notions of authorship can simply be dismissed with a lofty contempt. Heath's entire article, by the way, has the air of presenting itself as a "breathtaking achievement"—which, like Welles' movie, it is on a certain level, both authors being very much aware of and insistent upon their virtuosity.

Heath's attitude to authorship is succinctly outlined in a sentence that (almost) follows the above: "The sole interest here is in the author as an effect of the text and only in so far as the effect is significant in the production of the filmic system, is a textural effect." I am not at all clear as to the distinction between "an effect of the text" and "a textual effect": if Welles in an effect *of* the text (a finished product), how can he also produce an effect *on* it? (If there is no distinction the last phrase is redundant—but perhaps Heath did not write but was written at that point, i.e., he lapsed into a kind of lazy automatic doodling). Nor am I clear as to what either of these phrases actually means. If one reduces the term "text" (but of course one can't) to mean "narrative content," then Welles' all-pervading authorial flourishes are by no means its necessary product ("effect"); the narrative content of the extraordinary opening tracking shot (which lasts not "some two and a half minutes," as Heath asserts, but a few seconds over three, the time in which—as the opening close-up shows us—the bomb is due to explode, which is its whole point) could as easily have been rendered in a Hitchcockian montage of fifty shots or more. If "text" means (as it must) the film in its highly specific material entirety, then it is quite easy to show that, one or two brief nondescript passages apart, Welles' "signature" dominates every aspect of it, everything that gives a filmic text its texture: camera angle, camera movement, lighting, shot length, even most of the editing which (though strictly speaking it was taken out of Welles' hands) was obviously conceived as integral to the mise-en-scène. (The point is not contradicted by the fact that Welles' editing decisions would have differed in detail; infinite variations are possible within the same style).

The reduction of Welles to "an effect of the text" is a necessary step in Heath's ultimate reduction of *Touch of Evil* to a conventional "classical Hollywood narrative": its project turns out to be, yet again, the repudiation/repression of aberrant (i.e., nonpatriarchal) sexuality, and the construction of the heroine (Susan/Janet Leigh) as "good object." The reductivism (which finally overrides all the elaborate paraphernalia of an ultra-close reading, complete with pages of diagrams) brings to mind the reductivism of another virtuoso of modern film criticism, Raymond Bellour, who once remarked that *North by Northwest* and *Bringing Up Baby* are really the same film: both end with Cary Grant pulling the heroine up by her arm from a precipitous drop, constructing once again the heterosexual couple. One might well argue that the two films are in fact polar opposites: *North by Northwest* is about Grant learning to be responsible, *Bringing Up Baby* is about Grant learning to be *ir*responsible, both outcomes presented, within the very different dramatic and authorial contexts, in the most positive terms. If the two are linked it is in their disrespectful attitude to the patriarchal organization, skeptical in Hitchcock, openly derisive in Hawks. As for *Touch of Evil,* the ultimate overriding effect of the film—its seductive and insidious invitation to the spectator to accept corruption as a fact of existence, privileging Quinlan over Vargas—has almost nothing to do with the production of the "good object" (which the film treats in the most perfunctory way) and a very great deal to do with Welles' authorship. Heath's "reading" misses it entirely. Both Heath and Bellour have done much to push forward the bounds of film theory (the later chapters of this book are indebted in various ways to both of them),* which makes it the greater pity that the conclusions their analyses reach tend to be reductive, simplistic, and banal. It is not quite, but almost, the case that the mountains, in labor, produce a ridiculous mouse.

The *Cahiers' Young Mr. Lincoln* analysis, while it uses some of the same methodological/ideological apparatus and preconceptions, is quite different in effect. For all the apparent commitment to Barthesian notions of "plurality," it seems to me that Heath and Bellour both ultimately close off the texts they "read": they turn out to be the same old "classical narrative text" all over again. The *Cahiers* reading substantially opens up Ford's film, presenting it in terms of contradictions, internal strains, and tensions. Crucial to this is a perceptibly different attitude to authorship. Far from being merely "an effect of the text," Ford's (active) "inscription" is viewed as the prime factor in the production of contradiction, the intervention that, through its resistances, disrupts and throws off course a seemingly innocuous and conservative ideological project. This version of authorship strikes me as far more defensive, profitable, and politically suggestive than Heath's "textual effect." In fact, it has a lot to recommend it. On the one hand it rejects any equation of authorship with "the artist's conscious intentions"; on the other it acknowledges that the intervention of a particular auth.· may be a (the?) prime determinant of a film's interest, without reducing the film (the "text," a texture woven from many strands) to the author's exclusive property/creation. Yet I am not entirely happy with the acceptance of "inscription" as the answer to all our problems. There seems a certain ambiguity as to what (in practical, concrete terms) the word actually means: it can easily become synonymous with "direction," or even "visual style" (the *Cahiers* writers make much of the "excesses" of Ford's "writing," for example, the recurrent "castrating stare" of Lincoln), and that is not enough. Typically, the major Hollywood directors have been involved in their films at every state—choice of subject, construction of the scenario, shooting, editing, even (as with Hitchcock) promotion. It follows that one cannot simply talk of Ford's "inscription" producing strains, disruptions, etc., in preexistent material with an independent identity outside that inscription. The strains and disruptions must already be present in the inscription itself (if one takes the term to

* I have found the analytic tools developed by Bellour especially useful, as the subsequent chapter on *Blackmail*, will testify.

cover all of Ford's intervention throughout the realization of the project) and ultimately within the ideology itself.

I shall not propose an alternative term of my own as a solution. I rather like the one I have already introduced: "intervention": because it can refer to the entire spectrum of the author's possible activities, from choice of subject to editing. But I wouldn't wish to adopt it exclusively or claim it as an adequate answer to all the problems of authorship. Instead, I offer a series of loosely interconnected propositions which should serve as explanatory background if and when I refer to Hitchcock as the "author" of his films.

1. The author's intentions. There was indeed a person called Alfred Hitchcock who, over the course of a long career, achieved a quite unusual degree of control over his films, at all stages of their construction/creation. This is not to claim that he had unconstrained freedom of choice: restrictions existed in many forms, from the tangible and documented interference of powerful producers (Selznick, for example) to the less tangible but perhaps even more powerful circumscriptions imposed inwardly—the fear of losing money, of losing one's public, of exposing oneself too nakedly. To reject the "intentionalist fallacy" (the notion that an artist's *expressed* intentions have a definitive authority in interpreting his or her work; the complementary notion that the author's intentions are what the critic is supposed to interpret and evaluate) is not to reject the fact that on certain levels the creation of a work of art or an artifact constitutes an intentional act. Hitchcock generally knew— I repeat, on certain levels—why he wanted to place his camera where he did, why he wanted to move it, why he wanted to cut, why he wanted his actors to move in certain ways, turn their heads at certain moments, speak their lines with certain intonations. This fully conscious, intentional level cannot possibly account for everything in the film and cannot account for the more important, deeper levels of meaning; but I cannot see that it is irrelevant or unworthy of consideration.

2. The author's personal psychology. We are all constructed by our culture, yet each of us is unique. The semiological emphasis on the spectator who (already constructed by culture) is then constructed by film after film has been useful to a degree, but again it proves ultimately reductive on both sides of the camera/screen, reducing both filmmaker and film recipient: the uniqueness both of artist and spectator is overridden in favor of reproducing yet again the "classical Hollywood text" and its passive victim. Below the obviously intentional level of Hitchcock's films—the level of filmic skills—lies a shadowy level where the intended and unintended, conscious and unconscious, merge indistinguishably: the level of thematic content. It can be argued that Hitchcock's cinema, on all levels (thematic, formal, methodological), is built upon the struggle to dominate and the dread of impotence, and that within the films this most characteristically takes the form of the man's desire (frequently unrealized) to dominate the woman. It is easy to see that such a thematic belongs to much more than one individual filmmaker: it is "in the culture." Equally, however, one can argue that in Hitchcock's films it achieves a quite extraordinary intensity and complexity so that it takes on an importance it does not have in, say, the work of Renoir or Hawks. This is an example of what is meant by asserting that great films belong both to their authors and to the culture.

It follows that I don't consider biographical and autobiographical material entirely irrelevant to film criticism: there are valid uses to be made of Hitchcock's many personal anecdotes and of the *type* of work represented by Donald Spoto's *The Dark Side of Genius* (critical as one may be of the particular instance). One's initial impulse to reject such resources is well motivated: one is all too familiar with the kind of interpretation that starts from a biographical fact and proceeds to explain (or explain away) the films purely in reference to it. The legitimate use of such information is exactly the reverse: the biographical data may confirm or consolidate a reading arrived at from a careful analysis of the film itself. It follows that such a use is minor, incidental, and never necessary, it merely accords the satisfaction of confirmation. Thus Hitchcock's celebrated (and frequently reiterated) anecdote about his mock-incarceration, as a child, in a police cell (clearly an incident or fantasy of almost traumatic significance for him) has a clear if limited usefulness and interest in relation to my reading of *Blackmail*, though the anecdote was neither the source nor the conclusion of that reading. Or I find it interesting that, throughout the filming of *Vertigo*, Hitchcock compelled Kim Novak to wear certain kinds of clothing which she strongly resisted—precisely what James Stewart does to her within the diegesis. To *reduce* the film to that kind of anecdotal significance would be merely a way of rejecting or evading the implications of its profound and disturbing investigation of the sources and mechanisms of romantic love within our culture.

3. The author and ideological construction. "Personal psychology," of course, is not and cannot be *merely* "personal." The infant is born into ideology, expressed immediately in the way it is clothed. The traditional "blue for a boy, pink for a girl" is but the beginning, and crudest manifestation, of a whole long process of gender construction of which psychoanalytical theory has established the formidable power. Whether one accepts the Freudian model (the oedipal; trajectory) or the Lacanian (the entry into the Symbolic), it is clear that we are inevitably subjected to an inexorable socialization whose (largely unconscious) purpose is to construct us as secure subjects within the dominant ideological norms. Yet it is also clear that the socialization process doesn't entirely work (if it did, we couldn't become aware of it as such, because all alternatives and all resistance would be "successfully" repressed). Many, arguably all, human individuals within our culture set up an instinctive resistance to it in many forms, on different levels, and to greatly varying degrees, the resistance testifying to the fact that we are never "merely" ideological subjects or capable of being fully explained by such concepts. The socialization process, the perception that it begins at birth, the human individual's resistance to it, and the results of the struggle, were brilliantly encapsulated by Blake about two hundred years ago in his brief *Infant Sorrow,* a poem of which every phrase deserves pondering:

Infant Sorrow

My mother groan'd, my father wept,
Into the dangerous world I leapt;
Helpless, naked, piping loud,
Like a fiend hid in a cloud.

Struggling in my father's hands,
Striving against my swaddling-bands,
Bound and weary, I thought best
To sulk upon my mother's breast.

It is doubtless too simple to say that when the resistance becomes conscious (and healthy) it manifests itself as radicalism, and when it remains unconscious (and unhealthy) it manifests itself as neurosis: the relationship between the two (between conscious/unconscious, health/ unhealth, radicalism/neurosis) is likely to be far more complicated and interpenetrating than such a formulation suggests. What, after all, are the forms of neurosis but a kind of incoherent, unformulated radical protest? The meeting of psychoanalytical theory and concepts of ideology suggests that every human being in our culture is a battleground on which is fought, at both conscious and unconscious levels—always in a different form, always with a different outcome, the variations being infinite—the struggle between the forces of repression and the urge to liberation, the struggle in microcosm that we see being waged in the outside world of politics, national, international, sexual.

It can certainly be claimed that Hitchcock's work manifests this resistance to an extreme degree and in highly idiosyncratic ("personal") ways, with the result that the dominant ideological structures—especially those governing gender construction and gender relations—are repeatedly exposed, called into question, or ruptured. Many of the films therefore offer themselves very readily for appropriation as radical texts. It also needs to be said that the resistance should not be attributed exclusively to the workings of the unconscious, to impulses of which the artist has no awareness: it is manifested on all levels and is as much an attribute of intelligence and control as of repressed psychic drives.

4. Narrative patterns/Generic conventions. Like Shakespeare, Hitchcock invented neither his medium nor the genres that had developed within it (also like Shakespeare, he significantly explored and extended the potentialities of both). No artist starts from scratch, there can be no absolute new beginning, no *tabula rasa*. The Romantic-idealist craving for absolute, mystically inspired 'originality' found its ironic apotheosis, disguised as the ultimate in historical materialism, in Godard's repeated call, desperate and barren, for a "return to zero," a call already countered by Trotsky almost half a century earlier:

The main task of the proletarian intelligentsia in the immediate future is not the abstract formation of a new culture regardless of the absence of a basis for it, but definite culture-bearing, that is, a systematic, planful and, of course, critical imparting to the backward masses of the essential elements of the culture which already exists. (*Literature and Revolution*, p. 123)

Whether on the level of the individual or that of the political collective (a collective is composed of individuals), significant art arises out of the artist's appropriation and transformation of forms, structures, conventions, that already exist. Like the artist, those forms, etc., are ideologically determined, though, again, not in any simple, absolute, or exclusive way: like the individual, they exhibit, on inspection, the principles of resistance, conflict, and contradiction. The process of appropriation and transformation—as opposed to mere inert reproduction—is of course crucial: if a given form (a Hollywood genre, for example) is structured ideologically, it follows that a transformation of that structure also affects its ideological meaning. Whether or not the appropriation and transformation are conscious or unconscious is immaterial: again, the term "intervention" comes to mind as a means of suggesting an active and dynamic involvement that may or may not operate partly on the level of intention.

What applies to forms, genres, conventions also applies to the wider principles of so-called "classical narrative." Again, the intervention of the individual artist can have a transformative effect on the narrative's overall movement and on the precise significance of its closure. It is true that the basics of narrative—the principle that a story must have a beginning, a middle, and an end, and that these will correspond roughly to order/disturbance/restoration of (some form of) order—are likely to survive, and that some form of closure (however tentative or ambiguous) will assert itself. But these are not merely the principles of something called "classical narrative" or the "classical realist text," they are the principles of storytelling itself. It is time we resisted the temporarily pervasive notion that closure is a sort of bourgeois wish fulfilment, particularly exemplified by the nineteenth-century novel and the Hollywood film. I cannot think of a single folktale, legend, or myth that does not exhibit the principle of closure (if such exist they must be very rare); it is a characteristic of even the most primitive narratives. Tribal hunting rituals, in which one man dresses as a tiger while the others stalk him, appear invariably to culminate in the death of the "animal" in the interests of sympathetic magic. Crucial in reading the closure of a narrative are attitude and tone. If, in the Hollywood cinema, the privileged form of closure is the guaranteed union of the heterosexual couple, even a perfunctory glance at Hitchcock's American films will show how rare it is in his work that such a closure is presented convincingly, as the film's triumphant culmination, without irony or discord.

5. Signification/expression. The false opposition individual author/ cultural production gets its logical extension in the equally false opposition between personal expression and signification. The "advanced" position was usefully summed up ("usefully" in the sense that its perversity and reductivism are inadvertently exposed) in a passage from Tom Ryall's review of Raymond Durgnat's *The Strange Case of Alfred Hitchcock, Screen,* Summer 1975 (I have no reason to suppose that Ryall would stand by this today, and am not trying to "get at" him personally):

In those terms (i.e. the terms of "auteurist" criticism), the debate is about the director/auteur's management of his consciousness, and not about managing the problems of signification in the cinema. The latter orientation would depend upon recognizing that the work of the filmmaker uses materials (images/sounds) which are already charged with a multiplicity of meanings which can be underlined (remarked), or effectively suppressed by the filmmaker, and by a great many other factors. Accordingly, filmmakers succeed or fail depending upon their knowledge of signs and meaning in the cinema rather than their "genius" or "talent" or whatever.

Hitchcock, apparently, was simply a good student who mastered his signifiers, and this had nothing to do with any personal qualities (other than, presumably, application). One may well ask why, if Hitchcock's art consisted merely of learning and applying certain sets of preexistent signifiers, it is so distinctive, so different from the work of others? But the passage concedes something by way of answer: Hitchcock can underline or effectively suppress any quantity of that "multiplicity of meanings" with which the materials (images/sounds) are already charged. What is conceded here is in fact the vacuity of the entire either/or opposition on which the passage is structured. It is but a short step from conceding Hitchcock's ability to underline and effectively suppress meanings to arguing that he is also able, out of his materials, effectively to construct them. He also, of course, constructed the particular images and sounds that constitute his "materials," out of the vast range of options available to him within the culture and within the limitations of commercial cinema. There is no realistic opposition between the notion that meanings are culturally determined and the notion of personal cinema.

The demolition of the author is necessary and central to a wider operation, the demolition of art. For without artists there is no art—only various configurations of signifiers awaiting deconstruction. The experiences for which one used to go to art—experiences inextricably bound up with concepts such as intelligence, sensibility, complexity, a sense of value—have been declared invalid. They were, apparently, the exclusive preserve of the bourgeoisie, an aspect of bourgeois ideology, and anyway an illusion: if there are no artists, how can we attribute intelligence or sensibility to them? The notion of value—that the ultimate aim of criticism might be the establishment of (provisional) value judgments—is regarded as particularly reprehensible. If what we used to call works of art are mere ideological constructions, culturally determined, produced out of various combinations of codes, systems, and signifiers, then there is no point in choosing between them. All we need do is disassemble them to see how the mehanisms work—or, more commonly, to prove once again that the mechanisms work in exactly the ways we predicted. Further, to attempt to develop a mature and responsible sense of value by prolonged attention to works of art is apparently an undertaking that smacks of elitism. I have never quite understood why: Is any human endeavour that requires sustained effort and long experience elitist?—is it elitist to be good at football, physics, or mathematics? And how comes it, then, that the achievement of the lofty pinnacles of "deconstruction" and Lacanian psychoanalysis is somehow *not* elitist? Why a Marxist interested in the arts should not strive to develop a sense of value continues to elude me.

In fact, the whole either/or attitude of the semiotics/structuralist movement is based on a massive misapprehension. None of the valid achievements of that movement has rendered obsolete what T. S. Eliot called "the common pursuit of true judgment": indeed, what the most valuable of those achievements have done is to strengthen and more clearly define (and partly redefine) the criteria upon which that "common pursuit" can effectively be undertaken. It is important, if we are to pursue responsible value judgements, to develop a sense of how classical narrative works, what are its constraints and limitations, to what degree its "rules" (which can always be bent or broken) are determined by the patriarchal construction of gender differentiation. It is crucial to develop a concept of ideology, and of ideological contradiction, of the ways in which ideology functions as a force of repression—and hence of the forces it strives to repress that struggle against it. This will certainly affect our sense of value (which will be very different from T. S. Eliot's), in some ways transforming it; but there is no reason to suppose that the critical drive through analysis to evaluation has been discredited or rendered obsolete.

A NOTE ON "DECONSTRUCTION"

There was just a piece in the *New York Times* Magazine—something about the Yale critics. There's a big movement afoot there, and I can't begin to explain it—they're called deconstructionists. . . . I saw a woman pick a carrot out of the gutter on Columbus Avenue where now the rents for a store are twelve, fifteen thousand dollars a month. You know, money is flowing on that street, and here is this woman picking a filthy carrot out of the gutter in front of a Korean vegetable store. It's very peculiar—society is so hard to describe. (Arthur Penn, interviewed in *CineAction!* 5)

What went wrong?—how was the political impetus of the late '6os/early '7os lost, that manifested itself so strikingly in the field of film study? Basically, times changed, the revolution never happened: it is difficult to nurture a radical voice within a culture that doesn't want to listen to it, or where it is attended to only by a small, self-enclosed elite provided it wraps itself up in a more or less esoteric academic discourse. But one can be more specific: the cultural change itself—the shift from protest to recuperation—perhaps was responsible for certain choices that have determined the progress of film theory: choices of who and what should be the major influences. Semiotics/structuralism had (perhaps still has—one mustn't discount the possibility) great political potential. It provided tools that could be, and up to a point have been, used politically. One must insist upon a crucial distinction between using semiotics/structuralism as a set of political weapons and surrendering to it as an all-embracing system. The latter was the choice that was made, by and large, and it led to further choices that seem progressively disastrous: the adoption of the later Barthes, Lacan, and "deconstruction."

Barthes' earlier work *(Mythologies, S/Z)* had and retains its political usefulness, though the danger signals were already there, pointing to the

possible retreat into a new aestheticism that his later work on the whole
enacts. Lacan's pernicious essentialism might be compared to that of the
opening chapters of the Book of Genesis, the options it assigns women
being scarcely less ignominious: they can either resign themselves to their
subordinate place in the patriarchal Symbolic, or become psychotic. The
repeated feminist attempts to appropriate Lacan seem as perverse as if
the Jews had tried to appropriate the tenets of Nazism, or gays today
tried to appropriate the fundamentalism of Jerry Falwell. Of course, if
you are led to believe that Lacan—or Hitler, or Falwell—embodies "the
truth," you can't very well do anything else. This phenomenon is sometimes given the name "self-oppression."

Semiotics offered to lead us to the Promised Land. As far as I can see
we are still in the wilderness, in terms of social practicalities. The wilderness has a new name every few months. The last I heard it was called
"deconstruction." Like semiotics, deconstruction can of course be used
as a political tool, and this seems to be what Derrida himself intended.
But to appropriate it thus is to violate its basic premise: as language
itself is slippery and unstable, every text can be deconstructed: every
piece of knitting has a dropped stitch somewhere, and if you find the
right place and pull, the whole thing will come undone and we'll end up
with a big jumble of wool on the floor. Here of course politics vanishes
altogether: if every text can be deconstructed, then it makes no real
difference whether you choose to deconstruct conservative texts or radical ones, *Mein Kampff* or *Das Kapital:* the choice is merely arbitrary.
Nothing ultimately means anything and nothing ultimately matters. It's
the perfect gift for academics in the '80s, though something of a dead
end. When you've demonstrated that every text can be deconstructed, it
becomes fruitless to deconstruct more and more. You can, of course,
deconstruct the deconstruction, then deconstruct the deconstruction of
the deconstruction: the babushka-doll of contemporary aesthetics. Instead of the Promised Land we are left with Peer Gynt and his onion.
Meanwhile, old women are still bending down to retrieve carrots from
gutters all over the world, and the nuclear power is building in preparation for the holocaust, deliberate or accidental. We academics, of course,
can change things very little, but we can at least try to be ready in
position when the next cultural upheaval produces the next wave of
popular radicalism. There are widespread rumors now that student protest is once again beginning to mobilize—centered on the anti-nuclear

movement and the various enormities of Reaganism. If and when the time comes, I hope we shall be in the forefront rather than sitting in a back room deconstructing one another's texts.

Leavis, Marxism, and Film Culture

Now that the semioticians' trek to the Promised Land has ended in the wilderness of deconstruction, and we are looking around in bewilderment wondering if there is anywhere else to go before we starve to death, it seems a propitious moment to question the wisdom of summarily rejecting, at the trek's outset, the alternative direction of a critic and thinker who stood, above all, for "life." From its first appearance, *Hitchcock's Films* was identified (favorably or unfavorably, but generally the latter) as a work owing an immense debt to the literary criticism of F. R. Leavis. This is the time and place, then, to acknowledge the debt and to reaffirm a continuing—if continuously shifting and developing—relationship to the figure whom I still regard as one of the great heroes of twentieth-century aesthetics.

In attempting to revaluate the role of Leavis in the past history of criticism, and his potential role in its future, I am faced with some problems. To some of my readers Leavis may not even be a name, to many others little more; others still will believe that he was disposed of once and for all two decades ago, when the theoretical hegemony passed decisively to semiotics, and that there is little point in trying to resurrect a body of work that history has declared definitively dead and buried. A further problem: Leavis was a literary critic who showed not the slightest knowledge of or interest in the cinema, and regarded all contemporary popular culture as degraded beyond possible redemption: his relevance to the present and future of film criticism may seem negligible, an attempt to suggest otherwise merely perverse, the more so from a professedly leftist critic (he was explicitly anti-Marxist). It is necessary, then, to begin with some account of what Leavis stood for; the more necessary because, in order to discredit it, leftist British criticism found it expedient to reduce his position to the most simplistic parody, and it is the parody that survives: the occasional use of the term "Leavisite" in modern criticism is scarcely calculated to encourage the reader to explore its source.

This account will inevitably be colored by a strongly personal note.

Not just *Hitchcock's Films*, but all my early works—books on Hawks, Bergman, Penn, Satyajit Ray, etc.—were commonly characterized (generally with hostile intent) as "Leavisite" or, somewhat more positively, "Leavisian" (the distinction is that between blind discipleship and the acceptance of an influence). It is also widely believed (for a while I half-believed it myself) that I subsequently abandoned Leavis when I became committed to Marxist and feminist principles regarded (by, among others, Leavis himself) as incompatible with a Leavisian standpoint. I now feel that I have been more faithful to Leavis than I realized, and one impulse behind this present discourse—which many will regard as an unjustifiable digression, but which I feel to be central to the nature and aims of my work—is the desire to reaffirm a commitment that has continued undergound though a radical ideological shift, and which I hope can now resurface.

One factor—a crucial one—that immediately suggests Leavis' potential interest for a left-wing critical practice is his uncompromising hostility to the critical and cultural Establishment, for which he was virtually ostracized at Cambridge. As an undergraduate, I frequently saw his academic colleagues pass him by as if he didn't exist. He was repeatedly passed over for promotion, his work as far as possible marginalized by the faculty of which he was unquestionably the most distinguished member; his wife, also a critic and scholar of exceptional distinction and achievement, was never granted the recognition of a university lectureship. His crime was, essentially, a concept of "seriousness" totally at odds with most academic practice and with British literary culture generally. The fundamental Leavisian assumption is that a seriousness about art is inseparable from a seriousness about life. The seriousness that informs all Leavis' work places it, then, in opposition not only to the careerism of many academics but also to a rival concept of academic seriousness, the notion of "scholarship." Leavis' own scholarship was formidable, and he despised dilettantism. The opposition was not to the cultivation of knowledge but to the familiar academic tendency to lose all sense of the relevance of art to the urgent problems of living, of values, of choices and decisions in a world outside the secure confines of academe. The resistance to Leavis on all levels, from the popular press to the highest academic ranks, can only be read today as defense against a threat and as nervous rejection of a challenge.

Leavis' hostility was by no means directed narrowly toward academics. The force of his cultural analysis is generated partly by his perception that traditional academics, however insulated they may appear and may wish to be, are inevitably implicated in wider movements within a wider culture. Academics publish; their books are reviewed in literary periodicals, in weekly papers (such as the *Times Literary* and *Educational Supplements*), frequently by other academics, and are promoted by organizations such as the British Arts Council. Leavis saw all of this, correctly, as a network of interlocking clubs of which the main condition for membership was the readiness to scratch other members' backs and not rock the boat: a literary culture characterized, overall, by careerism, mutual back-scratching, "scholarship," and liberal platitudes, a culture that can attribute to a Kingsley Amis or a C. P. Snow a significance beyond the merely symptomatic, and in which "seriousness" can be regarded only as a threat. Beyond that culture was the wider culture of consumer capitalism and "entertainment," into the horrors of which Leavis seldom ventured (he had a secure grasp of its dominant characteristics, though not of the complexities and contradictions that underlie them). We are talking here of Britain in the '40s, '50s, and '60s, but the description will seem depressingly familiar today. Indeed, the era of "Postmodernism," and the types of "scholarly" and theoretical work it is producing, are peculiarly inimical to the Leavisian "seriousness"; its exponents will react to the challenge with ever greater hostility if they don't prefer the option (all *that* is, after all, so passé) of simply ignoring its existence.

It is not easy to define Leavis' critical position: it is magnificently embodied in his critical practice, the complexity, flexibility, and subtlety of which resist reduction to theoretical formulation. He vigorously opposed any notion that criticism could be "scientific" (which of course partly accounts for his rejection by semioticians). Adequately reading a great work of literature is a matter of sensitive and cultivated receptiveness; so, therefore, is teaching it, studying it, or writing about it critically. The emphasis on education provoked, predictably enough, the charge of elitism; yet the notion that one can only assimilate the full complexity of, say, *Anna Karenina* or *Hamlet* if one has been educated to do so does not seem unreasonable. As Leavis frequently noted, no one questions the need for training and discipline in the field of athletics, or suggests that it is elitist to exclude untrained and unqualified beginners from Olympic teams, yet to suggest that a university English literature program should not be automatically accessible to anyone who wishes to enter it is to risk being branded as anti-democratic. The same point applies, even more strongly, to university film study courses, habitually regarded (by students and many professors, including even some film professors) as "soft options" for a relatively painless grade.

Central to Leavis' work is the proposition that the ultimate aim and purpose of criticism is evaluation ("scholarship" being a means to that end, never an end in itself). For Leavis, a sense of value in the arts is the index of a sense of value in life. To understand (and the understanding must be authentic and personal, not a matter of accepting accepted opinion) that George Eliot was a greater novelist than Thackeray, for example, is also to understand a great deal more: the nature of true "seriousness," of "intelligence," of "significance" (three key Leavisian terms). For Leavis, "intelligence" is never synonymous with "intellectuality" (let along "cleverness"): to be "intelligent" is above all to be intelligent about "life" (another key word). It is of the essence of Leavis' position that these terms cannot be given a fixed definition: one might say that they are continuously redefined, for every age, by every great artist—the corollary of which (what Leavis's detractors would see as an impossible, unresolvable vicious circle) is that the great artist is definable as the one who redefines them.

It has become fashionable, in the age of semiotics, to argue that Leavis' sense that the most important critical concepts are not susceptible of fixed (or "scientific") definition is the greatest weakness of his position; it seems to me, on the contrary, its greatest strength. For one thing, it acknowledges the provisional and relative quality of all valid judgments: they are valid (at least in the precise form in which they find expression) for the time and the place, for the cultural moment. "Significance," "intelligence," "seriousness" answer to major human needs, but human needs, though a reality, are never fixed, are themselves undefinable except in terms of the specific cultural situation. There is a sense in which the values embodied in the finest work of Shakespeare, Tolstoy, George Eliot, have permanent relevance: as a model of "seriousness" and "intelligence" about living. But they cannot have the direct relevance that might enable us to read their plays or novels to cull practical moral suggestions as to how to conduct our own lives (certain of the dismissive parodies of Leavis have sought to reduce his position to idiotic notions of that kind). To put it bluntly: one reads Tolstoy to learn what it means to be serious and intelligent about "life" and human needs, not to be told which side one should take on the abortion issue. Leavis' favorite and famous formulation of the ideal critical exchange ("This is so, isn't it?"/"Yes, but . . .") itself testifies to the provisional nature of value judgments, that they are subject to continuous modification and refinement.

Leavis' insistence that crucial critical terms can't be "scientifically" defined calls into question the contemporary opposition Science/Ideology: on the one hand there is science (= knowledge), the demonstrably true, on the other hand ideology, the demonstrably false. It is time we recognized the unsatisfactoriness of this dichotomy, and in human terms its pernicious reductivism. As we are born into culture, our instincts, drives, primary emotions, inevitably take on ideological form, but that doesn't mean that they are merely *reducible* to ideology: in other words, yes, there is such a thing as "human nature," though we must see it as endlessly protean rather than as eternal and unchangeable. Love, for example, takes on different forms in different cultures and many forms in one culture, and all that we can define precisely ("scientifically") are the forms, which are ideological; yet this should not lead us to deny the reality of love, even if we can never know what that reality *divorced from its forms* is.

We must repudiate above all the notion that "human nature" is a construction of bourgeois ideology. Certainly, bourgeois ideology has attempted to impose its view of human nature as the only one, naturalizing itself and its institutions, passing them off as "real," hence unchangeable: this is one of Marxism's great, radical, seminal perceptions. But to leap from this to a belief that "therefore" there is no such thing as human nature is a most extraordinary and dangerous non sequitur. It is rather like asserting that, because certain florists try to make artificial flowers that can be mistaken for real ones, there are no such things as real flowers. If there were not such a thing as human nature there would never have been such a thing as human society. It is human nature that makes us able to interact, to cooperate, to wish to understand each other; although, at some stage very early in human history, two principles—purely contingent on material conditions—were instituted that have made that interaction and cooperation problematic: private ownership and the subordination of women. We must believe in human nature if the human race is to continue: in the ability and desire to communicate; in the need to give and receive love and tenderness; in the drive for fulfillment and self-respect. It is quite ridiculous to dismiss these as attributes of bourgeois ideology: did the bourgeoisie really invent love? The human nature and human needs I am positing are clearly very fluid: they could take on an infinite number of social forms and ideological clothings. The social forms in which they have currently become embodied—represented at their crudest by the opposed but complementary ideologies of Soviet Russia and the United States—can only be seen as an appalling perversion and corruption (the history of which can be clearly traced) of the "human nature" they profess to fulfill. It is only through a return to an overthrow of the origins of our contemporary disease (private ownership, the subordination of woman) that "human nature" can be liberated.

By this point it will be obvious that there is another reason for the rejection of Leavis by the semiotic/structuralist tradition: his position presupposes a notion of individual authorship, terms like "intelligence" and "seriousness" having meaning only in relation to a human source. In fact, the semiological school's attack on the idea of personal author-ship rests upon another false opposition (and another reductive parody): the alternative to the notion that works of art can be adequately ac-counted for as cultural products is proposed as the "Romantic" notion that they are produced out of the untrammelled inspiration of an indi-vidual genius. Both alternatives strike me as equally nonsensical, and Leavis' critical practice makes nonsense of both. For him, the great work of art is at once, and inseparably, the product of a culture and an individual living within that culture, an individual who is at once its product and something more. There is an obvious sense in which we are all "products" of our culture. The problem of the word is that it suggests a total passivity and helplessness. We are not "products" in the sense in which a can of beans is a product, because we are capable of understand-ing, criticizing, and, if we feel it necessary, repudiating, the culture that "produced" us. Another necessary Leavisian term (of which semiotics has perversely taught us to feel ashamed) is "creativity." Do we no longer believe in human creativity, because the latest "truths" of semio-tics have reduced everything to collections of signifiers awaiting decon-struction? If so, in the words recently immortalized by Bette Midler, "Why bother?"

Central to Leavis' concerns was a certain concept of the university and its role in cultural development; as this book will find its main readership among university lecturers and students, it seems appropriate to go into this here at some length. The background to the concept was a particular university, Cambridge, England, where I attended Leavis' lectures in the early '50s. Cambridge was far from realizing the Leavisian ideal, but it was so different from (and so much closer to it than) the contemporary North American model (not to mention the modern British universities which that model has influenced) that some account of it may be necessary here.

The phrase that epitomized Leavis' concept of the ideal university was "creative center of civilization." However one interprets terms like "human values," "human needs" (an orthodox Marxist will interpret them somewhat differently from a traditional humanist, let alone, for example, an orthodox Catholic), it is obvious that they are becoming increasingly submerged in the present drift of our civilization: any serious conception of "human needs" is not answered by consumerism, material greed, the quest for status and "upward mobility," or the cynical opportunism that characterizes "democratic" party politics. Leavis' "creative center of civilization" was, then, conceived of as functioning essentially in rigorous opposition to that drift. Like Leavis, the Cambridge English faculty at large saw itself as preserving a tradition within a world that threatened to render it obsolete, but the general conception of tradition was very different from Leavis'. For Leavis, any tradition worth preserving was dynamic and continuously developing and evolving, embodying a critique of the present and pointing toward possible futures. The "tradition" represented by most of his fellow lecturers *was,* in effect, obsolete: it looked to the past, and sealed itself off from the world it should have opposed. Leavis' claim that literature and the arts should be the vital center of the university could be argued only in terms of an ideal, not with reference to any producible actuality— apart, that is, from his own work and the achievements it generated, achievements most impressively and concretely incarnated in *Scrutiny,* the literary journal Leavis edited and sustained for over thirty years in collaboration with his wife, Q. D. Leavis. (Those who wrote for *Scrutiny* —mainly Leavis' own students—were seldom appointed to the Cambridge English school, which operated, again, on the principle of the "club": criteria for appointments appear to have been a readiness to conform to standards that Leavis could only repudiate. Again, the description is likely to evoke a strong sense of familiarity today.)

However, if Cambridge was very far from corresponding to the Leavisian ideal, it nonetheless had the potential to do so, as our contemporary universities have not. Crucial to that potential is its organization of the apparatus of study. At Cambridge, every student had a supervisor for whom one produced an essay every fortnight; the essay was read aloud and exhaustively discussed in a tutorial shared with one other student. Lecture courses were optional—one could attend ten a week or none, as one chose—and they involved no essay-writing, examinations, tests, or "quizzes" (the very word suggests how low we have sunk). One attended a course because one was interested, not because one needed another grade. This meant, inevitably, that many lecture rooms were almost empty after the first week or two (Leavis' were almost invariably crowded, with students sitting on the steps and standing at the back and sides). Motivation, obviously, is partly constructed by the environment, its organization, its material realities. Cambridge at its best constructed student motivation in terms of a commitment to study for the sake of understanding; our universities today construct it in terms of "making it": obtaining the necessary credits for the necessary degree to lead to the necessary job in the existing culture. (This is not to suggest that all students inertly submit to such construction; many, in varying degrees of consciousness, resist it. But, for lecturer and student alike, it breeds the cynicism with which anyone connected with a university today is all too familiar.)

In a famous incident at the time of the release of *Deux ou Trois Choses que Je Sais d'Elle*, Jean-Luc Godard appeared on French television and brought along a real-life prostitute. In answer to protests, he remarked that prostitution is doing something you don't want to do, for money, and that everyone working for television was a prostitute. If one accepts the definition, then it is clear that prostitution is one of the central defining characteristics of capitalist culture. The principle certainly extends to our educational system: our children are taught prostitution from a very early age, and the instruction now provides the basis for a university education. To take a course in order to get a credit is prostitution; so is writing an essay in order to get a grade. Anyone who teaches in a university is confronted daily with the practical results of this system: "What do I have to do to get a B on this course?—I need a B to graduate": the prostitution is now not uncommonly as shameless as that. The university as a "creative center of civilization"?—Leavis' challenging phrase now provokes little but a raised eyebrow. It is not the students' fault. Nor is it, on an individual level, the teachers': if we are honest we must recognize how difficult it is to refuse to become complicit, and how frequently we succumb, the disease being intrinsic to the system itself. The only possible effective response would be organization and mobilization, involving both teachers and students. But we are very far, at present, from a revolutionary situation. The educational system is deeply implicated in the requirements and ethos of consumer capitalism; so, too, are the universities' administrators (who will tell you that "we must attract students in a heavily competitive world"), their teachers (who will tell you that "we have to compromise if we are to keep students in our classes"), their students (who will tell you that "we have to prepare ourselves to find jobs, we must face reality"—i.e., move from one form of prostitution to another). All this is known familiarly as "being realistic about things." Interest any of the existing political parties in a program to reconstruct the university as "a creative center of civilization"? Don't make me laugh. There is no established political party that would not be directly threatened by such a move; and, besides, it wouldn't attract many votes.

The essential point is this: if not to the university, where, today, does one look for the "creative center of civilization"? The university was its last stronghold—and then in potential rather than actuality. We are constantly being told by the media how lucky we are to be living in a "free" democracy rather than a police state, and to an extent of course we *are*. But just how far *does* this luck—this freedom—extend? Where are we to look, today, within our culture, for any central, influential, and accessible location wherein a radical critique of that culture might be mounted? As the capitalist media gain ever-increasing dominance, infiltrating every corner, protest is correspondingly marginalized, pushed out into peripheries where it can do little harm: "Fringe" theater, countercultural (hence under-financed and under-distributed) papers and magazines, small and often clandestine political groups. Meanwhile, *within* the media, Marxism is conflated with Stalinism and radicalism becomes barely distinguishably from terrorism. The university remains, in theory, the one central location where a serious critique of our culture and its values might have effect; but the university has now been fairly thoroughly coopted by consumer capitalism. Instead of a place where students might be encouraged to undertake a searching examination of our culture and their positions within it, it has become increasingly indistinguishable from career-training institutes of "higher" education, its primary function being to slot students into positions within the status quo. No, we don't live in a police state (though we can scarcely doubt that its conditions could and would quite easily be imposed if it were found necessary—the machinery is in place); but capitalism has its own methods, the more effective for *appearing* noncoercive, of inhibiting if not prohibiting free speech and free inquiry. What "freedom of speech" amounts to within capitalist culture and a capitalist educational system is that we can ask any questions except the important ones.

The key document in the exposition of Leavis' view of the university, and one of his finest works, *English Literature in Our Time and the University*, (Chatto and Windus, 1969), originated as a series of lectures delivered in 1967. At that time it was still possible for Leavis to believe, though only with an obvious effort of will (disillusionment and desperation can be felt lurking just beneath the surface of the argument, threatening its poise, provoking its tendency to repetitiveness and over-insistence), that his ideal was somehow realizable within the conditions of modern capitalism. If that belief had finally collapsed, he would surely (given his honesty and his constant striving for the construction or affirmation of positive concepts) have felt compelled to rethink his attitude to Marxism, as the only available alternative. We can see now, clearly enough, that the Leavisian ideal was already impossible in 1967: even had it been possible to (re-)construct the university as a vital core of cultural development, it is impossible to believe that it could ever have significantly affected the general drift of capitalist civilization. That drift is plainly irreversible. The only hope for "life" must now lie in the collapse of the capitalist economy and the emergence of alternative systems out of its ruins. Leavis made the complementary errors of (more or less) equating Marxism with Stalinism and defining the "enemy" as industrialization rather than as the capitalist organization that has controlled and exploited it.

Yet the Marxist rejection of Leavis in the '60s/'70s now seems to parallel the feminist rejection of Freud: both rejections were perhaps necessary at a certain phase in the evolution of Marxist and feminist thought; both now appear in the long run misguided and impoverishing. Leavis, like Freud (or anyone else, for that matter), was partially circumscribed by the ideological formations of his time, place, class, and gender, yet (again like Freud) he produced concepts that can be developed to shatter those formations, concepts we simply cannot afford to jettison. The impoverishment, the ultimate sterility, of a Marxist aesthetic founded upon exclusive notions of the "scientific"—an aesthetic that has led us by an internal logic both inexorable and perverse into the contemporary wasteland of "deconstruction," an aesthetic that feels duty bound to renounce all ties with humanism—has by now become clear to many of us. Humanism and Marxism must, for the validity of either, exist not as irreconcilable contraries but in total, inseparable union. It is of vital importance that Marxist thinking be animated by the essential Leavisian concerns embodied in the key words: "values," "standards," "intelligence," "seriousness," "creativity," "life." Within a Marxist society, Leavis' concept of the university—or something sufficiently like it to bear a recognizable resemblance—might prove realizable; it would certainly be worth fighting for. One must add that— ideally—such a university would be run by the students; the problem being, of course, that today—thanks to the effectiveness of consumer-capitalist indoctrination and the educational system that serves it—most students by the time they reach university age are too thoroughly constructed within the ideological norms (the norms of prostitution) to be trusted to do more than repeat the existing patterns, perhaps with even laxer standards.

I have argued for the necessity of Leavis' rehabilitation: I feel that he should play a more central role in the development of a revolutionary Marxist aesthetic than, say, Roland Barthes. That should not, however, suggest that there must be yet another either/or opposition. In fact, the dismissal of Leavis by the semiological school rests partly on a confusion between practices (and purposes) which, while interactive within any healthy aesthetic, are also in important ways discrete: the practice of theory (broadly, how things work in terms of general principles) and the practice of criticism (the interpretation and evaluation of specific works). The theoretical exploration into the functioning of classical narrative (Barthes, Heath, Bellour . . .) has been of immense value to the critic in recent years, particularly in relation to the continuous process of refining and redefining criteria; it in no way renders the function of criticism obsolete. Nor are Leavisian principles (as embodied in the key words) rendered obsolete by the enormous advances in Marxist and feminist theory, the pervasive concern with ideology: they merely need to be expanded and reinterpreted, as Freud has had to be reinterpreted (occasionally against himself). It would be a curious and hopelessly impoverished form of Marxism or feminism that found no place for "seriousness," "intelligence," "creativity," or "life" (with the full weight the Leavisian context gives those words). I want to pass now to consider some of the problems and limitations of Leavis' position, as I see them.

1. English literature. The two words to be understood both as a single term and independently. Leavis, though intransigently hostile to the dominant movement of British civilization, consistently identified himself as "British," rooted in a peculiarly British tradition of thought and sensibility. He also saw literature—rather than the other arts—as central to cultural development, because it is the highest embodiment of language, our most direct and essential means of expression and communication. Much of the strength of Leavis' work—its concentrated energy and force—doubtless derives from this sense of rootedness, but (like most strengths) it can also be held to constitute a limitation. That my own work has never achieved the concentratedness and authoritativeness of Leavis' may be due to the differences in my position (as well as to personal deficiencies): though my own sensibility was similarly formed within a specifically British tradition which I have neither the desire nor the ability to repudiate, I feel no commitment to preserving and developing a specifically British culture. My "country" is Marxism, feminism, gay liberation . . . the major progressive movements of our age, which are necessarily international and transcultural (whatever particular inflections they may acquire within specific cultural situations). The essentials of Leavis' position are also extendable to the other arts: while Shakespeare, Donne, Blake, George Eliot have been and continue to be important to me, I also want (say) Bruckner and Ozu to play major roles in my spiritual, emotional, and intellectual life.

2. Popular culture. I automatically parted company with the "pure" Leavis position when I began writing on the Hollywood cinema in the early '60s. Leavis' attitude to modern "mass culture" was unambiguously dismissive: for him it constituted simply another aspect of all that threatened "life." He never found it necessary to explore a phenomenon like the Hollywood cinema and could not acknowledge the complexity of the issues it raises. This of course lays him open once again to the charge of elitism; it is worth pointing out that numerous Marxist approaches to mass culture have been equally dismissive. Adorno and Horkheimer are scarcely more helpful than Leavis in providing tools for an open and complex investigation of Hollywood films, though unlike Leavis they do offer a detailed and partially plausible rationale for their position in their analysis of capitalism.

3. Critical aims. One may agree that evaluation—one's sense of value in art corresponding to one's sense of value in life—constitutes the highest aim of criticism. There is a tendency in Leavis to make it the only one, so that once a work or writer has been judged inferior the work or writer can be dismissed from further notice. This has been the commonest objection to Leavis, and it requires careful qualification. One possible implication that might be drawn from it—that Leavis dissociated works of art from their cultural context, enshrining them in some metaphorical museum (or mausoleum) of Great Literature—is totally false: no critic has a surer or subtler sense of the interdependence of art and the culture within which it is produced. Far from viewing the artist as a god-created genius in isolation, he continually stressed the perception that different cultural situations make possible different kinds of art, and that some cultural situations are more favorable to art than others: the principle of evaluation, that is, extends beyond the artist to the culture. At the same time, the emphasis on great works tends to overwhelm the other kinds of interest one can legitimately derive from even very bad works: the interest of what they reveal about the culture that produced them. I don't think Leavis would have seen the point of devoting several years to the study of the American horror film, for example. It would not have occurred to him either that high value might be claimed for certain of its specimens or that the examination might produce important insights into ideological structures irrespective of the value of individual works. Neither would he have seen the point of devoting a book-length study to the films of Katharine Hepburn; but Andrew Britton's splendid work is quite unmistakably in the Leavis tradition.

4. "Positive" values. Leavis believed that the greatest works of art convincingly embody positive values—that, however tragic or pessimistic, they achieve affirmation through their feeling for and commitment to "life." I entirely agree. The qualification I want to make arises from the difference between Leavis' cultural situation (or his perception of it) and my own. As I have said, he clung tenaciously, with what looks like the desperation of a blind faith, to the belief that our civilization is somehow redeemable without changing its basic structures, that the battle for "life" within it has not already been lost. Hence his completely negative attitude to what he perceived—to some degree correctly—as the forces or symptoms of disintegration. When one jettisons such a belief, and replaces it with the belief that our civilization must effectively disintegrate before a new movement toward "life" becomes possible, then the problem becomes more complicated. Leavis' inability to accept that the cultural situation was already hopeless and to take the necessary step into a revolutionary position resulted in two failures of insight. (a) He failed to see that the "forces of disintegration" (he tended to lump together rock 'n roll, race riots, student protest) are not merely disintegrative but often carry strong positive implications within them. Not all student protest was merely irresponsible and nihilistic; even if it had been, the events of May '68 in France (some months after the lectures that make up *English Literature in Our Time and the University* were delivered) demonstrate how readily that irresponsibility and nihilism can be transformed into something quite other by the assimilation of Marxist theory. (b) If one relinquishes the belief that capitalist culture is redeemable, then the symptoms of disintegration become interesting in themselves—even take on positive connotations insofar as they can be read as pointing toward a cultural moment when revolution becomes feasible and popular.

5. Evaluative criteria. The fact that our criteria for judging works are likely to be somewhat different from Leavis' is more an apparent than real obstacle. Leavis' own sense of tradition as a process in continuous transition, development, and transformation itself implies that evaluative criteria will never be quite the same from one generation to the next. Closer reflection, however, suggests that there are fundamental criteria that do not change, or change only very gradually. My own experience has been that a radical change in ideological position has had little effect on which films I value but a fairly drastic effect on why I value them. The implication is that there are levels of creativity (for the artist) and of evaluation (for the critic) that transcend ideological difference: precisely, the levels indicated by the Leavisian key words such as seriousness, intelligence, complexity. What changes is not so much one's awareness of the presence or absence of such qualities but one's awareness of how they are manifested—of how an artist's seriousness and intelligence not only produce statements about "the human condition" but involve him or her inevitably in the movement of culture and the conflicts within it. My commitment to Marxism and feminism has revealed entire new levels of meaning, and new possibilities of interpretation, in films like *La Règle du Jeu*, *Blonde Venus*, *Letter from an Unknown Woman*, *Tokyo Story*, that were previously closed to me.

There is a passage of D. H. Lawrence (it occurs in *Lady Chatterley's Lover*) that Leavis was fond of quoting: "It is the way our sympathy flows and recoils that really determines our lives. And here lies the importance of the novel, properly handled: it can lead the sympathetic consciousness into new places, and away in recoil from things gone dead." One can make the same claim for criticism "properly handled": its function should equally be to "lead the sympathetic consciousness into new places," and that involves a constant readiness to change and modify one's own position as one's perception of human needs changes. Which is not the same—is likely to operate in total opposition to—the common critical practice (at all levels from the journalistic to the academic) of drifting with the latest fashions, the latest fashions generally proving to be merely "things gone dead" in new disguises, the critics functioning as morticians applying a semblance of life to corpses.

It seems appropriate to conclude by attempting to apply Leavisian principles (suitably modified, along the lines I have suggested) to a recent film in order to suggest the kind of judgments to which they lead. I have chosen *Blue Velvet*, partly because it is a work of undeniable distinction, partly because it relates directly to the work of Hitchcock, partly because it has received such critical acclaim: clearly headed, like its predecessor *Eraserhead*, for "cult" status, it has already headed the "Ten Best" lists for 1986 of a number of influential journalist critics, and was selected as the best film of the year by America's National Society of Film Critics (a "Leavisian" judgment on the film is unlikely to be popular). From the

noun "distinction" derive two adjectives with somewhat different connotations, and in claiming distinction for Lynch's film I have in mind
"distinctive" rather than "distinguished." Like all Lynch's work it is
highly idiosyncratic (whatever one may think of *Eraserhead* one must
grant that its weirdness is authentic rather than merely manufactured),
with all the stylistic signifiers of a "personal statement." Unlike *The
Elephant Man* and *Dune*, it seems the work of someone—at least on a
superficial level—completely in control of his material: the effects, that
is to say, achieved through dialogue, acting, mise-en-scène, decor, composition, editing, etc., have a precision that convinces one that they are
exactly what Lynch wanted. For many critics, of course, it is enough if a
film embodies an idiosyncratic personal vision: its maker is then a "visionary" and nothing more need be said. But the "vision" of *Blue Velvet*,
while indeed personal, also belongs very much to its period, and the
phenomenon of the film's critical success cannot be explained in simplistic terms (what Richard Lippe calls "bastardized auteurism"). The personal vision, the way it expresses itself, the way it is received, the almost
unanimous critical adulation, have all to be understood in relation to a
particular phase of cultural development.

Taking a cue from one particularly excessive manifestation of that
adulation—the notion that *Blue Velvet* "transcends" Hitchcock (Jay
Scott, Toronto's *Globe and Mail*)—I want to compare the film briefly to
Shadow of a Doubt. The choice is by no means arbitrary, the two films
sharing a common thematic: the "innocence" of small town American
life; the apparent opposition of that innocence to a corrupt, perverted,
and dangerous "under-world"; the revelation that the two are in fact
intimately interrelated and interdependent; the resultant questioning as
to whether "innocence" has the positive value commonly attributed to
it. One small detail is symptomatic of the vast differences between the
two films: both Hitchcock and Lynch introduce their small towns with
low angle images of benevolent and protective patriarchal figures, but
while Hitchcock's traffic policeman outside the Bank of America is a
resonant and evocative figure, Lynch's fireman beaming at the audience
from his itinerant firewagon is merely ridiculous, a cliché rendered
laughable, introducing the tone of parody/pastiche that immediately
locates the film within the era of Postmodernism. *Shadow of a Doubt* is
built upon a complex dialectic in which each side carries weight; in *Blue
Velvet,* small town values, "innocence," goodness, are offered from the

outset as patently absurd and risible, their emptiness a "given" that precludes any need for dramatic realization.

Crucial to *Shadow of a Doubt* is Hitchcock's commitment to Young Charlie (Teresa Wright)—(that he is also committed, on another level, to her murderous uncle is crucial to the enactment of the dialectic). Her goodness and innocence are revealed as in a certain sense limitations (she has to learn to become aware of the evil her society produces and nourishes), but we are never invited to find them ridiculous. Indeed, it is precisely because they are convincingly realized as genuine and positive that the film is so authentically disturbing. (It is a characteristic of our world that to invoke such a concept as "human goodness" is to risk inviting "sophisticated" laughter, and it is no coincidence that the same world has declared *Blue Velvet* a masterpiece). Lynch's treatment of his "innocent" characters (Jeffrey/Kyle MacLachlan and Sandy/Laura Dern) is very different.

It is fascinating to watch *Blue Velvet* with a large mixed audience: the spectators seem about equally divided between those who believe themselves to be laughing *at* the film and those who believe themselves to be laughing *with* it (it is possible to argue that the film is laughing at both categories). In fact, Lynch operates a double standard throughout, and one must admire the skill and precision with which he treads his difficult tightrope. The presentation of "normality" (the "innocent" heterosexual couple, their small town suburban family backgrounds) can be taken absolutely "straight" by the more naive members of the audience (those poor shmucks) or as wittily and hilariously "knowing" by the more sophisticated (those who laugh *at* the film presumably being somewhere on the borderline, seeing the absurdity but mistaking it for *Lynch*'s naiveté). This might at first sight seem similar to the different levels of involvement permitted by Douglas Sirk's melodramas, where a sophisticated awareness of style and technique (composition, framing, color, the use of glass, windows, mirrors, etc.) can create a (loosely speaking) "Brechtian" distance which appears not to have been perceived by the films' contemporary audiences (let alone reviewers). But Sirk never treats his characters, or any section of his audience, with contempt; in his films the level of Brechtian distanciation is never incompatible with a commitment to the themes and quandaries of the melodrama. If spectators weep during *Imitation of Life* or *Written on the Wind,* Sirk isn't laughing at them: he is weeping too. Although the the double standard of *Blue*

Velvet does not appear to operate along class lines, one might relate the impulse behind it to Lynch's treatment of class in *The Elephant Man:* refined and sensitive bourgeois characters contrasted with a unanimously grotesque and brutal proletariat whose debasement requires no explanation or analysis beyond a few generalized images of urban industrial squalor. It is a characteristic of Lynch's brand of humanism (in any case a very dubious commodity) that it enables him to identify with an abused and outcast "freak" but not with any wider instance of societal oppression.

The two points where the double standard operates most clearly are Sandy's speech about the robins and the final sequence which answers it. On the one hand Laura Dern has been directed to deliver the speech "straight"—if one attended only to the performance one might find it quite touching. On the other hand the speech is written not as an expression of innocent faith but as a parodic reduction (when the robins return love will be reborn and the world will be transformed). Finally, the backdrop for this is the lighted stained glass windows of a church. Religion (whether as social or metaphysical observance) plays no role in the film whatever: the church is, deliberately, a signifier without substance, the image's total lack of resonance strongly underlining the foregrounding of cliché, which some might wish to call Brechtian but which in fact expresses a cynicism totally alien to Brecht. (No wonder our bourgeois journalist critics love the film so much: they epitomize the audience it flatters).

The final sequence is the conventional closure of classical narrative, once again foregrounded as cliché. Lynch certainly understands the conventions and their ideological significance. We are given: (a) the restoration of patriarchy in the figures of two fathers (Jeffrey's now recovered from the stroke he suffered at the beginning of the film), one of whom is a policeman, now friends as well as neighbors; (b) the restoration of Dorothy (Isabella Rossellini), seemingly cured of the "disease" of sadomasochism she caught from Frank (Dennis Hopper), to her socially correct role as mother; (c) the construction of Jeffrey and Sandy as the new healthy heterosexual couple, guarantee of the perpetuation of "normality." Finally, there is the appearance of the robin, first in the tree, then on the windowsill crushing a black bug in its beak. Lynch has pointed out with evident pride that it is a *mechanical* robin. Again, some might wish to invoke Brecht, and the distinction between "representation" and "presentation" (the former invites the spectator to succumb to the illusion of a "reality" that is in fact heavily ideological; the latter "presents" the signifiers of that illusion, exposing them as constructions). On a fairly elementary level one can concede that this is what is going on. The effect ceases to be Brechtian in any important sense the moment one asks some obvious interconnected questions: For what purpose are we being asked (those of us who are sufficiently sophisticated) to deconstruct these conventional signifiers of normality? What attitude are we being encouraged to take to them? What *alternative* are we meant to envisage?

The last question seems to me the crucial one, and leads directly to a consideration of the film's presentation of normality's "underside," the world of the repressed, the world of subversive sexuality. This is clearly where the film's energies lie; it is also the aspect of the film that especially attracts and impresses the critics, who are fond of informing us, with minimal variations of phrasing, that what is remarkable about Lynch is that he has a direct pipeline to his unconscious. I agree that the sequences involving Frank are the most impressive part of the film: they have a brutal intensity that might certainly be read as betokening a strong personal involvement. What the critics appear not to notice (or not to mind?)—and this is particularly striking in the case of would-be radical reviewers like the *Village Voice*'s J. Hoberman and David Edelstein—is that the film's treatment of sexuality is totally and unambiguously reactionary. The bedroom scene (in which Jeffrey, hiding in a closet, watches Frank subject Dorothy to sadistic sexual violence) is the most powerful and fascinating thing in the film, its power lying in its explicit connecting of sadomasochistic sexual behaviour with the patterns of domination and submission inherent in the patriarchal nuclear family structure: Frank forces Dorothy to call him "Sir" and "Daddy," he addresses her as "Mommy"; he can achieve orgasm only by untying and restoring the umbilical cord (the blue velvet sash, one end of which must be held in each partner's mouth). The psychoanalytical perception here—together with the intensity of its dramatic realization—suggests that it is not after all inconceivable that Lynch might one day produce work comparable to that of Buñuel and Hitchcock (to whom the journalists are already, and prematurely, so fond of comparing him)—though probably not within the present cultural climate. The connotations of the "primal scene," the attribution of the dominance/submission attitudes of sadomasochism to the father/mother, husband/wife roles our civilization calls "normal," Jeffrey's subsequent fascination with all of this and partial, horrified surrender to it: given a very different context, a film that was actually thought through, a film capable of developing such perceptions "intelligently" and "seriously," the sequence would deserve the adulation that has been showered upon it. But it exists in isolation, without organic connection to anything else. How, for example, are we supposed to relate it to Jeffrey's own familial relations, which are presented in a manner at once perfunctory and parodic? Frank's assertion that Jeffrey is just like him is left unexplored.

Worse: the kind of sexuality represented by Frank is offered as the only alternative to the conventional "normality" the film ridicules. Frank and his entourage (including the grotesquely stereotypical "faggot" portrayed by Dean Stockwell) come to embody quite a compendium of alternative sexual practices, but they are treated with unequivocal horror and disgust. (If the journalists are right and this underworld is Lynch's representation of his own unconscious—an allegation not exactly flattering and conceivably libelous—then the disgust is also self-hatred, but that scarcely makes it more interesting or progressive.) The scene in which Frank smears his own mouth with lipstick and kisses Jeffrey with a kind of horrified and horrifying passion before brutally beating him certainly has its auteurist significance in that it repeats the hysterical homophobia of *Dune*. Its point here seems to be the lumping together of bisexuality and sadomasochism as equal and equally loathsome components of the alternative to the "normal" sexual conventions the film despises. One could easily argue that the two are diametrically opposed —that whereas sadomasochism is the entirely logical product of the patriarchal norms, bisexuality is what those norms strive to repress and deny. In any case, it is quite unhelpful to present either in terms of simple disgust and revulsion.

Where, finally, does this leave the film as a whole? Right back with what it purports to ridicule: suburban/bourgeois "normality," patriarchy, women as wives and mothers (and nothing else), the heterosexual couple restored to their idyllic innocence. If Frank represents—as the film seems to suggest—an unrepressed version of Jeffrey, then what is left but to restore repression? It leaves the film, to be precise, with a mechanical robin, as an image of a renewal and transformation it not only doesn't believe in but feels obliged to negate by parody and ridicule. The image epitomizes the film's essential emptiness and bankruptcy. Far from "leading the sympathetic consciousness into new places, and away in recoil from things gone dead," *Blue Velvet* is a supreme example of the mortician's art, a corpse with eyes staring open, its mouth fixed in a grimace, garish makeup applied. It belongs—with its cynicism, its negativity, its contempt—to the '80s as surely at *E. T.* and the *Star Wars* trilogy (the other side of the same coin): it reinforces all those aspects of our culture that a major artist would strive to repudiate or transcend. The film parodies certain basic structures of classical Hollywood narrative while remaining helplessly locked within them. To label it "Postmodernist" may sound impressive (for many critics to affix a label to a work is mysteriously to justify it), but if *Blue Velvet* can be held adequately to represent Postmodernism, then a critique of Postmodernism and the cultural situation that has produced it is urgently needed.* A civilization gets, by and large, the art that it deserves.

POSTSCRIPT: A NOTE ON THE ENGLISH LANGUAGE

It seems (but nowadays isn't) a truism to suggest that a critic's quality is inseparable from how he writes. Leavis developed one of the great English prose styles, so flexible and precise in its inflections that it is capable of expressing nuance and complexity to a degree perhaps incomparable within modern critical writing. Yet many purportedly educated people (undergraduates in their final year, for example) today appear to find him virtually unreadable. Far from reflecting adversely on Leavis, this fact can be taken as marking the extreme degree to which the English language has been eroded.

Obviously, the main culprit is journalism. The majority of students today seem reluctant to tackle any writer who produces sentences extending beyond one-and-a-half lines. I have myself been through many dispiriting struggles with editors (even "academic" ones) who have attempted to remove most of my colons, semicolons, and brackets and replace them with fullstops, producing a choppy journalese and depriv-

* For such a critique, see Andrew Britton's article in *CineAction!* 13/14.

ing me of the opportunities for annotating vocal inflection and relative emphasis that punctuation affords. Leavis' style never loses touch with the spoken language and the subtle movement of the speaking voice (it is of course significant that most of his critical writings had their origins as lectures). The long, complex sentences, with their many qualifying clauses, demand to be not merely read but *listened to*, and with total concentration: you can't read Leavis if you don't hear him. The slick, clipped sentences of journalism are utterly incapable of conveying that delicacy of nuance, that sense of poised and considered judgment and the awareness of the complexity of serious issues that it implies. But then when has journalism shown any interest or ambition in such areas?

More insidious, it seems to me, has been the devastation wrought upon English critical prose by semiotics/structuralism. Central here is the proposal that criticism should be "scientific." If the notion that a critic should possess an educated sensibility is implicitly scorned by journalism, it has been explicitly repudiated by the semiotics school. It is not simply a matter of the acquisition of a jargon—though that is bad enough. If criticism is scientific, then it has fixed rules, which anyone with a sufficient I.Q. (something very different from Leavis' "intelligence") can master; having mastered them, you can write criticism. The notion of an individual voice becomes not only irrelevant, it becomes anathema. Try an experiment: cull, at random, a dozen paragraphs of semiological explication by a dozen different writers; then see if you can distinguish them stylistically. (You will be able to single out Stephen Heath, if you have been fortunate enough to fasten upon something of his.) Unlike Leavis, semiologists are not elitist. If there is the small problem that only a tiny group of initiates can understand them, that is because everyone else is too lazy to learn the rules (or master the jargon). If we bothered to learn the rules we could *all* write like that, indistinguishably. So democratic.

I end, then, with a plea to my fellow critics to rediscover the rich resources of the English language (and with those resources their own voices), its capacity for precision, nuance, and complexity, its quality as spoken language. They could not do better than begin with Leavis himself: for example, *Revaluation, The Great Tradition, The Common Pursuit, The Living Principle, English Literature and the University in Our Time, Nor Shall My Sword* . . . (all published by Chatto and Windus). They will find plenty with which to disagree, much to infuriate them; yet the proposition that these works should continue to have currency and a substantial influence on critical theory and practice seems to me beyond question. As John Keats remarked when he discarded his unfinished, Miltonic, latinized *Hyperion*, "English must be kept up."

BOOK ONE

HITCHCOCK'S FILMS

I
INTRODUCTION (1965)

Why should we take Hitchcock seriously?

It is a pity the question has to be raised: if the cinema were truly regarded as an autonomous art, not as a mere adjunct of the novel or the drama—if we were able yet to *see* films instead of mentally reducing them to literature—it would be unnecessary. As things are, it seems impossible to start a book on Hitchcock without confronting it.

Hitchcock has expressed repeatedly his belief in "pure cinema"; to appreciate his films it is necessary that we grasp the nature of the medium. We are concerned here with much more than is normally meant by the word "technique." Let us look at an example.

In *Marnie,* Mark Rutland (Sean Connery) tries to "persuade" Strutt (Martin Gabel) not to take action against Marnie for robbing him (the money has been returned). Strutt protests that the lenient attitude asked of him is "fashionable," but "just wait till *you've* been victimized." Then we see Marnie enter the house. She has just been through a terrible accident, has had to shoot her beloved horse, still carries the pistol in her hand: she is distraught, and quite bereft of free will or the power of rational consideration. Reduce this to literary "content" detached from the images (from the movement of the images, and the movement from image to image) and there isn't much there: a straightforward dramatic situation with a rather dislikeable man making things unpleasant for the poor heroine. But compare this account with the force of the images on the screen. The cut from Strutt to Marnie gives us, first, an ironic comment on Strutt's word "victimized." We see Strutt, complacent, self-righteous, a man devoid of human warmth and generosity taking his stand on a rigid, standardized morality; then we see Marnie, haggard, drawn, face drained of all color, clinging to a gun without realizing she is holding it, moving forward like a sleepwalker, "victimized" indeed by a whole complex past. It defines for us our moral attitude to Strutt's moral attitude, and is a comment on Strutt himself and all he stands for (he stands, in the film, for quite a lot: a whole attitude to life, a whole social milieu). There is also color: Mark wears a brown-flecked tweed suit and a brown tie, so that he blends naturally with the "natural" colors—predominantly browns and greens—of the decor of the Rutland house: the hard blue of Strutt's tie clashes with the green of the sofa on which he is sitting, making him out of place in the decor as his attitude to life is out of place in the Rutland milieu. The point, like so much that is important in the film, is *felt* rather than registered consciously by the spectator.

A novelist could give us some kind of equivalent for all this, could make us react along the same general lines; but he couldn't make us react in this direct, immediate way, as image succeeds image—he couldn't control our reactions so precisely in time. He could describe the way Strutt was sitting, but he couldn't *show* us Strutt sitting in precisely that way: we would all imagine it differently. He couldn't place us at a certain distance from Strutt to watch his awkwardness, his gestures, his changing expressions from a slightly low angle, so that we are aware at once of his absurdity and of his power. He could describe Marnie's appearance and analyze explicitly her emotional state from within (as Hitchcock can't); he couldn't show us her face, her way of moving; he couldn't place us in front of her and make us move with her, at her speed, so that we are caught up in her rhythm of moving, so that we share for a moment her trance-like state. The novelist can analyze and explain; Hitchcock can make us experience directly.

I have purposely chosen here a quite unremarkable (in its context) example which contains nothing obviously "cinematic": it could be paralleled from almost any sequence in *Marnie*. It seems to me a fair representative specimen of that local realization that one finds everywhere in recent Hitchcock films, realization of theme in terms of "pure cinema" which makes the audience not only see but *experience* (experience rather than intellectually analyze) the manifestation of that theme at that particular point.

Or consider the moment in *Psycho* when Norman Bates carries his mother down to the fruit cellar. In literary terms there is almost nothing there: a young man carrying a limp body out of a room and down some stairs. Yet in the film the overhead shot with its complicated camera

movement communicates to us precisely that sense of metaphysical vertigo that Hitchcock's subject requires at that moment: a sense of sinking
into a quicksand of uncertainties, or into a bottomless pit; communicates
it by placing us in a certain position in relation to the action and
controlling our movements in relation to the movements of the actors.
The cinema has its own methods and its own scope. We must beware of
missing the significance of a shot or a sequence by applying to it assumptions brought from our experience of other arts.

The cinema—especially the Hollywood cinema—is a commercial
medium. Hitchcock's films are—usually—popular: indeed, some of his
best films *(Rear Window, Psycho)* are among his *most* popular. From
this arises a widespread assumption that, however "clever," "technically
brilliant," "amusing," "gripping," etc., they may be, they can't be taken
seriously as we take, say, the films of Bergman or Antonioni seriously.
They *must* be, if not absolutely bad, at least fatally flawed from a serious
standpoint. And it is easy enough for those who take this line to point to
all manner of "concessions to the box office," fatal compromises with a
debased popular taste: Hitchcock returns repeatedly to the suspense
thriller for his material; he generally uses established stars who are
"personalities" first and actors second; there is a strong element of
humor in his work, "gags" and "comic relief" which effectively undermine any pretensions to sustained seriousness of tone. To one whose
training has been primarily literary, these objections have a decidedly
familiar ring. One recalls that "commercial"—and at the time intellectually disreputable—medium, the Elizabethan drama; one thinks of
those editors who have wished to remove the Porter scene from *Macbeth*
because its tone of bawdy comedy is incompatible with the tragic atmosphere; of Dr. Johnson's complaints about Shakespeare's fondness for
"quibbles" and conceits; of Robert Bridges' deploring of the bawdy
scenes in such plays as *Measure for Measure*. The argument, in all these
cases, was basically much the same: Shakespeare allowed himself these
regrettable lapses from high seriousness merely to please the "groun-
dlings"; or, if we can't bear such a thought, we can comfort ourselves
with the reflection that perhaps they were interpolations by someone
else.

Now one does not want to deny Shakespeare his imperfections, or
Hitchcock his: indeed, a strong objection to much current French exe-
gesis of Hitchcock, as to so much current critical work on Shakespeare,

is that the writers tend to start from the assumption that their hero can do no wrong, and quite fail to make necessary discriminations between different works, or admit occasional failures of realization within works. Such treatment does much harm, by erecting barriers between artist and audience that are very difficult to break down: one is not responding at first hand to a work of art if one approaches it in a spirit of uncritical veneration. But what one does not want either Shakespeare or Hitchcock deprived of is precisely the richness their work derives from the sense of living contact with a wide popular audience. To wish that Hitchcock's films were like those of Bergman or Antonioni is like wishing that Shakespeare had been like Corneille (which is what his eighteenth-century critics *did* wish). This implies no disrespect to Corneille (nor to Bergman and Antonioni) who can offer us experiences that Shakespeare cannot; it is meant to imply that Shakespeare can offer us richer experiences, and that if we somehow removed all trace of "popular" appeal from Shakespeare and Hitchcock, then we would have lost Shakespeare and Hitchcock.

That there are important distinctions to be drawn between Shakespeare's audience and Hitchcock's, and important resulting distinctions between the oeuvres of the two artists, I would not, of course, wish to deny. And Hollywood is not as conducive to great art as Elizabethan London, for many reasons too obvious to need recounting here. But it is a matter of approaching these alleged concessions and compromises from the right end. I remember once expressing great admiration for Howard Hawks' *Rio Bravo*. I was promptly told that it couldn't be a very good film, because Hawks had used a pop-singer (Ricky Nelson) and then introduced a song sequence quite arbitrarily to give him something to sing. It didn't apparently occur to the person in question to consider the song sequence on its own merits in its context in the film (in terms of strict thematic unity it is easier to justify than the role of Autolycus in *The Winter's Tale,* which no one nowadays wishes away, though it represents a "concession to popular taste" that, one feels, delighted Shakespeare's heart very much as the *Rio Bravo* song sequence delighted Hawks). It seems clear that the relationship of a Hitchcock or a Hawks to his art is much more like Shakespeare's than is that of a Bergman or an Antonioni; the sense of communication on many levels precludes that self-consciousness of the artist that besets the arts today, and fosters true artistic impersonality. All one asks for Hitchcock is that people *look* at his films, allow themselves to react spontaneously, and consider their reactions; that, for example, instead of assuming that *Vertigo* is just a mystery thriller (in which case it is a very botched job, with the solution divulged two-thirds of the way through and the rest, one supposes, total boredom), they look without preconceptions at the sequence of images that Hitchcock gives us, and consider their first-hand responses to those images. They will then be led, very swiftly by the straightest path, to the film's profound implications.

It is precisely this refusal to look, react, and consider that vitiates most British criticism of Hitchcock's films. The characteristic "Establishment" line may be fairly represented by the article "The Figure in the Carpet" by Penelope Houston in the Autumn 1963 issue of *Sight and Sound:* the immediate stimulus being in this case the appearance in England of *The Birds.* The article is in fact so characteristic, not only of the line on Hitchcock, but of the *Sight and Sound* critical approach in general, that it is worth studying as a representative document, in some detail: which I do not propose to do here. A few comments, however, seem in order. What is most striking in the article is its almost exclusively negative character. Miss Houston examines cursorily some of the more obvious and easily dismissible excesses both of the book on Hitchcock by Eric Rohmer and Claude Chabrol, and of Jean Douchet's articles in *Cahiers du Cinéma;* when one looks for some clear positive lead one finds almost nothing. Miss Houston appears to include herself in that "general agreement that (Hitchcock) is a master"; yet nothing she finds to say remotely supports such a valuation. There is continual evasion of critical responsibility, a refusal to follow any line of enquiry rigorously to its conclusion. Of *Vertigo* (which Miss Houston seems now to like, though it is impossible to discover why or how much or in what way) we learn that it "hypnotises . . . The first half moves like a slow underwater dream. The second half . . . has the hallucinatory quality of a nightmare. By the end of the film, the audience ought to be as mad as James Stewart appears to be." And that is all. If we ask for some effort to explain this "hallucinatory quality"—its method, its purpose, its moral implications (for good or ill, intentional or unintentional)—we get no answer from Miss Houston. One is left to assume that any film is vaguely acceptable if it has a "hallucinatory quality."

Most of Miss Houston's article seems to rest on two supports, both critically insufficient to say the least: what Hitchcock has said, and what she herself assumes to have been his intentions in this or that film: and never, as far as one can judge, on a detailed first-hand study of the films themselves. Her closing paragraph (on *The Birds*) is representative: ". . . If *The Birds* is really intended as a doomsday fantasy, one can only say it's a lamentably inadequate one . . ." It is at least equally inadequate if "really intended" as Oedipus Rex, Winnie the Pooh, or a pair of kippers: unfortunately, what concerns (or should concern) the critic is not what a film is "really intended" to be, but what it actually *is*. Miss Houston's remark also implies a set notion of what a "doomsday fantasy" ought to be like; anyway, her inability to cope with a complex work like *The Birds* is sufficiently revealed in that desire to package it neatly and tie on a ready-to-hand cliché label. ". . . But why not try the birds as the Bomb; or as creatures from the subconscious; or start from the other end, with Tippi Hedren as a witch? . . ." Why not, indeed? Go ahead, Miss Houston! ". . . One could work up a pretty theory on any of these lines . . ." (except that a minute's consideration of the film would be enough to show that one couldn't) ". . . if only one could suppress a conviction that Hitchcock's intention . . ." (intention again!) ". . . was an altogether simpler one. He scared us in *Psycho* enough to make us think twice about stopping at any building looking remotely like the Bates motel. He tries it again in *The Birds*, but we will happily go on throwing bread to the seagulls, because the film can't for long enough at a time break through our barrier of disbelief . . ." And one cannot, at this point, suppress a conviction about Miss Houston's conviction: that it existed before she saw *The Birds*, which was accordingly judged by the criterion, Is this frightening me as much (and in the same way?) as *Psycho* frightened me? ". . . And a director who has told us so often that his interest lies in the way of doing things, not in the moral of a story, invites us to take him at his own valuation . . ." An invitation any serious critic ought, one would have supposed, to decline, politely murmuring "Never trust the artist—trust the tale." The whole article—with its apparent assumption that a few odd quirks are enough to justify the description of a director as a master, and one needn't look deeper, needn't at all inquire what this or that film actually *does*—is typical of the dilettantism that vitiates so much British film criticism. One respects far more— while considering them mistaken—those who find Hitchcock's films morally repulsive: at least their attitude is based on the assumption that a work of art (or entertainment) has the power to affect us for good or ill, and that one needs to examine a work in detail and in depth (in Paddy Whannel's words, "teasing out the values embedded in the style") before one can offer any valuation of it. This bland disregard of the need for moral concern (I would say commitment, had the word not become so debased by oversimplification) in some form links up with the astonishing confusion (or absence?) of values revealed by the fact that the issue of *Sight and Sound* that contained Peter John Dyer's contemptuous review of *Marnie* (another interesting representative specimen) also awarded *Goldfinger* three stars in its "Guide to Current Films" ("Films of special interest to *Sight and Sound* readers are denoted by one, two, three, or four stars"—do *Sight and Sound* readers accept such blackening of their characters?), and printed Dyer's eulogy of Roger Corman's vulgar and pretentious Bergman plagiarism, *The Masque of the Red Death*.

It is a fact, I think, that the chief obstacle in the way of a serious appraisal of Hitchcock's work for many people is Hitchcock's own apparent attitude to it; and it seems worth insisting for a moment on the fundamental irrelevance of this. What an artist says about his own work need not necessarily carry any more weight than what anyone else says about it: its value can only be assessed by the test to which one must subject all criticism or elucidation, the test of applying it to the art in question and asking oneself how much it contributes toward either understanding or evaluating it. The artist's own utterances are more likely to have an indirect relevance, by telling us something further about his personality and outlook. I used to find maddening Hitchcock's refusal to discuss his work with interviewers on any really serious level; I have come to admire it. It seems so much in keeping with the character of the films themselves that their creator should be such a delightfully modest and unassuming man who makes no claims for his art outside the evidence of the films. He leaves that to the commentators—it is their job, not his. The attitude can be illustrated with that splendid moment in the interview in *Movie 6*. Hitchcock has been asked to express an opinion on the thematic "broadening out" of his later films: "Well, I think it's a natural tendency to be less superficial, that's Truffaut's opinion—he's been examining all these films. And he feels that the American period is much stronger than the English period . . ." He is the least self-conscious of great artists: that delight in creation of which the films themselves speak sufficiently clearly is accompanied by no sense of artistic self-importance. One cannot help thinking again of Shakespeare, content apparently to leave supreme masterpieces to the mercy of producers and actors, not even considering (as far as we know) that perhaps some of them ought to be preserved in print. The delight in creation was its own reward, its own justification.

But when one turns from British to French criticism of Hitchcock one is not made altogether happier. Eric Rohmer and Claude Chabrol deserve our gratitude for their pioneer work: their book on Hitchcock constitutes a very serious attempt to account for the resonances his films can evoke in the mind. One admires its many brilliant perceptions and the authors' interest in the moral qualities of Hitchcock's films. It leaves one unsatisfied, however; with the feeling that, if that is all Hitchcock offers, the authors overrate him, and a complementary feeling that, no, that is not all he offers. Their analyses—they set out to cover all Hitchcock's films, British and American, up to and including *The Wrong Man*, more than forty films in 150 pages of text—have the effect of depriving the films of flesh and blood reducing them to theoretical skeletons. And one is always aware, behind the enterprise, of the authors' sense of the need to make Hitchcock seem "respectable." Accordingly, they play down the suspense element and the comedy, and strip each film down to some bald intellectual postulate. The sort of thing I mean is suggested by the remarks Miss Houston quotes in her "Figure in the Carpet"—the work immediately under consideration is *Strangers on a Train*: "One must consider Hitchcock's work in exactly the same way as that of some esoteric painter or poet. If the key to the system is not always in the door, or if the very door itself is cunningly camouflaged, this is no reason for exclaiming that there is nothing inside." This seems to me most misleading. The meaning of a Hitchcock film is not a mysterious esoteric something cunningly concealed beneath a camouflage of "entertainment": it is there in the method, in the progression from shot to shot. A Hitchcock film is an organism, with the whole implied in every detail and every detail related to the whole. In Spenser's words,

> For of the soul the body form doth take;
> And soul is form and doth the body make.

If we can't find the "soul" of a work of art expressed in its body, informing and giving life to every limb, then we may be pretty sure it is not worth looking for.

The Rohmer-Chabrol book suffers also from a refusal to look at the films empirically: the authors have decided in advance on their thesis and the films have to be made somehow to fit it: they are Catholic films. Hence the significance of *Rear Window* "is impossible to grasp without a precise reference to Christian dogma." Were this true, the film would surely have to be accounted a failure: a successful work of art must be self-sufficient, its significance arising from the interaction of its parts. [1]* But the assertion is of course, ridiculous and it leads Chabrol and Rohmer to distort the film drastically. According to them, for instance, the last shot of the film shows James Stewart and Grace Kelly "in the same state, exactly as if nothing had happened"; yet at the start of the film Stewart was on the point of breaking with Kelly, and at the end they are engaged to be married; and his back is now turned to the window. [2] Again, according to Rohmer and Chabrol, *Rear Window* offers us a straightforward denunciation of curiosity. A strangely equivocal denunciation, surely, that has most people coming away from the cinema peering fascinatedly through other people's windows. And the curiosity has, after all, brought to light a peculiarly hideous murder and saved a woman from suicide. Hitchcock's morality, with its pervading sense of the inextricability of good and evil, is not so simple.

The articles of Jean Douchet, published in *Cahiers du Cinéma* under the title "La Troisième Clef d'Hitchcock," seem to me, for all their interpretative excesses and, again, a tendency to reduce things to abstractions, more generally persuasive; especially the accounts, in the last installment, of *Rear Window* and *Psycho* (*Cahiers du Cinéma*, No. 113). Douchet is not in the least embarrassed by Hitchcock's popularity or by his suspense techniques: indeed, these become the starting-point of his analyses. But, again, I feel he oversimplifies, through a fixed determination to pursue one line of approach. To see the flats across the courtyard in *Rear Window* as a sort of cinema screen on which James Stewart "wish-fulfills" his secret desires is splendidly illuminating; but by the end of the argument we seem to have forgotten the fact that the murderer is a real man who has murdered a real woman, deposited real limbs around the country, and buried a real head in a real flower bed. Douchet's insistence on black magic, initially interesting, seems eventually to limit the significance of Hitchcock's films rather seriously. His treatment of

* Note numbers in brackets refer to endnotes for and commentary upon earlier editions. They will be found in a separate section following book 1.

Psycho, from the point of view of Hitchcock's control and manipulation of audience reaction, seems to me—despite disagreements over detail—brilliant, but it covers only one aspect of a complex film. Nevertheless, Douchet's work—and the Rohmer-Chabrol book—are so far beyond anything the British "Establishment" has given us in intelligence and critical rigor that one feels ungrateful in advancing any criticism of them. Even their moments of lunacy seem more intelligent than the relentless triviality of "Establishment" reasonableness. The worst harm done by using black magic or "precise reference to Christian dogma" to explain a Hitchcock film lies in the resulting suspicion that the films cannot stand up without such support.

But, it will be objected, I am not answering my opening question: what can one adduce, positively, once all the false preconceptions have been cleared away, to encourage the doubters to believe that Hitchcock deserves serious consideration as an artist? To answer such a question it will be necessary to advance claims and make assertions that only detailed analysis can justify, and this I shall try to provide in subsequent chapters. Meanwhile I can only ask skeptical readers not to dismiss the assertions before they have given some attention to the attempted justification that follows.

First, then, one might point to the *unity* of Hitchcock's work, and the nature of that unity. I mean of course something much deeper than the fact that he frequently reverts to mystery thrillers for his material; I also mean something broader and more complex than the fact that certain themes—such as the celebrated "exchange of guilt"—turn up again and again, although that is a part of it. Not only in theme—in style, method, moral attitude, assumptions about the nature of life—Hitchcock's mature films reveal, on inspection, a consistent development, deepening, and clarification. Now almost any body of work by a single person will reveal unity of some sort: not only the oeuvre of an Ian Fleming, but of an Agatha Christie and even an Enid Blyton. But this steady development and deepening seems to me the mark of an important artist—essentially, that which distinguishes the significant from the worthless. There is discernible throughout Hitchcock's career an acceleration of the process of development right up to the present day, when the rate is such that the critic can perhaps be forgiven if it sometimes takes him a little time to catch up.

But within this unity—and this is something which rarely receives the emphasis it deserves—another mark of Hitchcock's stature is the amazing *variety* of his work. No need to point to the obviously "different" films like *Under Capricorn*: consider merely Hitchcock's last five films, made within a period of seven years, *Vertigo, North by Northwest, Psycho, The Birds, Marnie*. There are plenty of points of contact: the use of identification techniques to restrict the spectator, for a time, to sharing the experiences of a single consciousness, in *Vertigo* and *Psycho;* the birds in *Psycho* and *The Birds;* the theme of the parent-child relationship in *Psycho* and *Marnie;* the "therapeutic" theme in all five films (common to almost all Hitchcock's mature work). But even more striking is the essentially *different* nature of each work, in tone, style, subject matter, method: though one is constantly aware that all five are manifestations of a single genius, there is no repetition; each film demands a different approach from the spectator.

The thematic material of Hitchcock's films is much richer than is commonly recognized. True, he never invents his own plots, but adapts the work of others: again, one cannot resist invoking Shakespeare. Hitchcock is no more limited by his sources than Shakespeare was by his. The process whereby Greene's romance *Pandosto* was transformed into the great poetic drama of *The Winter's Tale* is not unlike that whereby Boileau and Narcejac's *D'Entre les Morts* became *Vertigo:* there is the same kind of relationship. Shakespeare found it necessary to make no greater changes in Greene's plot than did Hitchcock in Boileau and Narcejac's; the transmutation takes place through the poetry in Shakespeare and the mise-en-scène in Hitchcock. Nor is this a matter of mere decoration: Shakespeare's poetry is not an *adornment* for Greene's plot, but a true medium, a means of absorbing that plot into an organic dramatic-poetic structure; precisely the same is true of Hitchcock's mise-en-scène in *Vertigo*. Naturally, this transmutation of material does not always take place so successfully, without leaving intractable elements: Shakespeare has his *Cymbeline*, Hitchcock his *Spellbound*. In such cases, the artist tends to return later to a richer, more organic treatment of material which is closely related but from which the intractable elements are absent: thus Shakespeare writes *The Winter's Tale,* and Hitchcock makes (though this somewhat exaggerates the relationship to the earlier work) *Marnie*.

The mystery thriller element is, in fact, never central in Hitchcock's best films; which is not to deny its importance. We could put it this way: "suspense" belongs more to the method of the films than to their themes (insofar as any distinction is possible, such distinctions applied to organic works being necessarily artificial). Look carefully at almost any recent Hitchcock film and you will see that its core, the axis around which it is constructed, is invariably a man-woman relationship: it is never a matter of some arbitrary "love interest," but of essential subject matter. This will be readily granted, one supposes, of *Notorious, Vertigo,* or *Marnie;* but it is equally true of *Rear Window* and *North by Northwest.* Of the obvious exceptions, *Psycho* derives most of its power from its sexual implications and overtones—from the impossibility, for Norman Bates, of a normal sexual relationship—and *Rope* much of its fascination from the equivocal relationship between the two murderers (the whole action can be seen as a working out of suppressed homosexual tensions). Of other partial exceptions, *Strangers on a Train* would be more completely satisfying were its central love relationship more fully realized; and the failure of *I Confess* seems due in part to the fact that the protagonist is a priest—the most interesting sequences are those dealing with his past love affair.

It is true that one can find a profound theme underlying almost anything if one is predisposed to search it out sufficiently diligently; what distinguishes a work of art is that this theme should be seen, on reflection, to inform the whole—not only the "content" (if there is such a thing as distinct from treatment; for what is the content of a film but sounds and images, and where else can we look for its style?), but the method. Think seriously about *Vertigo* and *Psycho,* and you will find themes of profound and universal significance; think again, and you will find these themes expressed in the form and style of the film as much as in any extractable "content." The subject matter of Hitchcock's *Vertigo* (as distinct from Boileau and Narcejac's) is no longer a matter of mere mystery thriller trickery: it has close affinities with, on the one hand, Mizoguchi's *Ugetsu Monogatari,* and on the other, Keats' "Lamia." To adduce these generally respected works is not to try to render *Vertigo* respectable by means of them—there is no sleight-of-hand involved of the "A is like B so A is as good as B" variety. *Vertigo* needs no such dishonest apologia, having nothing to fear from comparison with either work (it seems to me, in maturity and depth of understanding as in formal perfection, decidedly superior to Keats' poem if not to Mizoguchi's film). I want merely to ensure that the reader considers Hitchcock's film, not the plot on which it is based; the merits and demerits of Boileau and Narcejac are as irrelevant to *Vertigo* as are those of Greene to *The Winter's Tale.*

More practically, perhaps, in answer to my opening question, one can point to the disturbing quality of so many Hitchcock films. It is one of the functions of art to disturb: to penetrate and undermine our complacencies and set notions, and bring about a consequent readjustment in our attitude to life. Many refer to this quality in Hitchcock but few try to account for it: how often has one heard that a certain film is "very clever" but "leaves a nasty taste in the mouth" *(Shadow of a Doubt, Rope, Strangers on a Train, Rear Window . . .).* This "nasty taste" phenomenon has, I believe, two main causes. One is Hitchcock's complex and disconcerting moral sense, in which good and evil are seen to be so interwoven as to be virtually inseparable, and which insists on the existence of evil impulses in all of us. The other is his ability to make us aware, perhaps not quite at a conscious level (it depends on the spectator), of the impurity of our own desires. The two usually operate, of course, in conjunction.

This disturbing quality is frequently associated with the Hitchcockian "suspense," and it is this which I would like to consider next. It is very rarely a simple thing, very rarely "mere" suspense; but it is not easy to define, since it has many functions and takes many forms. Jean Douchet's definition—"the suspension of a soul caught between two occult forces, Darkness and Light"—although one of those phrases that sounds better in French than in English, strikes me as too abstract and generalized to be much help. Starting with something concrete, let us attempt two obvious but illuminating exercises in "practical criticism."

Compare, first, the crop-dusting sequence in *North by Northwest* with the helicopter attack in *From Russia with Love* (there is a fairly clear relationship between the two). The difference in quality will seem to some readers too great and too obvious for the comparison to be worth making; but its purpose is not to score easily off a bad film but to help us define the quality of the suspense in Hitchcock. It is worth, perhaps, pointing out that *From Russia with Love* represents precisely that pandering to a debased popular taste that Hitchcock is widely supposed to be guilty of; the most hostile commentator would find difficulty in paralleling its abuses of sex and violence in any Hitchcock

film. The film itself, in fact, need scarcely detain us: it will be generally
agreed that the sole raison d'être of the helicopter sequence is to provide
a few easy thrills. From a purely technical viewpoint (if such a thing
exists) the Hitchcock sequence is clearly incomparably superior: it is
prepared with so much more finesse, shot with so much more care, every
shot perfectly judged in relation to the buildup of the sequence. Delicacy
and precision are themselves strong positive qualities. In comparison,
the Bond sequence is messy and unorganized, the mise-en-scène purely
opportunistic. But there is far more in question here than the ability to
construct a "suspense" sequence: the suspense itself in *North by Northwest* is of a different order. The suspense in the Bond sequence is
meaningless: the attack is just an attack, it has no place in any significant
development, there is no reason apart from plot—no *thematic* reason—
for it to happen to Bond then or to happen in the way it does; it has no
effect on his character. The suspense consists solely of the question: Will
he get killed or not?; and as (a) we know he won't and (b) there seems
no possible reason to care if he does, it has no effect beyond a purely
physical titillation. In *North by Northwest* the crop-dusting sequence
has essential relevance to the film's development. The complacent, self-
confident Cary Grant character is shown here exposed in open country,
away from the false security of office and cocktail bar, exposed to the
menacing and the unpredictable. The man, who behaved earlier as if
nobody mattered except himself, is here reduced to running for his life,
scurrying for cover like a terrified rabbit; he is reminded—and we, who
found him smart and attractive in his accustomed milieu, are reminded
—of his personal insignificance in a vast, potentially inimical universe.
The sequence marks a crucial stage in the evolution of the character and
his relationships, and, through that, of the themes of the whole film. If
the character were not attractive, for all his shortcomings, our response
would be merely sadistic, we would delight in the spectacle of an unpleasant man getting his deserts; but we have become sufficiently identified with him for our suspense to be characterized by a tension between
conflicting reactions to his predicament.

   North by Northwest is not, however, one of the Hitchcock films that
evokes a really disturbing or complex response. The instance I have
given, however stunning, shows Hitchcock's suspense at its simplest (in
the context, that is, of his recent work). A second comparison will take
us a stage further, and once again I shall choose a film that bears a clear

relationship to Hitchcock's work: Robert Aldrich's *Whatever Happened to Baby Jane?*, made a few years after the great box office success of *Psycho*. The comparison is the more interesting in that Aldrich's film has its defenders, and Aldrich himself some intellectual pretensions. Consider the sequence in which Joan Crawford, the crippled sister, struggles downstairs to telephone for help while Bette Davis, who is victimizing, perhaps killing her, is on her way back to the house from town. One is aware here primarily of a sense of great effort which is not entirely explicable in terms of an attempt to convey the agony of the crippled woman's rung-by-rung descent. Indeed, if almost nothing in the film works, it certainly is not for want of trying: every incident is milked for every drop it can yield and more, so that one often becomes embarrassedly aware of Mr. Aldrich tugging determinedly at a dry udder. But what is the purpose of this particular suspense sequence? To arouse our pity for a helpless woman? But it is totally unnecessary to go to these lengths to do that; so we cannot help suspecting that we are rather being asked to relish her suffering. The suspense seems to me entirely gratuitous, in fact. It carries no implications beyond "Will she or won't she?"; no overtones or resonances. The cross-cutting between the sisters has no purpose beyond prolonging the agony. Since Bette Davis is unaware of what is happening, there is no complementary struggle on her side and the moment of her return is entirely fortuitous. In any case, the film's trick ending, in the manner of *Les Diaboliques,* makes nonsense of everything that has gone before.

Compare, first, the cross-cutting between the tennis match and the murderer's journey to deposit the incriminating lighter in *Strangers on a Train*. The tension generated here has meaning in that it arises from a trial of skill and endurance for both men (the winning of the match, the regaining of the lighter from the drain); all manner of resonances are aroused in the mind (stopping just short, perhaps, of a fully formulated symbolism) by the cross-cutting between the hand straining down into darkness and the struggle for victory in the match in brilliant sunshine; and the most complex reactions are evoked in the spectator, who cannot help responding to the effort of *both* men. Or compare with the Aldrich sequence the scene in *Rear Window* where Grace Kelly is surprised while searching the murderer's rooms. Our suspense here is inseparable from the suspense of James Stewart, who is responsible for her danger but quite powerless to *do* anything: it is as if *we* had sent her there and must now watch her pay for *our* curiosity. In other words, the suspense has that characteristic Hitchcockian *moral* quality, the experiencing of the suspense being an essential factor in the evolution of the James Stewart character and an integral part of its complex meaning.

Instances could be multiplied: the celebrated Albert Hall sequence from *The Man Who Knew Too Much* (1956 version), where the suspense is the outward projection of the agonizing conflict within the heroine's mind—Hitchcock's way of making us share that conflict; the descent of the staircase at the end of *Notorious,* where Ingrid Bergman is being rescued from much more than a gang of spies and death by poisoning, and where our response is further complicated by a certain compassion for the Claude Rains character. Enough has perhaps been said to demonstrate the complexity of this concept of "suspense" in Hitchcock's films. I said earlier that it belonged more to his method than to his themes (while denying that any clearcut distinction between the two was possible). It is sometimes his means of making the spectator share the experiences of the characters; it sometimes arises from a tension in the spectator between conflicting responses; it is sometimes not entirely distinct from a growing discomfort as we are made aware of our own involvement in desires and emotions that are the reverse of admirable. It is one of the means whereby we *participate* in Hitchcock's films rather than merely watch them; but this does not constitute a definition: we must always bear in mind the complex moral implications of the experiences we share or which are communicated to us.

In fact, of the many Hitchcock imitations I have seen, the only one (Riccardo Freda's *Terror of Dr. Hitchcock* is in a different category, being less an imitation than a homage, with a highly personal character of its own) that catches something of the true quality of Hitchcockian suspense—and that only for a few moments—is Stanley Donen's *Charade.* I am thinking of the sequence near the end among the pillars outside the Comédie Française where Audrey Hepburn has to choose, in a matter of seconds, between two men who are both demanding her trust, and the suspense is the projection of the conflict within her between instinct and reason—shall she trust the man she loves but whose behavior has been extremely equivocal, or act rationally and give the treasure she is carrying to the other man? These moments apart, the film is a shallow pastiche.

The theme adumbrated here—the necessity for trust above all, whatever the risks—is the theme of one of Hitchcock's early, and not entirely satisfactory, Hollywood films, *Suspicion*. I pass to this now because it offers a convenient focal point for disentangling two threads which run through Hitchcock's later work and, while they do not in themselves *explain* his films, offer a means of access to them. I had better say that the mystery surrounding the genesis of this film—whether or not Hitchcock reversed the ending at the last moment, and whether, if he did, it was against his own wishes, is irrelevant: we are concerned only with the finished work. Such a last-minute decision might help to explain the slightly "uncooked" quality of much of the film; since its whole significance, as we have it, depends on the ending as it stands, it is difficult to believe that Hitchcock was strongly opposed to it.

First, what I call the *therapeutic* theme, whereby a character is cured of some weakness or obsession by indulging it and living through the consequences. Joan Fontaine falls in love with and marries Cary Grant. He is soon revealed as a liar and she comes to suspect that he is a murderer—eventually, that he is trying to murder *her*. The suspicions poison their marriage, making any open communication between them impossible. Only when they are eventually forced into the open is the fallacy exposed and, in the film's very last shot, a new start made. Two shots are worth singling out. The first gives us the moment of crystallization of the suspicions. The couple are playing a word game with the husband's best friend; as the two men talk, the woman's hands finger the letters on the table absently arranging them, and suddenly they have formed the word "murder." [3] Immediately she "realizes" that her husband is planning to kill the other man. A marvelous depiction of the way the conscious mind can be guided by the subconscious: in its context, of how deeply entrenched values can manipulate conscious thought. For Joan Fontaine, at the outset, is a dowdy, repressed young woman, a colonel's daughter, who has led a sheltered life characterized by the rigid values of respectability and a total ignorance of the outer world. She is irresistibly attracted to the man who represents glamor and reckless, carefree abandon; but he represents also a total rejection of everything her family background and upbringing have stood for: subconsciously, she *wants* him to be a murderer.

The second shot occurs later in the film, a long shot where we see Joan Fontaine, now certain that her suspicions are justified, standing in a black dress before a window whose framework casts around her a shadow as of a huge web. She is feeling herself the victim, the fly caught in the trap. But the image suddenly gives us the truth—she is in reality the spider, fattening herself on her suspicions in the center of the web she has herself spun; or she is both spider and fly at once, victim of her own trap. The image anticipates the even more powerful one in *Psycho* where Norman Bates, sitting in his room beneath stuffed birds of prey, becomes, simultaneously, the bird (from his resemblance to it) and its victim (from his position under it).

The second thread is the extension of this "therapy" to the spectator, by means of encouraging the audience to identify. The outlook of the Joan Fontaine character is a very common one, certainly not restricted to colonels' daughters. From the time of her marriage onward, we are restricted to the one consciousness: we know only what she knows, see only what she sees: we share her suspicions and learn from experience with her. With her, we find the Cary Grant character attractive: he is so romantic and dashing, so careless of mundane cares and restraints. But with her, we are gradually dismayed by his excesses: the reckless abandon with other people's money—and other people's feelings—comes to appear very unpleasant. So we become ashamed of having found him so attractive: if he were a complete blackguard, now, we would be exonerated, merely the victims of deceit, and we would be revenged on him when his downfall came. As Joan Fontaine's fingers arrange those letters into the word "murder," the camera places us in her position: they are *our* hands. The film endorses the man's attitude to life no more than the woman's: if the limitations of her inhibited, sheltered respectability are chastised, so is their inevitable complement—the attraction toward total irresponsibility. And always it is our own impulses that are involved, not only the characters'. [4]

I have tried, in this introduction, to give some rough basis for the analyses of seven films that follow.* I decided on Hitchcock's five most recent films for detailed study: first, because they seem to me to constitute an astonishing, unbroken chain of masterpieces and the highest reach of his art to date; second, because they offer such variety; third, because they are likely to be revived frequently in coming years, enabling interested readers to submit my analyses to the test of re-seeing the films;

* A chapter on *Torn Curtain* was added for the second edition.

finally, because they have received very little serious critical attention in this country. This last consideration, admittedly, would be little help in the matter of selection; but it is worth drawing the reader's attention here to the work on Hitchcock that appeared in early issues of *Movie:* especially V. F. Perkins' article on *Rope (Movie 7)* and Ian Cameron's two-part analysis of *The Man Who Knew Too Much (Movie 3* and *6).* I have decided to add discussions of *Strangers on a Train* and *Rear Window* partly because of their intrinsic merit and their importance in relation to Hitchcock's oeuvre as a whole, partly because they are widely known, having been frequently revived. Before this, however, I shall glance cursorily at a few other films. Any attempt at a complete survey is rendered impossible by the unavailability of certain key films—*Shadow of a Doubt* and *Under Capricorn,* for example. Comprehensiveness being impossible, I have simply followed whim; the reader is asked to attach particular significance neither to my selection nor to the proportion of space allotted to any given film, which does not necessarily correspond to my evaluation.

One day, perhaps, we shall rediscover Hitchcock's British films and do them justice; they are so overshadowed by his recent development as to seem, in retrospect, little more than 'prentice work, interesting chiefly because they are Hitchcock's (just as *Two Gentlemen of Verona* is interesting primarily because it is by Shakespeare). One can, of course, find most of the later themes and methods adumbrated in them; but who wants the leaf-buds when the rose has opened? The notion that the British films are better than, or as good as, or comparable with the later Hollywood ones seems to me not worth discussion. A delightful little comedy thriller like *The Lady Vanishes* gives us the characteristic Hitchcock tone in a primitive state, with its interweaving of tension and light humor; *Rich and Strange,* for all its clumsiness and uncertainities of touch—its clearly experimental nature—gives us the characteristic preoccupation with the marriage union. Ralph Thomas' shamelessly plagiaristic remake of *The 39 Steps,* with its intolerably clumsy handling of suspense and cheaply pornographic humor, nicely sets off the technical finesse and moral purity of Hitchcock's original; on the other hand, *North by Northwest,* with its far greater thematic cohesion, shows the limitations of the early film it superficially resembles. There is about these early films a freshness and spontaneity that the far more carefully composed later films lack; the latter, however, are characterized by a creative intensity that makes a preference for the British films analogous to preferring *The Comedy of Errors* to *Macbeth.* [5]

Of the Hollywood films, one might start with the three made for Selznick: *Rebecca, Spellbound,* and *The Paradine Case,* both chronologically and in ascending order of satisfactoriness. *Rebecca* (1940) was Hitchcock's first Hollywood film, an expensive production, and one guesses he didn't have much say in the script. In any case, the film fails either to assimilate or to vomit out the indigestible novelettish ingredients of Daphne du Maurier's book, and it suffers further from Olivier's charmless performance, which finally destroys our sympathy with the heroine, doting on such a boor. But there are rewards: an excellent scene where Olivier and Joan Fontaine, watching the films they took on their honeymoon, quarrel miserably, and we see simultaneously their past happiness and present wretchedness, two stages in a crumbling marriage (though we are perhaps slightly distracted by wondering how a fixed camera without an operator managed a tracking shot); [6] a "confession" scene that anticipates *Under Capricorn;* and the best scenes in the film, those built around George Sanders, which arouse something of the characteristic Hitchcockian complexity of response in our simultaneous attraction and repulsion. [7]

If the more interesting aspects of *Rebecca* suggest a sketch for *Under Capricorn, Spellbound* (1945) strikes us—with its central case history of traumatic shock—as superficially a sketch for *Marnie;* though it is in its own right more interesting than *Rebecca.* The trouble here is a split in the thematic material. The chief tension is generated by the development of the Ingrid Bergman-Gregory Peck relationship, the growth of mutual trust, the breaking down of barriers and inhibitions on both sides. The final detection of the murderer is arbitrary and not very interesting, for all its audience-suicide shot and scarlet flash (camera in murderer's position, hand holding gun follows Bergman to door, then gun turns toward us and Bang! we're all dead), one of the rare instances I can think of in Hitchcock of a *pointless* use of identification technique, since none of us wants to shoot Ingrid Bergman and we feel no connection of any kind with the murderer. One senses the artist playing about with technique for its own sake because he is not much engaged by his material at that point. Nor do the Salvador Dali dream sequences really belong in a Hitchcock film. [8]

Spellbound is perhaps the most interesting of the three Selznick films; *The Paradine Case* (1947), much less adventurous, is more satisfying. It points forward this time to *Vertigo:* the fascination of Alida Valli for Gregory Peck clearly foreshadows that of Kim Novak for James Stewart: the temptation is of the same kind, but it is here given little of the extraordinary universal significance it has in the later film, the conception being inherently more conventional. The film is marred by the miscasting—against Hitchcock's wishes—of Louis Jourdan. The courtroom denouement is masterly, with its complex and adult moral sense: we never cease to feel sympathy for Valli, and our (and Peck's) last sight of her is very haunting.

Lifeboat (1943) proves a far more complex film than I had expected: childhood memory had simplified it into a rather crude anti-Nazi piece in which the survivors in the lifeboat rescue a German, gradually discover that he is irredeemably wicked and treacherous, and batter him to death, with Hitchcock and the whole film solidly behind them; which is far from being so. The Nazi, as played by Walter Slezak, is by no means a stock villain; he bears a close resemblance to the charming devils of certain other Hitchcock films. Charm he certainly has—a seductive charm that in no way mitigates our final verdict on the deeply embedded doctrines on which he acts, but which keeps also in our minds the sense of the different man he might have been, a sense of his potential human excellence. On the other hand, the other characters, even the good and gentle radio operator and nurse, reveal a latent brutishness when they turn on him and kill him. Certainly there is provocation: the Nazi has murdered the seaman whose leg he earlier amputated: but Hitchcock's treatment of the scene leaves no doubt as to his response and ours. The killing is characterized by a messy, uncontrolled violence in which we are shocked to see the nurse (especially) participating: a response confirmed by the protest of the only character who holds back from what amounts to mob violence and lynch law—the Negro. The scene is extremely disturbing because we share the fury of the attackers sufficiently to feel ourselves personally involved in the killing, and are at the same time made to feel ashamed of that involvement. The film conveys the sense that the attackers' primary motivation is a desire for revenge on a man who has made fools of them.

We find in the film that typical Hitchcockian counterpointing of despair and optimism. The despair—amazing, really, for an American film made in 1943—arises from the sense that the Nazi is the only person who can control the situation, and that his strength is the strength of the Nazi doctrines—the strength of ruthlessness and inhumanity, of complete lack of scruple in achieving an end. And it is a strength that can serve good ends. Joe, the seaman (William Bendix), would certainly have died from his gangrenous leg if the Nazi (a surgeon in civilian life) had not amputated it; and it is clear that no one else has either the ability or the willpower to perform the operation without him. It is made almost unendurably horrible by the implied primitiveness: the shot of the jackknife held over the flame to be sterilized makes the blood run cold: the Nazi performs it without the slightest loss of composure. We cannot help admiring him, and it becomes very difficult for us, in the course of the film, to retract our admiration: to draw the line between what is admirable and what detestable, since both spring from the same source. The Nazi is dangerous (as so many film Nazis are not) because there is so much to be said for him. Besides him, the morally pure characters are impotent. And it is significant that the character who comes nearest to being a "hero"—the Marxist stoker (John Hodiak)— is the nearest (the point is made explicitly) to the Nazi in outlook, having a similar ruthless determination whose effect is softened, however, by our awareness that it springs from warm human sympathies. If Hitchcock shows himself, in *Lifeboat* and in *Rope,* a committed anti-fascist, he does not on the other hand show himself a committed democrat. The alert reader may think ahead to Mark Rutland in *Marnie;* though it should be insisted that Hitchcock would probably not endorse the translation of Mark's behavior into political terms: it is made valid only by being rooted in a deep instinctive-sympathetic flow.

The optimism that qualifies this implicit despair is revealed in a variation on the experience-therapy theme. The Tallulah Bankhead character is marvelously realized throughout the film, a very precise, complex attitude to her defined: points for, points against. What we watch, as the film develops, is the gradual stripping away of all the artificial barriers she sets between herself and life—seen primarily in her cynical toughness, partly a pose, partly the manifestation of a real strength—until the real woman emerges. The last stage is reached when her much-vaunted diamond bracelet (she has sworn she will never part with it, and it acquires a symbolic importance, as a trophy, as a means of self-exhibition, as an embodiment of false values) is lost after being used in an attempt to catch fish. Her uncontrollable laughter, we are made to feel, manifests not so much hysteria as a sense of release: she has lost all the external trappings that seemed to compose her identity, and finds that nonetheless she still exists, she is still *there* as a human being. *Lifeboat* may not be mainstream Hitchcock in method—the spectator is left unusually free throughout to regard the action from an objective, detached viewpoint, and there is no clear central figure—but it is central enough in its underlying themes and its complex moral position. [9]

Notorious (1946) is such a rich film that one hesitates to attempt an assessment of its significance in a few lines. I shall content myself with pointing to the sensitivity and insight with which the Grant-Bergman relationship is developed, passing through its phase of mutual destructiveness to become mutually healing, and the complexity of response that arises from its juxtaposition with a second love relationship, that of Sebastian (Claude Rains) and his mother (Madame Konstantin), many subtly moving effects being achieved through the subsequent modification of the spectator's sympathies and interest. It is perhaps Hitchcock's most fully achieved film to that date. The progress of the relationship is summed up in two love scenes: a progress from the desperate sensuality, betraying the underlying instability, of the lovers' kissing on the balcony near the beginning, to the sure, wondering, protective tenderness of the embrace when Grant at last comes to rescue Bergman from the situation into which he has perversely allowed her—even encouraged her—to be plunged. [10]

Kisses in Hitchcock, one may remark parenthetically, are often used to reveal or epitomize a whole relationship and (if one works outward from that) the sense of a whole film. Consider, besides the present instance, the contrasted relationships between husband and wife, wife and lover, stated simply by cutting from kiss to kiss in *Dial M for Murder;* the stiff embrace, quite lacking in real intimacy, between Farley Granger and Ruth Roman in *Strangers on a Train;* Grace Kelly covering with kisses the unresponsive face of a James Stewart engrossed in his obsession in *Rear Window;* the prolonged and detailed kiss with 360° camera track, to convey at once the near triumph of illusion and the growth of doubt in *Vertigo;* the kiss in *North by Northwest* with Cary Grant's hands encircling Eva Marie Saint's head as if to crush it; the awkward, tentative embrace in the kitchen in *The Birds;* the poignance of the kisses in *Marnie,* with the man's masculine protective tenderness trying to penetrate the woman's frozen unresponsiveness, revealed in huge close-up.

Rope (1948)—apart from its very first shot—takes place entirely within a single apartment and is filmed entirely in ten-minute takes, with an attempt at unbroken continuity not only of time but of *regard*. Some said, absurdly, that it was mere filmed theater. On the contrary, it is one of the most cinematic of films, carrying one of the defining characteristics of the medium—its ability to use a camera as the eye of the spectator, to take him right into an action, show him round inside it as it were —to its ultimate conclusion. Even were we allowed, however, to go up on the stage and prowl around among the actors, peering into their faces, studying their gestures, their movements, their reactions, this would still not offer a real analogy. For, in *Rope,* if we say that the camera becomes the spectator's eye, we must add that it is an eye that sees only what Hitchcock wants it to see, *when* he wants to see it. The camera, used constantly to link one action or gesture or glance to another in a continuous movement, generates terrific tension, the spectator's eye guided relentlessly to the significant detail at the significant moment. The ten-minute take is one manifestation of Hitchcock's suspense technique. As a piece of virtuosity the film is extraordinary, with timing, in complex actions involving several actors and complicated tracks, that takes the breath away. But technique—suspense itself—is here, as in all the films in which one feels Hitchcock really engaged, the embodiment of moral purpose; or, if "purpose" suggests something too cut-and-dried, a "film with a message," then the vehicle for conveying Hitchcock's complex moral sense.

The main line of development of the film is less the gradual process whereby the murder is brought to light than that whereby the James Stewart character—Rupert—is brought to realize how deeply he is implicated in it; the two processes in fact coincide, and the quality of the suspense depends partly on this duality of development. But the spectator is caught up in this suspense from the start, for we implicate ourselves by wanting—against our better judgment—these two quite unforgivable young murderers to get away with it, and the suspense of *Rope* is basically the tension between this and our conflicting desire that they be brought to justice. There are more ways than one of making an anti-fascist film (or an anti-anything film). There is the straight denunciation that generally has the effect of sending the spectator out with a

comfortable feeling of being on the right side, his complacency reinforced; or there is Hitchcock's method, which makes us subtly aware
that the evil tendencies are there in all of us, a potentiality rooted in
human nature against whose upsurging we must be constantly on our
guard. I believe that a film like *Rope* (or *Lifeboat;* or *Rear Window*—to
make it clear that the argument can be extended far beyond fascism) is
more socially beneficial than a film like Kubrick's *Paths of Glory,* which,
stating its subject and its attitude in terms of simple black-and-white,
gives us (for all the disturbing force of the execution sequence) the easy
satisfaction of telling the Bad People (through the mouth of Kirk Douglas) what we think of them. Hitchcock (in some respects—*vide* his TV
programs, his trailers, the advertising he either promotes or permits—
the least uncompromising of great artists) never compromises on one
basic artistic essential: his films never make explicit statements, their
"meaning" being conveyed entirely in terms of concrete realization,
entirely dramatized; but even the least alert spectator must go out of
Rope feeling uneasy and disturbed, because the tensions of the film—for
all the marvelous sense of release when the window is at last opened and
the shots fired—are never fully resolved. Art, as opposed to propaganda,
because of its necessarily inexplicit nature cannot operate directly on the
entirely unaware spectator (or reader); yet a film like *Rope,* while giving
such a spectator no "message" to take away, cannot fail to bring nearer
to the surface of consciousness those feelings which are first subtly
encouraged, and then (dramatically, not explicitly) denounced. There is,
of course, a very basic artistic principle involved here: to make clear the
range of application, one could point out that Jane Austen used much
the same method in *Emma.*

Consider one tiny point, which will have to stand as representative of
a moral tone and a method diffused through the whole film. We listen to
the clever talk of Rupert and his ex-pupil Brandon (John Dall) about the
right of the "superior being" to place himself above accepted morality,
even to kill. It is all light-hearted, on Rupert's side at least, his manner
relaxed and engaging; we respond to his charm and to the outrageousness—the freedom and irresponsibility—of his joking. But underlying
this amused response we are never allowed to forget what this philosophy, adopted as a code of life, has led to. The camera tracks away from
Rupert and Brandon to the right, where Kentley (Cedric Hardwicke) sits
in growing uneasiness, and, just as the camera takes him in, turns to

look out of the window. We know he is looking to see if his beloved and belated son is coming—the son whose murdered body is in the chest in the middle of the room—and the smile freezes on our face. The effect is achieved not only through the actor's performance (which is superb) but by means of the camera movement, which links the father's movement with the other men and at the same time integrates it in the entire situation; a cut there would have made the point much too obvious, and dissipated the emotional effect by losing the continuity of gaze. The camera movement makes us respond simultaneously to two incompatible attitudes whose conflict forces us (whether or not on a conscious level) to evaluate them.

Rope has two weaknesses. Hitchcock carries his decision to preserve continuity to the point of trying to cover up inevitable breaks between ten-minute takes by tracking right up to, then out from, something dark. The effect when Rupert blacks out the screen by throwing open the lid of the chest is electrifying; but there are several points where no dramatic purpose is served by our being led right up to, and then away from, a character's back: a straightforward cut would have been less distracting. The second weakness is that the spectator wants—and I think needs— to know just how Rupert *did* mean his teaching to be taken. [11]

In *Stage Fright* (1950) one feels the creative impulse at a comparatively low ebb. Hitchcock for once loses his grip on the spectator and about halfway through one realizes that one is not much interested in finding out what is going to happen. The film, however, if highly unsatisfactory considered as a self-sufficient work, is extremely interesting to anyone interested in Hitchcock, since it abounds in ideas relevant to his development. It is a series of variations on a theme common to films as different as *Notorious, Vertigo,* and *North by Northwest:* the discrepancy between Appearance and Reality (behind the credits, a safety curtain rises to reveal, not a stage, but real London backgrounds), and their equivocal nature. Running through the film is an extended comparison between two women, both actresses: "corrupt" star Charlotte (Marlene Dietrich) and "innocent" R.A.D.A. student Eve (Jane Wyman). That Corruption emerges on the whole more sympathetically than Innocence is not due *entirely* to the casting. *Acting* is a leading motif: both women act parts continually and habitually, so that there is constant doubt as to the real nature of each. From the start, it is made clear that Eve is not nearly so much in love with Jonathan (Richard Todd), the poor young dupe framed for a murder we see from the flashback in the opening sequence he didn't commit, as she thinks she is: she is in love with the situation, which enables her to make life into a drama with herself as romantic heroine Charlotte, in fact, the woman who has framed Jonathan, reveals at one point (when her mask of outrageous callousness and cynicism slips for a moment) that, although not emotionally involved with him, she feels for his predicament more genuinely than Eve does. [12] Eve gradually discovers real love for the handsome Inspector (Michael Wilding), and there is an interesting scene in a taxi (horribly overplayed by Jane Wyman, however) which begins as conscious, calculated seduction to help Jonathan, the pretense imperceptibly merging into reality so that no one, least of all Eve, is certain where one begins and the other ends. She remarks (about Charlotte), "Who knows what goes on in a woman's mind?—*I* don't know."

But, in a sense, Jonathan himself is the central character, and the subject of a potentially fascinating Hitchcockian experiment. The flashback sequence (where he tells Eve how Charlotte has committed the murder and is framing him) is handled (partly through subjective camera technique, partly because we see everything, inevitably, from the narrator's viewpoint, knowing only what he tells us) in such a way as to make us identify very strongly with Jonathan in his predicament: Jonathan's fate becomes our fate. We watch the film with a certain complacency, knowing that this nice young man will win through somehow; but we are disturbed by our constant uncertainty as to the sincerity of *both* the women with whom his fate rests. Then, at the end of the film, we suddenly learn that Charlotte hasn't framed him at all: he really *is* the murderer; the ground is cut away from under our feet. The flashback was a deliberate lie (and, whatever Rohmer and Chabrol may say, the images lie as well as the words, quite indisputably). Consequently, our response, when Eve (who set out to save Jonathan) indirectly brings about his death by safety curtain, is highly complex: we are still sufficiently involved with Jonathan to find it a betrayal, we are left with a disturbing sense of participating both in his guilt and in his death, cut off from all possible simple attitudes.

Or so, it seems, we would be if *Stage Fright* were the masterpiece that it ought to have been and sounds on paper. In fact, the meanderings of the scenario in the middle stretches of the film, combined with an oddly lethargic mise-en-scène, have dissipated our concentration; Jonathan has been lost sight of for so long that identification has been broken; and the script is conventional enough to allow us to reflect, as Eve falls in love with another man, that Jonathan is probably the murderer after all. It is a film more interesting in retrospect than while viewing.

When Chabrol and Truffaut told Hitchcock during an interview that of all his films (this was before *Vertigo*), they preferred *Under Capricorn* and *I Confess*, he replied, "I find them too serious": a characteristically self-depreciatory response with which, in the case of the later film (the earlier I cannot comment on, it is too long since I saw it) one cannot help agreeing. *I Confess* (1952) is earnest, distinguished, very interesting, and on the whole a failure: it would be, one would have thought, sufficient answer to those who wish to claim Hitchcock as an overt Catholic apologist. If one looks in this film for any genuine response to the Catholic religion, one looks in vain. The "impressive" use of church architecture is an external substitute, uneasily offered, for any effective realization of the priest's dilemma—for any conveyed sense of what religion, and the confessional law, mean to him: his vocation comes across as just a factor in the data, nothing more. And the moment where he is seen, in high-angled long shot, walking along a street, with the foreground of the screen occupied by a statue of Christ bearing the cross, is one of the few moments in all Hitchcock's work where the word "pretentious" rises to one's mind. A significance which has no realized dramatic life is being externally stressed.

The film bears a very close relationship to the one that immediately preceded it: *Strangers on a Train*. For once, the earlier work is the better. The priesthood in *I Confess* is to Father Logan what the political world is to Guy Haines, a world of order which offers a legitimate escape from a disordered past. But *Strangers* has the following advantages: (a) Though very important to the plot, the world of politics is not *central* to it: there is no need for Hitchcock to go into Guy's vocation (such as it is) in detail. *I Confess*, on the other hand, is centered upon a point of Catholic church law: the hero's commitment to his beliefs is of fundamental importance. (b) In *Strangers* Hitchcock feels free to suggest that Guy's vocation is in fact suspect, not untained by a shallow opportunism; in *I Confess*, while failing to convince us of Logan's dedication, he seems unable or unwilling to imply any criticism of it, or to realize Logan's actual attitude clearly in dramatic terms. (c) The conception of Keller, the murderer, though convincing enough, is far more conven-

tional, less detailed, suggestive, and complex, than that of Bruno Anthony in *Strangers*. (d) The famous theme of the interchangeability of
guilt, of the hero's involvement with the murderer on more levels than
that of plot, not entirely satisfactorily confronted in *Strangers,* is shirked
even more in *I Confess* (if indeed it can really be said to be there at all).
(e) In the world of *Strangers* Hitchcock seems at his ease, in *I Confess*
one senses a constant constraint; where the earlier film has a marvelous
combination of tautness and fluency, the later strikes one as labored.
The constraint is clearly not due to theme, or to faulty construction, but
to milieu. It may well be that it is the result, not merely of unfamiliarity,
but of the lingering, imperfectly assimilated influence of Hitchcock's
early Jesuit upbringing. In any case, *I Confess* seems to me to bear the
sort of relationship to his work that *The Princess Casamassima* bears to
Henry James'. The cost of the somewhat obtrusive "seriousness" to
which Hitchcock retrospectively objected is the sacrifice of so much of
the characteristic complexity of tone, the "seriousness" here largely
precluding the interplay of irony and humor. The general constraint can
be localized in some small uncertainties of touch, a failure on the director's part to respond to a *whole* situation. As the murderer's wife dies
and begs for Logan's forgiveness, he seems virtually to ignore her; yet
one doesn't feel that any criticism of his lack of humanity is implied, nor
indeed that Hitchcock is really aware of the implications of the scene.
And Anne Baxter's final withdrawal with her husband, leaving the man
she loved in a situation of extreme peril, showing neither concern nor
interest, is very awkward and indeterminate in aim.

It is the Anne Baxter character, however, that is the most interesting
and successful thing in *I Confess,* both in itself and as an anticipation of
Annie Hayworth in *The Birds.* The scene on the boat where she admits
to Logan that she still loves him generates more tension than any of the
scenes involving Keller. The sense we are given in all her scenes of a life
willfully wasted on a self-indulgent clinging to romantic fantasy (one
thinks of *Vertigo* as well as of Annie Hayworth here) carries a powerful
moral charge. Especially, one can single out the brilliant use of subjective
flashback (during her confession scene), both to characterize her and to
evoke the necessary moral judgment on the quality of her life. The
flashbacks are extremely stylized in a naively romantic manner, each
stage in her relationship with Logan seen in terms of sentimental cliché.
This is how she sees the past, this is the dream for which she is perversely

sacrificing any possible fulfillment in reality; and this romantically gush-
ing girl descending the steps to her waiting lover, to the accompaniment
of a sentimental love song, is her cherished image of herself. The flashbacks are usually laughed at in a superior, knowing way, on the assumption that it is Hitchcock who is being naive: he is often too sophisticated
for the sophisticated. A particularly subtle touch is the visual suggestion
contained in the flashbacks that the lovers did in fact commit adultery:
we discover later, through Logan's obviously sincere testimony, that they
did not, and realize we have been given a beautiful description of wish
fulfilment. *Stage Fright* is not the only Hitchcock film to contain a lying
flashback.

The other Hitchcock film with overt religious content is *The Wrong
Man* (1956); and it seems to confirm in part the impression of *I Confess*,
though it is a far more successful film. Its first half can stand comparison
with anything Hitchcock has done. Particularly, one might point out the
thematic connection with *The Birds,* a film so different in tone and
subject matter (indeed, they are in some respects at opposite poles, being
respectively the most "realistic"—in the narrow sense—and the most
fantastic of Hitchcock's recent films): the theme of the precariousness
and vulnerability of the little order we can make in our lives. The
imprisonment of Henry Fonda becomes more than a case of mistaken
identity, through the very intensity of the images: the treatment of his
progress, the gradual stripping away of his means of identification, his
personal possessions, the reduction of a man depicted form the start as
passive, gentle, slightly ineffectual, lacking any strong identity, to the
total anonymity with which he is threatened, makes of it a descent into
the underworld—into a chaos world underlying the surface reality,
where all men are one man, where values cease to exist, where all
particularity is merged. For Balestrero, prison becomes a vision of Hell.

The second half of the film fails to maintain this intensity. The change
of the focus of interest to Balestrero's wife (Vera Miles), instead of
evoking a more complex response, tends to dissipate the spectator's
interest. The failure seems to lie in the realization, in the actual scene-
by-scene plotting of the scenario, rather than in the basic conception.
We are shown Balestrero, after his preliminary prison experiences, hovering on the brink of breakdown. Yet it is his wife who goes mad, and it
is her madness that saves him. By taking away his chief prop, it places
the whole burden of holding together the family unit, on the preserva-

tion of which the couple's sense of identity depends, on his shoulders. He is forced to discover unknown strengths within himself, and the film associates this with his discovery of God through prayer. Hitchcock attributes the partial failure of the latter half of the film to the fact that working from a factual story limited his freedom to plan the scenario as he wished. A further cause, on internal evidence, seems to be uneasiness with the dénouement, with its suggestion of miracle. The crucial scene in the film, if one takes it as essentially a religious work—the scene where Balestrero's mother exhorts him to pray for help—is, significantly, as labored and conventional in execution as in writing. It will be recognized that a very delicate problem of belief is involved here. I must confess that I find the same kind of unsatisfactoriness in certain other Catholic works, for example in Hopkins' poem "That Nature Is a Heraclitean Fire and of the Comfort of the Resurrection." Hopkins' treatment of "nature's bonfire" is magnificent in the vitality of its imagery; in his treatment of the resurrection theme the imagery abruptly weakens, becomes unrealized, rather banal, even glib. Similarly, Hitchcock's response to the undermining of a precarious order in the first half of *The Wrong Man* seems so much stronger than his response to the idea of *religious* salvation in the latter. One could perhaps argue that the flaw in both works is caused by the essential incommunicability of the unknowable; it *looks* more like a lack of real conviction, a desire to believe rather than belief itself.

In the final sequences, Hitchcock finds his form again. The confrontation of "Wrong" and "Right" men, where Fonda, by his firm stare at the real criminal, proclaims his preservation, indeed the definition, of the identity that was in danger of being submerged, has great force, and the final scene with the wife in the mental home takes us right into the world of *The Birds*. That Hitchcock's Catholic background has relevance to the assumptions about the universe that underlie his films I would not deny; but it seems to me an indirect relevance. The notion that his cinema is the vehicle for a committed Catholicism is made more than dubious by close inspection of the film which seems, superficially, to endorse it most of all.

2

STRANGERS ON A TRAIN

The first shots introduce us to two pairs of men's feet as their owners arrive at a station. The two are characterized by means of their shoes: first, showy, vulgar, brown-and-white brogues; second, plain unadorned walking shoes. A parallel is at once established in visual terms: or, more precisely, a parallel is imposed by the editing on what would otherwise be pure contrast. Each shot of the first pair of feet is promptly balanced by a similar shot of the second. On the train, we are shown the feet again, moving to the same table. It is always Bruno's feet that we see first—he arrives at the station first, he sits down first, it is Guy's foot that knocks his accidentally, under the table, leading directly to their getting into conversation. Thus Hitchcock makes it clear that Bruno has not engineered the meeting, despite the fact that he knows all about Guy ("Ask me anything, I know the answers") and has the plan for exchanging murders ready to hand: it is rather as if he is waiting for a chance meeting he knew would come. This gives us, from the outset, the sense of some not quite natural, not quite explicable link between the two men.

The contrast between them is developed explicitly in the dialogue. Guy is planning a career in politics: in Hitchcock's films, politics, government, democratic symbolism (the Statue of Liberty in *Saboteur,* the Capitol in this film, Mount Rushmore in *North by Northwest*), are always associated with the idea of an ordered life, set against potential chaos. Bruno, on the other hand, has been expelled from three colleges for drinking and gambling, and lives mostly for kicks. Guy wants to marry Ann Morton, a senator's daughter; Bruno is associated with his mother (by means of the ornate tiepin, a gift from her, which bears his name). Bruno, despite the fact that he has flown in a jet and driven a car blindfold at 150 mph, and has a theory that "you should do everything before you die," envies Guy: "I certainly admire people who do things";

and, "It must be pretty exciting, being so important—me, I never do anything important." We register this sense of impotence as probably, at bottom, sexual: it links up with Bruno's voyeuristic prying into Guy's love life.

Yet, behind the contrast, the parallel established by the editing of the opening shots becomes manifest. Both men, like so many of Hitchcock's protagonists, are insecure and uncertain of their identity. Guy is suspended between tennis and politics, between his tramp wife and his senator's daughter, and Bruno is seeking desperately to establish an identity through violent, outré actions and flamboyance (shoes, lobster-patterned tie, name proclaimed to the world on his tiepin). His professed admiration for Guy is balanced by Guy's increasing, if reluctant and in part ironically amused, admiration for him. Certainly, Guy responds to Bruno—we see it in his face, at once amused and tense. To the man committed to a career in politics, Bruno represents a tempting overthrow of all responsibility. Guy fails to repudiate Bruno's suggestive statements about Miriam ("What is a life or two, Guy? Some people are better off dead") with any force or conviction. When Bruno openly suggests that he would like to kill his wife, he merely grins and says, "That's a morbid thought"; but we sense the tension that underlies it. When he leaves the train he is still laughing at Bruno; but he leaves his lighter behind. This lighter, on which our attention has already been focused by a close-up and some commentary in the dialogue, is to be of crucial importance in the plot. It was given to Guy by Ann Morton, and bears the inscription "A to G" with two crossed tennis racquets: it is through his tennis that Guy's entry into politics has become possible. Guy's forgetfulness at this moment belies his dismissive joking air when Bruno asks if he agrees to the exchange of murders ("Of course I agree—I agree with *all* your theories"). He is leaving in Bruno's keeping his link with Ann, his possibility of climbing into the ordered existence to which he aspires. The leaving of the lighter is one of the visual equivalents Hitchcock finds for the interior, psychological analysis of the Patricia Highsmith novel that was his source.

Guy, then, in a sense connives at the murder of his wife, and the enigmatic link between him and Bruno becomes clear. Bruno is certainly a character in his own right, realized in detail with marvelous precision; but he also represents the destructive, subversive urges that exist, though suppressed, in everybody: he is an extension, an embodiment, of desires already existing in Guy. In their first conversation, as they face each other, the cross-cutting between them gives us Guy's face unshadowed, Bruno's crossed with lines of shadow like the shadow of bars. He is continually, in these early stages of the film, associated with shadows and with darkness; the development of the film can partly be seen in terms of his forcing himself into the light for recognition. He understands Guy's darker motives better than Guy does himself: "Marrying the boss's daughter—the short cut to a career": nothing later in the film, and especially not the uneasy, formal relationship between the lovers, contradicts this assessment.

The next sequence introduces us to Miriam and defines Guy's position more clearly. Miriam—hard, mean, slovenly, at once contemptible and pathetic in her limitations—is one of those Hitchcock characters created in the round with the utmost economy in a few seconds: a gesture of the hands, a drooping of the mouth, a slovenly way of turning the body, dull yet calculating eyes peering shortsightedly through those spectacles. She is more than a character. We are introduced to her in the record shop where she works, and the association of her with revolving objects (taken up later in the fairground sequence) suggests the futile vicious circle of her existence, the circle from which Guy wishes to break free. We have already seen Guy's lack of insight into other people in his inability to deal firmly with Bruno, and seen too that this lack is basically one of self-awareness; so we have no difficulty in accepting the premise of his involvement with Miriam.

After the row in the record shop, during which Guy "warns" Miriam and shakes her violently, the phone call to Ann: "You sound so savage, Guy"—"I'd like to break her foul, useless little neck . . . I said I could strangle her"—shouted over the roar of an approaching train. Cut to Bruno's hands—his mother has just manicured them, and he is admiring them, flexing the fingers. The cut finally clinches the relationship between the two men, making Bruno an agent for the execution of Guy's desires.

The fairground and amusement park is a symbolic projection of Miriam's world: a world of disorder, of the pursuit of fun and cheap glamor as the aim of life, of futility represented by the circular motion of roundabout and Great Wheel that receive such strong visual emphasis in almost every shot. The whole sequence is realized with a marvelous particularity and complexity. Through Miriam, Hitchcock evokes a whole social milieu, small town life in all its unimaginativeness and restriction. The sequence is introduced by the long shot of Miriam's home, from Bruno's viewpoint, as he waits for her to emerge: respectable-looking, white-fronted house, mother sitting outside on porch, calling, "Now don't be out late" to Miriam as she runs down the steps with her two boyfriends, holding hands, giggling childishly. We think back to the sullen girl in the record shop. At the fairground, she makes the boys buy her an ice-cream cornet, talking at the same time about hot dogs, and they tease her about eating so much. We remember that she is pregnant. She talks about her "craving"—the boys laugh: "Craving for what?" She turns, gazing round the fairground through her spectacles, licking at her ice cream like a spoiled schoolgirl, looking at once childish and sensual, and her eyes fix on Bruno, watching her from a distance. Not only is the character rendered with precision: an attitude to her is precisely defined, an attitude totally devoid of sentimentality, astringent yet not without pity. She is not pathetic in herself—she is never aware of needing anyone's compassion—but her situation, the narrow, circumscribed outlook, the total lack of awareness, is both pathetic and horrible. And what is being defined, ultimately, is the world from which Guy is struggling to escape: contaminated by that world (remember the impurity, exposed by Bruno, of his motives for wanting to marry Ann), he cannot free himself cleanly as he wants.

The sequence of events leading up to the murder throws further light on both Miriam and Bruno: the strangling is invested with a clear sexual significance. Miriam, at her first glimpse of Bruno, sees something more intriguing—more *dangerous*—than she can find in her two very unmysterious boys. She gives him the "come-on," unmistakably, demanding to go to the Tunnel of Love loudly, so that he will hear. As her boys fail to ring the bell at the "Test Your Strength" machine, she looks round for him, and when he materializes mysteriously on her other side, she smiles at him. He shows off his strength to her ("He's broken it!"), first proudly flexing his hands, which are emphasized by the low camera angle, afterward waggling his eyebrows at her. Then the roundabout: circling motion, raucous music, painted, prancing horses, more flirtation from Miriam. She calls—loudly again, like an announcement—for a boat ride. More revolving in the backgrounds as they get the boats: the Big Wheel behind Bruno, huge waterwheel beside the Tunnel of Love ahead of Miriam. From here, the sexual symbolism accumulates strikingly. They pass through an archway to the boats, above which is written "Magic Isle"—where Miriam will shortly be murdered; the boats cross the lake, enter the tunnel (where Bruno's shadow ominously overtakes Miriam's), out again onto the lake. Miriam runs away on the isle, purposely losing the boys. Then a lighter is trust before her face and struck: "A to G": "Is your name Miriam?" "Why, yes," she smiles seductively, and Bruno drops the lighter and strangles her.

Her glasses fall off, one lens shatters, and the murder is shown to us reflected in the other lens, inverted and distorted. The lens itself recalls lake and tunnel and is a further sexual symbol. The shot is one of the cinema's most powerful images of perverted sexuality, the murder a sexual culmination for both killer and victim. It ends with Bruno's hands enormous in the lens as he moves back from the body. We see the lighter, "A to G", on the grass, and remember Guy's words on the phone: "I could strangle her." Having retrieved it, Bruno returns to his boat through a chaos of promiscuity—pairs of lovers on the grass all round: the chaos world has been finally defined, the "Magic Isle" be- comes an island of lost souls. The association of sexual perversion with the sense of damnation will be taken up again more forcefully in *Psycho*. Bruno, with his close relationship with a crazy mother, is an obvious forerunner of Norman Bates.

As he leaves the fairground, Bruno helps a blind man across the road. At the time, it seems merely a cleverly ironic touch, a trifle glib; but in retrospect it takes on a deeper meaning. Henceforth Bruno will be haunted by the memory of Miriam's eyes looking at him through her spectacles in which the lighter flame is reflected; his helping of a blind man with dark glasses is an act of unconscious atonement. The sequence ends with Bruno looking at his watch: cut to Guy, on a train, looking at *his:* the visual link again used to enforce the connection between them.

Later, we see Guy reaching his rooms in Washington. On one side of the street, stately, respectable houses; towering in the background, on the right of the screen, the floodlit dome of the Senate House, the life to which Guy aspires, the world of light and order. On the other side of the street, deep shadow and tall iron-barred gates from behind which Bruno calls. The light-and-darkness symbolism—Guy turning from the lighted doorway of the house toward the shadow, away from the Senate House —is simple, but not naive or ridiculous, and handled naturally and unobtrusively. Bruno beckons, a shadow among shadows. Again we see him with bars across his face: at the start of the ensuing dialogue he is behind the bars, Guy in the open. He gives Guy the spectacles, reminds him about the lighter—"I went back for it, Guy." Guy is horrified. Then: "But, Guy, you *wanted* it . . . We planned it together . . . You're just as much in it as I am . . . You're a free man now." The phone rings in Guy's rooms, a police car approaches, stops outside, and Guy promptly joins Bruno behind the bars, in shadow: a free man. He says, "You've got me acting like I'm a criminal," and we have a subjective shot of the police from Guy's position behind the bars. The scene gives a beautifully exact symbolic expression to Guy's relationship to Bruno and what he stands for.

More light-and-darkness in the next sequence: Guy answers his phone, Ann tells him to come round. Right of screen: a large, lighted lamp, Guy holding the receiver to his ear, Ann's voice coming through. Left of screen: heavy shadow, Miriam's spectacles dangling downward in Guy's other hand. The hands remind us of a pair of scales. We then see Guy and Ann together for the first time, and Hitchcock shows us their rather remote, uneasy relationship. Ann strikes us as the older, certainly the maturer, the more completed: the dominant partner. Their kiss lacks real intimacy or tenderness. She tells him she loves him and he replies, "Brazen woman, I'm the one to say that": an odd, endistancing, defensive kind of joke. As Ann, her father, and her sister Barbara break the news, and Guy makes a feeble attempt at surprise, our view of the lovers' relationship is confirmed by Ann's obvious suspicions that Guy has killed Miriam: she tells him, with heavy significance, "She was strangled"; and she is visibly relieved when he explains his alibi. If the world from which Guy wishes to escape is defined for us by Miriam, then Ann —formal, rather hard, rather cold, in Ruth Roman's unsympathetic performance—defines the life to which he aspires: a life of imposed, slightly artificial orderliness. As for his guilt, Hitchcock makes it very clear that what he can't bear is not the idea that he has been indirectly involved, at any rate by desire, in the death of a human being, but the fear of being found out: it is the only feeling he reveals in his conversation with Bruno, and all that he and Ann reveal in this scene. The moral point is made clearly when Senator Morton rebukes Barbara for saying, of Miriam, "She was a tramp," with the remark, "She was a human being." The rebuke, for the audience, has relevance to the lovers as well.

Yet, despite the critical attitude adopted toward the lovers' relationship, we are made aware of its importance for Guy. Ann is more than a way to a career, she represents in herself something of the ordered world he aspires to. Thus the kiss that closes the sequence, which Guy, eyes looking straight into the camera, scarcely returns, is in contrast to the kiss that opened it: the *potentialities* of the relationship are threatened by the concealment of his involvement in Miriam's murder.

In the ensuing sequences Bruno increases the pressure on Guy to murder his father. First, the phone call to Ann's house: Guy hangs up. Second, the scene where Guy and Hennessy (the detective detailed to watch him) walk together past the Senate House. In the setting of spacious, ordered architecture, Guy says, "When I'm through with tennis I'm going into politics," and looks across to see Bruno watching from the steps, tiny in long shot. Third, the letter from Bruno pushed under Guy's door. Fourth, the scene where Ann sees Bruno for the first time. She and Guy are in the Senate House when Bruno calls Guy from among the pillars: "You're spoiling everything . . . You're making me come out into the open." Fifth, Guy receives the plan of, and key to, Mr. Anthony's house. Then, at last, the famous shot of Bruno watching Guy at the tennis court, all other heads turning to follow the ball, Bruno's conspicuous because motionless, his eyes fixed on Guy: a moment at once funny and unnerving. He now manages to meet Ann while Guy practices.

These scenes work beautifully in terms of suspense, but here as elsewhere it is necessary to ask, of what exactly does his suspense consist? We feel uneasy not just because pressure is being brought to bear on Guy to make him commit a murder; rather, it is because that which he wants to hide is indeed "coming out into the open." Think back to a character I have hitherto neglected: Ann's sister Barbara. In the first scene at Senator Morton's house, Barbara's function is clearly to express, directly and unhypocritically, what everyone—including the spectator —is slightly ashamed to find himself thinking: that it is really an admirable thing from all points of view that Miriam is dead. Her frank and shocking remarks recall Bruno's justification of killing—"Some people are better off dead"—and therefore involve the spectator with Bruno; they also prompt the senator's rebuke—"She was a human being." In other words, conflicting, apparently mutually exclusive responses are set up in the spectator, with disturbing results. We respond strongly to Barbara's no-nonsense honesty, but we are made ashamed of that response. It is this conflict within the spectator that is the essence of the ensuing suspense: we, as well as Guy, are implicated in Miriam's murder. Bruno's symbolic progress, each step bringing him closer and clearer —telephone, distant figure, closer figure lurking among shadowy pillars, figure sitting in full sunlight, young man in conversation with Ann, intruder from the chaos world into the world of order—represents the emergence of all we want concealed: our own suppressed, evil desires.

Bruno's appearance at the party marks his final eruption into the world of order: the demand for recognition of the universality of guilt by a world that rejects such an assumption. The centerpiece of the scene —in some respects of the whole film—is Bruno's near-strangling of Mrs. Cunningham. It derives its disturbing power again from a subtly aroused conflict, the attractiveness and the danger of that connivance at common guilt which Bruno represents. First, we are disarmed by Bruno's casually irreverent deflection of a dignified, self-righteous judge: how is he able to sit down to dinner after sentencing someone to death? The way the judge responds to the insolent question plainly makes the point that his way of life depends on such questions never being asked. The lightly humorous treatment releases us from some of the uneasiness we feel at responding to Bruno and prepares us for the next step—Bruno's conversation about murder with Mrs. Cunningham.

Here the underlying assumption of the film (subversive, destructive desires exist in all of us, waiting for a momentary relaxing of our vigilance) becomes explicit. Mrs. Cunningham's denial that *everyone* is interested in murder breaks down abruptly when Bruno asks if there haven't been times when she has wanted to kill someone—*Mr.* Cunningham, perhaps? There follows the richly comic exchange of murder methods, culminating in Bruno's demonstration of silent strangling— the method he used on Miriam—with Mrs. Cunningham as guinea pig. As his hands close on the old woman's throat, Barbara comes up behind her, Bruno sees her and, for the second time, is reminded by her (dark hair, round face, glasses) of Miriam. He goes into a "sort of trance," Mrs. Cunningham is nearly killed, and the sequence ends with Barbara, who has realized that Bruno was really strangling *her*, in tears. The scene is a superb example of the Hitchcock spectator trap. First, belief in established order has been undermined in the deflation of the judge; then the dialogue with Mrs. Cunningham and her friend, because of its light tone, gives us license to accept the notion of common guilt as something of a joke, to connive at it, allowing ourselves to be implicated in the "game" of murdering Mrs. Cunningham, who is anyway a rich, trivial, stupid old woman. Then abruptly the joke rebounds on us: we have nearly been implicated in another murder: swift modulation of tone has seldom been used to such disturbing effect. We are horrified to find that we have momentarily identified ourselves with Bruno (the sequence contains a number of subjective shots, where we are placed in his position). We have the feeling, even, that we, through a lack of vigilance, have released these destructive forces by conniving at them. But the final emphasis is on Barbara; and we recall that earlier it was she who was used to make explicit our conventionally suppressed feeling that Miriam's murder was all for the best. She seemed before to give validity to the release of the anarchic forces of desire: now she is punished by the very forces she helped release, and we with her. The scene leads us straight to the essence of Hitchcock: that ordered life depends on the rigorous and *unnatural* suppression of a powerfully seductive underworld of desire: and we see the reason for the stiff formality of the world of order in the film.

The scene is rich in other ways too. The three minor characters, the judge, Mrs. Cunningham, and her friend, are realized with marvelous economy and precision, the realization being, as always, as much a crystallization of an attitude toward them as the objective description of character: there is nothing indulgent about the humor with which these representatives of the world of order are presented. The incident also further illuminates Bruno, whose symbolic function in the film is by no means undermined by the fact that he is also a character created in the round. Mrs. Cunningham, like Bruno's mother, is rich, spoiled, foolish, and indulgent; he is able to handle her so adroitly because he is used to managing his mother, manipulating her reactions. This is the kind of relationship he can manage, a relationship based entirely on power, wielded through a combination of cunning and insidious, self-insinuating charm—his ability to involve others in his sickness. Finally, the sequence shows the toll his life and actions are taking of him, his thoroughgoing cynicism and complete lack of remorse belied by his obsession with Barbara's (i.e. Miriam's) glasses and neck, the ineradicable memory of that other relationship expressed in the shot of his anguished face as he tries to strangle Mrs. Cunningham. As his hands are pulled away from her throat, he falls back in a swoon.

It is the near-strangling of Mrs. Cunningham that forces the spectator to come to terms with his attitude to subversive desire, and prompts Guy, under pressure from Ann, to divulge the truth to her: without, however, acknowledging any personal guilt, of which he obviously remains quite unaware. He tells Ann, "I'd do his murder, he'd do mine"; to which she responds suggestively, "What do you mean—*your* murder, Guy?" Her first reaction was, "How did you get him to do it?" The removal of doubts between the lovers marks a necessary stage in the action. Their relationship is now on a surer footing, giving Guy the strength to take steps to extricate himself. The next sequence, in which he visits Mr. Anthony's house at night, is a turning point and a critical crux.

The emphasis is, again, on suspense: in successive shots we see Guy take the gun Bruno has sent him, elude his "tail" by using the fire-escape, and cross the moonlit lawn of the Anthony grounds in long shot, like a shadow. We don't know at all clearly what he intends to do or what will happen to him. Suspense is built up as he enters the house (using the key Bruno had sent), consults Bruno's map to find the father's room, encounters a snarling mastiff on the stairs, subdues it, finds the room, transfers the gun, hesitating for a moment with it in his hand, from his breast pocket to his side pocket, creeps into the bedroom, approaches the bed, calls in a whisper, "Mr. Anthony . . . I want to speak to you about your son . . . about Bruno." The dark figure on the bed switches on a lamp and reveals himself as Bruno.

At first glance this seems, indeed, to be that "mere" suspense that is all Hitchcock's detractors see in his films: externally applied, rather cheap. And if we assume that Guy knows precisely what he is going to do in Mr. Anthony's house, the criticism is unanswerable. Hitchcock is cheating, basing the suspense on a deliberate misleading of the spectator. There are, however, points which suggest that this is too superficial a reading: that Guy has indeed made up his mind to visit Mr. Anthony, but there remains a possibility, right up to the moment of hesitation outside the bedroom door that he will change his mind and shoot him. With this in mind, the sequence assumes quite a different aspect.

The first hint comes in fact several scenes earlier, when Guy is talking to Hennessy in his rooms before the party. The camera looks down as Guy opens the top drawer in which Bruno's gun is lying, and we see the two men with the gun strongly emphasized in the foreground of the screen. Guy has just been telling Hennessy he will have an early night: he is in fact planning to visit the Anthony house. But they are now discussing Hennessy's suspicious colleague, Hammond, and, as we see the gun in the drawer, Hennessy says "He doesn't trust anybody—not even himself." The whole shot is framed and directed in such a way as to give a particular significance to the remark, linking it with the gun. Then, in the house, we have the moment of hesitation itself. This is either the decisive moment of the scene or a very cheap trick indeed: cheap, because it falsifies a character's behavior for the sake of producing a shiver—if the gesture doesn't imply uncertainty as to what to do with the gun, then it has no meaning at all. Finally, shortly after the discovery that it is Bruno on the bed, Guy tells him, "You're sick," adding, "I don't know much about those things . . ." It is the nearest to an explicit statement in the film of that lack of self-awareness so plentifully illustrated elsewhere. The "suspense" of the sequence, then, has a point: the spectator's uncertainty as to what Guy is going to do corresponds to the character's own inner uncertainty. And the moment of final decision is the turning-point of the film: henceforward, Bruno is openly *against* Guy, no longer wanting anything but revenge. The conflict has changed levels, and the struggle for self-preservation is the price Guy must pay for his involvement; an involvement partly expiated by the decision taken outside Mr. Anthony's bedroom.

But, this said, it must then be admitted that to raise such doubts is to acknowledge a dissatisfaction with the sequence. Guy's uncertainty is not sufficiently realized, a fault due perhaps to the limitations of Farley Granger as an actor, which led Hitchcock to put more weight on that one gesture with the gun than it can stand. But the criticism is of a misjudgment, a local failure of realization, not a major lapse in artistic integrity. [—Now, I'm not so sure. The compromise over the hero figure that fatally flaws *Torn Curtain* offers a close parallel, and one cannot but feel that Hitchcock's uncertainty of handling in the scene of Guy's visit to Bruno's house has its roots in his fears of the effect of so morally dubious a "hero" on box office response. "Major lapse in artistic integrity" is perhaps not too strong a description—R. W. 1968.]

Ann's interview with Bruno's mother is the next step in the working out of the situation on its new level, the protagonists now ranged openly against one another. In Mrs. Anthony's insanity we see (as we are to see it later, more extremely, in the amalgam of Norman Bates and his mother at the end of *Psycho*) the ultimate extension of the chaos world. The woman's very existence depends on the complete rejection of all value judgments, the final denial of responsibility. In fact, "irresponsibility" is the word she uses to excuse Bruno: with a smile of maternal indulgence, a little knowing shake of the head, she says, "Sometimes he's terribly irresponsible." To which Ann returns a moment later, "He's *responsible* for a woman's death."

The famous cross-cutting between the tennis match and Bruno's journey with the lighter gives us a very different sort of suspense—simpler, less disturbing than before, as befits this phase of the action. The tension we feel now is not uncomplicated by conflicting responses (who hasn't *wanted* Bruno to reach the lighter?), but the struggle has become clear and simple, the forces of good and evil are now separate and clearly aligned. Despite this, some very interesting points arise.

First, the development of that elementary yet elemental light-darkness symbolism: Guy fights for victory on the brilliantly sunny tennis court as Bruno struggles to reach the lighter which has slipped through a grating down a drain. One doesn't want to reduce the film to simple, pat allegory (Hitchcock resolutely defies any such treatment), but the cutting between sunny open court and shadowy enclosed drain carries powerfully evocative overtones: underlying the whole action of the film, we can see as its basis the struggle for dominance between superego and id. Second, we remember that tennis has been established from the start as Guy's means of access to the ordered word, his ladder from the previous life with Miriam to his projected political career: it is therefore appropriate that his fate should depend now on his ability at tennis. Furthermore, this test is made explicitly one of character, even of character development. Guy, in his desperation to finish the match in time, has to change his whole manner of playing (as the commentator points out)— he abandons his usual cautious long-term strategy in favor of a "grim and determined" open battling style. His whole career—even the desire to marry Ann—has been a matter of careful strategy: now he is forced to fight openly for what he wants. Third, it is significant that the outcome of the entire film should be made to depend upon the retrieving of the lighter, symbol of Guy's involvement with Bruno, of his placing himself in Bruno's hands. Great emphasis is laid on it—and on the "A to G" inscription—every time it appears. It is Guy's strongest *concrete* link with the ordered world; now he must reenter the chaos world in order to retrieve it, thereby risking final submersion.

The fairground climax gives us the ultimate development of that world in its magnificent symbol of the roundabout that gets out of control. Guy struggles for his life—for more than his life—on the insanely whirling machine beneath the metallic hoofs of hideously grinning and prancing dummy horses: the horses on which Bruno, with Guy's implicit consent (the lighter) set about "seducing" Miriam. Guy is denied the satisfaction—we are denied the release—of a straightforward victory: the roundabout terrifyingly breaks down, Guy is thrown clear, Bruno is crushed under the wreckage. He dies obstinately refusing repentance, and Guy seems involved forever. Then, as he dies, Bruno's hand opens: the lighter is in his palm.

The very last scene of the film (where Guy and Ann move away pointedly from a friendly clergyman on a train) shows us, with light humor, Guy, united with his senator's daughter, resolutely—even somewhat extremely and rigidly!—resisting the possibility of further temptation. The stiff unnaturalness of the couple's behavior is perfectly logical: Guy's involvement with Bruno has been worked out in action—he has never faced its implications, and his personality remains to the end unintegrated, his identity still potentially unstable, the threat of disorder to be held back only by rigid control.

Strangers on a Train draws together many themes already adumbrated in earlier films, which will be taken further in later ones: the theme of what Conrad calls the "sickening assumption of common guilt" (developed especially in *Psycho*); the theme of the search for identity *(Vertigo);* the theme of the struggle of a personality torn between order and chaos (perhaps the most constant Hitchcock theme); and, in close conjunction with this, the notion of experience therapy—the hero purged of his weaknesses by indulging them and having to live out the consequences *(Rear Window)*. We find here, too, the characteristic Hitchcock moral tone: the utterly unsentimental and ruthless condemnation of the forces that make for disorder, coupled with a full awareness of their dangerously tempting fascination; a sense of the impurity of motives: does Guy love Ann, or is she merely the way to success? Clearly both: good and evil are inseparably mixed. And, running through the film, there is that Hitchcockian humor which itself represents a moral position: it is the manifestation of his artistic impersonality, of his detached

Blackmail. Alice White (Anny Ondra), the first of Hitchcock's "guilty women," is mocked by the jester as she is about to resume her "respectable" dress after the death of Crewe.

The morning after the manslaughter. Alice at breakfast with her parents; in the background the gossiping neighbor who won't stop talking about the "murder"; in the foreground, Alice's father with the breadknife.

The triangle: Alice silent between Frank (John Longden) and Tracy (Donald Calthrop) in their struggle for domination.

The 39 Steps. The film's pivotal moment: Professor Jordan (Godfrey Tearle) reveals his telltale mutilation to Hannay (Robert Donat).

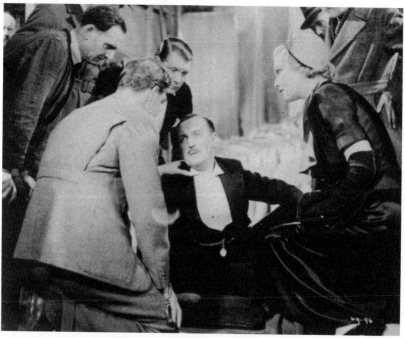

The death of Mr. Memory (Wylie Watson). Hannay (still bearing the handcuffs) and Pamela (Madeleine Carroll) are about to join hands; the chorus line is dimly visible in the background.

Young and Innocent. The birthday party. The image, remarkable for its intricate patterning of looks, balances the tentative future couple (Derrick de Marney, Nova Pilbeam) with the established older couple (Basil Radford, Mary Clare).

Shadow of a Doubt. Uncle Charlie (Joseph Cotten) with his cigar and his adoring sister (mother? lover?) (Patricia Collinge).

Uncle Charlie and young Charlie (Teresa Wright) confront each other over the mutilated newspaper.

Young Charlie has grasped that her beloved and idealized uncle/lover is in fact the "Merry Widow" murderer.

Ingrid Bergman: complexities of a star image (see chapter 15). a) The "natural" woman *(For Whom the Bell Tolls;* **b) the great lady** *(The Visit).*

Bergman: "niceness" *(Adam Had Four Sons).*

The "good" woman in a morally ambiguous situation *(Rage in Heaven).*

Bergman: saintliness *(Inn of the Sixth Happiness).*

Bergman: sickness *(The Bells of St. Mary's).*

Bergman: the smile *(Eléna et les Hommes)*. Asked why he made the film, Renoir replied simply that he "wanted to see Bergman smile."

Bergman as goddess: an episode cut from the Salvador Dali dream sequence in _Spellbound._

Notorious. The end of the party: Alicia and alcohol.

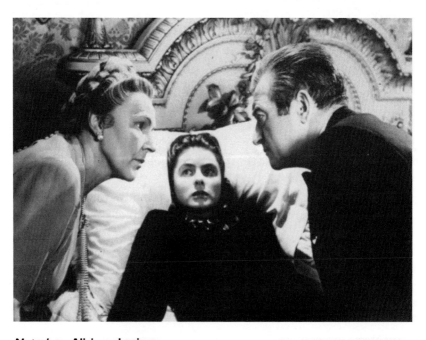

Notorious. Alicia and poison.

Notorious. A contrite Devlin rescues Alicia from death.

Under Capricorn. **Mrs. Flusky, restored to her status, image, and maiden name as "Lady Henrietta Considine" by Charles Adare (Michael Wilding), continues to betray an emotional resistance to his appropriation of her.**

and impersonal attitude to themes which clearly obsess him. Yet the film leaves one unsatisfied (not merely disturbed). The fault may lie partly with the players: Farley Granger, a perfect foil to John Dall in *Rope,* is too slight a personality to carry much moral weight, so that we feel that Guy's propensity for good or evil is too trivial: Ann (Ruth Roman) is a cold, formal woman, so that there is little sense, at the end, that Guy has won through to a worthwhile relationship. There is not enough at stake: his triumph over too slight an evil (in himself) has won him too equivocal a good. Consequently, the effect seems at times two-dimensional, or like watching the working out of a theorem rather than of a human drama, and the film, if not exactly a failure, strikes me as something less than a masterpiece.

One has no qualifications about Robert Walker's Bruno, or about any of the scenes built around him. The film's two classic sequences, in fact, seem to me the first fairground sequence and the scene of the Mortons' party. Here the characteristic Hitchcockian moral tone is felt in all its disturbing complexity. [13]

3
REAR WINDOW

Rear Window is perhaps the first of Hitchcock's films to which the term masterpiece can reasonably be applied; and at the time of writing no copy of the film is available in this country, either for public or private viewing. I mention this unhappy fact by way both of apology and of protest. Apology, because this chapter is necessarily based on three-year-old memory and a few notes scribbled in the cinema: if there are inaccuracies, and if my analysis is here less particularized, the reader's forgiveness is asked, on these grounds.

There seem to be two ways, in general, of looking at *Rear Window:* (a) It constitutes a whole-hearted condemnation of curiosity, prying, voyeurism, *libido sciendi* and *delectatio morosa* (see Rohmer/Chabrol); (b) A corrupt, distasteful film, it shamelessly exploits and encourages curiosity, prying, etc, etc. . . . Neither of these extremes can stand up to a rigorous analysis of the actual film and of the reactions it provokes in the spectator; the fact that the second is much the easier to defend is no doubt what has forced many of the film's admirers into the false position of defending the first. In fact, the morality of the film is far subtler and more profound than either suggests.

The chief objection to the second view is that we are made to feel far too uneasy, in the course of the film, about the morality of prying, to find it really pleasurable: by explicit discussion in the dialogue (Jefferies and Lisa, hence the audience, are "the most frightening ghouls . . . plunged into despair because we find a man *didn't* kill his wife"), by placing Lisa in grave danger, by our discovery that the murderer is as pitiable as monstrous. The chief objection to the first is that the final effects of Jefferies' voyeurism are almost entirely admirable. If he hadn't spied on his neighbors, a murderer would have gone free (and whatever our views on capital punishment, most of us will agree that it is undesirable that a man capable of murdering a helpless, if maddening, woman, cutting her up in little bits and distributing them round the country, should retain his liberty), a woman would have committed suicide, [14] and the hero would have remained in the spiritual deadlock he had reached at the beginning of the film. If I say at once that I regard *Rear Window* as the clearest statement in Hitchcock of what I have called the therapeutic theme, it will be guessed that I attach great importance to this last point.

First, however, I want to consider another aspect of the film: that suggested by Paul Mayersberg in *Movie 3* when he described it as Hitchcock's "testament," and expounded in a somewhat different form by Jean Douchet in the last of his series "La Troisième Clef d'Hitchcock" in *Cahiers du Cinéma* (no. 113). Douchet's interpretation of the film roughly equates Jefferies (James Stewart) with the spectator in the cinema, the flats across the court with the screen: what Jefferies sees is a projection of his own desires. The parallel is, up to a point, rewarding. Jefferies is presented as a man who has never come to terms with himself; his lack of self-knowledge and consequent tendency to lapse into compulsive behavior make him an archetypal Hitchcock protagonist. A news photographer, he has frequently courted death; he refuses all commitment, all personal involvement, escaping from responsibilities by pursuing danger and hectic action recklessly. As Lisa (Grace Kelly) says, he is like "a tourist on an endless vacation." Before the film begins, his leg has been smashed and he is restricted to a wheelchair in his apartment: in other words, he is thrown upon himself, all his usual escape routes cut off. Lisa, who wants to marry him, is becoming very pressing. He, consequently, is trying to break with her: whenever the question of marriage crops up, his leg itches under the plaster, he feels an uncontrollable urge to scratch. Stella, his visiting nurse (Thelma Ritter), tries to make him see the dangers of his condition, his need for self-knowledge: "We've become a race of Peeping Toms. People ought to get outside and look in at themselves." Jefferies's only means of escaping from examining his own condition is by spying on other people —the people in the flats across the courtyard. Stella tells him she can "smell trouble right in this apartment . . . Look out of the window, see things you shouldn't see." He is "like a father": in fact, we realize that his gazing gives him a sense of power over those he watches, but without any accompanying responsibility. He tells Stella in reply that "there *is* going to be trouble . . . Lisa Freemont": from the first, a clear link is established between his relationship with Lisa and his spying on the neighbors. He watches the occupants of the flats opposite as a means of escape from his problems, just as the average cinemagoer goes to the movies to escape his; but the people he chooses to watch (the element of choice is made clear: Hitchcock shows us one happy, seemingly united family in whom Jefferies shows no interest whatever: Stella calls him a "window-shopper") all in some way reflect his own problems, so that his problems are worked out through his gradually growing involvement with them. This is very much how a Hitchcock film works on the lowest level—the level, that is, of the least aware spectator. Jefferies regards Lisa as an encumbrance, and their relationship as a threat to his freedom, to his irresponsibility; he sees a man opposite plagued with a nagging, invalid wife. He would like to get rid of Lisa; he deduces (rightly, as it turns out, though the deduction involves a considerable amount of guesswork) that the man has murdered his wife and is disposing of the body.

Jefferies himself (the resemblance to the hero of *Strangers on a Train* will be clear) never becomes conscious of the connection between what he sees and his personal life, though what is in effect a substitute for that consciousness is forced on him when the murderer invades his apartment. Connections with the other tenants are less obvious but still demonstrably there. Each apartment offers a variation on the man-woman relationship or the intolerable loneliness resulting from its absence, and only the one contented couple is passed over and forgotten. The sterile couple who have made a dog their chief object of affection; the newlyweds stifling (metaphorically) behind closed shutters; "Miss Lonelyhearts," forever enacting romantic situations: all can be taken as representing possibilities before Jefferies and Lisa. The difficulties of human relationships, the horror that marriage can be and the comparable horror of frustrated singleness, are much stressed; and the fact that Jefferies morbidly concentrates—while preserving an apparent ironic detachment—on failed relationships and failed lives, taken in conjunction with his recklessness with his own life, reveals to us the essential features of his spiritual condition.

All this offers clear parallels with the spectator watching the screen. We tend to select from a film and stress, quite unconsciously, those aspects that are most relevant to us, to our own problems and our own attitude to life, and ignore or minimize the rest; and we tend to use such identification—again, usually unconsciously—as a means of working out our problems in fantasy form: often, as it proves with Jefferies, a dangerous tendency but sometimes—again, as with Jefferies—a valuable one. There is an obvious point at which the parallel breaks down: Jefferies sees what, within given limits, he chooses to see; the spectator sees what Hitchcock chooses to show him. And this is especially true, it must be emphasized, of a *Hitchcock* film. When watching, let us say, a Preminger movie—*Exodus* or *The Cardinal*—we are left unusually free to select, to reflect upon the action and reach our own decisions; but in late Hitchcock our responses are themselves very carefully controlled and organized. But despite this objection the parallel largely works because we are led from the outset to identify ourselves with Jefferies, to such an extent that the discrepancy between what *he* sees and what *we* see is considerably narrowed: if the whole film is his enactment of a therapeutic experience, it becomes, by extension, a therapeutic experience for the spectator too.

Rear Window is Hitchcock's most uncompromising attempt to imprison us, not only within a limited space, but within a single consciousness. From the beginning of the film to the end, we are enclosed in the protagonist's apartment, leaving it only when he leaves it (precipitately, through the window!). With one brief exception (when Jefferies is asleep, we see Thorvald, the murderer, leave his apartment with a woman), we are allowed to see only what he sees, know only what he knows. The exception is very important, in fact: the woman *could* be Mrs. Thorvald, and this brings home to us the fact that Jefferies *could* be wrong: by making the identification of the spectator with Jefferies' consciousness not *quite* complete, Hitchcock enables us to feel just that small amount of uneasiness necessary for us to question the morality of what he is doing—our own morality since we are spying with him, sharing his fascinated, compulsive "Peeping-Tom-ism." I have already hinted at the other limitation on identification: the fact that, in the course of the film, we become more consciously aware of the nature of Jefferies' involvement with what he watches than he is himself. But these points apart, identification is forced on us to an unprecedented extent, and preserved throughout the film, as it is not in *Vertigo* or *Psycho*.

The difficulty of the Lisa-Jefferies relationship lies in the refusal of either to compromise. The lack of any give-and-take makes it essentially artificial, sterile, incapable of development. Its essence, and its relationship to Jefferies' spying, is given us, with characteristic economy, on Lisa's first entry. We see Jefferies asleep; then a shadow falls over his face: it is Lisa. She bends over him, kisses him tenderly, and he wakes up. Instantly the relationship becomes an act, Lisa is forced into giving a performance: she could be natural only when he was asleep. "Who are you?", Jefferies asks; and at once she moves back from him, then swirls round the room switching on lamps: "Reading from top to bottom: Lisa"—first lamp—"Carol"—second—"Freemont"—third. We watch a woman become a mannequin, or even a magazine illustration: it is all Jefferies can accept. She turns herself into a public performance, a spectacle to be watched from the other side of the footlights. It is a splendid example of the ability of Hitchcock, or a happy conjunction of director and scriptwriter, to find a means of crystallizing a whole situation or relationship or idea in a single image, when he is working at full pressure: the difference between this film and most of *Stage Fright,* or much of the second half of *The Wrong Man.* Soon, over wine, Lisa tries to "sell" Jefferies a new identity ("I could see you looking very handsome and successful in a dark blue suit") which he resolutely rejects. And of course rightly: the issues in Hitchcock are seldom simple. She goes out to fetch the dinner, and Jefferies immediately turns to spy on the neighbors. He sees first Mrs. Thorvald, the nagging, invalid wife, then "Miss Lonelyhearts," the pathetic spinster, welcoming an imaginary guest, pouring out wine for two. Clearly what he is seeing are two grotesquely distorted images of Lisa: two possible Lisa-identities.

What happens in the Thorvald apartment represents, in an extreme and hideous form, the fulfillment of Jefferies' desire to be rid of Lisa. Because of its extremeness, he reacts against it with horror; and his overcoming of Thorvald (the victory is equivocal) corresponds to the casting out (also, therefore, equivocal) of this desire. Two climactic scenes carry particular significance. The first is where Lisa explores Thorvald's flat and is trapped by him: we watch with Jefferies, sharing his sense of anguish and impotence. It is the turning point in their relationship. He comes to respect her for the courage and initiative (virtues he can appreciate) which he didn't know she possessed (and she does it, obviously, to demonstrate these to him, to make him *see,* not from any abstract desire for justice). But more than that, and simultaneously with it, his desire to be rid of her is abruptly given a form so direct as to be unacceptable: dream has become nightmare. It is this, as much as his new respect for Lisa's pluck, that brings about a recoil in him, allowing the deeper but suppressed need for a permanent relationship to rise to the surface.

In the second climactic scene, Thorvald bursts into Jefferies' apartment. Because of the relationship established between Jefferies and what he watches, the scene carries overtones of a confrontation with a *doppelganger;* or of the eruption of a monstrous force from the underworld of the subconscious, demanding recognition. The effect is made more, not less, frightening by the fact that Thorvald is presented, not as a monster, but as a human being, half terrible, half perplexed, and pitiable. If he were merely a monster we could reject him quite comfortably; because our reaction to him is mixed, we have to accept him as representative of potentialities in Jefferies and, by extension, in all of us. In him is adumbrated one of the leading themes of *Psycho,* more clearly here than in any previous Hitchcock film. We watched him, earlier, with Jefferies, through the telephoto objective, washing the axe, wrapping up the saw and carving knife, then lying down to sleep: our common humanity involves us all in his actions, he is not *only* a brutal murderer, but also a man who has to sleep sometimes. We are left to speculate, to *feel* about, the state of his mind, as we are to be later about the mind of Norman Bates. As he bears down upon Jefferies, a great looming, menacing shadow, Jefferies tries to fight him off with his only weapon of defense —his camera, repeatedly loaded with dazzling flashbulbs—and alternately we are placed in the positions of Jefferies and the murderer, emphasizing his significance as a kind of potential alter ego. The flashbulbs become symbolic: Jefferies' camera is his means of keeping life (which includes his knowledge of himself) at a distance, of remaining a spectator, of preserving his detachment. It takes up the image of Lisa and the lamps. But ultimately it cannot save him: the dazzlement is ineffectual, Thorvald bears down upon him and pushes him headlong over his balcony. Jefferies's victory is, I have said, equivocal: it looks very much like defeat; and with him we hurtle groundward, terrifyingly, helplessly plunging toward darkness.

But the confrontation is in itself a kind of victory: a clarification—on one level the murderer is exposed and caught, on another Jefferies is ready to accept marriage. He has been confronted by the darkness that Hitchcock sees as underlying—or as surrounding—all human existence:

the chaos of our unknown, unrecognized "Under-nature" (a term A. P. Rossiter uses when discussing Shakespeare's tragedies in *Angel with Horns*) which is also the unknownness of the universe. This may strike the reader as an absurdly inflated and pretentious way of talking about a film which is, on the surface, a light comedy thriller; but I think anyone willing to expose himself to the disturbing undercurrents of the film (as a "light comedy thriller" it is often found vaguely unsatisfactory because it "leaves a nasty taste") will find it justified. When we emancipate ourselves from a response exclusively on the "comedy thriller" level, the images—light flashes against the murderer's shadowy bulk—take on great power; moreover, it is impossible not to associate them with Tippi Hedren's struggle to ward off the attacking birds in the attic by waving her torch at them, at the end of *The Birds,* where, whether one likes the film or not, at least a gesture toward metaphysical significance will be allowed. The flashbulbs (and the torch) sum up for us the inadequacy of human knowledge against this "under-nature." The Hitchcock hero typically lives in a small, enclosed world of his own fabrication, at once a protection and a prison, artificial and unrealistic, into which the "real" chaos erupts, demanding to be faced: consider Henry Fonda's descent into Hell in *The Wrong Man,* or Cary Grant deprived of the security of office and cocktail bar in *North by Northwest.*

The ending of *Rear Window* shows us the achievement of an uneasy equilibrium. Jefferies' development has been made possible through his submitting to a process, the indulging of morbid curiosity and the consequences of that indulgence: a process which in itself is a manifestation of his sickness. Only by following it through does progress become possible for him. At the end, with *both* legs in plaster, he is seated with his back to the window, while Lisa, ostensibly engrossed in a news magazine, surreptitiously reads *Harper's Bazaar.* None of the problems between them has been solved; but the fact of their engagement, and Jefferies' symbolic back-to-window position, tells us that they have been at least in a sense accepted. Parallel to this, and on one level expressing it, is the resolution of the problems of the various tenants opposite: we see "Miss Torso's" true love coming home, "Miss Lonelyhearts" receiving a nice young man, [15] and so on: to cap it all comes the songwriter's new, saccharine-sweet inspiration, "Lisa." The very neatness of all this tying up of loose ends emphasizes its superficiality, and we are left with the feeling of the precariousness of it all. The ending is by no means permitted to obliterate for us the memory of the woman's denunciation of the "society" the apartments epitomize, when she finds her dog poisoned: "Was it because he *liked* you?" Nor does the happy ending offset the sense the film, with its stylized presentation of flats and occupants, has established, of semi-live puppets enclosed in little boxes: yet puppets whose frustrations and desperations can drive them to murder or suicide. Order is restored, within and without—in the microcosm of Jefferies' personality, and in the external world which is on one level an extension or reflection of it; but we are left with the feeling that the sweetness-and-light merely covers up that chaos world that underlies the superficial order.

4
VERTIGO

Vertigo seems to me Hitchcock's masterpiece to date, and one of the four or five most profound and beautiful films the cinema has yet given us. This is a claim that may surprise, even amuse, the majority of my readers; but I think an analysis of the film, by revealing an entirely satisfying and fully realized treatment of themes of the most fundamental human significance, can justify it.

The film is adapted from a mystery novel by Boileau and Narcejac—authors also of *Les Diaboliques*—called *D'Entre les Morts:* the two books share the same formula, a squalid exercise in sub-Graham Greenery with a "brilliant" surprise twist at the end that reverses (and in so doing makes nonsense of) the significance of everything that has gone before. Both books are saturated with that easy pessimism that is as much a sentimental self-indulgence as its opposite, characterized by a willful refusal to see any worthwhile possibilities in human life and human relationships; the characters are either helpless devitalized dupes damned from the outset, or the ingeniously malignant intriguers who trap them. The Clouzot version of *Les Diaboliques* (despite its reversal of the sexes of the original's victim and victimizer) does full justice to the book, the director's temperamental and moral affinity with the authors being continuously in evidence.

Hitchcock took very little from *D'Entre les Morts* apart from the basic plot line, and then proceeded to minimize the importance even of that. Boileau and Narcejac's cherished surprise solution—the whole raison d'être of the book—is revealed to us, in one of the cinema's most daring "alienation effects," about two-thirds of the way through the film; and with lordly indifference to such trivia Hitchcock never bothers to tell us whether or not the murderer gets caught. The objection has frequently been made that the plot hinges on a wild improbability: not so much that a man who has seen the woman he loves fall from a height should not stay to make sure she's dead, as that the murderer should count on his not doing so. But if one is going to approach the film in this way, a moment's thought will make it clear that the whole plot is quite fantastic—no one would ever set about murdering his wife in *that* way. Most of Shakespeare's plays can be demolished in the same way, and with just as much validity. As in Shakespeare's plays, in fact, the organization of *Vertigo* is thematic; plot, characterization, psychology, all are strictly subordinated to thematic development.

Whatever aspect we choose to consider, in passing from book to film, we find total transformation. The difference in significance in the locations, for example, is not simply a matter of transposition from France to America: the novel offers no equivalent for the sequoias, and the complex thematic and emotional deepening that comes with them. The characters are quite altered and an important new one (Midge) introduced. Of even greater consequence is the difference in the attitude to them: in Boileau/Narcejac they are despised like so many ignominious worms, and we are invited to look down upon them, and to regard life as squalid and ignoble; in Hitchcock they become entirely acceptable representatives of the human condition, whom we are permitted to regard—for all their weaknesses and limitations—with respect and sympathetic concern: no question here of any failure of awareness of human potentiality, flawed and imperfect as the protagonists may be. The drab, willful pessimism of *D'Entre les Morts* is an essentially different world from the intense traffic sense of *Vertigo,* which derives from a simultaneous awareness of the immense value of human relationships and their inherent incapability of perfect realization.

But that *Vertigo* is superior to a poor book does not of course justify my large claims for it, and I must now turn to the film itself. Granted an unfaltering continuity of development, it can be seen to fall conveniently into a brief prologue and three main acts or *movements* (I prefer the latter term). The prologue gives us the incident that precipitates Scottie's vertigo; the first movement his consent to watch Madeleine, his following her, the gradual deepening of his involvement; the second takes us from her attempted suicide and their meeting, through their developing relationship to her death and his breakdown; the third begins with his

meeting with Judy, and passes through the development of their relationship, his attempted re-creation of Madeleine, to Judy's death and the
curing of Scottie's vertigo.

One aspect of the theme of *Vertigo* is given us by Saul Bass' credit
designs. We see a woman's face; the camera moves in first to lips, then
to eyes. The face is blank, mask-like, representing the inscrutability of
appearances: the impossibility of knowing what goes on behind the
mask. But the eyes dart nervously from side to side: beneath the mask
are imprisoned unknown emotions, fears, desperation. Then a vertiginous, spiralling movement begins in the depths of the eye, moving
outward as if to involve the spectator: before the film proper has begun,
we are made aware that the vertigo of the title is to be more than a
literal fear of heights. This credit sequence is linked by the music that
accompanies it to the scene of Judy's metamorphosis into Madeleine in
the beauty salon: the only scene where the same music returns, again as
accompaniment to a close-up of a woman's face—a face that is transformed into a mask.

The first image is of a horizontal bar standing out against a blurred
background: a single object against an undefined mass. The shot is held
for a moment, then two hands grab the bar, the camera moves back, the
focus deepens, to reveal a city spread out beneath the night: suggestions
of clinging and falling set against a great wilderness of rooftops. There
follows the accident, with Scottie (James Stewart) clinging to a collapsing gutter while a policeman, trying to save him, plunges past him to his
death hundreds of feet below. The sensation of vertigo is conveyed to
the spectator by the most direct means, subjective shots using a simultaneous zoom-in and track-back that makes the vast drop telescope out
before our eyes; we watch, from Scottie's viewpoint, the policeman
hurtle down. The sensation has been explained, I believe, by psycholo-
gists as arising from the tension between the desire to fall and the dread
of falling—an idea it is worth bearing in mind in relation to the whole
film. In any case, we, with Scottie, are made to understand what it feels
like to be so near death, and to have death made so temptingly easy, yet
so terrifying, a way out of pain and effort: to live, he must hold on
desperately to the gutter, his arms and body agonizingly stretched, his
fingers strained, his mind gripped by unendurable tension; to die, he has
only to let go. When we next see Scottie, he is sitting in the apartment of
Midge (Barbara Bel Geddes). We do not see, and are never told, how he

got down from the gutter: there seems no possible way he *could* have got down. The effect is of having him, throughout the film, metaphorically suspended over a great abyss.

Midge and her apartment (that contrasts markedly, we see later, with Scottie's own, which is furnished largely with antiques) represent one of the possibilities before Scottie. The assessment of Midge herself is made with that complexity and economy so characteristic of Hitchcock (though it is only completed by the contrast offered by Madeleine); it is an assessment not only of a clearly defined character but of a whole milieu, even of modern culture itself. It is a very sympathetic portrait: Midge is practical, realistic, emancipated, eminently sane, positive and healthy in her outlook: but from the outset the inadequacies revealed later are hinted at. A trained artist, she devotes her energies to sketching the advertisements for brassieres. In her cluttered studio-cum-living-room, Miros on the wall are juxtaposed indiscriminately with fashion designs. Entirely devoid of mystery or reserve, the kind of sexuality she represents is suggested by her smart sex-chat about corsets and brassieres ("You know about those things, you're a big boy now"), she reduces everything to the same matter-of-fact level. Yet one senses already a discrepancy between what she is and what she might be: a depth of feeling, of constancy, is hinted at, more visually than verbally, which is at odds with the superficiality of the cultural environment her flat evokes. Her look at Scottie when he reminds her that it was she who broke off their three-week-long engagement is one of those moments that reveal the basic strength of the cinema, because it suggests things not really formulable in words: one could say that the rest of the film defines why she broke it off. If there is something a little boyish about her, there is also something—Scottie actually uses the word—"motherly." She reminds one a little of that other sympathetic young mother figure, the Doris Day of *The Man Who Knew Too Much:* she disapproves of Scottie's leaving the police, she supervises his attempt to "lick" his vertigo (by climbing her portable steps) as a mother might help a child to master a bicycle, alternately urging and restraining.

He tells her, in his habitually noncommittal manner, that he is still available—"That's me, available Ferguson"; the phrase recalls his decision to "do nothing" to give us the full extent of his "availability" and suggests one aspect of that metaphorical suspension: he is suspended both in work and in personal relationships. That characteristic Hitchcockian economy and directness in organization connects this "availability" with Elster, whom Scottie goes on at once to mention. The scene ends with the attempt to overcome the vertigo, culminating in the startling subjective shot of the street over which Scottie hung, [16] which he sees again when he looks down from the top of Midge's steps. In the foreground of the shot, we see ornaments and a bowl of flowers that keep the reality of Midge's room before us; but that reality—Midge's world, charming, uncomplicated, safe, superficial—is shattered by the vision. Scottie has seen death, and the experience has undermined all possibility of his accepting Midge and the life she represents as adequate fulfillment. It is Midge's room that becomes unreal, the vision (a great abyss apparently in the middle of that room,) that is "real." Hitchcock cuts from her "motherly" frightened comforting of him to the exterior of Elster's offices.

What I have called the *thematic* organization of the film can be seen in the transition from the smart modernity of Midge's apartment to the discussion about the past in Elster's office. Behind Elster we see shipbuilding in progress, and there is a model ship in the room, carrying a suggestion of escape. The walls are covered with prints of San Francisco in the "old days": Scottie and Elster examine one as they talk. Elster bears a clear thematic relationship to Scottie. Shipbuilding—modern development—bores him; he has a nostalgia for the past, where a man had "freedom" and "power": the words are echoed twice later in the film, in the bookshop (linking Elster with the man who destroyed Carlotta Valdes) and at the end. There is in Elster a hint of the inexplicable—of the diabolical—in his intuitive understanding of Scottie's psychological traits (the metaphorical, as well as the literal, vertigo), in his fastening on them and *using* them: at the end of the film, Scottie's insistent question, "Why did you pick on me? Why *me?*" never gets an explicit answer. Elster, like other Hitchcock villains (Bruno Anthony, for example), besides being a clearly defined character in his own right, is related to a weakness in the hero. We shall see how important for Scottie are a nostalgia for the past and a desire for "freedom" and "power."

The long expository dialogue between the two men is given tension by the exactness in the use of cutting and camera movement to express that control. In a cut to close-up we see the effect on Scottie of Elster's abrupt, unobtrusive "Someone dead" (in answer to Scottie's question as to who may harm Elster's wife); then the camera immediately moves back to take in Elster standing over him, dominating, *imposing* his story. Scottie rejects it: he is "the hard-headed Scot": but rejects it, with his insistent reiteration that all the wife needs is a psychologist, too emphatically. We are very much aware of the tension in him between natural skepticism and an attraction toward the fantastic story, with its associations of Elster's wife with the past and with death. Madeleine, Elster tells him, sits by a lake looking at pillars across the water, pillars that are called "The Portals of the Past." The "wandering" theme—picked up both verbally and visually many times later in the film—the theme of being lost in life, of having no clear aim—is stated here by Elster ("She wanders—God knows where she wanders"). It is natural to link it with Scottie's expressed lack of purpose (his "doing nothing") and hence with the "vertigo" idea. He is sufficiently intrigued to agree at least to see Madeleine before he rejects the case.

There follows about quarter of an hour without dialogue, showing us the growth of Scottie's obsession with Madeleine. She herself is introduced by a camera movement different from any that has preceded it, that sets a new mood, maintained throughout the ensuing sequences up to Scottie's next meeting with Midge. We are in Ernie's, the restaurant where Scottie is to see Madeleine. Close-up of Scottie seated at the bar, looking across. The camera swings over in a slow, graceful movement disclosing the decor of the restaurant, which evokes immediately the gracious living of the past, then tracks slowly in toward a table, gradually focusing our attention on the bare back of a woman in evening dress leaning in a graceful attitude, almost statuesque. Then, in a subjective shot from Scottie's viewpoint, we watch her cross the restaurant with an easy, gliding motion, and pause near him so that her face is clearly visible, beautiful, smooth, without definable expression.

The fascination Madeleine exerts over Scottie—and over us—is complex. One is immediately aware of the contrast between her and Midge. Where Midge is an entirely known quantity, Madeleine is surrounded by an aura of mystery. She is always remote from Scottie and from us: we see her only as Scottie sees her. When she goes to a flower shop, she enters by a back door, down a side street, passing through dingy, cobwebby storerooms; later, she apparently disappears from a house: she may be herself a ghost. She represents a completely different sexuality from Midge's: one has only to compare Midge's demonstrating the latest brassiere "based on the principle of the cantilever bridge" with Madeleine's hesitant grace of movement and attitude later as she comes to stand in the doorway of Scottie's sitting room wearing his dressing gown: Madeleine is so much more erotic because of this combination of grace, mysteriousness, and vulnerability. She is from the start the representative of another world, of experience beyond the grasp of the cards-on-the-table reality of Midge. A higher reality, or an illusion? Or, to shift to the Keatsian terminology, "vision," or "waking dream"? It seems more reasonable to adduce "Lamia" or the "Nightingale Ode" in this connection than to make the conventional classification of *Vertigo* as "mystery thriller"; [17] and it is worth pointing out that we find in Hitchcock a far more secure and mature balance of sympathy and interest between the real world and the visionary, and certainly a no less complex awareness of the issues, than Keats was capable of. If it be objected that Madeleine does in fact turn out to be pure illusion, I shall answer that the matter is by no means so simple.

Madeleine certainly is presented as a dream, in some sense; and she becomes our dream as well as Scottie's. If her own movements, in their grace, their air of remoteness, are dream-like, the effect of dream is intensified by Hitchcock's use of the camera. Leisurely, steady-paced subjective tracking shots characterize the sequences in which Scottie follows Madeleine; we are placed behind the windscreen of his car in the driver's seat as he follows her around the streets of San Francisco, pursuing a dream through modern surface reality; we wander at his walking pace round the graveyard; we watch Madeleine continually through his eyes, her distance, her silence, his and our inability to understand her, help her, protect her, are all a part of the fascination. The effect of romantic dream is especially strong in the churchyard sequence, everything steeped in hazy sunlight as Madeleine stands, statue-like, minute in long shot, over an unknown grave.

The settings to which she leads Scottie (Spanish church, graveyard, art gallery, old house) in and around San Francisco, seem nonetheless not to belong to the city; they are little pockets of silence and solitude, another world. She leads him back always to the past—the grave, the portrait, the house of a long-dead woman. Finally, and perhaps most important of all, she is continually associated with death, and the fascination she exerts is the fascination of death, a drawing toward oblivion and final release; the yearning for the dream, for the Ideal, for the Infinite, become logically a yearning for death: Scottie's and our vertigo.

This death wish—or more exactly, in "vertigo" terms the simultaneous longing for and fear of death—culminates in the scene among the sequoia trees: "the oldest living thing." The dialogue stresses the fear:

SCOTTIE: What are you thinking about?
MADELEINE: All the people who were born and died while the trees went on living . . .
SCOTTIE: Its real name is Sequoia Semperviva. [18]
MADELEINE: I don't like it . . . Knowing I have to die.

They examine a cross-section of a felled tree. The camera moves across it, outward from the core, taking us through centuries in seconds; Madeleine puts her fingers tentatively near the circumference, murmuring, "Somewhere here I was born, and there I died. It was only a moment for you, you took no notice." She moves off, and disappears among the trees. Disappears, as she previously disappeared in the Carlotta Valdes house: Scottie follows but can't find her, and we get a slow, sinuous tracking shot of "ever-living" tree trunks and sunlight which precisely realizes the significance of the quoted dialogue, the pitiful brevity and transience of the individual life most beautifully and disturbingly conveyed. The whole scene is bathed in an atmosphere of romantic dream —its great visual beauty intensified by the emotional overtones, by the whole context—which counterpoints the dread of death expressed in the dialogue with a sense of yearning for peace and oblivion.

The sequence culminates in the kiss by the sea, the mutual capitulation to love. From Scottie's point of view, the significance of this *as* a culmination is clear—his love for Madeleine becomes identified with his death-yearning. Earlier, gazing in his car at a reproduction of the Carlotta Valdes portrait, he saw the dead woman and Madeleine as interchangeable (in terms of film, dissolve from the portrait to Madeleine and back). On one level there is a strong element of romantic cliché in the image of the lovers embracing against a background of crashing waves, an effect which crystallizes for us another aspect of the film: for many spectators, the cinema itself is a kind of dream, an escape world in which reality can be evaded and forgotten. In one way Hitchcock is throughout the first half of *Vertigo* using his audience's escapist expectations, the fact that they go to the cinema in order to see a "hero," with whom they can identify, involved in romantic wish fulfillments: hence at this climactic moment dream and romantic cliché merge. But, at a deeper level, the sea as the culmination of this part of the film has another significance: if the sequoia trees are "the oldest living thing," the sea is older still, beating eternally against the rocks, eroding, wearing down; and it is against such sea associations that the two embrace on the cliff edge, a tiny, precarious moment placed against eternity. But this is perhaps merely to suggest why the cliché itself still has emotional validity.

Before this sequence there has occurred the nearest to a meeting between Midge and Madeleine that ever takes place: Midge, driving up to Scottie's apartment, sees Madeleine drive away. That the two women never appear, beyond this, in the same scene brings home to us the incompatibility of the worlds they represent. Midge's reappearance immediately after the beautifully sensitive, tentative groping toward a relationship between Scottie and Madeleine, makes us aware of her exclusion from certain levels of experience and her inadequacy to combat the sort of rivalry Madeleine offers; yet at the same time it makes us aware of her as representing a healthy normality to set against the element of neurotic sickness in Scottie's attraction to Madeleine. Now, after the sequoia sequence, we have the scene in Midge's apartment where she shows Scottie the parody portrait of herself as Carlotta. She is trying to make him see *her,* to substitute herself for the woman who obsesses him, at the same time making the obsession ridiculous by satirizing it, and the attempt reveals both her anti-romantic down-to-earth normality and her inadequacy. It finally destroys Scottie's connection with her: he resents the attempt to shatter the dream. There is a marvelous shot, superbly balanced between pathos and humor, of Midge seated beside her self-portrait, the two images in the same attitude, the Carlotta portrait with Midge's unglamorous, bespectacled face; but the figure in the portrait holds the posy Madeleine carried with her through the graveyard and the art gallery, and Midge's hands are empty. The portrait is Midge's attempt at an "alienation effect," its purpose the breaking of an involvement; but its effect is to alienate Scottie from *her.* We recall the moment in his car when the image of Madeleine was superimposed on the portrait reproduction. Reality is defeated, the dream is too strong; and Midge is left tearing her hair, with her sense of inadequacy.

There follows the sequence at the Mission of San Juan Baptista, culminating in Madeleine's suicide. Here, in the livery stable, amid the decor of the past, Scottie makes his last effort to explain the dream, to make it reality. The suicide itself has a shattering effect on the spectator which is by no means to be explained solely in terms of visual impact, strong as this is—the bell tower, the unnerving "vertigo" shots down the stairwell, the body falling past the aperture then spread out lifeless on the roof below. On one level, again, we have Hitchcock capitalizing on audience expectations by abruptly defeating them: no one, I think, seeing *Vertigo* for the first time unprepared, thinks that Madeleine is going to die halfway through. She is the heroine of the romance, the medium through which the escape wishes are to be fulfilled: we are prepared for a happy ending, or perhaps for final grand tragedy, but not for this brutal midway rupture. But Madeleine, as I have suggested, represents wish fulfillment on a deeper and more valid level than that normally offered by the Hollywood film: by this point in the film she has evoked in us all that longing for something beyond daily reality which is so basic to human nature. We are in fact by this time so thoroughly identified with Scottie that we share his shock, and the resulting sense of bewildered desolation, in the most direct way, just as we share his sense of helplessness, even of responsibility. We are stunned, the bottom is knocked out of the world, we cannot at all see where the film is going, what possible sequel this event can have: all is chaos. It is an effect that Hitchcock is to match, two films later, in *Psycho* with the shower bath murder.

We have already been placed, then, in a position to understand, sympathetically, Scottie's breakdown. It is preceded by the inquest, in which a brutal coroner places the responsibility for Madeleine's death on him, and which closes with the shot of his leaving the courtroom, a vast expanse of ceiling seeming to weigh down oppressively over the tiny figures in long shot.

The breakdown is precipitated by Scottie's nightmare. This begins with an image of disintegration from earlier in the film—the posy which Madeleine plucked to pieces, dropped in the water and watched floating away immediately before her first suicide attempt. Again the posy (suggestive of a tight, unnatural order) disintegrates, only in the dream Hitchcock uses cartoon—crude cartoon at that—to show it: the image of real flowers'turned to paper flowers suggests that the possibility that the whole Madeleine ideal is a fraud is already nightmarishly present in Scottie's subconscious. The next dream image goes back to the inquest, with Scottie and Gavin Elster by the courtroom window, but now Carlotta Valdes stands between them, dressed as in the portrait. Carlotta now "possesses" Madeleine as completely as Mrs. Bates possesses Norman at the end of *Psycho:* possesses her in death. Madeleine's identification with the portrait (one of the sources of her fascination) is now complete, and the essential paradox of Scottie's desires crystallized: he has sought an identification of reality and dream, of life and death, and now there is only the face from the portrait looking at him tauntingly. The image also intensifies the sense of the possibility of fraud, because of its incongruity: Gavin Elster and the supernatural simply don't belong in the same world (or in the same shot), and the image tells us—retrospectively at least—that we should never have trusted his story. With the elliptical logic of dream, we next have Scottie walking, purposefully yet in a void, without seeming to know where he is going yet unable to stop; walking through the graveyard; walking to Carlotta's now open grave. We become him by means of camera identification, and fall forward into the grave, into darkness, a bottomless pit. The subsequent images prolong the falling sensation, until we see the *man's* body falling on to the roof where Madeleine fell; but the roof dissolves and he hurtles into endless space, blindingly white. Scottie wakes up screaming. Here, at the center of the film, is the clearest statement about the nature of the "vertigo." In his dream he achieves identity with Madeleine: first by sinking into her grave (as described by her earlier in the scene by the sea), then by falling onto the roof. He wants to die in her place, or to join her in death; but looking back we can see his whole attraction to her as a matter of identification—the desire for annihilation. The continued use of subjective technique during the nightmare serves both to render Scottie's sensations (hence his breakdown) directly comprehensible, and to make us experience the logical outcome of our identification with his basic driving impulse. We may think back to Scottie's, and our, vision of the street during the attempted cure in Midge's room: the film conveys a terrifying impression of external reality as a sort of fragile shell which we pierce at our peril: once beyond it, we are whirling uncontrolled in chaos. We may be led to think back, in turn, to the credit designs: the mask-like face of Appearance, the vertiginous, spiraling movement drawing us down into the depths behind the eye.

The scene in the mental home in which Midge tries to break through to a Scottie completely withdrawn into melancholia makes us view him objectively, look in the face the condition into which his alienation from reality has led him. Music lovers will wince at the use of Mozart here—

his music clearly identified with the superificial externality of Midge's world—but objections on musical grounds are hardly relevant. The point of the music, its total inability to reach Scottie, lost as he is in the abyss he has fallen into, is defined by its context, and in fact the very superficial and shallow interpretation of the andante of the 34th Symphony (taken at a ridiculously brisk tempo) that Midge plays him fulfills its function admirably. The music as played suggests both a poise and an artificiality that admirably epitomizes for us the fragile shell.

The scene ends with Midge's acknowledgment of defeat. After moving around the entirely passive and immobile Scottie, vainly caressing him ("You're not lost—Mother's here"), she takes off the gramophone record and tells the doctor, "I don't think Mozart's going to help at all": a line given great poignance by the actress' delivery, which conveys her sense not only of Mozart's inadequacy but of her own. We see her—it is her last appearance in the film—walk away down the hospital corridor; and as she reaches the end the screen darkens around her, so that the darkness seems to swallow her. This is a unifying image of great importance. It recalls immediately the shot of Scottie descending the bell tower stairs after Madeleine's death, where the camera, pointing straight down into the well, made it look like a tunnel into which the figure, moving away from the camera, was disappearing. By linking the two moments visually Hitchcock draws our attention to a similarity beyond the visual, as a means of universalizing his themes. At both points in question the person disappearing has failed to help or save the person he or she loves: both have been made aware of the ultimate impossibility of getting through to another person in the deepest essentials. And in both cases a relationship has been irreparably broken on whose continuance and development future happiness and fulfillment seemed entirely dependent. But there is another, perhaps more obvious link: the dream which Madeleine described to Scottie as they stood by the sea: ". . . walking down a long corridor . . . When I come to the end there's nothing but darkness." There is also a grave—"an open grave. It's my grave"—the grave which swallowed Scottie into darkness in the nightmare. With the two visual links, the corridor image takes on a universal symbolism, connecting all three principal characters, exposing that point at which every human being is essentially alone, beyond the help of others. If I point to the clear link (through bell tower and nightmare) with the "vertigo" theme, the full force of the word "organic" applied to *Vertigo* will perhaps be felt. To anticipate, it is the significance that has accrued to the corridor image that gives the scene of Madeleine's re-creation—Judy's return from the beauty salon with face and hair transformed—such emotional intensity: she appears at the end of the hotel corridor in the light, walking toward Scottie (us), precisely reversing the previous corridor images and thereby intensifying that effect of resurrection that is the more poignant in that we know it, then, (as Scottie doesn't) to be in normal senses illusory.

That phrase "normal senses" will seem either willfully mysterious or merely vague; but the qualification it implies will soon become clear. We enter now the third movement of the film, and the revelation that drastically alters—at first glance simplifies, at second renders enormously more complex—most of what has gone before. Scottie, partially recovered but still obsessed by Madeleine, wanders around the places she frequented, seeing her in other women—imposing the dream on reality. Then he sees a girl in the street who bears little superficial resemblance to Madeleine (unlike the other women)—indeed, seems to provide on the surface, in clothes, makeup, manner, gestures, way of moving, nothing but contrast—yet whose face is sufficiently like Madeleine's for Scottie to follow her to her hotel room. Her first appearance is introduced by a shot of a flower shop window with, prominently displayed, posies identical to the one Madeleine carried, the posy that changed into disintegrating paper flowers in Scottie's nightmare. Five minutes later we see, in flashback showing the girl Judy's memory, what really happened: she was Madeleine, Madeleine was a fraud, the body falling past the aperture a woman Scottie has never seen. Two big questions are now raised: why did Hitchcock choose to break the first law of the mystery thriller and divulge the "surprise" solution two-thirds of the way through the film? And what difference does the revelation make, in retrospect, to the significance of what has preceded it? I shall leave the answer to the first question—which primarily affects the last third of the film—aside for the moment and try to answer the second.

Our immediate reaction to the revelation, I think, is extreme disappointment. This can exist on a purely superficial level: we have come to see a mystery story and now we know it all, so what is the use of the film's continuing? Why should we have to watch the detective laboriously discovering things we know already? Much popular discontent with the film can be traced to this premature revelation, and in terms of audience reaction it was certainly a daring move on Hitchcock's part. Yet our feelings of being cheated, if we analyze them, reveal a deeper cause. We have been, up to the revelation, very largely identified with Scottie, we have involved ourselves deeply in his weaknesses and his desires, in his longing to fulfill a dream as a means of escaping from or of rising above daily reality. We experienced directly his shock at Madeleine's death: now we experience a further, and worse shock: not only is she dead—she never existed. The effect is not merely of discovering that we have been deceived by an ingenious murder plot: one of our most vulnerable moral spots, our discontent with reality, has been penetrated, we have been caught off our guard. Some of the best films that have come from Hollywood, films as different in tone and in overt subject matter as Howard Hawks' *Monkey Business* and Nicholas Ray's *Bigger Than Life,* have had as their core this theme of discontent with the actual world, but none has explored it as profoundly or brought it home to the spectator by such direct, inescapable means, as *Vertigo.* The revelation cuts the ground away from under our feet, and makes us painfully aware of the degree of our previous involvement in what is now proved to be a cheap hoax.

Yet this reaction, which the film certainly provokes at this point, has to be modified on reflection. If we re-see the film, or carefully reconstruct the first two-thirds, we shall see that we have not yet taken the full measure of the subtlety and complexity of Hitchcock's conception. For such a reviewing or reconstruction will show us that the illusion is not *just* an illusion: Judy was not *merely* acting Madeleine—up to a point she *became* Madeleine. Our very incredulity that the Judy we see could ever have been trained to act the part of Madeleine works for Hitchcock here. Judy—on her first appearance, and in her treatment of Scottie when he follows her to her hotel room—appears hard and vulgar, over made-up, her attitude at once defiant and cheaply provocative; she is playing up the tartiness to deceive him, and her underlying vulnerability is gradually exposed, yet she is never depicted as intelligent. But she was, as Scottie tells her at the end of the film, "a very apt pupil." If we mentally juxtapose her stance and manner in the doorway of the hotel room—her way of holding her body, her expression, her intonation, her vulgarized version of what is in part their love story—with, again,

Madeleine's entry from Scottie's bedroom, her way of moving and standing, her hesitant words, her reticence and *pudeur,* we shall see that Madeleine was not just an acted role but another persona.

It is not difficult to see that the pretense partly became reality. Most obviously, there is the point that Judy was to make Scottie fall in love with her by pretending to fall in love with him, and then she really *did* fall in love. Her behavior before the "suicide" is full of obvious ambiguities ("It wasn't supposed to happen this way . . . If you love me, you'll know I loved you and I wanted to go on loving you"—the remarks mean something quite different depending on whether we think of them as spoken by Madeleine or by Judy), and if we look further we shall see that in fact every moment of the relationship is ambiguous, it is impossible to distinguish pretense from reality. Is her nervousness during the car journey to San Juan Baptista real or feigned—Judy pretending to be Madeleine becoming distraught, or Judy becoming distraught as she gets nearer to what she has agreed to do? Her scream as Mrs. Elster falls, the scream Scottie so insistently questions her about at the end: is it the scream that was (presumably) planned to accompany the fall, or the scream of a woman trying, too late, to prevent an outrage at which she has connived?

Madeleine says to Scottie, "One shouldn't live alone . . . it's wrong": Judy lives alone. Later, by the sea, telling Scottie her fragments of memory: ". . . A room. I sit there alone—always alone." The room in the McKittrick hotel, of course. Or Judy's hotel room? We see Madeleine once when Scottie can't see her—as she watches him from her car going to close the door of his apartment before they drive out to the sequoias: she is watching him tenderly, sadly, as if attracted to him—is she still acting? When he tries to make her tell him, under the trees, why she jumped into the Bay, she appears to panic, reiterating "Please don't ask me, please don't ask me": again, Judy pretending to be a woman on the verge of breakdown, or Judy falling in love and terrified at the situation she is in? And the fears of death: when Madeleine says, "I don't want to die—there's someone within me says I must die," she could be speaking for Judy, for all of us; she is not only Judy pretending to be Madeleine possessed by Carlotta. Yet Judy, we feel (the Judy of the last third of the film), is not a girl who would ever allow herself to become explicit about, perhaps even conscious of, such fears: she hasn't the intelligence, the self-awareness, or (despite her evident capacity for suffering) the depth. The fears can only be released in her through her being Madeleine: in a sense, it is Madeleine who is the more "real" of the two, since in Madeleine all kinds of potentialities completely hidden in Judy find expression. The pretense was that Carlotta was taking possession of Madeleine; in reality, Madeleine has taken possession of Judy. Scottie and Madeleine are linked verbally—at many points—by the fact that both are "wanderers" (with all the overtones the word accrues in the course of the film). In fact, it becomes clear that Judy as well, in surrendering to the Madeleine identity, is abandoning herself to the fulfillment of a dream. There is, up to the revelation, only one subjective shot from Judy/Madeleine's viewpoint, and it clinches this thematic connection between her and Scottie: the shot, as she stands by the water before flinging herself in, of the torn flowers drifting away on the current—the disintegration symbol of Scottie's dream. The shot can also be taken as an imaginative-subjective shot from Scottie's viewpoint: he can't *see* the flowers drifting away from where he is standing, but he can see Madeleine tearing and throwing them. So the shot links the two consciousnesses, and we are made to feel that the image has much the same significance for both. With this, and Judy's absorption in Madeleine, in mind, it is an easy step to see an *element* of reality in all her supposedly artificial behavior. We cannot say that Madeleine's attempted suicide, her fears of madness, express nothing of Judy. The painfully limited, enclosed Judy, in fact, becomes articulate in Madeleine, whose *potential* reality to some extent validates the dream she represents. The theme of unstable identity is reflected in Scottie, the "wanderer" who is going to "do nothing": he is "Johnny" or "Johnny-O" to Midge, "John" to Madeleine, "Scottie" to Judy: the identity is created in part by the relationship.

The "vertigo" of the title, then, expands from the man's fear of heights into a metaphysical principle, and the metaphysic of the film is "peculiarly terrifying." I am thinking of T. S. Eliot's remarks about Blake, where he speaks of Blake's "peculiarity" as revealing itself as "the peculiarity of all great poetry . . . It is merely a peculiar honesty which, in a world too frightened to be honest, is peculiarly terrifying." (He also remarks that this honesty "is never present without great technical accomplishment.") The world—human life, relationships, individual identity—becomes a quicksand, unstable, constantly shifting, into which we may sink at any step in any direction, illusion and reality constantly ambiguous, even interchangeable. To such a response to life, Hitchcock's authoritarian attitude to film-making, each film predestined down to the smallest detail before shooting starts, each camera movement and camera angle rigorously thought out, the actors strictly controlled, nothing left to chance, is clearly relevant.

Why did Hitchcock divulge the solution so early? Clearly, the decision entailed sacrifices, and not only on the "popular thriller" level: if the spectator's identification with Scottie had been preserved to the end, so that we identified throughout his attempt to re-create Madeleine from Judy, the fascination of the "dream" would also have been preserved, and only at the very end would we have been left stranded with "reality," to leave the cinema in some perplexity. Imagine the last hour of the film with the "revelation" scene cut out: we would be in a position to share Scottie's feelings toward Judy very exactly, our interest in her restricted to the lurking suggestion there of Madeleine. We would have shared (as she undergoes her transformation) Scottie's wonder at her resemblance to Madeleine, and like him we would have been torn between surrender to the re-created dream and suspicion of the possibility of some cruel fraud. The Hitchcockian "suspense," in short, with its characteristic undercurrent of moral division, would have held us to the end. Yet the very act of imagining the film without the revelation will convince the spectator of the rightness of Hitchcock's decision.

First, most obvious, the effect of the revelation is to detach us from Scottie's consciousness: suddenly, and for the first time in the film, we know something about Madeleine that he doesn't know. From here on we shall be watching him as much as watching *with* him. But our involvement with him has been such that this is in essence like watching ourselves, and what we see is again, right up to the final clarification, deeply ambiguous: simultaneous drives toward sickness and toward health. As Scottie re-creates Madeleine, is he impelled by a desire to rebuild a dream in which he can lose himself, or by an undeviating (though obscure) determination to reach the truth? If the former is the more obvious, the latter is, as we shall see, indisputably expressed in the film, which offers a particularly beautiful example of that Hitchcockian sense of the inextricability, in human life, of good and evil. Like Jefferies in *Rear Window,* Scottie can achieve health (or, if you prefer, enlightenment) only by following through to the end an obsession that has its source in a spiritual sickness. We could have been made (as we were in

Rear Window) to share in this process; Hitchcock elected to have us study it.

Why this is in this case the better alternative arises from the second difference the revelation makes. Without it, Judy would remain, necessarily, as inscrutable as Madeleine had been; with it, we are constantly made aware of her feelings as well as of Scottie's. The gain in richness and complexity is great; the sacrifice in "suspense" is compensated for by a gain in poignancy that makes this last part of the film profoundly disturbing to watch, by a tension set up in the mind of the spectator between conflicting responses. Knowing the truth, we also have far more opportunity, during the last part of the film, to consider the implications of what we see.

The detachment itself is achieved with a startling abruptness: some find the introduction of the flashback very clumsy, but it seems to me that the abrupt brutality is essential to the effect. Throughout the middle part of the film—since Madeleine's "death"—we have been feeling increasingly at sea. We can't see where the film is going—where Scottie is going. There seems no firm ground, no sense of direction: in fact, we are being made to share Scottie's state of mind once again. Then, suddenly, we are in the room alone with Judy: the withdrawal of Scottie from the scene is like the withdrawal of our own consciousness, we have nothing to cling to. Then the screen darkens around Judy and the flashback begins. Few moments in the cinema produce a greater *frisson:* this rather cheap, shallow-seeming girl is suddenly associated with Madeleine's dash up into the church tower. We experience a moment of total bewilderment in which all sense of reality seems terrifyingly to dissolve; then, abruptly, the vertigo is over for us: over, anyway, until we begin to reflect on the quicksand of reality and illusion the film presents.

We watch Judy compose her letter to Scottie, and the intolerability of her situation comes home to us. She is deeply in love with him, while he is still in love with Madeleine; yet she *is* Madeleine—or Madeleine is potentially within her. As she writes her letter the camera half circles her, and the shade on her table lamp fills a large area of the screen, at one point obliterating her. The image recalls the scene where Madeleine came to Scottie at dawn to tell him her dream. She sat at his writing table, leaning forward in the light from his table lamp as she described her terror of "darkness." The effect was of the pitiful inadequacy of human illumination to combat the enveloping metaphysical darkness (compare the flashbulbs in *Rear Window* and the torch in *The Birds*). By linking the two scenes through this image (the lamp and shade get great visual emphasis in both) Hitchcock links Judy's present situation and her inability to cope with it with Madeleine's "darkness." Later, Judy (now dressed like Madeleine but still a brunette) sits in Scottie's room where Madeleine sat in the earlier scene, the light on her as it was on Madeleine. The two scenes also resemble each other in that in both Scottie stands over her in a dominating attitude: in the earlier sequence he was trying to compel the dream to become real, in the later he is trying to compel the reality to become a dream.

After Judy has torn up the letter, she hides Madeleine's gray suit right at the back of her cupboard, selecting a dress as unlike it as possible: is she afraid Scottie might see it? Or is she vehemently rejecting her Madeleine identity? Later, in the dress shop, when Scottie buys her the clothes she wore as Madeleine, her attitude ("No, I won't *do* it . . . I don't *like* it") betrays panic: is she afraid Scottie will learn the truth if she dresses like Madeleine? Or does the thought of slipping back into being Madeleine, the sense of dissolving identity, terrify her?

Throughout these scenes, our consciousness is split between the two characters. By means of this split, Hitchcock makes us aware of the painfulness of the relationship, the tension of which becomes a distillation of the tensions in all human relationships. Scottie can neither accept nor even really *see* Judy: all that holds him to her is the ghost of Madeleine that lurks within her. He takes her to Ernie's, where he first saw Madeleine. While he gazes fascinated at a woman who, until she gets near, in her movements, figure, and clothes resembles Madeleine, the woman who was (and, somewhere, still is?) the real Madeleine sits helplessly, ignored—he "doesn't even know she is there," as Midge said to him in the mental hospital. Judy, in fact, has now taken over from Midge in some respects: it is she, now, who fights, as unsuccessfully as Midge, to keep him in the "real" world. Her insistence that he see *her*, that he like *her*, reminds us of Midge's clumsy attempt to destroy the dream with the portrait. The irony of the scene in Ernie's brings home to us forcefully that Scottie has not been in love with a woman so much as with—almost in the platonic sense—an Idea. Later Scottie takes Judy walking by a lake: it was the first thing associated with Madeleine, the lake Gavin Elster described her as sitting by, gazing across at the pillars

we now see—the appropriately named "Portals of the Past." Judy yearn-
ingly watches couples kissing on the bank: Scottie isn't even holding her
hand. Later, in his apartment, she tells him, "You don't even want to
touch me." By now, the film has defined very thoroughly all that was
behind that look of Midge's when Scottie reminded her that it was she
who broke off their engagement. But, if Scottie represents an extreme
case (we classify him by now, certainly, as a sick man), this rejection of
life for an unattainable Idea is something fundamental in human nature, his sickness still, potentially, our sickness. The tendency in relationships to form an idealized image of the other person and substitute it for
the reality is relevant here.

But it is during the sequences showing Scottie's attempt to turn Judy
into Madeleine that the emotional effect of our feeling *with* both of them
at once rises to its greatest intensity. In Scottie we see revealed the duality
of impulse I mentioned earlier. When Judy asks him "What good will it
do?" his "I don't know" is clearly genuine: he is not *only* bent on re-
creating a dream. In Judy we watch the gradual submergence of her
identity as her Madeleine persona is reassumed. As she sinks down on to
the cushions Scottie places for her before his fire—the cushions he
placed there earlier for Madeleine—we sense her awareness that she is
slipping helplessly into something she won't be able to control. As he
waits for her to emerge from her bedroom with her hair up—the final
item in the re-creation—we see in his face a fear mixed with longing, a
nagging doubt and uneasiness. The bedroom door opens, and the camera
remains on his face. For a moment he can't bring himself to look round
at her: if what he sees *is* Madeleine, then Madeleine was a hoax. When
she appears, we see her through his eyes, dazzling but blurred, a realized
dream. As Judy, now Madeleine again, moves forward to him, her face
expressing a beautiful erotic yearning, we see that it is not only clothes
and hairstyle that have changed: her way of moving is different, her
expression again has Madeleine's sensitivity. There follows the kiss during which the camera performs a 360° tracking movement around them.
In the middle of it, Hitchcock back-projects behind them the carriage in
the livery stable at San Juan Baptista. Past and present, illusion and
reality, merge. It is at once the triumph of illusion, the perfect re-creation
of the dream, and the expression of the painful nagging doubt that
necessarily accompanies the sense that this is indeed Madeleine. During
the kiss we see Scottie's face troubled and perplexed, divided between

surrender and suspicion; while Madeleine clings to him as she clung to him when they kissed by the sea, seeming to hang on him for help, protection, security, as if drowning.

When Judy/Madeleine reenters after dressing for dinner, it is Madeleine we see moving, Madeleine we hear talking: Judy is quite submerged. She wants to go to Ernie's ("Well, after all it's our place"). She has reentered the Madeleine world. When she makes the fatal, apparently so stupid and obvious, mistake of putting on the Carlotta Valdes necklace and asking Scottie to link it for her, it is simply the final surrender of her identity as Judy: she *is* Madeleine again. We are shown Scottie's realization subjectively: the necklace on Judy's throat in the mirror is juxtaposed with the same necklace in Carlotta's portrait. Because we have long since known the truth, we cannot share his shock of comprehension, though the use of identification technique helps us to understand it.

But there is more to this beautiful moment than that. From the close-up of the necklace around Carlotta's neck the camera tracks back to take in Madeleine staring in the art gallery, her posy beside her: the shot draws together with poignant effect various strands of emotional reaction: our (and Scottie's) past feeling for the dream locks with our present feeling for (and Scottie's bitter reaction against) Judy. Also, the backward tracking shot contrasts with the frequent forward tracking shots that characterized the earlier part of the film, to suggest recoil, Scottie extricating himself from the quicksands of illusion. The earlier shots in the art gallery took him (and us) forward into the dream, tracking in on the posies, and on the similarly styled hair, of Madeleine and Carlotta, hair arranged in a spiral that evoked the patterns of the credit titles and the whole vertigo theme. Now the camera sweeps back: the effect is in some ways analogous to that of the car reemerging from the swamp at the end of *Psycho*.

The ending of the film perfectly knots all the strands. Scottie's vertigo is cured, not by forcing himself to go higher, nor by the "emotional shock" that Midge told him might do it (he had that the first time Madeleine died), but by finally learning the whole truth: after he has forced the confession from Judy, he can look down the well of the tower without dizziness: the symbolic nature of the vertigo is thus finally emphasized. Judy's death, on the face of it an accident, contains elements both of murder and suicide. It is clear, as he drags her up the tower stairs, that he wants to kill her—he takes her by the throat and shakes her violently. He hates her for not being Madeleine—for destroying for him the possibility of escape into fantasy. Even after he knows the whole truth, he can still cry out bitterly, "I loved you so, Madeleine," without being aware of the name he is using. As for Judy, she protests frantically and yet allows herself to be dragged up the stairs. During and after her confession, we have a terrifying sense of watching a personality disintegrate before our eyes: she talks sometimes as Madeleine, sometimes as Judy. We remember Madeleine's cry to Scottie after the sequoia sequence: "If I'm mad, that would explain it." She is already quite broken before she falls. As for the nun, there is really no need to read any Catholic significance into her. We see her through Judy's eyes rise up like a ghost, and Judy falls, destroyed by Madeleine's return from the dead as Madeleine was supposed to be by Carlotta's. The shadow materializing as a nun can stand as a symbol of Scottie's illumination: a far more satisfactory one than the Buddhist monk who rescues Genjuro the potter from *his* dreamworld in Mizoguchi's *Ugetsu Monogatari,* because her appearance corresponds to a development within Scottie's consciousness.

The film ends with the magnificent image of Scottie looking down from a great height to where Judy has fallen: magnificent, because it so perfectly crystallizes our complexity of response. Scottie is cured; yet his cure has destroyed at a blow both the reality and the illusion of Judy/Madeleine, has made the *illusion* of Madeleine's death real. He is cured, but empty, desolate. Triumph and tragedy are indistinguishably fused.

Vertigo seems to me of all Hitchcock's films the one nearest to perfection. Indeed, its profundity is inseparable from the perfection of form: it is a perfect organism, each character, each sequence, each image, illuminating every other. Form and technique here become the perfect expression of concerns both deep and universal. Hitchcock uses audience involvement as an essential aspect of the film's significance. Together with its deeply disturbing attitude to life goes a strong feeling for the value of human relationships. To object that the characters' motives are not explained in terms of individual psychology is like demanding a psychological explanation of the sources of evil in Macbeth: Hitchcock is concerned with impulses that lie deeper than individual psychology, that are inherent in the human condition. The film's only blemish is the occasional inadequacy of Kim Novak as Judy.[19] Her performance as Madeleine, lovingly molded by Hitchcock, is flawless, but there are moments when one wants more inwardness from Judy. The taxing long take of her composing the letter reveals this slight inadequacy: one becomes uncomfortably aware of the director behind the camera telling her "Now you do this . . . Now you do that . . ." But this weakness is not serious enough to detract from the poignancy of these last sequences. In complexity and subtlety, in emotional depth, in its power to disturb, in the centrality of its concerns, *Vertigo* can as well as any film be taken to represent the cinema's claims to be treated with the respect accorded to the longer established art forms.

5

NORTH BY NORTHWEST

There are no symbols in *North by Northwest*. Oh yes! One. The last shot, the train entering the tunnel after the love-scene between Grant and Eva-Marie Saint. It's a phallic symbol. But don't tell anyone.— Alfred Hitchcock, *Cahiers du Cinéma*, No. 102.

Of Hitchcock's six most recent films, *North by Northwest* is that which corresponds most nearly to the conventional estimate of him as a polished light entertainer. That, beside its immediate neighbors, it is a lightweight work, a relaxation, in which we see Hitchcock working at something less than full pressure, I do not deny. That it is trivial or frivolous, not worth serious attention, I reject absolutely. When I spoke of the unbroken series of masterpieces from *Vertigo* to *Marnie*, I had not forgotten *North by Northwest*.

A light entertainment can have depth, subtlety, finesse, it can embody mature moral values; indeed, it seems to me that it *must*. If I fail to be entertained by *Goldfinger*, it is because there is nothing there to engage or retain the attention; the result is a nonentity, consequently tedious. The essential triviality of the James Bond films, in fact, sets off perfectly, by contrast, the depth, the charm, the integrity of Hitchcock's film.

A film, whether light entertainment or not, is either a work of art or it is nothing. And the basic essential of a work of art is that it be thematically organic. *Goldfinger* is a collection of bits, carefully calculated with both eyes on the box office, put end to end with no deeper necessity for what happens next than mere plot; nothing except plot develops in the course of it, and, obviously, the essence of an organic construction is development. But *Goldfinger*, I shall be reminded, doesn't take itself seriously: so much the worse for it. And if it doesn't why should anyone else?—for I find it difficult to see how the adult mind can occupy itself with something that cannot, in some sense, be taken seriously. *North by Northwest,* on the level of plot (if one can imagine its plot divorced from its subject, which is more difficult than may at first appear), also doesn't take itself seriously: we are not, in other words, expected to believe, literally, *this could happen.* But it is a very superficial glance that sees no more there than the plot. The tongue-in-cheek element on plot level has the function of directing our attention to other levels. On the other hand the self-mocking aspect of the Bond films is merely a very shrewd means of permitting the spectator to indulge any penchant for sadism and sexual "kicks" he may have without any accompanying discomfort.

The sociologist and the critic have territory in common, certainly; but *Goldfinger* and its success, the wide popular and critical success of a film that has scarcely more to offer than a boys' comic paper, seems to me to belong strictly to the sociologist. Even to compare it with *North by Northwest* will seem slightly ridiculous to Hitchcock's admirers, but a moment's reflection will be enough to remind them that the obvious distinction between the two films has not been made everywhere.

I have allowed that *North by Northwest* is a comparatively relaxed film, a divertissement; that is to say, one must not demand of it the concentrated significance, the extraordinarily close-knit organization of *Vertigo* and *Psycho.* Nevertheless, it has a coherent and satisfying development, a construction sufficiently strong and clear to assimilate the occasional charming but irrelevant little *jeux d'esprit* (the strange lady's reaction to Cary Grant's nocturnal passage through her bedroom as he escapes from the hotel in which the head of the C.I.A. has imprisoned him) permissible in a work of this nature. Like *Vertigo* (to which it is also linked through its equivocal heroine), it can be regarded as falling into three movements corresponding to the main stages in the evolution of the hero's attitude. The first lightly sketches all that is relevant (for the purposes of the film) of his general situation and outlook, and has him mistaken for George Kaplan and wanted by both spies and police; it closes with the revelation that George Kaplan doesn't exist. The second sees him involved with Eve Kendall and traces the abrupt shifts in his relationship with her as he (as well as the spectator) becomes increasingly frustrated, baffled, disillusioned, by the ambiguity of her position and behavior. The last movement begins when he learns the truth about her and—the real turning point of the film—voluntarily accepts his role as Kaplan, and culminates in the cementing of their relationship.

North by Northwest bears an obvious resemblance to both *The 39 Steps* and *Saboteur;* its immense superiority to both films scarcely needs to be argued, but it is worth noting that Hitchcock himself, when asked why he had remade *Saboteur,* replied that in the earlier film the characters were not interesting, and that he made an elementary mistake in having the villain, not the hero, dangle from the top of the Statue of Liberty. The second point is by no means a trivial one, and is intimately connected with the first. It is not so much a greater complexity of the characters in *North by Northwest* that makes them more interesting, but their relationship to the action. Both *The 39 Steps* and *Saboteur* have heroes quite unpredictably and abruptly plunged into hair-raising adventures, but the adventures bear no really organic relationship to the men; there is not the same point in these things happening to Richard Hannay and the hero of *Saboteur* as there is in their happening to Roger Thornhill. Similarly, there is no point at all in having Fry (the "saboteur" of the title) hang by his coat sleeves from the Statue of Liberty, beyond the prolonging of a simple suspense as an end in itself; there is every point in Roger Thornhill, the previously irresponsible, unattached advertising man, having to hang onto a ledge on Mount Rushmore by one hand, holding the woman he loves by the other, while the homosexual spy Leonard, the film's ultimate representative of the sterile and destructive, grinds the hand with his foot.[20] The difference can be summed up (with some unfairness in simplification to the earlier films) by saying that *North by Northwest* has a subject as well as a plot.

In fact, at a deeper level the film has more in common with *Rear Window* than with *Saboteur* or *The 39 Steps.* The film begins with shots of New York traffic and New York crowds: a sense of apparently aimless and chaotic bustle and movement. From this emerges Roger Thornhill, dictating to his secretary on his way home by lift, crowded pavement, taxi: emerges from it as its typical representative and product. In an exposition of masterly compression we learn all the essential things about him: he is brash, fast-talking, over-confident on the surface; entirely irresponsible and inconsiderate of others (he cheats two people out of their taxi by pretending his secretary is ill, then cheerfully justifies this to her by telling her he has made the other man "feel like a Good

Samaritan"); a heavy drinker; a divorcé (twice, it transpires); surprisingly dominated by his mother, who, he says, is "like a bloodhound" in still sniffing his breath to find out if he has been drinking. Indeed, he is a man who lives purely on the surface, refusing all commitment or responsibility (appropriately, he is in advertising), immature for all his cocksureness, his life all the more a chaos for the fact that he doesn't recognize it as such; a man who relies above all on the exterior trappings of modern civilization—business offices, cocktail bars, machines—for protection, who substitutes bustle and speed for a sense of direction or purpose: a modern city Everyman, whose charm and self-confidence and smartness make him especially easy for the spectator to identity with, so that at the start we are scarcely conscious of his limitations as a human being. We can quite happily and thoughtlessly attach ourselves to his smug confidence in being in control of his environment.

And then, abruptly, within ten minutes of the start of the film, the ground is cut away from under his/our feet. Hitchcock's sense of the precariousness of all human order has never been more beautifully expressed (though conveyed elsewhere—in *The Wrong Man* and *The Birds,* for instance—with greater intensity and overt seriousness) than in the mistake, due to sheer chance, by which Thornhill, going to send a telegram to his mother, finds himself kidnapped by gunmen. In the lobby of a crowded hotel, in whose lounge bar he has just been drinking with associates, chaos abruptly takes over.

The remainder of the film's first movement is devoted to a systematic stripping away of all the protective armor of modern city man on which Thornhill relies for his safety. In the midst of crowds, he becomes completely isolated. The opportunist has been defeated by chance. The man who deprived others of their taxi is imprisoned in a car he can't get out of, unable even to attract attention. He is taken to the house of a Mr. Townsend where all his "proofs" of identity are disdainfully refused. The heavy drinker is forced to gulp down immense quantities of Bourbon as a preliminary to a "drunk driving accident." The fact that he is a heavy drinker, of course, makes it feasible that he should be able to frustrate his potential murderers by escaping his "accident"; but we are also left to reflect on the appropriateness of such a death—it is precisely the way in which Thornhill might eventually have died. The hair-raising drive in a car almost out of his control is a logical extension of his basic situation. And Hitchcock is so little interested in his spies *as* spies, the spectator is so little encouraged to inquire into the precise nature of their activities, that it becomes very easy to accept them as simply the embodiment of the forces of disorder and subversion: we are no more interested in their rational motivation than we are in that of the birds two films later. Like the birds, they are not so much a projection of the chaos underlying modern order as the agents whereby that order is destroyed, the chaos forced upon the characters' consciousness.

Thornhill's sense of personal identity is clearly weak, and undermined by the spies' unshakable conviction that he is George Kaplan; and indeed as an integrated human being he has about as real an existence. At the police station, he tells his mother on the phone, very emphatically, "This is your son, Roger Thornhill"—as if he had been brought to the point of doubting it. The only relationship of any apparent strength, with his mother, proves worse than useless, her skepticism undermining him at every step; it is parodied when he returns with the police to the Townsend mansion by the false Mrs. Townsend's effusive, motherly, yet equally cynical, treatment of him. The parallel is emphasized by Hitchcock's having the two women (who look very much alike) stand in similar postures, hands folded before them. One of the film's funniest and most uncomfortable moments comes when, descending from their exploration of Kaplan's rooms in the hotel lift, Thornhill's mother remarks gaily to the two men who almost sent her son over a cliff the night before, "You gentlemen aren't *really* trying to kill my son, are you?", and the whole lift load—mother, killers, other passengers—laugh uproariously at the joke while Thornhill stands helplessly in their midst.

With characteristic Hitchcockian outrageousness, Thornhill's final plunge into chaos is set in the supreme symbol of potential world order, the United Nations building. After the knifing of the real Townsend, we see Thornhill running frantically, a microscopic figure, in a shot taken from the top of the building, looking directly down on him; the smug, self-confident advertising man, so sure of the effectiveness of his personality, reduced to an almost indistinguishable speck, and a completely isolated speck, for he is now (as Thornhill) pursued by the forces of order as well as disorder (as Kaplan). It is at this point that we leave him for a moment to learn the truth: the meeting in the Intelligence Bureau reveals that Kaplan (on whose whereabouts Thornhill's fate depends) doesn't exist—is a convenient invention, a "nonexistent decoy " designed to divert the spies' attention from the *real* agent. What is to be done to protect Thornhill? Nothing. He is to be left to fend for himself, thrown back on his own resources, all civilized protections removed. The first movement of the film ends with the secretary's epitaph on an unknown nonentity: "Good-bye, Mr. Thornhill, whoever you are!"

The second movement begins with Thornhill, in the station, again among crowds, into which we see him, in long shot, disappear. The ensuing sequence gives us the train journey, Thornhill's meeting with Eve Kendall, and the first stage in their relationship. The superficial Eve —it is all we see for some time—suggests that she is the perfect counterpart for Thornhill: worldly, amoral, quite without depth of feeling, quite uncommitted to anything or anyone, taking sex as she would a cocktail (she says to him, with a sly suggestiveness, "It's going to be a long night, and I don't particularly like the book I've started . . . know what I mean?"). There is a slight hint of nymphomania. She seems to be offering exactly the kind of relationship he would want: love-making without involvement, sex without responsibilities. But already, as they begin to make love after she has hidden him in her wall-bed from the searching police, one begins to be aware of undercurrents. He wonders why she isn't afraid of him, a supposed murderer; she asks him if he is planing to murder her. He asks, "Shall I?"; she murmurs "Please do," and they kiss. It is all playful on the surface; but as they kiss his hands encircle her head as if either to strangle or to crush her, and hers move to his to draw him down, in an attitude of surrender. We realize his sudden sense of the danger of involvement and also her barely concealed weariness and yearning. It is all done with a marvelous delicacy which is in fact profoundly characteristic of Hitchcock, although this is not often recognized. The scene ends with a shot of her looking over his shoulder, her eyes deeply troubled; then she sends the message along to Vandamm: "What do I do with him in the morning?"

What she does is to arrange for him to be machine-gunned from a plane. The attempt on his life is prefaced by their parting, which ends with the beautiful shot of his hand tentatively covering hers on the handle of her case, as she draws back: their mutual involvement is suggested with remarkable economy. What we seem to have here (for we still take Eve very largely at her face value) is the old cliché of the wicked woman drawn into true love against her will. A cursory comparison with what Guy Hamilton makes of the Pussy Galore/James Bond relationship will reveal the extent to which a "light entertainment" can have grace, sensibility, and moral depth if it is directed by Hitchcock.

The crop-dusting sequence is justly famous and seems widely accepted as one of Hitchcock's most brilliant set pieces. What is not so often noticed, however, is its dependence for much of its effect on its context. Certainly, it is brilliant in itself, an object lesson in the building up of a suspense through the repeated cheating of the audience's expectations, ending in the *frisson*-producing line, "That plane's dusting crops where there ain't no crops," and the subsequent explosion into violent action. Yet the sequence retains its magic however many times one sees the film —even after one knows, shot by shot, what comes next, and it is worth asking why this should be. The sequence occurs at almost exactly mid-point in the film. Immediately behind it is our knowledge of Eve Kendall's treachery (*we* know Thornhill is going to be attacked, though *he* doesn't) and all the emotional tension generated by their relationship. But there is much more behind it than that. Hitherto in the film, Thornhill has always been *inside:* inside cities, buildings, vehicles: and we know him as a man at home in the complacency-encouraging security of office and cocktail bar. Now, suddenly, he is in open country. And not merely open country: a flat landscape, treeless, houseless, shelterless, parched, stretching away apparently to infinity on all sides. In the midst of this he stands, an isolated speck with the whole world against him, absolutely exposed and vulnerable: modern man deprived of all his amenities and artificial resources. The bus—his last contact with other people, with civilization—moves away, the crop-dusting plane turns and flies toward him . . . It is a marvelous conception, central to the film in more ways than position.

Thornhill's first image of Eve is now shattered; the second is equally misleading—though both bear some relationship to the real Eve. When they meet again in the hotel, she runs up to him, and we see her relief: relief not only that he isn't dead but that she hasn't been responsible for his death. His hands go round her head again to embrace her, in the gesture he used on the train; only this time they don't quite touch. He hesitates, moves away, makes a sarcastic remark about "togetherness." Another familiar Hitchcock theme is touched on: the necessity for a trust based on instinct, even when it is quite unreasonable. Their separation is expressed by restless crosscutting, their partial reconciliation (on his side clearly provisional and suspicious) by a beautiful camera movement that unites them in one image as she moves toward him. She helps him remove his jacket to have it cleaned, and he says, "When I was a little boy I wouldn't even let my mother undress me"; she tells him he is a big boy now. It is one of those unobtrusive, almost offhand exchanges that reveals a great deal. Before she leaves, he asks her, "Have you ever killed anyone?"—we are made to remember that (whatever her motives) she did in fact connive at the attempt on his life.

This middle movement of the film closes with the auction scene, which gives us Thornhill's view of Eve at its most bitterly disillusioned ebb. Vandamm is standing behind her, his hand closing round the back of her neck in what constitutes at once a caress and a threat. A close-up emphasizes this, and we connect it with Thornhill's embraces, but this is far more sinister, and expresses the precariousness of Eve's position (before we know the truth about her). Thornhill calls her a "statue" and tells her: "Who are you kidding? You *have* no feelings to hurt." We see, but he doesn't, that she is in tears: the sequence is a condensed recapitulation of *Notorious*. This is not so banal as it sounds. We are aware by this time of the potentially healing power of the relationship on both sides (though we still don't know the real nature of Eve's need); but it appears—as Thornhill escapes, thanks to the police—irremediably broken.

The final movement opens with the reversal of this situation. At the airport, the head of the C.I.A. tells Thornhill the truth about Eve, and he accepts his role as Kaplan for her sake. Immediately before, he uses a phrase that unites his two images of her: "That treacherous little tramp." Suddenly he learns that her life may depend on him, and, in agreeing to be Kaplan, he is accepting his responsibility and his involvement in a deep relationship. The sexual basis of his previous refusal of commitment, rejection of responsibility, is clear: he has survived two marriages which have left him, apparently, completely unaffected. As he accepts, his face is suddenly illuminated by the light of the plane; and we cut to the first shot of Mount Rushmore. The cut has great emotional effect, because it abruptly defines for us, with marvelous economy, the evolution of the hero. For if the significance of Mount Rushmore is dramatic rather than symbolic, it is because "symbolic" suggests something too precise and too simple. It is not a symbol of democracy standing against the wicked agents; but certainly, in its emotional effect it suggests the order and stability toward which Thornhill is progressing, and to which

the acceptance of a strong relationship with its accompanying responsibilities is the essential step.[21]

The scene of his reconciliation with Eve (after the false shooting) is
perhaps the most beautiful in the film. First, the location: for the first
time in the film we are among trees, cool calm sunlight and shade—the
effect is more a matter of context than of the intrinsic beauty of the
scenery, and (as usual in this film, indeed in all Hitchcock's work) more
of overtones and associations than of overt, clear-cut symbolism; it is an
apt setting for the beginning of new life. Second, the mise-en-scène. As
the "dead" Thornhill gets out of the back of the car, the camera tracks
back to reveal Eve standing by *her* car to the right. We see them in long
shot gazing at each other from the extremities of the screen, across the
space of trees and filtered sunlight, everything still, the two hesitant, as
if shy of each other. Then a shot of Thornhill as he begins to move: the
camera tracks with him, left to right. Cut to a shot of Eve as *she* starts
forward: the camera tracks with her from right to left. And so they are
united: Hitchcock beautifully involves the spectator in their movement
toward each other, their movement toward the "togetherness" that was
earlier (for Thornhill) a contemptuous sneer.

We, and Thornhill, see at last the real Eve; or perhaps it is truer to
say that the real Eve now *emerges:* her true identity is created—or at
least crystallized—by the relationship, superceding (or perhaps assimilating) her two earlier personae. But it is made clear that those earlier
Eves, partly artificial, are what she could have become, just as the real
Judy Barton contains elements of her two adopted "personalities" (in
Vertigo the distinction between them is of course much greater). It is the
real Eve who tells Thornhill, with a touching gentleness, how deeply his
words hurt; but almost at once, we get a glimpse of the first Eve, the Eve
of the train journey, in her description of her relationship with Vandamm: "I had nothing to do that weekend, so I decided to fall in love."
Then her comment on her decision to help Intelligence ("Maybe that
was the first time anyone ever asked me to do anything worthwhile")
gives us the potentially ruthless Eve—ruthless in a good cause—who
could send Thornhill (with whatever qualms) to his death, and who is
still ready to sacrifice their relationship for the "cause." The strands are
drawn together in the ensuing dialogue exchange: "Has life been like
that?" he asks her, and she assents. "How come?"—"Men like you!"—
"What's wrong with men like me?"—"They don't believe in marriage."

He tells her he's been married twice: her comment, "See what I mean?" Circumstances have steered her toward being one or other of the earlier Eves; now, in the relationship with Thornhill, her true self can be realized.

She makes it clear that this marriage is one, at last, that he will not easily escape. His reaction is jocular, cynical—"I may go back to hating you: it was more fun." His expression and tone belie the words, but they serve to bring before us the man's previous fear of real involvement, of responsibility. Hitchcock—here and in *Rear Window*—gives us no simple "redemption through love," no abrupt transformation; just a delicate intimation of the potential healing power of a balanced, permanent relationship. Eve reminds him that he "is meant to be critically wounded" he replies, "I never felt more alive."

That charming father figure, the head of the C.I.A., whom Jean Douchet appears to suggest is some kind of Divine Instrument, seems to me to come out of things pretty badly. The film is surely solidly behind Thornhill in rejecting the use of a woman to "get people like Vandamm": prostitution, in however admirable a cause, remains prostitution. Mixed morality—the pursuing of a good end by conventionally immoral means like Mark Rutland's in *Marnie*—is justified by Hitchcock only as the outcome of powerful instinctive drives, of basically right feelings, not when it comes to cold calculation: justifiable, therefore, only on the personal level, not on the political. We are entirely behind Thornhill, then, in his attempts to extricate Eve—in the determined positive action that results from his acceptance of personal responsibility.

Before the Mount Rushmore climax, we have Thornhill's attempts to rescue Eve from Vandamm's house, Vandamm's discovery of her true nature, and his plans to dispose of her over the sea. Leonard is built up here as the incarnation of destruction and negation. His motive is sexual jealousy—jealousy of Eve, his rival for Vandamm. He discloses the truth about Eve in a melodramatic, vindictive way, by "shooting" Vandamm with her blank-loaded revolver.

The climax is played out on and around the imperturbable stone faces of the Presidents, with their suggestion of stability and order forming a background to Thornhill's desperate struggle to save himself and Eve for life. As they dangle from a ledge by their hands, they discuss—with total absurdity on a naturalistic level—Thornhill's first two marriages: "My wives divorced me . . . I think they said I led too dull a life." The struggle for life against the destructive elements (the spies) is thus combined with the cementing of the relationship, the sealing off of the past. The joining of the lovers' hands derives some of its emotional and moral force from our view of it as the climax of a sequence of shots of their hands touching (to mark phases in the relationship) earlier: her sensuous caressing of his hand over the lunch table on the train, when she looked at his "R. O. T." bookmatches; his pressure on her hand at the Chicago station as they say good-bye, after she has arranged the "meeting" with Kaplan. Eventually, Thornhill is hanging by one hand, holding the dangling Eve by the other, a great abyss beneath them: final test of stamina, with everything staked on his powers of endurance and determination. Leonard stands above them; Thornhill's "Help! Help me!" is given great force. Then Leonard treads on Thornhill's hand. Thornhill survives the trial for long enough: Leonard is shot down. We see Thornhill pulling Eve to safety. An abrupt cut, but with overlapping dialogue, makes the action culminate in his pulling her up into bed on a train, as "Mrs. Thornhill"—a beautiful way of expressing the link between his survival of the ordeal and their relationship. The last shot is of a train entering a tunnel: the "phallic symbol" toward which the whole film has moved.

It will be objected that this account of *North by Northwest* makes it far too serious. But its charms, its deftness, the constant flow of invention, its humor and exhilaration, are there for all to see. All I have tried to do is adjust the balance: not to turn a light comedy into an unsmiling morality play, but to suggest why *North by Northwest* is such a very, very good light comedy.

6
PSYCHO

. . . . function
Is smother'd in surmise, and nothing is
But what is not.—*Macbeth*

But if you look at the matter from a theoretical point of view and ignore this question of degree you can very well say that we are all ill, i.e. neurotic; for the conditions required for symptom-formation are demonstrable also in normal persons.—Freud, *Introductory Lectures on Psycho-Analysis*

You have to remember that *Psycho* is a film made with quite a sense of amusement on my part. To me it's a *fun* picture. The processes through which we take the audience, you see, it's rather like taking them through the haunted house at the fairground . . ."—Hitchcock, interview in *Movie 6*

Psycho opens with a view of a city. The name of the city appears, followed by a precise date and a precise time, as the camera swings over the rooftops and apartment blocks. It hesitates, seems to select, tracks in toward one particular block, hesitates again before all the windows, seems to select again, then takes us through one slightly open window into a darkened room.[22] Arbitrary place, date, and time, and now an apparently arbitrary window: the effect is of random selection: this could be any place, any date, any time, any room: it could be *us*. The forward track into darkness inaugurates the progress of perhaps the most terrifying film ever made: we are to be taken forward and downward into the darkness of ourselves. *Psycho* begins with the normal and draws us steadily deeper and deeper into the abnormal; it opens by making us aware of time, and ends (except for the releasing final image) with a situation in which time (i.e., development) has ceased to exist.

The scene we witness between Marion Crane (Janet Leigh) and Sam Loomis (John Gavin), while carefully and convincingly particularized in terms of character and situation, is ordinary enough for us to accept it as representative of "normal" human behavior. A leading theme emerges, unexceptional both in itself and in the way in which it is presented, though it subtly pervades the whole scene: the dominance of the past over the present. The lovers cannot marry because Sam has to pay his dead father's debts and his ex-wife's alimony; "respectable" meetings in Marion's home will be presided over by her (presumably) dead mother's portrait. From this "normal" hold of past on present, with its limiting, cramping effect on life (the essence of life being development), we shall be led gradually to a situation where present is entirely swallowed up by past, and life finally paralyzed. That the lovers are meeting surreptitiously, doing things that must be concealed from the outer world, provides a further link (still within the bounds of normality) with Norman Bates. And in both cases the "secrets," normal and abnormal, are sexual in nature.

Everything is done to encourage the spectator to identify with Marion. In the dispute between the lovers we naturally side with her: Sam's insistence on waiting until he can give her financial security annoys us, because it is the sort of boring mundane consideration we expect the romantic hero of a film to sweep aside, and we are very much drawn to Marion's readiness to accept things as they are for the sake of the relationship. This is in fact the first step in our complicity in the theft of the $40,000. It is Sam's fault that Marion steals the money, which has no importance for her. It is simply the means to an end: sex, not money, is the root of all evil. Indeed, the spectator's lust for money, played upon considerably in the early stages of the film, is aroused only to be swiftly and definitively "placed": the fate of the money, after the shower murder, becomes an entirely trivial matter, and Hitchcock by insisting on it evokes in us a strong revulsion.

Our moral resistance is skilfully undermined during the office scene. The man with the money—Cassidy—is a vulgar, drunken oaf; he has plenty more; his boast that he "buys off unhappiness," that his about-to-be-married "baby" has "never had an unhappy day," fills us with a sense of unfairness even as we realize how far his boast probably is from the truth: whatever he is, Cassidy does not strike us as a happy man.

The whole fabric of the film is interwoven with these parent-child references: even Marion's fellow office girl has a prying mother, and Marion's room is decorated with family photographs which look down on her as she packs. Cassidy's relationship with his "baby" takes us a step into the abnormal, because it is highly suspect: she will probably be better without the $40,000 house, which is clearly a symbol of her father's power over her. That Marion will also be better without it is a reflection we do not allow ourselves, any more than she does. By minimizing our moral opposition to the notion of stealing $40,000, Hitchcock makes it possible for us to continue to identify with Marion, involving ourselves in her guilt as easily and unthinkingly as she herself becomes involved. There is no clear-cut moment of decision: she takes the money home, changes, packs her suitcase, but the money lies on the bed and she constantly hesitates over it: her actions tell us that she has committed herself, but she doesn't consciously accept that commitment. We are able to commit acts we know to be immoral only if we inhibit our conscious processes: Macbeth never really knows why he *"yields* to that suggestion whose horrid image does unfix his hair. . . ," but the yielding itself involves the paralysis of his conscious moral faculties. So it is with Marion: the decision having gripped her (rather than been taken), she necessarily forfeits her powers of conscious will. She drifts helplessly, and we drift with her.

Her inability to control her actions rationally is illustrated in numerous incidents. As she drives, she imagines voices, conversations: Sam, her boss, Cassidy. She knows Sam will be horrified, will reject the money (she cannot finish the imaginary conversation with him); yet she drives on. Her boss notices her as her car is held up by traffic lights, and she sees him notice her; yet she drives on. Everything she imagines stresses the impossibility of getting away with it and the uselessness of it anyway; yet she drives on. A suspicious policeman sees her changing cars, and she knows that *he* knows what her new car looks like, and what its number is, and that she is throwing away an irretrievable $700 quite pointlessly; yet she goes through with the exchange. Throughout the journey Hitchcock uses every means to enforce audience identification—the staging of each scene, the use of subjective technique, the way in which each subsidiary character is presented to us through Marion's eyes, Bernard Herrmann's music and Hitchcock's use of it, all serve to involve us in Marion's condition. With her, we lose all power of rational control, and discover how easily a "normal" person can lapse into a condition usually associated with neurosis. Like her we resent, with fear and impatience, everything (the policeman, the car salesman) that impedes or interferes with her obsessive flight, despite the fact that only interference can help her; just as, two films later, Marnie will be helped only by events that are entirely contrary to her wishes, everything she wants being harmful to her. As Marion drives on (after the exchange of cars) we share her hopelessness and her weariness. The film conveys a sense of endless journey leading nowhere, or into darkness: as the imagined voices become more menacing, darkness gathers. Driving through darkness, she imagines Cassidy learning of the theft of the money: "I'll replace it with her fine soft flesh": Marion's verdict on herself, hideously disproportionate to the crime, will find its hideous enactment. Rain begins to fall on the windscreen before Marion—before us. She pulls up at the Bates Motel, which seems to materialize abruptly out of the darkness in front of her. She has by her actions penetrated the shell of order, and like Macbeth plunged herself into the chaos world, which finds here its most terrifying definition.

The confrontation of Marion and Norman Bates (Anthony Perkins) is in some ways the core of the film: the parallel made between them provides the continuity that underlies the brutal disruption when Marion is murdered. It is part of the essence of the film to make us feel the continuity between the normal and the abnormal: between the compulsive behavior of Marion and the psychotic behavior of Norman Bates. In the "parlor" behind his office, surrounded by Norman's stuffed birds and paintings of classical rapes, they talk about "traps." Marion is brought face to face with the logical extension of her present condition. Norman tells her, "We're all in our private trap. We scratch and claw, but only at the air, only at each other, and for all of it we never budge an inch": he is defining the psychotic state, the condition of permanent anguish whence development becomes impossible, a psychological hell. The parallel between the two is clinched when Norman says to her, "We all go a little mad sometimes. Haven't you?"

It is her perception of Norman's condition that gives Marion her chance of salvation, which she takes. In answer to his question, she says, "Sometimes just one time can be enough. Thank you." She decides to return the money the next morning. The decision this time is clearly made: she has regained her freedom of will, her power of rationality. The scene prepares us for the transference of our interest from Marion to Norman. We see Marion under the shower, and her movements have an almost ritualistic quality; her face expresses the relief of washing away her guilt.

It is not merely its incomparable physical impact that makes the shower bath murder probably the most horrific incident in any fiction film. The *meaninglessness* of it (from Marion's point of view) completely undermines our recently restored sense of security. The murder is as irrational and as useless as the theft of the money. It also constitutes an alienation effect so shattering that (at a first viewing of the film) we scarcely recover from it. Never—not even in *Vertigo*—has identification been broken off so brutally. At the time, so engrossed are we in Marion, so secure in her potential salvation, that we can scarcely believe it is happening; when it is over, and she is dead, we are left shocked, with nothing to cling to, the apparent center of the film entirely dissolved.

Needing a new center, we attach ourselves to Norman Bates, the only other character (at this point) available. We have been carefully prepared for this shift of sympathies. For one thing, Norman is an intensely sympathetic character, sensitive, vulnerable, trapped by his devotion to his mother—a devotion, a self-sacrifice, which our society tends to regard as highly laudable. That he is very unbalanced merely serves to evoke our protective instincts: he is also so helpless. Beyond this, the whole film hitherto has led us to Norman, by making us identify with a condition in many ways analogous to his: the transition is easy. After the murder, Hitchcock uses all the resources of identification technique to make us "become" Norman. He is a likeable human being in an intolerable situation, desperately in need of help and protection yet by the very nature of the case unable to obtain it. As he cleans up after his mother's hideous crime, the camera becomes subjective; they are our hands mopping away the blood. At the same time we cannot forget Marion; the intense anguish aroused in the spectator arises, as usual, from a conflict of response. Our attention is directed repeatedly to the last lingering trace of Marion which Norman almost overlooks: the money, becomes now a mere squalid bundle of paper, an ironic reminder of her life, her desires, her relationship with Sam.

Psycho is Hitchcock's ultimate achievement to date in the technique of audience participation. In a sense, the spectator becomes the chief protagonist, uniting in himself all the characters. The remainder of the film is an inquiry into the sources of the psychological hell state represented by Norman Bates: a descent into the chaos world. The other characters (Sam, Lila, Arbogast), perfunctorily sketched, are merely projections of the spectators into the film, our instruments for the search, the easier to identify with as they have no detailed individual existence. Each stage in the descent adds to the tension within us: we want to know, and we dread knowing, we want the investigators to find the truth and put an end to the horrors, yet we have involved ourselves in those horrors through our identification with Norman. One is struck (bearing in mind the care with which Hitchcock always selects his players) by close physical resemblances between certain characters. That between Vera Miles and Janet Leigh can be easily explained: they are sisters; but what of that, still more striking, between Anthony Perkins and John Gavin? As they face each other across the counter of Norman's office, we have the uncanny feeling that we are looking at two sides of the same coin; and the scene in question, which seemed at first mere suspense, useful only in its plot context, becomes one of the most moving of the film. The two men look at one another, and we look at them, and we realize suddenly that they are interchangeable: each seems the reflection of the other (though a reflection in a distorting mirror), the one healthy, balanced, the other gnawed and rotted within by poisoned sex. Similarly, Vera Miles is the extension of Janet Leigh, and what she sees and that character, is, potentially, inside herself. The characters of *Psycho* are *one* character, thanks to the identifications the film evokes, is us.

Lila's exploration of the house is an exploration of Norman's psychotic personality. The whole sequence, with its discoveries in bedroom, attic, and cellar, has clear Freudian overtones. The Victorian decor, crammed with invention, intensifies the atmosphere of sexual repression. The statue of a black cupid in the hall, the painting of an idealized maiden disporting herself at the top of the stairs, a nude goddess statuette in the bedroom, are juxtaposed with the bed permanently indented with the shape of Mrs. Bates' body (the bed in which, we learn later, she and her lover were murdered by Norman), the macabre cast of crossed hands on her dressing table, the stifling atmosphere of stagnation: one can almost *smell* it. The attic, Norman's own bedroom, represents the sick man's conscious mental development: strange confusion of the childish and the adult, cuddly toys, grubby unmade bed, a record of the *Eroica* symphony; the unexplained nature of all this carries the suggestion that what we see are mere superficial hints of underlying mysteries, a suggestion confirmed by the clasped, untitled book that Lila never actually opens (a Bates family album?).[23] Consequently we accept Norman more than ever as a human being, with all the human being's complex potentialities. The cellar gives us the hidden, sexual springs of his behavior: there Lila finds Mrs. Bates. It is a *fruit* cellar—the fruit is insisted upon in the mother's macabre joke about being "fruity'": the source of fruition and fertility become rotten.

Our discovery of the truth, of course, partly changes our attitude to what has gone before. It adds, for example, many complexities to our understanding of the shower murder, which we see now as primarily a sexual act, a violent substitute for the rape that Norman dare not carry out, and secondarily as the trapped being's desire to destroy a woman who has achieved the freedom he will never achieve: a point that gives added irony to the fact that it is her awareness of Norman that gives Marion that freedom. What it cannot do is remove our sense of complicity. We have been led to accept Norman Bates as a potential extension of ourselves. That we all carry within us somewhere every human potentiality, for good or evil, so that we all share in a common guilt, may be, intellectually, a truism; the greatness of *Psycho* lies in its ability, not merely to *tell* us this, but to make us experience it. It is this that makes a satisfactory analysis of a Hitchcock film on paper so difficult; it also ensures that no analysis, however detailed, can ever become a substitute for the film itself, since the direct emotional experience survives any amount of explanatory justification.

The effect of forward tracking shots in the film (from the opening right through to Lila's exploration of the house) is to carry us always further inside or into darkness. All the time we are being made to *see*, to see more, to see deeper: often, to see things we are afraid to see. Hence the insistence on eyes, into which the camera, our own eyes, makes us look, to see the dark places of the human soul beyond. And hence the dark glasses of the policeman: he is the only character whose eyes we never see, because it is he who is watching Marion, and hence ourselves. By the end of the film, Hitchcock has placed us in the policeman's position: we watch Norman Bates as the policeman watched Marion, and he is as conscious of our gaze as Marion was of the policeman's. On the other side of the cinema screen, we are as inscrutable, hence as pitiless, as the policeman behind his dark glasses. We may recall Norman's remark about "institutions" in the dialogue with Marion: ". . . the cruel eyes studying you." Norman is finally beyond our help. Much of the film's significance is summed up in a single visual metaphor, making use again of eyes, occurring at the film's focal point (the murder of Marion): the astonishing cut from the close-up of the water and blood *spiralling* down the drain, to the close-up of the eye of the dead girl, with the camera *spiralling* outward from it. It is as if we have emerged from the depths *behind* the eye, the round hole of the drain leading down into an apparently bottomless darkness, the potentialities for horror that lie in the depths of us all, and which have their source in sex, which the remainder of the film is devoted to sounding. The sensation of vertigo inspired by this cut and the spiralling movement itself, are echoed later as we, from high above, watch Norman carry his mother down to the fruit cellar.

The cellar is another clear sex symbol. And what Vera Miles finds there at the end of the quest are once again eyes: the mocking "eyes" of a long-dead corpse as a light bulb swings before its face: the eyes of living death, eyes that move without seeing, the true eyes of Norman.

The psychiatrist's "explanation" has been much criticized, but it has its function. It crystallizes for us our tendency to evade the implications of the film, by converting Norman into a mere "case," hence something we can easily put from us. The psychiatrist, glib and complacent, reassures us. But Hitchcock crystallizes this for us merely to force us to reject it. We shall see on reflection that the "explanation" ignores as much as it explains (the murder as symbolic rape, for example). But we are not allowed to wait for a chance to reflect: our vague feelings of dissatisfaction are promptly brought to consciousness by our final confrontation with Norman, and this scene in the cell, entirely static after the extremes of violence that have preceded it, is the most unbearably horrible in the film. What we see is Norman, his identity finally dissolved in the illusory identity of his mother, denounce all the positive side of his personality. "Mother" is innocent: "she" spares the fly crawling on Norman's hand: it is Norman who was the savage butcher. Thus we witness the irretrievable annihilation of a human being. The fly reminds us of Marion, who wasn't spared: the act constitutes a pathetic attempt at expiation before the pitiless eyes of a cruel and uncomprehending society. For a split second, almost subliminally, the features of the mother's ten-year-dead face are superimposed on Norman's as it fixes in a skull-like grimace. The sense of finality is intolerable, yet it is this that makes our release possible: we have been made to see the dark potentialities within all of us, to face the worst thing in the world: eternal damnation. We can now be set free, be saved for life. The last image, of the car *withdrawing* from the dark depths of the bog, returns us to Marion, to ourselves, and to the idea of psychological liberty.

Psycho is one of the key works of our age. Its themes are of course not new—obvious forerunners include *Macbeth* and Conrad's *Heart of Darkness*—but the intensity and horror of their treatment and the fact that they are here grounded in sex belong to the age that has witnessed on the one hand the discoveries of Freudian psychology and on the other the Nazi concentration camps. I do not think I am being callous in citing the camps in relation to a work of popular entertainment. Hitchcock himself in fact accepted a commission to make a compilation film of captured Nazi material about the camps. The project reached the rough-cut stage, and was abandoned there, for reasons I have not been able to discover: the rough-cut now lies, inaccessibly, along with vast quantities of similar raw material, in the vaults of the Imperial War Museum. But one cannot contemplate the camps without confronting two aspects of this horror: the utter helplessness and innocence of the victims, and the fact that human beings, whose potentialities all of us in some measure share, were their tormentors and butchers. We can no longer be under the slightest illusion about human nature, and about the abysses around us and within us; and *Psycho* is founded on, precisely, these twin horrors. For Hitchcock it was a "fun" picture, and a streak of macabre humor ("Mother . . . what is the phrase? . . . isn't quite herself today") certainly runs through it. Is it, then, some monstrous perversion? Many have found it so, and their reaction seems to be more defensible than that of those (must we include Hitchcock himself?) who are merely amused by it (". . . make us think twice about stopping at any building looking remotely like the Bates motel . . ."). David Holbrook, for example, remarks (presumably with *Psycho* in mind, since his book appeared in 1962), "Of course, if we lived in the world of detective stories and Hitchcock films we may take all this sordidness in a light-hearted spirit as a snuff-like piece of stimulation. But if we are responding to poetry and drama our senses should be sharpened . . ." (*Llareggub Revisited*). Yet this seems to be a short-sighted and insensitive verdict: if one is responding to *Psycho*, one's senses should be sharpened too. No film conveys—to those not afraid to expose themselves fully to it—a greater sense of desolation, yet it does so from an exceptionally mature and secure emotional viewpoint. And an essential part of this viewpoint is the detached sardonic humor. It enables the film to contemplate the ultimate horrors without hysteria, with a poised, almost serene detachment. This is probably not what Hitchcock meant when he said that one cannot appreciate *Psycho* without a sense of humor, but it is what he *should* have meant. He himself—if his interviews are to be trusted—has not really faced up to what he was doing when he made the film. This, needless to say, must not affect one's estimate of the film itself. For the maker of *Psycho* to regard it as a "fun" picture can be taken as his means of preserving his sanity; for the critic to do so—and to give it his approval on these grounds—is quite unpardonable. Hitchcock (again, if his interviews are to be trusted) is a much greater artist than he knows.

7

THE BIRDS

My own experience with *The Birds* has been varied and disconcerting. At first it seemed to me a great disappointment; now, after repeated viewings, it seems to me among Hitchcock's finest achievements. Talking oneself round to the point of view one wishes to hold is a not uncommon phenomenon, and for a time I distrusted my own deepening response to the film for this reason. But I don't think my experience of *The Birds* has been of this kind: rather, it has been a matter of breaking down a number of misleading preconceptions, so that only at the fifth or sixth viewing did I feel that I was really seeing the film, instead of being frustrated because it wasn't what I had assumed it was going to be and ought to have been; only then did it begin to make complete, instead of merely fragmentary and intermittent, sense.

For those who come to it with Hitchcock's preceding films—and especially *Psycho*—fresh in their minds, *The Birds* raises in particular two major red herrings: 1) The mother-son relationship, which leads one off the track into speculation about possessive-incestuous involvement, despite Hitchcock's explicit warning (through Annie Hayworth) that Lydia is not a "jealous, possessive mother" (a diagnosis amply confirmed later in the film in the development of Lydia herself). 2) The rather tentative use of those audience-identification techniques familiar from *Vertigo* and *Psycho* to involve us with Melanie Daniels in certain parts of the film. This can lead us to feel that we are being asked to *be* Melanie as in the first part of *Psycho* we were Marion Crane, and if we approach the film with this preconception it can seem only a disastrous failure. In fact, the identification Hitchcock encourages in *The Birds* is of a far more delicate and intermittent nature: the method of the film is quite unlike that of *Psycho,* both in the mise-en-scène and in the construction of the scenario. These errors of approach arise from too simple a notion of an artist's line of development, which rarely takes the form of such a straightforward extension of theme and technique from film to film.

Certain visual reminiscences from *Psycho* can also be misleading, though less drastically. Melanie's ascent of the stairs to her near-death in the upper room is treated in a manner recalling that of Lila Crane's exploration of the Bates house; and the birds' actual assault on Melanie carries strong reminders of the shower bath murder. Neither of these parallels is of any *direct* help in reaching the core of the film. Melanie is much more than an audience projection à la Lila, and she is not used as our instrument for "discovering what is up there" since we already guess; and Melanie's agony has a significance quite different from Marion's. Yet if there *is* a clue to *The Birds* in *Psycho*, it is certainly the shower murder, and it is not irrelevant to recall that Norman Bates, when carrying out his murders, becomes a bird of prey.

Then there are the birds themselves: what do they mean? everyone wants to know; or why do they attack? 1) *The birds are taking revenge for man's persecution of them.* Hitchcock is at pains to encourage this view in his rather lamentable misfire of a trailer. In fact, one neither accepts nor rejects it: it does so little toward explaining the film as to appear merely irrelevant. 2) *They are sent by God to punish evil humanity.* Scarcely, unless we postulate an unusually monstrous and callous God: an Old Testament God, not a Christian one: the indiscriminate nature of the attacks is the stumbling block to a theory one is quick to reject as quite foreign to the tone and temper of the film. 3) *The birds express the tensions between the characters.* This is more interesting, and seems to gain some support when one considers the original attack on Melanie by the seagull. But objections soon pile up: the birds attack innocent schoolchildren and kill Dan Fawcett, of whose possible tensions we know nothing.

The film itself is quite insistent that either the birds can't be explained or that the explanation is unknown; and it seems reasonable to start from this. Consider the totally arbitrary and pointless nature of the shower murder in *Psycho* from the point of view of Marion and her development at that point. From her point of view—which is after all that from which we have been watching the film—the murder has no dramatic, symbolic, or thematic justification. If she were still in her compulsive state, if she had not just been released from it and made her free decision to return the money, the murder could be taken as having some validity as retribution (though grossly disproportionate), or as a symbolic representation of the irrevocability of her descent into the chaos world. But Marion is saved. It is partly because the murder is— again, from her point of view—entirely arbitrary and unpredictable that its effect is so shattering. We are made to feel at that moment the precariousness, the utter unreasonableness, of life.

This disturbing sense of precariousness, of unpredictability, is of course very common in Hitchcock, who delights in disrupting a normal, every-day atmosphere with some alarming event. But usually, hitherto, the event has some justification. If Guy Haines meets Bruno Anthony, it is because something of Bruno exists already in him; if Ben and Jo (*The Man Who Knew Too Much*) get involved with spies, it is because, in the near stalemate of their marriage, they crave some external excitement; if Roger Thornhill is mistaken for Kaplan, the disorder of his life makes the mistake appropriate. But the murder of Marion Crane is in no way and to no extent either provoked or deserved.

And this seems to me the function of the birds: they are a concrete embodiment of the arbitrary and unpredictable, of whatever makes human life and human relationships precarious, a reminder of fragility and instability that cannot be ignored or evaded and, beyond that, of the possibility that life is meaningless and absurd. Hitchcock said that his film was about "complacency."

The opening shots of the film, as so often in Hitchcock, state the theme with almost diagrammatic simplicity. Melanie Daniels (Tippi Hedren) crosses a street in San francisco; overhead, birds mass in ominous dark clouds. She enters an expensive pet shop; she is surrounded by birds in ornamental cages. Outside, reality, with its constant menace of instability; inside, the "safe" artificial world that sophisticated human beings fabricate and call reality. The light comedy of the opening sequence is not merely there to lull the spectator into a state of unpreparedness for the coming horrors. The triviality is the point: the triviality of constant, even habitual playacting. Indeed the essential point about Melanie is revealed (with characteristic lack of fuss) before she even enters the shop: the determined elegance, which is very close to awkwardness, of her walk, gives us a girl whose sophistication is a disguise for underlying insecurity; she is whistled at, and turns with a smile of enjoyment at once self-conscious and childish, welcoming any boost, however vain, to her ego; then she promptly looks up, uneasily, at the birds flocking far overhead. The point is made explicit by Mitch Brenner's "parallel" as he slips the canary back into the cage: Melanie is imprisoned in a gilded cage of sophisticated triviality, an inability to be sincere which is an inability to live. We see that she is both exasperated and attracted by Brenner (Rod Taylor): her practical joke is motivated by contradictory impulses—to make a fool of him and to be mastered by him.

The "parallel" is developed in the ensuing scenes. As Melanie stands in the lift taking the lovebirds to Brenner's apartment, the camera (following the gaze of the fellow occupant) moves up from her legs and the hand holding the bird cage to her face, and we see that, in her tense and affected stance, head cocked self-consciously on one side, she is curiously bird-like. Her behavior and her attitude, like the stance, are unnatural and dehumanizing—life rendered insignificant in the gilded cage of artificiality.

But such reflections scarcely occur to us at this stage of the film, where the tone is of brittle comedy. Melanie's behavior, like the girl herself, seems cute and smart, we respond with an indulgent smile. It is later developments that condemn, retrospectively, her behavior, our response, and the tone itself; for brittle comedy is based on the assumption that relationships don't really matter, and are a kind of game we play until we are bored. In retrospect, then, these opening sequences assume serious overtones already, and Melanie, instead of seeming cute, seems already pathetic.

The drive to Bodega Bay has superficial affinities with Marion's drive in *Psycho:* both girls seem trapped in a pattern of behavior from which they cannot extricate themselves, and which they cannot view objectively, each successive step involving them in it more deeply. But the treatment, defining the spectator's relationship to the action, is completely different. When Marion was driving, we were restricted almost exclusively to her vision and her emotions; in *The Birds* we cut from a forward-moving close-up of Melanie (with ugly back-projection) to a vast static view of the landscape from high above. Identification, in other words, is not insisted upon. *The Birds* is far more "open" than *Psycho:* we are at liberty to respond in different ways. Though our indulgence is invited by the light tone of the film so far, we are free to be critical of Melanie if we wish. We are also free, therefore, to contemplate her behavior and ponder her motives, as we were not free to contemplate

Marion. And we find ourselves in a state of extreme uncertainty. Are we watching a completely fatuous and pointless game? Just what is the delivery of the lovebirds meant to achieve? On the conscious level, there seems no satisfactory answer: going to endless trouble to perform a service seems a peculiar way to avenge an insult. We are left to conclude that Melanie knows why she is doing it even less than we do. Clearly she can't leave Mitch Brenner alone: he constitutes a challenge, though of what sort we can't yet say. All that is clear is that she is giving him something, and something that he associates with her, that is even for him a symbol of her: birds in a gilded cage. We deduce, then, a split between supposed motives and true motives. Consciously, she is playing a silly, trivial trick (the birds, we learn later, were to be accompanied by a "smart" note hoping that lovebirds will "do something" for Brenner's personality); subconsciously, she is trying to continue the relationship and provoke further developments; perhaps to show him she is a nice girl after all; perhaps even to offer herself to him (to his masculine protection?) symbolically. This concealment—or, on a conscious level, rejection—of deep needs beneath a deliberately cultivated shallowness is the essential theme of these opening sequences.

It is during the sequence of the delivery of the lovebirds by boat that deliberate identification techniques are most in evidence: though again, much less consistently than in *Psycho*. Before this, our sympathy for Melanie has been carefully increased. We see her charm the kindly old storekeeper, whose warmth and natural directness makes a strong contrast with the maddening fussiness and insincerity of the manager of the bird shop. Journeys in Hitchcock's films always represent more than a method of getting a character from place to place: Melanie has progressed in behavior since we saw her in San Francisco, and the change of background reflects something of this development: she is slightly less tense, her inner concern is rising nearer the surface. Like the old man, we admire her determination and efficiency. We note her anxiety when the old man talks of "the Brenners" and her relief when she learns that Mrs. Brenner is Mitch's mother, not his wife. She seems to be allowing herself to understand more of her motives. We are sufficiently softened not to rebel against being invited to be her temporarily as she leaves the lovebirds and makes the return journey—an invitation made through the now familiar means of subjective shots and camera movements.

Even here, however, the tendency to identification is offset by certain endistancing effects. During the journey across to the Brenners' landing stage we are made to look *at* Melanie, not with her. For the close-ups and medium shots back-projection is used again, as in the car journey. Arguments along these lines are admittedly dubious, but there seems some evidence to suggest that the use of back-projection in *The Birds* is a matter of deliberate choice rather than of mere convenience: there are several perfectly straightforward shots in the middle of sequences clearly made on location where back-projection is used, and they are always shots of Melanie. Whether intentional or not, it certainly has the effect of giving an air of unreality to her situation, of isolating her from the backgrounds, of stressing her artificiality by making it stand out obtrusively from natural scenery. These close-ups are interspersed with long shots that give us Melanie isolated, a tiny, defenseless figure in a vast open space. Behind her, flocks of gulls bob on the water. Advance publicity apart, the title of the film, the nerve-jangling credit sequence, the birds massing over San Francisco, all warn us that there is going to be trouble from birds, and we expect Melanie to be attacked at any moment: they have her in a peculiarly vulnerable situation. This makes it impossible to identify with her completely as she delivers her present: *we* are expecting birds to attack, but she isn't. If we share with her something of her amusement at a joke that is becoming increasingly positive in its tendency (she tears up the letter to Mitch, substitutes one to Cathy), and share too her tension in case something goes wrong, she gets caught and made a fool of, we feel at the same time a deeper tension that she doesn't feel, as of something ominous and terrible hanging over these harmless proceedings, putting them in a different, disturbing perspective.

Melanie waits for Mitch to find the lovebirds, and we watch with her. We see him come out, look around, see her, raise fieldglasses to his eyes. She grins, bobs quickly down in the boat; Mitch grins too: she has got him, he is responding, we see him run to his car. But again Hitchcock clouds our amusement and deliberately interferes with our involvement: just before we see Mitch's response, the tranquility of the shot is disrupted by seagulls abruptly fluttering and squawking across the foreground of the image: we think for a second that the attacks are beginning. There follows the race back to Bodega Bay—Melanie in the boat, Mitch in his car—and again any sense of exhilaration is clouded over by an anxiety not shared by the characters: she is out in the open again, far from help, exposed. But she reaches the other side, switches off the motor, drifts toward the jetty, timing her arrival beautifully to coincide with Mitch's. Both are pleased—indeed, delighted—and, as Melanie now seems safe, we relax to enjoy the reunion. But Melanie (annoyingly? amusingly?) must go back to playing with him: she puts on an affected, coquettishly aloof expression, head on one side, suddenly bird-like again —and a seagull, hovering over her, abruptly swoops and pecks her head, drawing blood.

There are two ways in which Hitchcock could have made this sequence. Melanie could have been made more completely sympathetic, the reminders of her exposed isolation and of potential menace could have been eliminated, and we could have been led to become completely identified with her and her attitude; the seagull's attack would in this case have been aimed directly at us. Or her irritatingness and affectation could have been emphasized, the reminders of possible danger strengthened, and no identification set up by technical means; the attack would then have expressed *our* exasperation at her. In the event, Hitchcock rejects both methods; or combines them, if we prefer: it amounts to the same thing, in effect. Quite contradictory impulses are set up in the spectator. Hitchcock here is undertaking something more delicate and difficult to realize than the direct identification demanded by *Psycho:* the precise controlling of a partial and intermittent response to Melanie's attitudes, balanced by a sense of their insufficiency. We identify with Melanie enough to understand her, and enough to become aware of our own proneness to admire the sort of smart "cleverness," with its trivializing effect on relationships, that she represents. Instead of encouraging a deep involvement that the spectator will only later be able to judge, Hitchcock here makes involvement and judgment virtually simultaneous.

Also, the two possible treatments I have suggested would give the seagull's attack too simple a significance. Although there is some appropriateness (derived from Melanie's attitude) in the attack occurring at that moment, there have been plenty of preceding moments when it would be just as appropriate. The birds are not a straightforward *punishment* for complacency; they are not *sent* to break down the characters' attitudes so as to enable them to form relationships—nothing so schematic or explicable. Indeed, we have been led to believe (despite Melanie's moment of affected aloofness) that the two were on the point of manoeuvering toward a viable relationship. Melanie is neither admirable nor contemptible; nothing in her behavior could be dignified with the name "evil." And if all Hitchcock were after were a straightforward breaking down of a woman's complacency, he would have found characters in whom complacency was far more deeply embedded than in the obviously precariously balanced and vulnerable Melanie Daniels. If the film were simply the deliberate destruction of Melanie by the birds it would be unpardonably sadistic, the systematic torture of a child, the punishment monstrously disproportionate to any discernible crime. But the disproportion is at least part of the point: what happens to Melanie is neither the chastisement of the guilty nor the martyrdom of the innocent, for she is very carefully depicted as neither. The question we are left with, "What do you suppose made it (the seagull) do that?", is not meant to have an answer.

The ensuing scene in the café introduces Mrs. Brenner and certain parallels between the women that afford clues to an understanding of the film. Verbal parallels—and the common attitudes they express—link Mrs. Brenner and Annie Hayworth. The earlier scene, when Melanie visited Annie to learn Cathy Brenner's name, ended with Annie inquiring about the birds and, on learning that they were lovebirds, exclaiming with an air of significance, "Oh, I see." The café scene ends almost identically, only this time the query and the significant "Oh, I see" are given to Lydia (Jessica Tandy). The link tells us for the moment only that both women regard Melanie's relationship with Mitch with anxious concern, perhaps jealousy. What matters at this stage is that the two women be linked in our minds, so that we retain the sense of a *thematic* connection between them. A visual parallel, on the other hand, links Lydia and Melanie: quite simply, the fact that they look remarkably alike, with the same shaped faces and very similar upswept hairstyles: almost, we feel, we are seeing Melanie as she will look in thirty years' time. Hitchcock also supplies an almost subliminal link between Melanie and Annie, by having both women speak at moments with a similar intonation. These links are the more important in that in *personality* the three women are very strongly contrasted. Hitchcock is pointing to connections that lie deeper than personality, connections that link the three in terms of the human condition itself.

The introduction of Cathy when Melanie goes for dinner at the Brenners' puts the pattern of relationships in a slightly new perspective. Cathy rushes up to Melanie and hugs her, as soon as she has ascertained

who she is, in gratitude for the lovebirds; she is rebuked by her mother
for referring to Mitch's San Francisco acquaintances (he is a lawyer) as
"hoods," but continues to insist that that is what they are and everyone
knows it; and when Melanie declines to stay for her birthday party, she
asks right out, "Don't you like us?" Where the adults are circuitous and
evasive, the child is direct. The child accepts Melanie at once as she is
now, without question; Lydia and Mitch—to different degrees and from
different viewpoints—hold her past against her. Relationships are easy
for the child because they are uncomplicated by considerations other
than intuitive like or dislike; the adults' relationships are constantly
arrested or threatened by habitual attitudes. As Mitch sees Melanie off,
telling her he'd like to see her again, they immediately fall into just such
habitual attitudes, she adopting her smart aggressive-defensive manner,
he leaning on the car door as if on the witness-box, cross-examining her.

Melanie's conversation with Annie when she gets back clarifies the
pattern that is now emerging. Annie was and still is (as we and Melanie
have guessed) in love with Mitch; their relationship was broken up by
Lydia, whose husband had just died. Through Annie, Hitchcock makes
it clear that what he is after is not the analysis of an Oedipus problem:
"She's not afraid of losing Mitch," Annie tells Melanie, "She's afraid of
being abandoned." She goes on to say that she herself came to Bodega
Bay to be near Mitch after it was all over. We see Annie's living room,
the room of a cultured woman (reproductions of Braque; long-playing
records of Wagner), and we have seen something of Bodega Bay: we see
how isolated her life must be and recall our introduction to her, coming
round from her garden, describing her "tilling of the soil" as "compulsive." The point of the earlier suggestion of a link between her and Lydia
now becomes clear: Annie too is "afraid of being abandoned"; she can't
face the truth that she lost Mitch long ago—her behavior toward Melanie suggests a whole fantasy world of fulfilled love that reminds us
strongly of the heroine of *I Confess,* a suggestion intensified by the
records of *Tristan und Isolde* prominent in the decor. Although she is
certainly "afraid of losing Mitch," or of having to admit she has lost
him, it is her isolation that is insisted on. The hopelessness of her
position is conveyed by one tiny movement—the closing of her eyes as
Melanie, talking on the telephone to Mitch, agrees to stay for Cathy's
party. With isolation becoming such a prominent theme, we think back
to other images of isolation: Melanie alone in the bay with the birds on

the water behind her: and to the very tentative and brittle nature of her relationship with Mitch. At the end of her telephone conversation she says to Annie, "Oh, it seems so pointless!" She asks Annie if she should go, and Annie tells her to—gives her permission to develop her relationship with Mitch. A bird thuds into the front door.

Looking back to the previous sequence, we find a further strengthening of the connection between Annie and Lydia and clarification of the significance of the birds (not an *explanation* of them). The bird that attacked Annie's door becomes associated with her isolation; earlier, while Lydia talked on the phone about her chickens' refusal to eat their feed, and Mitch and Melanie talked in the background, the only fragment of their conversation that was allowed to come through clearly was Melanie's question (indicating a painting) "Is that your father?" And as Melanie drove away, after her unsatisfactory, apparently final conversation with Mitch, he gazed up at birds massing on the telegraph wires. The implication is not that the birds attack people with broken relationships—nothing so schematized; any temptation to interpret the film along these lines is quickly shattered by the more generalized attacks (on schoolchildren and townspeople) that make up much of the central section of the film. But a link of some kind between isolation and the threat the birds constitute has clearly been established.

The next sequence gives us the important dialogue between Mitch and Melanie and the first mass attack by the birds. The setting chosen for the dialogue—sand dunes by the sea—and the action that introduces it—the couple clambering up the dunes in formal dress, Mitch carrying glasses and bottle—serve to emphasize the sense of precariousness in the relationship and in the very basis of the characters' lives: Melanie with her background of wild living and scandal, Mitch with his unsatisfactory home situation. With this precariousness of decor and situation intensified by our apprehension at the constant potential menace of bird attacks (the characters are out in the open again, unprotected) Melanie talks proudly of her job: she is studying semantics at Berkeley university and "helping a little Korean boy through school." Of Rome she says, "It was very easy to get lost there"; and so "I keep myself busy." It is the thinness of her life that one feels most—the sense that the "jobs" of which she speaks with pathetic complacency are feeble substitutes for any real sense of purpose or fulfilment; distractions more constructive than getting thrown into fountains in Rome, but distractions nonetheless. Then, with one of those swift transitions of which Hitchcock is such a master—the preceding frivolity of tone throwing into relief an intensity of feeling awkward and embarrassing in its abruptness—we pass from Melanie's aunt's myna bird to her relationship (or lack of it) with her mother. Gesture, stance, and intonation, the setting of sea and dunes, the incongruity of the characters' physical position, are employed with a marvelous precision. The effect of Melanie's revelations is to neutralize any lingering contempt we may feel for her triviality by showing us why she is like that—by making the triviality quite plainly a neurotic symptom over which she has little command; and to show us finally how superficial is her complacency, how easily shattered her confidence.

Their return to the children's party is watched by Lydia and Annie with similar expressions of anxiety, the developing relationship between Mitch and Melanie producing in both women the dread of aloneness and waste. Then immediately, the bird attack begins.

The destruction of the children's party by the birds crystallizes for us in a series of superbly realized images—the upsetting of cakes and cartons of fruit squash, and, particularly, the bursting of balloons—that awareness of fragility and insecurity that is the basis of the whole film. The scene ends with the tear-stained faces of two terrified children gazing anxiously up at the sky. That children are the victims of the attacks in these middle sequences is not mere sensationalism on Hitchcock's part. The children are completely innocent—there can be no "reason" for the birds to attack them—and they are, even more than the grown-ups, defenseless. The film derives its disturbing power from the absolute meaninglessness and unpredictability of the attacks, and only by having children as the victims can its underlying emotions of despair and terror be conveyed. To demand consistency and any form of divine or poetic justice from the attacks is to miss the point altogether.

The sequence depicting the attack of small birds down the chimney is the one point in the film where realization—inevitably, one feels—falls short of conception. The superimpositions are very obvious here, and the "attack" never looks like an attack—just a lot of frightened birds fluttering around. None of the characters involved receives even so much as a scratch (not surprising, as the vast majority of the birds are so obviously on separate strips of film). However, one sees why Hitchcock found the scene necessary. We have grown accustomed to the imposed

and impeccable neatness and order of Lydia's house. The heavy masculine decor shows us how she clings to the past, to the idea of her dead
husband, and the determinedly imposed order suggests the importance
the house and furniture have for her. Into this decor the birds irrupt:
there is no safety from them, no shelter or screen behind which one can
find security. When the attack is over, the ineffectual policeman questions the characters. Officials of the law are always ineffectual in Hitchcock: as representatives of a superficial, unnaturally imposed order they
are unable, or refuse, to see the abysses: compare sheriff Al Chambers'
dismissal of any suggestion of mystery in the Bates motel with the
present policeman's inane refusal to accept the fact of the attack. While
he talks to Mitch, Lydia stoops over the shattered crockery (smashed
when Mitch upset the table to use it to barricade the fireplace), and,
human beings forgotten, broods over her "things," a look of bewilderment and desolation on her face. And we see Melanie watching the older
woman, and are again aware of the resemblance between them. Melanie
stares at her as if wondering: the scene is the clearest possible visual
communication of the unspoken questions: "Has life any purpose? Has
this woman's life any purpose? Has *my* life any purpose?" Melanie
watches, while Lydia carefully, abstractedly straightens the portrait of
her dead husband.

In a work of art as organic as *The Birds* it is possible to pick on
almost anything as the "key" to the meaning; but it is perhaps permissible to attach a particular importance to the sequence of Lydia's visit to
Dan Fawcett's farm and the effect on her of what she sees there. First,
the truck passing over that wonderfully evocative and disturbing landscape: calm-seeming, yet ominous in its stillness; beautiful, yet somber
beneath the dullish sky; the farm open to the sky amid its range of fields,
the truck moving in long shot along the dusty road. Then Lydia's entry
into and exploration of the house ("Dan, are you there?"); her discovery
of the cup handles hanging uselessly from hooks on the kitchen dresser.
The image, given strong impact by a sudden track-in that emphasizes the
cup handles by reframing the shot and directly conveys to us Lydia's
shock of perception, links back to the previous image of her bent over
her own smashed teacups, thereby connecting Lydia with Fawcett. The
corridor (everything ominously silent), the bedroom; more wreckage and
disorder; the horrible-beautiful image of the dead gull caught in the
smashed window; the empty double bed; finally, in a series of relent-

lessly nearing shots, the mutilated body: we are given Lydia's experience directly, and we have sufficient knowledge of her now to appreciate its effect on her. The isolated man by the bed amid the wreckage of old, treasured furniture and bric-à-brac: Lydia's already precarious hold on life is cruelly undermined. We see her stagger, retching, speechless, back along the corridor, out past the bewildered farmhand; we see the truck travel rapidly back across the same still, ominous, beautiful landscape. From driver's seat position we see Mitch and Melanie together in the drive of the Brenner home as the truck sweeps up. They come to help the distraught woman as she clambers out, she looks at them, utters a terrible cry of despair, and pushes them violently aside.

The effect of the experience on Lydia calls to mind the effect on Mrs. Moore of her experience in the Marabar cave in E. M. Forster's *A Passage to India*. Hitchcock's image is more powerful and terrible than Forster's, it arises more naturally from its context and seems less "applied": one is never quite convinced that an echo could mean all that. And film—as used by Hitchcock—can convey the experience to the spectator far more directly than can Forster to the reader. If *The Birds* lacks, certainly, the density and complexity of characterization of Forster's novel, the comparison does not seem to me entirely disadvantageous to Hitchcock, for the Hitchcock of recent years is a more rigorous artist than Forster, quite free of those uncertainties of touch that Dr. Leavis has analyzed in Forster's novels, and what may at first seem a comparative thinness in Hitchcock's films appears rather, on further reflection, as a toughness and self-discipline, a strict reduction of material to essentials to give extreme clarity and force to the presentation. In fact, a Hitchcock film—and *The Birds* is a particularly good example of this—is more analogous to a poem than a novel: Hitchcock focuses the attention and perceptions of the spectator, controls his reactions, through the rhythms of editing and camera movement as a poet controls those of the reader through his verse rhythms; and his films derive their value from the intensity of their images—an intensity created and controlled very largely by context, by the total organization—rather than from the creation of "rounded" characters.

Lydia's situation is defined more explicitly for us in her dialogue with Melanie as she sits in bed drinking tea: defined not only in the dialogue itself, but in gesture, expression, and intonation. Before this, however, we have witnessed a new development in the relationship between Mitch and Melanie, a development touchingly conveyed in the tentative, tender kiss they exchange in the kitchen before Mitch goes to the Fawcett farm. Just the Hero kissing the Heroine, a weary Hollywood banality? Look again: as directed by Hitchcock, the moment conveys perfectly the beginning of sincerity in the characters, their acceptance of the human need for a relationship grounded in mutual respect and tenderness. It reveals the essentially positive bent of an undermining and ruthless film: in counterpoint to the breaking down of Lydia, the building up of a fertile relationship.

For it is precisely the dread of a solitary, sterile existence that terrifies Lydia. She is tormented not only by her immediate experience ("I keep seeing Dan's face") but by the loss of her husband, her sense of which the experience has abruptly intensified: "I wish I were a stronger person . . . I lost my husband four years ago . . . It's terrible how you depend on someone for strength." The emphasis is on the sense of valuelessness arising from a life lived without deep relationships. She has the teacup in her hand, a reminder, almost like a leitmotiv, of fragility and of her dependence since her husband's death on "things." She tells Melanie how she still gets up to get her husband's breakfast: "There's a good reason for getting out of bed . . . And then I remember . . ." She lives in a state of constant tension ("I wish I could relax—I wish I could sleep"). She feels her grasp on her children slipping, and again it is the loss of the father that is felt as responsible: "Frank . . . had the knack of entering into their world, becoming part of them. I wish I could be like that." Then suddenly: "Oh, I miss him!" It is a very basic reality that Hitchcock is presenting here. We are not to see Lydia as a neurotic woman: or, if neurotic, then made so recently by the frustration of certain basic human needs. Her fear of Melanie is not the outcome of an unhealthy involvement with her son, but of the dread of a life of loneliness and futility. The scene culminates in her cry, "But you see—I don't want to be left alone—I don't think I could bear to be left alone." It conveys positively a sense of the value of human relationships—marriage, family unity—and at the same time stresses their fragility: the fragility brought home to us and the characters by the birds. In the intimation we get of the close interdependence of the family and its resultant strength when the father was alive, we understand Mitch's individual strength. Yet the subtlety of the film, the delicacy of its feeling, lies in the way in which every point made is qualified by others, giving a touch of uncertainty to every action, every position, however simple it appears. We recall Mitch's conversation with Melanie on the dunes about their mothers. Melanie asked, "Do you know what a mother's love is?" and Mitch replied, "Yes, I think I do." His tone was so equivocal that she asked, "You mean it's worse?"; and his denial was hesitant, rather stiff, as if considering the possibility. Our sense of the value of relationships is qualified by the emphasis on the difficulties and complexities that they entail—the conflicting responsibilities that make it impossible that relationships be complete, that everyone be satisfied.

At the end of the scene in Lydia's bedroom, when Melanie has agreed to go to the school to fetch Cathy, we are given again the positive trend, the reaching out toward the formation of viable relationships, in Lydia's tentative acceptance of Melanie as she thanks her for the tea and calls her for the first time by her Christian name: a very simple point, but, in its unobtrusive naturalness, a beautiful depiction of the beginnings of trust. There is a similar, more equivocal but no less beautiful instance in *Marnie,* where Marnie uses Mark Rutland's Christian name for the first time.

The next two attacks—on the fleeing schoolchildren and on the townspeople—scarcely require elucidation; but they furnish some of Hitchcock's most brilliant and disturbing images. On the one hand the world of order and tranquillity: the school, with its association of education, of the growing and developing young, of the transmission of tradition and culture, hence of mankind's hopes; the small, easygoing little town realized for us earlier in the film through its general store with its associations of community life, friendliness, familiarity, security. And on the other hand the birds, and their arbitrary destructiveness. The image of the terrified children running down the hill as the great flock of crows whirrs up from behind the school, looming over it and seeming to darken the sky, and later images of disorder in the town—horses out of control pulling a cart that overturns, the unmanned firehouse twisting and squirting uselessly—bring home to us in more general terms than before the frailty and precariousness of ordered, meaningful existence. One might single out particularly the stunning aerial long shot of the town with its blazing center, with bird after bird hurtling down to attack from behind the camera: *we* are suddenly the birds, looking down on defenseless humanity; but we are also human beings, and the image gives us a vertiginous sense of our own vulnerability.

Between the two attacks comes the debate in the café, with the two extreme attitudes to the birds expressed by Mrs. Bundy, the ornithologist, who refuses to believe the attacks are happening, and the town drunk, who airily proclaims, with considerable pleasure and satisfaction, that "It's the end of the world." Both attitudes are over-simplified and equally complacent; but "It's the end of the world" and "It's all impossible" are both attitudes likely to be common among the film's less perceptive spectators, and we know how carefully Hitchcock keeps his audience in mind when he prepares his films. By making these extreme attitudes explicit and ridiculous, Hitchcock prevents us from maintaining them during the crucial last stretches of the film. This is important to his purposes, despite the fact that the "end of the world" theory is logically tenable: we are nevertheless not to simplify the complex pattern of uncertainties the film presents into an ornithological *On the Beach*. By making us reject simple attitudes to the birds, Hitchcock focuses our attention on the development of character, situation, and relationship, on the birds' *effect* rather than on the birds themselves, and on complex effects rather than simple effects.

It is after the second attack, back in the café, that we are placed (camerawise) in Melanie's position in order to be told that we have caused the bird attacks and that we are evil. The accusation is made by the hysterical mother, and we respond promptly (through Melanie) by slapping her face. The incident is remarkable, and not nearly as simple as it first appears. Certainly, it is a direct attack on the audience, and we find it difficult to look in the face the woman who stares straight at us with such intensity. If Melanie is guilty, then certainly we are all guilty, for she is no more "evil," and scarcely more complacent, than we are; and there is peculiar appropriateness in the accusation coming from the one character in the film who is entirely without complacency—she accepts the birds, terrified, as a terrible fact. Yet the accusation remains quite irrational and we are (Melanie is) right to reject it emphatically: Hitchcock is making us reject another over-simplified attitude: the birds have not been sent as a punishment for evil—they just *are*.

Yet there is another way in which we have provoked the attacks—as a cinema audience we have come demanding to be thrilled, perhaps shocked; demanding bloodshed and horror. We may recall Bruno Anthony remarking with severe distaste when the fairground attendant told him the public were flocking to see the murder spot, "I don't think that's very nice." When, a few minutes before the accusation, we were given our birds' eye view, placed in the birds' position far above the town, we would certainly have been disappointed if the birds had flown away without doing anything, even as we shuddered at the helplessness of humanity. This is not the first time Hitchcock has made us aware of the impurity of our feelings: not the first time we have been encouraged to reveal our impure feelings in order to have them chastised.

This whole central section of attacks and debate opens the film out further: the birds are there for everybody, they exist for all of us. But the discovery of Annie Hayworth's dead body reminds us that they have a special significance for those who are alone. The sequence also brings home to us afresh our helplessness against the birds, in Mitch's furious, impotent gesture at them with a stone: the birds cannot be fought, no aggressive action can be taken against them. The force of this moment derives from the fact that Mitch is the "hero" of the film, and (by the standards of Hitchcock's pre-*Marnie* heroes) unusually capable and stable, in control of most situations. The birds make the concept of "hero" untenable.

There follows the boarding up of the house, and we reach the last phase of the film, where its underlying concerns and emotions are communicated with the greatest intensity. The house becomes a cage, as previously car and phone box became cages: worse than a cage: a sunless box, in which the prisoners must come to terms with themselves and each other or finally succumb to the birds; and perhaps must die anyway.

If *The Birds* is about the Day of Judgment (another of Hitchcock's descriptions), then it is the value of life itself that is on trial. In this context, every gesture, every action, however trivial, becomes an object of closest scrutiny. Just after Cathy's questions and Mitch's admitted inability to answer them ("Why are they trying to kill people?" — "I wish I could say"), Lydia rises abruptly from the corner in which she is huddled. We watch her move into the foreground of the image, pick up a tray of cups and saucers, carry it out of the room, come back, resume her seat and her clenched, despairing attitude. Hitchcock shows us this in a single take in which nothing of any "importance" happens, and he shows us it deliberately and with emphasis, though it is an emphasis achieved quite naturally, entirely free from any pretentious ostentation; it can hardly be taken as a "bit of business" to fill in while we wait for the next attack. It links Lydia to crockery again, of course, to the sense of fragility; but more than this, it typifies for us all those small routine actions that make up our day-to-day existence, and, by putting these in the context of the bird attacks, setting them against the tension shared by characters and spectators, raises in us the fundamental questions: Has life any purpose, any meaning? Is there any sense in our carrying on a daily routine with the knowledge that death may come to any of us at any moment, and must come, one day, to us all? Has anything a value that justifies this continuation? And these are not questions to which the film proposes any glib or comforting answers. The significance of Lydia's action itself is left ambiguous: is she rousing herself from her sense of futility for a moment to perform a positive action—however slight?—or is she merely mechanically repeating a meaningless and pointless routine? The ambiguity remains because of Hitchcock's refusal to resolve it through any kind of directorial comment, the motionless camera simply recording it objectively; it ushers in a whole series of similarly unresolved ambiguities in the last stages of the film.

In the moments before the attack on the house, Lydia is sunk hopelessly into her sense of futility—her cave echo; it is Melanie who helps Cathy when the latter is sick, the mother seeming either unnoticing or indifferent. Then the attack begins, bringing the extraordinary shots of Melanie pressing herself back against the walls, against the sofa, upsetting the lamp shade, as if seeking to hide herself from some unendurable scrutiny. But the girl's movements have themselves an ambiguity: they reveal an intolerable anguish, but in their abandonment one senses something almost sensual, like a voluptuous surrender. She is roused from this only by the necessity of bandaging Mitch's torn and bleeding hands.

The attack dies down, mysteriously and arbitrarily, at the very moment when it seems that no available barricades will keep the birds out. We have the three successive shots of ceiling and upper wall slowly filled by the characters' heads—Mitch, Melanie, Lydia, in that order—rising up from the bottom of the screen, hesitant and fearful, straining to catch sounds in the sudden silence. The shots are angled and framed so that the ceiling seems to press down on them, so that the very instant of relief seems laden with a sense of doom. There follows exhausted sleep, from which Melanie is aroused by the sound of birds restlessly fluttering somewhere in the house.

Why does she go upstairs alone? The question was put to me by one of Hitchcock's detractors: the implied answer was that there *is* no reason, it is merely a pretext for staging some cheaply sensational thrills. Let us answer it first on its own level: Melanie tries to rouse Mitch to get him to go, but he is sleeping exhaustedly, his hands sore and ripped and swathed in bandages, so she decides to go herself and let him sleep. She doesn't know that she is going to be trapped in a roomful of birds— she has heard noises which suggest that one or two birds may be getting in somewhere, and she goes to check: if there is any danger, she will come back and report to Mitch. This is a perfectly adequate, rational explanation supplied quite clearly by what we see on the screen; it accounts sufficiently for Melanie's conscious motivation, and indeed combines with her competent handling of Cathy to suggest the strength (albeit tentative) that her experiences are revealing in her character, in contrast to her self-prostration during the attack.

However, I would insist that the film as a whole invites us to ask the question on more serious levels, and I put forward the following suggestions: on a level just below the conscious, Melanie retains the sense, despite all she has been through, that nothing very awful will happen to *her:* she retains, that is, a residuum of complacency which has yet to be beaten out of her. This accounts for one aspect of the sequence— Hitchcock's use of subjective camera technique to enforce audience identification as Melanie climbs the stairs. This is similar in manner to Lila's exploration of the Bates ménage, but not in effect: we dreaded Lila's entering the house, but we also wanted her to go in, to have our curiosity satisfied—we were still unsure what she would find. In *The Birds* we know what Melanie will find (she will find birds) and we are dragged up the stairs protestingly: we have already had so much bloodshed. We do, however, to some extent share her residual complacency: she is the heroine, a beautiful young girl, she will be rescued before anything very terrible happens to her: we must therefore share her disillusionment, her personal experience of the birds.

But the treatment of the attack itself reveals a deeper level of subconscious desire. Some of Melanie's gestures before the birds are gestures, again, of voluptuous surrender and prostration, her attempts to escape feeble. Her shallow sophistication and brittle smartness have been stripped away, revealing an apparent emptiness underneath; now she is giving herself to the birds as a terrible sort of fulfillment—almost like D. H. Lawrence's "Woman who rode away" accepting the sacrificial knife.

And her frantic, yet curiously half-hearted and ineffectual, beating at the
birds with her torch brings home to us again the inadequacy of our
defenses against all that the birds represent: the torch links with the car
horn Melanie honked frantically, which clearly didn't frighten the birds
away (the attack just happened to end then); with the phone box in
which she was trapped, its possibilities of protection inadequate and of
communication useless; with Mitch's powerful wooden barricades, which
the birds easily peck through. (Impossible? Indeed it is; which only goes
to prove that this isn't just a film about birds.) Underlying the fight
against the birds there is an inner conflict in Melanie between the tentative positive qualities that were emerging and a despairing desire for
annihilation.

And I must insist that whether or not Hitchcock consciously intended
these interpretations is quite immaterial: the only question worth discussing is whether they are sufficiently *there,* in the film, and I think they
are. There is nothing arbitrary about this: the interpretations I have
suggested become inevitable, it seems to me, if one sees *The Birds* in its
context in Hitchcock's oeuvre, and there is no need to suppose them
consciously worked out. If Hitchcock himself told me tomorrow that the
whole sequence was shot purely to give the audience "kicks," that the
only reason why Melanie doesn't escape is that if she did the "kicks"
would stop, I would merely quote him my favourite aphorism of D. H.
Lawrence: "Never trust the artist—trust the tale." The sequence, on
which Hitchcock spent so much time and trouble, contains, in its close-
up details of hands and face, gesture and expression, as the birds tear
and batter the collapsing girl, some of the most horrific and beautiful
images he has given us—some of the most desolate, conveying the
extremity of human anguish. The appeal is not sadistic: there is too
strong a sense of participation: we know it is *our* agony, *our* anguish
that we are witnessing, for the birds are waiting for all of us.

But the most beautiful and moving moment of all is reserved for
Melanie's regaining of consciousness downstairs. Mitch carries her down
unconscious, Lydia rousing herself to help: the girl's suffering awakening
in the woman her first positive reaction for some time, a sense of
compassion. Mitch gives Melanie brandy. She comes round not knowing
where she is, hands beating the air to ward off imaginary birds. Mitch
grips her hands, quiets them, their eyes meet, they exchange a long, deep
look, and slowly she relaxes and subsides, her eyes still fixed on his, her

face conveying a deep trust. The essential meaning of the film, it seems to me, is contained in that moment: that life is a matter of beating off the birds, and the only (partial) security is in the formation of deep relationships.

A bleak enough message; and in the last sequence of the film—the departure by car through the massed, waiting birds—the effect of bleakness is intensified by the uncertainties. For uncertainty is the keynote of the film: Hitchcock allows himself and us no easy comfort. Under this sense of judgment, of intense scrutiny, every action becomes ambiguous. The carrying of the lovebirds out to the car: is it a touching gesture (through the child) of continuing faith, despite all, in the goodness of nature and the possibility of order, or an absurd clinging to a sentimental view of life, a refusal *still* to face reality? The mother's cradling of Melanie in her arms and the shot of their interlocking hands: is it a gesture of acceptance (hence creative and fertile) or a new manifestation of maternal possessiveness? Melanie's broken condition: does it represent the possibility of development into true womanhood, or a final relapse into infantile dependence? All these questions are left open: if we demand a resolution of them we have missed the whole tone and temper of the film. We can say, at best, that there is a suggestion of a new depth, a new fertility in the relationships—Lydia has become the mother Melanie never had. The point about the ending is that the degree of optimism or pessimism it is felt to contain must depend on ourselves: what Hitchcock gives us is the questions.

In all of Hitchcock's last five films the very last shot has great importance as the culmination of the whole action, the whole thematic progress. The ambiguity of the last shot of *The Birds* is dictated by these preceding uncertainties: the birds are letting them through; the birds are massing for the next assault. This last shot represents a perfect balance of the sense of precariousness that runs through Hitchcock's work and the positive, therapeutic tendency that is an equally constant characteristic of it.

8

MARNIE

The general critical reception accorded to *Marnie* in Britain would appear quite staggeringly obtuse if one had not been well prepared for it by many precedents. However, as the notion that this film—one of Hitchcock's richest, most fully achieved and mature masterpieces—represents a falling-off, a proof of senility, or worse (he has become so cynical, apparently, about "audience gullibility" that he just doesn't bother any more) is widespread, it seems worth attempting to deal with the main lines of attack, removing certain false preconceptions as a preliminary to establishing what *Marnie* really is.

The following seem to be the main objections (in ascending order of intelligence):

1. The film is full of absurdly clumsy, lazy, crude devices, used with a blatant disregard for realism: hideous painted backdrop for Mrs. Edgar's street; ugly and obvious back-projection for Marnie's horse-riding (and, during the hunt, for Lil Mannering's); zoom lens for the final attempted theft; red flashes suffusing the screen every time Marnie has a "turn"; thunderstorms arriving coincidentally at climactic moments.

2. Connected with this technical naiveté, a psychological naiveté: Marnie's case is much too simple and schematized to be taken seriously, the single traumatic experience, as shown in the flashback, wouldn't affect her in these ways. Besides, there are actual inconsistencies, obviously due to mere carelessness: Marnie passes a red chair during the Rutland office robbery and doesn't react; she almost touches a scarlet magazine, actually laying the pistol on it, when taking Mark's key, again without reacting.

3. (Though most people don't take the film seriously enough to reach

this conclusion)—Marnie's "case" is much too extreme for the film to have any universal validity.

The first objection, as usually phrased, seems to me based on that conventional rule-making that is invariably detrimental to art, since it seeks to impose limitations on the artist's freedom. There is absolutely no valid reason why a film should be "realistic," why a director shouldn't use obviously painted sets, back-projection, zoom lens, etc., if the context justifies these things. The question is, then, not "should a serious director stoop to these?" but "Do they work?" Here we are clearly on more arguable ground; I can only state my case for believing that they do: the film would be weakened by their absence. Whether they were *consciously intended* to create certain effects I refuse—as usual—to discuss; though the very abundance and obtrusiveness of these devices makes it seem extraordinarily unlikely that Hitchcock merely "thought he could get away with it."

The backdrop of the ship needs to be considered as part of the set it dominates: the street in which Mrs. Edgar lives. Unbroken rows of tall ugly brick houses which give us a sense of imprisonment, claustrophobia, all possibility of freedom and openness shut out; at the end, the ship looming up ominously, as if blocking the exit. When we first see the image it is not precisely explicable, but it conveys admirably—if our responses are open, and free from preconceptions about "realism"—the intolerable constriction of Marnie's life. Only at the end, when the crucial role played by a sailor in the arresting of her development becomes clear, does the huge, blocking ship taken on a more precise symbolism. Perhaps something of the same effect—though it could scarcely have looked so ominous—could have been achieved with a real ship and a real street; but this would have sacrificed the most important aspect of all: the constrictedness of Marnie's life belongs essentially to the world of unreality, the trap she is caught in is irrational and her prison will be finally shattered by true memory: at the end, the storm over, the sky a clear blue (as it never has been behind the ship before), she and Mark drive away past the ship, turning off where we had not previously been aware of the existence of a road. (They have arrived, by the way, apparently at nightfall, and leave ten minutes later in broad daylight: surprising that none of our literal-minded critical friends has commented on this, unless I have missed it.) Far from being a fault, the false, painted set is a magnificent inspiration. I reject equally the notion that this and similar "artificial" devices are "ugly." Ugliness or beauty in a film is a matter of context: we cannot look at a shot as if it were a painting, to be judged for its intrinsic aesthetic beauty. The street set, seen in context and understood, is very beautiful.

The first specimen of offending back-projection immediately precedes our first view of the offending ship. We see Marnie achieving her release from her adopted personality (slinky brunette) in the freedom of horse-riding. But, because of the back-projection, she doesn't look released at all, though her face tells us that she *thinks* she is. And, of course, that is the point. The back-projection gives a dream-like quality to the ride, but no sense of genuine release. The effect is clinched by the cutting: from the riding we cut immediately to the taxi driving up the mother's street toward the ship: change of "vehicle" apart, it is presented as part of a single movement, a single state.

The use of zoom lens and red suffusions brings us to something more fundamental in Hitchcock's art. Let it be insisted that they are not desperate attempts to cover up inadequacies in Tippi Hedren's perfor-mance: they are much too clearly in line with the whole audience identi-fication trend in Hitchcock's development to be explained away like that. The acting in *Marnie* is flawless: at no point does one feel that a player has failed to give Hitchcock precisely what is needed in any given shot. The blame—if blame there is—is Hitchcock's, not the admirable Miss Hedren's. The red suffusions are—obviously—more than just blood symbolism. Because of her traumatic experience, the color red, seen either under conditions of great tension or in a way that directly evokes the experience itself (the *spreading* red ink on the blouse sleeve, the red blotches on the jockey's shirt), acts as a release mechanism for Marnie's suppressed tensions—the tensions that are with her, to some extent, continually. Its immediate effect is to provoke a sort of hysterical swoon, a panic reaction, as the terrifying, buried memory forces itself danger-ously near the surface of consciousness, which in turn produces a sense of unreality. Now, Hitchcock is not Preminger: he doesn't want merely to *show* us a woman caught in this condition, he wants to convey to us the feeling of the condition itself—wants us to experience it directly as Marnie experiences it, as far as that is possible. What better, simpler, more beautifully economical and direct way than by these red flashes that suffuse the whole screen, filling us, too, with a feeling of panic (we know no more than Marnie what they mean), conveying this sense of being plunged abruptly, arbitrarily, into unreality? Similarly with the zoom shots of the money. A director who wanted to *show* us Marnie at the moment when her compulsion to steal has been broken would use complex acting; Hitchcock wants us to *feel* her violent emotional condition, and the zoom shots, simple and crude as you please, offer much the most direct way of conveying this simultaneous attraction-repulsion.

As for the thunderstorm that accompanies and blends with the flashbacks, it is ridiculous to take it as coincidence, because the film doesn't work in the naturalistic manner to which such considerations are relevant. The stylized treatment of the storm (and the earlier one) forbids such an approach, as does the equally stylized use of the thunderclaps to punctuate the flashback and intensify certain of Marnie's shocks: the sailor's slamming of the door, for example, cutting the child off from her mother, coincides with a thunderclap in the flashback and also, apparently, with one in present time; the thunderclaps emphasize what was most significant to the child and what is most significant in memory. The use of storms to symbolize acute mental stress is so time-honored (and has such respectable past employers) that it has surely become convention more than cliché.

But the final justification for these devices is not in these individual arguments, but in the way in which they are absorbed into their context, the context of the entire film. In his most recent work, Hitchcock has achieved such absolute mastery of his medium that he can feel free to use anything, to *dare* anything. This bold, direct use of devices one would normally shudder at is perfectly fitting in a film where every idea unerringly finds its most fluent, most economical, most direct expression, from the opening track on the yellow bag to the final long shot of the car turning away as it passes the ship.

There are two possible answers to the accusation that a given film is psychologically naive: that it isn't, and that it wouldn't matter if it were. In the case of *Marnie* the truth lies in a combination of these two. Scarcely more here than in *Psycho* is Hitchcock offering us the detailed analysis of a clinical case; the essentials of Marnie's mental disorder and of the preliminaries to its cure are given us with great force and clarity, but we are not given a *detailed* study of her behavior, her symptoms, or the minor components of her neurosis. To demand this is to demand an entirely different film: Hitchcock uses, as usual, all he needs and no more, and the film would be in no way improved if it went into Marnie's case in more detail. On the other hand, the psychology, though simplified, is by no means as simple as one would gather from reading the various dismissive accounts of the film. It seems to be the common assumption that one incident in childhood has caused Marnie's condition and the recollection of that incident automatically cures her. A moment's reflection will make it clear that the remembering is but one stage in the cure. We watch successive stages in it throughout the film, of which the honeymoon and attempted suicide, the breakdown after the "free association" game, and the shooting of Forio are the most obvious; but the whole development of Marnie's relationship with Mark is movement toward cure. Nor are we given grounds for believing Marnie "cured" at the end of the film; a start has been made, but the hopefulness of the last shots is offset by the reminder, through the mother, of the difficulty of outgrowing habitual attitudes.

And Marnie's troubles do not stem entirely from one traumatic experience. The child we see in the flashback is already a very disturbed child who can't bear a man to touch her, the mother already a hysterical, neurotic woman, a prostitute so filled with disgust at her work that she frantically beats with both hands the sailor who is trying to soothe and comfort her little girl. We needn't ask whether Marnie, at that age, has actually witnessed intercourse: she knows from her mother's attitude that something horrible and disgusting goes on behind that door whenever she is shut out; she is terrified of the sailor—who is gentle and kind —touching her; and it is clear, I think, that the image she somewhere retains of the twisted legs and her mother crying out in pain will stand subconsciously for her conception of sexual intercourse in her subsequent life. Further, because of the sailor's relationship to her mother, in killing him she is symbolically killing her father (just as in beating the man for touching Marnie, the mother is beating the man who deserted her when she became pregnant, refusing to allow the father any part in the child). Then there is Marnie's whole implied upbringing to be considered, at the hands of a mother who has indoctrinated her (if it were needed!) with a belief in the filthiness of sex and the evilness of men, and who has also withheld all love from her. The girl is possessed by the mother's attitudes, in danger of being swallowed up in her mother as Norman Bates was in his. Her entire life is a sort of symbolic prostitution, working for wealthy men, gaining their confidence—and interest —by the deliberate use of her charm (and by her very reticence and modesty: we remember Strutt's description of her "pulling her skirt down over her knees as if they were a national treasure," a gesture we watch her perform later at Rutland's), than taking their money and disappearing. Her involvement with her mother is summed up perhaps in her insistent mis-remembering of the childhood experience: "I hit him —I hit him with a *stick.*" We have just seen her kill the sailor with an iron poker: it is the mother who, because of her "accident," habitually carries a stick. The point gains further overtones from the fact that the mother has just attacked Mark Rutland, beating him with her hands as she beat the sailor: her attitude and Marnie's, her guilt and Marnie's, are interchangeable.

The money, of course, has a further significance: it is Marnie's way both of taking and of trying to buy love. The child who can't get affection steals; and Marnie uses what she steals to try to buy affection from her mother. Neither woman can give affection where it would be natural to give it: the mother's maternal impulses are instinctively suppressed and withheld from the daughter who is a constant reminder of her guilt (not merely of prostitution—the guilt has many ramifications); she lavishes affection on another child. And Marnie's substitute object for her repressed sexual impulses is the horse Forio: "Oh, Forio, if you want to bite somebody, bite me!" The outline of a case history that Hitchcock gives us is perfectly satisfying psychologically: the more satisfying the more one follows the implications.

Hitchcock uses far more drastic simplifications, of course, to convey Marnie's symptoms. If he were offering a clinical study, they would be unpardonable. But he is offering—to anyone reasonably responsive— much more than that and the simplifications (those red suffusions again: Marnie's reactions to red, to the thunderstorms, to tapping, her recurring nightmares) constitute an artistically valid shorthand. Again, what seem to many faults are, properly regarded, shining virtues. With superb daring, Hitchcock sweeps aside all the distracting encumbrances of detailed psychological analysis—distracting that is, from the real theme of the film. It is by stylizing in this way that Hitchcock prevents the significance of his film from being limited to Marnie's "case."

As for the inconsistencies—the moments when Marnie *doesn't* respond to red—the two instances are quite distinct and must be considered separately. The instance of the chair in the office which we see Marnie pass twice during her robbing of the safe one would be inclined to pass over with a shrug—the objection is the merest naturalistic pedantry—did it not offer a very interesting example of how a great artists operates and raise a fundamental question. We shall not appreciate any work of art if we remain insensitive to the kind of realization it offers at any given point—if, instead of maintaining an open, sensitive, flexible response we set ourselves to deliberately working *against* it. In *Marnie* it is inherent in the "red" shorthand that it can be used, quite arbitrarily, as Hitchcock pleases, precisely because it is not a naturalistic device, as long as the film evokes the required response in the spectator; since the red chair is never connected visually with Marnie, we do not, if we are working *with* the film, respond to it as we do to the gladioli or the jockey's shirt. It is like the famous question of "How many children had Lady Macbeth?" At one point she has "given suck," at another Macbeth "has no children." Now, there are all kinds of possible explanations if we care to think of them: Lady Macbeth's child had died, Macbeth was her second husband, she was a parvenue ex-wet-nurse, etc. Similarly, explanations can be found in *Marnie* for the heroine's indifference to the offending chair (not the least convincing being that she has presumably seen it every day for some weeks and had plenty of chance to get used to it). But such explanations are irrelevant: neither play nor film operates in that way, and if we ask such questions we are simply failing to respond to the kind of realization that is being offered. Both Macbeth's childlessness and his wife's breastfeeding have clear dramatic relevance in their contexts; similarly, important use is made of that chair, but it is a use different from the use of other red objects elsewhere. One could quote in this connection Hitchcock's delightful response when asked why James Mason's supposed wife in *North by Northwest* comes in to ask her husband to receive guests who don't seem to exist: "I know nothing about it. I don't know the lady in question, I've never met her. I don't know why she came in then, or why she said that . . ."

Hitchcock uses the burglary sequence to convey to us, by the now familiar means of direct experience, the constant tension under which Marnie lives and the precariousness of her whole existence, which can hang on something as slight as a dropped shoe. We see her prepare to burgle the safe, leave the office door open, work the combination. Then the camera is set down for a long take in which we see her, in long shot, in the center of the screen, carry out the theft. On the right of the screen is the red chair, on the left an empty passageway. Then a cleaner appears round the corner at the end of the passageway and begins to mop, drawing nearer and nearer as Marnie, quite unaware of her, goes on lifting the money. The tension depends on several factors. We share Marnie's own tension, certainly—we become aware of the tight-rope precariousness that is her whole life. But our tension is greater than hers: we know the charwoman is there, she doesn't. Further, we want her to get away with it, and we are slightly ashamed of wanting this: stealing is wrong; more than that, stealing isn't going to help Marnie, who clearly needs psychological aid—getting away with it won't help her. It is scarcely too much to say that this tension between our emotional involvement in Marnie's wishes and our rational awareness that their fulfillment would do her nothing but harm is the basic suspense principle of the film. The tension is assisted by a characteristically daring use of sound (or lack of it). The soundtrack here is doubly subjective: we don't hear the slap of the cleaner's mop because Marnie, from inside the inner office, can't hear it; we hear only the slightest muffled sound, scarcely audible, of the heavy safe door closing, because that is all the cleaner (who, as we find out later, is very deaf) would hear. And counterpointed with all this, and intensifying it, is a color tension. The cleaner, far left, is dressed in a cerise smock; the scarlet chair occupies an almost exactly symmetrical position on the right of the screen, producing a jarring clash that acts on the eye as the other tensions on mind and ear.

And the red magazine? That is a very different matter. Marnie looks straight at it, lays the pistol on it; and her not reacting to it *at that moment in the action* is precisely the point. She has just shot Forio after the accident: an action of highly complex significance. First, there is the purely physical shock experience, the importance of which Hitchcock's realization of the accident emphasizes: seldom, surely, has physical sensation been so intensely conveyed in a film. There is the use of subjective time: the repeated tracks toward the wall, giving us a time monstrously prolonged, convey that agonizing nightmare-feeling of an interminable moment we get at times of extreme terror; then the camera positions and the rhythm of the cutting are conceived so as to convey the maximum physical impact. We remember Marnie's fear of death—her immediate association of the idea of death with herself—in that peculiarly revealing moment in the "free association" game; and here she, and the spectator, are brought face to face with the possibility of death in an unusually violent and, for Marnie, particularly appropriate form: a helpless, uncontrollable whirling toward destruction. But it is Forio who dies, Marnie who insists (from any rational point of view unnecessarily) on killing him herself. The shooting is, clearly (though we don't know it at the time), a reenactment of the killing of the sailor, a reliving without remembering of the traumatic experience: the death of the horse is linked with the end of the memory later by Marnie's "There—there now." And there is another point: the love Marnie lavishes on Forio has been a substitute for sexual fulfilment; the shooting of the horse occurs very shortly after the first obviously hopeful signs of her being capable of achieving a valid relationship with a man. Coming straight from the shooting, in a trance-like state of shock, Marnie no longer responds to red. Her tensions are partially resolved; she has reached a stage beyond that where they require a simple stimulus to secure their release in panic reactions. It is immediately afterward, it will be remembered, that Marnie finds herself unable to steal: the obsessive-compulsive behavior is breaking down, because the tensions that necessitated it are disintegrating. She is ready for the final stage in the preliminaries to cure: the domination of the past through memory.

Before I leave the red suffusions, there is one more point to note about them, which is that they are used not only as a convenient shorthand, but structurally. They are not random, but form a clear progress. Each one takes us a step nearer in the reality of the traumatic experience, and Marnie a step deeper in her descent into memory. First, her reaction to the red gladioli associates her tensions—consequently her compulsive behavior—with her mother; and with her mother's relationship with the child Jessie. The second red suffusion occurs during the first dream, in the mother's house, bringing together a number of other associations: the tapping (associated at the end of the scene with the mother's stick, hence with the "accident"), the sensation of cold, etc. The fourth suffusion associates Marnie's tensions with thunderstorms (in Mark's office), the remaining component of the memory. The most obvious progression is formed by the third, fifth, and sixth suffusions: the spreading red ink on the white sleeve, the scarlet blotches on the jockey's shirt, the scarlet hunting jacket (given a disturbing glare by the lighting), which lead naturally to the presentation of the memory itself, stylized and subjective, of the bloodstained sailor's shirt.

As for that third objection (that Marnie's "case" is too extreme to have universal validity), I seem to have invented it myself, since I cannot recall encountering it anywhere, but it seems worth answering. I have already suggested a partial answer: we are not concerned with Marnie's case simply as a case. Hitchcock gives us here, in fact, a sort of quintessence of neuroticism rather than a clinical case history, and if Marnie is extreme, she represents an extreme of something relevant to us all: the grip of the past on the present. If few of us are Marnies, there is something of Marnie in all of us. We are all to some extent dominated by the past, our present psychological liberty limited and interfered with by unremembered and unassimilated past experiences. Even Mark Rutland, who, as created in the film, is as exceptionally free of the past as Marnie is exceptionally gripped by it, is led to recognize motivations behind his behavior of which he was not entirely aware. Nonetheless, this balancing of one extreme by another is one way in which Hitchcock universalizes his theme, and one must not allow oneself to be prevented, by the fact that the film is so firmly and deliberately centered on the evolution of Marnie herself, from giving due attention to the character of Mark and the positive values he embodies. Indeed he represents a new stage in the development of Hitchcock's heroes: not only is he unusually free of inner compulsions and of his own past life, he sees clearly and accepts the fact of the inextricability of good and evil—the fact that every moral action carries within it its inextricably interwoven thread of immorality—that we have seen as one of the essential components of Hitchcock's moral sense.

Another way in which *Marnie* achieves universal significance is through the reminder—hardly necessary if we are familiar with Hitchcock's past work, but clearly if simply realized in the film and necessary to its completeness—that anyone, given the circumstances, could be Marnie. Consider the ending: Marnie, the traumatic experience remembered, comes out of her mother's house with Mark. The storm is over, it is broad daylight. A gang of children is playing beside the step. They interrupt their game to look at the haggard woman in the riding suit: shot of them gazing up at Marnie, of Marnie returning their gaze. We remember the Marnie of the flashback, a child of about this age, caught in an experience she had done nothing to bring about (the fact that her panic precipitates the killing can hardly be held to her blame) and over which—and its consequences for herself—she could exercise no control. As Marnie and Mark drive away, the children resume their play, a ritualistic game with a chant we heard when we saw Marnie first arrive at the house: "Mother, mother, I am ill/ Send for the doctor over the hill . . ."

Retrospectively, we can see the point also made through Jessie, the little girl Mrs. Edgar looks after, and on whom she lavishes the affection she cannot give Marnie. The use of Jessie is quite complex. She seems at first merely to be there to provoke Marnie's jealousy: a jealousy childish, certainly, but rendered with extreme poignance. One instance, moving in itself, but more moving in the context of the whole, since it is one of the unifying links used to establish the film's essential progression: Marnie has just given her mother the fur wrap, draping it tenderly round her neck. Mrs. Edgar calls Jessie to have her hair brushed, and removes the wrap, laying it aside. Marnie kneels beside her mother, placing her own head in the position necessary for her hair to be brushed. Mrs. Edgar moves her away, saying, "Marnie, mind my leg." Jessie, with a triumphant glance at Marnie, sits on the edge of the chair, pressed right up against the aching leg, and turns to Mrs. Edgar, who begins to brush her hair, which is roughly the same color and length as Marnie's. Close-up of Marnie watching with sad eyes, then subjective shot from her viewpoint. The camera tracks in on the hair and the brush, which moves over it with such tenderness. It is a beautiful example of Hitchcock's ability to make the spectator share, hence understand, a character's feelings. At the end of the film, after her recalling of the past, Marnie kneels again in the same position beside her mother's chair. Close-up of Mrs. Edgar's hand reaching out to touch her daughter's hair. Then, instead, she moves restlessly: "Marnie, you're achin' my leg." Marnie gets up, resigned. Mark Rutland takes her, and strokes and tidies and smoothes her hair with his hands, saying, "There, that's better," and Marnie accepts the action. The moment—so unobtrusive and unforced—is perhaps (more even than the flashback) the climax of the film: it expresses, with that simplicity which is the prerogative of genius at the height of its powers, the transference toward which the whole film has been progressing.

But Jessie is also used to parallel Marnie. We see her first through Marnie's eyes, and therefore share Marnie's reaction to her; but Marnie's treatment of her is too unkind, too neurotic, and we soon dissociate ourselves from it and see the child as essentially vulnerable and pathetic, fatherless, left all day by her mother, quite at the mercy of an obviously neurotic old woman who pampers her extravagantly and (no doubt) fills her head with nonsense about the bestiality of men, and a neurotic young woman who is irrationally beastly to her. The child's likeness to Marnie both in situation and appearance (Mrs. Edgar is reminded of Marnie's hair when she was little) is emphasized, and we see the vulnerable child and the woman who has never been able to grow up as interchangeable: Jessie could be Marnie—any of us could be Marnie.

The theme of *Marnie* is universalized partly through Lil, Mark's sister-in-law. She is presented throughout as a contrast to Marnie, in personality and general orientation as much as in appearance. Hitchcock gives us through her a marvelous and touching picture of female sexuality—she *exudes* it in all her scenes with Mark—to set against (and set off) Marnie's frigidity. Yet her behavior is in some ways curiously like Marnie's: her lying (about her wrist), eavesdropping, prying into others' private papers, underhand destructiveness (inviting Strutt to the party), parallel Marnie's criminal activities. We saw in *Psycho* how the compulsive behavior of a psychotic was made relevant to us all by its parallel in the compulsive behavior of a "normal" person; similarly in *Marnie*, the "normal" Lil acts in a way that borders on the compulsive, providing an extension into normality of Marnie's neuroticism.

A final means whereby Hitchcock universalizes *Marnie's* significance: almost exactly halfway through the film, during the honeymoon cruise, Mark tells Marnie about a beautiful jungle flower. When you get close to it, you find that its intricate pattern is composed of thousands of tiny insects, who have adopted this formation as protective camouflage against birds. The immediate application of this to Marnie herself is obvious enough: she can only survive by preserving a carefully cultivated, artificial exterior personality; this shattered, she would be in danger of disintegrating into fragments and of becoming a prey to "the birds." But by expressing it in this parabolic form at this central point in the film where Marnie's "artificial" personality is endangered by the relationship forced on her by Mark, Hitchcock gives the idea far wider extension: the whole *Vertigo-Psycho* theme of the relationship between appearance and reality is suddenly crystallized in a single image, an image that epitomizes the basic Hitchcock assumption (leading theme of *The Birds* itself) of the precariousness of order, the glimpse of the underlying chaos when that order is disturbed.

In *Marnie*, in fact, most of the concerns underlying Hitchcock's recent films become fused. Most obvious are the links with *Psycho*. There is the mother/child relationship, bringing with it the theme of the swallowing up of one personality by another: Marnie is in danger of becoming her mother—in all essentials—as Norman became Mrs. Bates. In both cases this involvement arises from a mutual guilt, which in *Marnie* becomes an especially complex entanglement, both mother and child sharing in the killing, each provoking the other's reactions. Marnie herself is a curable Norman Bates; or a combination of Norman and Marion Crane. With this comes the characteristic Hitchcockian preoccupation with the contrast between seeming and being, the public mask and the private truth, appearance and reality. The film contains a number of striking (whether intentional or not) reminiscences of *Psycho:* Marnie's mother lurching downstairs with her stick immediately evokes—in stance, attitude, rigidity of movement—Mrs. Bates; Mrs. Edgar's attitude to men is Mrs. Bates' attitude to girls; her attack on Mark, beating him with raised fists, reminds us of Mrs. Bates' knife attacks; at the end of the film, when Marnie and Mark leave, lighting and makeup give Mrs. Edgar's face a corpse-like appearance—she seems almost an embalmed body, a living death.

But there is a less obvious link to a previous film, that can be put like this: had Hitchcock elected to tell *Marnie* from the point of view of Mark Rutland, we would have something strikingly resembling (if significantly different from) *Vertigo*. Look at the film from this point of view and the triangle Mark-Marnie-Lil closely resembles in essentials the triangle Scottie-Madeleine-Midge. Marnie first intrigues, then fascinates Mark because of her inscrutability and mysteriousness, her very abnormality. Scottie falls in love with Madeleine because she is remote, dreamlike, inaccessible; and in one of the crucial sequences of *Marnie*, Marnie rounds on Mark with "Talk about dream worlds! You've got a pathological fix on a woman who's not only a criminal but who screams if you come near her." Like Scottie, Mark rejects a known reality for this "dream world." Lil's ineffectual struggle to win him back reminds us of Midge's parody portrait. And as in *Vertigo* our reactions are complicated by a certain sympathy for the rejected woman. Lil is at once more ruthless and less mature than Midge; yet the moment when she watches Marnie and Mark drive away after the wedding has something of the force of Midge's final exit down the corridor: a subjective shot puts us, for a matter of seconds, in Lil's place, we watch the car disappearing down the drive. Then the camera rests unbrokenly on her face as Uncle

Bob goes on and on with his grumbling about Mark's recklessness with money, and we see that the car was bearing Lil's life away with it.

But such parallels cannot be pressed too far: ultimately, it is the differences between the resemblances that are important. If Mark is Scottie, then he is Scottie without the vertigo: a Scottie become mature, responsible, and aware. Perhaps the most striking thing about *Marnie* is this new development in the Hitchcock hero, for of all Hitchcock's male protagonists, Mark is the one most in charge of situations, most completely master of himself and his environment, most decisive and active and purposive. In a sense, he is the reverse of Scottie: where Scottie struggled to re-create the dream of Madeleine—the illusory Idea—Mark struggles to destroy the unreal shell of Marnie—the protective exterior —in order to release the real woman imprisoned within it.

His capability is insisted on as specifically a freedom from the trammels of the past, embodied particularly in his attitude to Stella, his dead wife. When the branch shatters the display cabinet in his office and Marnie solicitously picks up a damaged vase from Stella's pre-Columbian collection, he takes it from her and casually smashes it, saying, "Well, we've all got to go sometime." In this attitude to the ancient vase he is rejecting more than domination by the memory of his dead wife: he is symbolically rejecting the whole grip of past on present. And later, at the party, he has no hesitation in allowing people to think he knew Marnie—suspiciously—for several years before their marriage. Lil, startled, begins, "Before Stell . . . ?" and Mark cuts in with an offhand, "Yes, didn't you know?" Lil's suspicions worry Marnie: "Lil thought . . ."; but Mark merely remarks, "I don't give one infinitesimal dime what Lil thought or thinks." It is this freedom from the past (combined with this refusal to be limited by "what people think") that makes him peculiarly able to help Marnie. The character carries, in the context of the film and of Hitchcock's work as a whole, great moral force. He embodies a powerful and mature life quality that is set against Marnie's helpless readiness to let the past swallow her: that corpse-like face of the mother represents the spiritual death from which Marnie has been saved.

Given this vitality, it is fitting that Mark should also embody a clear-eyed acceptance of the inseparability of good and evil in such a complex world. In answer to Marnie's "Talk about dream worlds . . . ," he is able to reply, with a calm accepting smile, "Well, I didn't say I was perfect." It is partly this acceptance of necessary moral imperfection that gives him his maturity—seen as a willingness to accept responsibilities and follow them through whatever this entails. The morality of the film is, in an unobtrusive way, very unconventional and subversive, arising from the assumption that a "pure" morality is impotent and useless, that often the only true morality is *conventionally* immoral. Hence Mark *forces* Marnie to marry him, using quite unfair and unscrupulous means: it is the only way he can help her. Not that he is acting altruistically, merely for her good: he is quite clear on the boat in referring to himself as a "sexual blackmailer"—"*Some other* sexual blackmailer would have got his hands on you." Equally clear, however, is his distinction between himself and other potential "blackmailers": his description makes us think of the lecherous but conventionally moral—indeed, self-righteous —Strutt, and an essential difference is that Mark is aware of and accepts the impurity of his motivation.

The complexity of the values embodied in Mark—of our attitude to him—seems hardly to have been noticed, but its reality is perhaps attested by the directly contradictory reactions the character provokes. Different people have said to me that Mark is (a) incredible because such a saint and (b) unacceptable because morally so vicious. Since he embodies—so actively and energetically—the underlying moral assumptions of the later Hitchcock, it is worth considering his position in some detail.

When he forces Marnie to marry him he is acting neither simply for her nor simply for himself. If he let her go he would be (as he tells her in the café) "criminally and morally responsible" for her actions and for what became of her. If she were caught she would go to prison: we must remember that he has not yet fathomed the depth of her psychological disturbance: if she has not exactly responded to his kisses, she has managed not to recoil from them. But it is equally clear that he forces her into marriage because he loves her and wants her. He is motivated, in other words, not so much by a desire that she be helped, as by a desire that *he* should help her: he wants her cure to develop out of their relationship. And his desire for her, it is clear, is aroused partly by the very fact that she needs help: his love for her is not entirely distinct from desire to possess, control, even—Pygmalion- or Scottie-like—create. It is his intellectual interests, zoology and psychology, instinctual behavior, that first attracted him to Marnie: she is both an interesting "case" and a potentially dangerous animal. This latter comparison is developed visually as well as in the dialogue (for example, during Mark's disclosure in the car that he loves her: "You think I'm some kind of animal you've trapped"—"That's right, you are"); as they are about to leave the roadside café Mark watches her as he would watch a dangerous animal; on the boat, Marnie cowers from him against the sofa arm, and we are irresistibly reminded of a dangerous yet terrified animal cowering from its tamer; later, when she "gets herself up like a cat burglar," the camera restlessly follows her movements as she paces the bedroom like a caged animal, conveying her sense of constriction and her nervous restlessness to the audience. With all her repressions, she represents something more vital, potentially more alive, than the Rutland environment.

Marnie makes Mark realize the nature of his attraction to her in the car when he makes his "proposal." Obeying the dictates of "acceptable" morality would make him powerless to help her. It is only by following through his basic instinctive drives that anything can be achieved, and those drives, necessarily impure in themselves, demand morally impure methods of fulfillment. The implied "doctrine" (if it can be called that) is of course very dangerous, and the dangers are not minimized by the film: the emphasis given to the attempted suicide and Mark's panic-stricken searching of the ship is but the most obvious example.

The attempted suicide is provoked by Mark when, faced with Marnie's dread of sex, he promises not to sleep with her and then a few nights later breaks that promise. There is no more devastatingly beautiful scene in the whole of Hitchcock, and the beauty arises not merely from the fluency of expression but from the awareness of moral complexity that underlies it. Mark, who has been drinking heavily (to weaken the grip of his superego?), desperate from frustrated desire—which is both desire *for* Marnie and desire to help her—follows her into the bedroom. She asks him to leave if he doesn't want to go to bed; he replies that he "very much wants to go to bed." She understands, cries out "No!" in panic, and he rips off her nightdress. The sequence of shots is then as follows: 1) Marnie's bare feet and legs. 2) Her head and bare shoulders. Mark says, "Sorry, Marnie." 3) Both of them. He removes his dressing gown, wraps it round her. She stands stiffly, in a sort of tense, rigid resignation. He kisses her. 4) Overhead shot of the kiss. His hands stroke her tenderly. 5) Low-angle shot. We see his lips moving over her unmoving, expressionless face, her lips making no response whatever. She is like a statue. His protective gestures—the dressing gown, his stroking hands, his tenderness—tenderness inseparable from sexual passion—

combines with her hopeless, unresponsive immobility to give us that sense of a longing for the unattainable that is the essence of *Vertigo*; the angles—overhead shot to suggest protectiveness and solicitude, low-angle to reveal in detail the tenderness of the man's touch—add to the desolating sense of his helplessness, his inability to reach her. 6) Close-up, Marnie's face. She sinks down, the camera following her, peering into her eyes with their terrible, unfathomable emptiness, like the eyes at the beginning of Vertigo. 7) Close-up, Mark's face, huge and ominous, shadowed, the eyes seeming to bore into her. We share simultaneously his pity and desire and her terror, we see how in him desire for her and desire for power *over* her are not clearly distinguished. 8) Close-up, Marnie again. Then the camera pans round across the bedroom, coming to rest on a porthole. A sexual symbol, certainly, which conveys the sexual act; but more than that: for beyond the porthole is the sea, empty, desolate, gray, and the shot also completes our emotional response to the whole scene. The complexity here is both moral and emotional, conveying to the spectator a sense at once of the beauty and tragic pathos of human relationships. The scene offers one of the purest treatments of sexual intercourse the cinema has given us: pure in its feeling for sexual tenderness. Yet what we see is virtually a rape. To the man it is an expression of tenderness, solicitude, responsibility; to the woman, an experience so desolating that after it she attempts suicide. Our response depends on our being made to share the responses of both characters at once.

Mark's treatment of Strutt constitutes one of the clearest moral statements in Hitchcock. In an impure world, he has no hesitation in resorting to the most impure means—blackmail—to defeat the conventionally pure Strutt. He is quite clear about this—and Hitchcock makes it quite clear where, as between Mark and Strutt, the moral superiority lies. What gives Mark this right? Simply that he is acting for life, against the deadening self-righteousness of conventional morality; his right derives from the rightness of his instinct, which is basically sexual instinct. For if evil in Hitchcock's late work (*Psycho*) derives primarily from perverted sexuality, so good has its root in true sexuality and the true flow of sympathy that stems from it. Only the essential validity of Mark's feeling for Marnie—feeling not altruistic, not "pure," because not distinct from power urge, but rooted in his sexuality—justifies his actions. If *Psycho* was a mainly negative statement, its magnificent fearlessness and robustness implied a strong underlying positive; and that positive finds its expression, quite unequivocally, in *Marnie*. Mrs. Edgar, when she attacks Mark, may remind us of Mrs. Bates with her knife, but Mrs. Bates was irresistible, whereas Mrs. Edgar is easily overpowered by a man who embodies qualities which have no equivalent in *Psycho*.

It is Mark's self-awareness and his acceptance of necessary moral impurity, that makes him able to deal with the business world effectively (he has put the firm of Rutland back on its feet). That business world is superbly rendered in the film, through four clearly differentiated and evaluated characters: Mr. Strutt, Mr. Ward, the man who approaches Marnie at the racetrack, and Uncle Bob. Ward's absent-mindedness is more than a necessary plot maneuver, and a little more than a manifestation of that balanced, ironic Hitchcockian humor that has its contribution to make to the overall tone of *Marnie*; it suggests the inorganic nature of the man's life, the failure of "business" to engage the human being caught up in its machinery. The man at the racetrack, with his air of furtive indecency and his inability to meet Mark's eyes, suggests a whole sordid world of petty intrigue, financial and sexual. And if the business world is presented slightly more sympathetically in Uncle Bob —who is after all a Rutland, with something of the more humane culture the Rutlands represent—his financial preoccupation, expressing itself in a rigidity of stance, a hardening of the mouth, is morally placed by its juxtaposition with Lil's emotional preoccupation, her sense of loss as Mark and Marnie drive away.

But the Rutland culture itself is by no means endorsed by the film. Mark's father, and the environment in which we see him—his home, his furniture, his estate, his stables—represent a true gentility, a mellowness, that shows up the world of the Strutts for the raw, inhuman thing it is; yet Hitchcock emphasizes the hermetic aspect of this world, and its air of stagnation, and eventually, in the fox hunt, the unthinking brutality with which it can associate itself (the hunters, beautiful in long shot, made to look stupid and trivial by the suddenly cut-in back-projection shot of Lil bouncing complacently up and down on horseback). The sense of abrupt alienation Marnie feels on seeing and hearing the insensitive laughter of the hunters as they watch the fox torn to pieces is marvelously communicated to the audience: communicated, as usual in this film, with such economy and directness: this is not mere anti-fox-hunting propaganda, but a sudden revelation of the limitations of what has hitherto seemed a generally attractive world, limitations of sensibility that go with the sense of stagnation. The point—the necessary linking up of our diverse responses—is made through Marnie's denunciation of Lil after the accident: "Are you still in the mood for killing?" The reference is plainly to much more than the death of the fox: one thinks at once of Lil's compulsive destructiveness in inviting Strutt to the party. Again, the comparison of Marnie at several points in the film to a wild animal makes us connect her at once with the fox, and the callousness of the hunters links with Strutt's self-righteous vindictiveness: his word "victimized" draws together a number of emotional threads. The Rutland world is without real vitality or flexibility, the father's responses limited and obvious. His remarks on traveling (when Mark and Marnie return from their honeymoon) sum up the enclosedness of his existence. The way of life the Rutland home represents is "placed" by Mark himself: by his flexibility of response, his alertness, his decisiveness and vitality, his range of interests.

But, crucially important though Mark is, both in relation to this film and to Hitchcock's whole development, it is Marnie's film, and in her Hitchcock gives us the most definitive statement so far of that "therapy" theme we have seen running through all his work. Every sequence of *Marnie* is constructed as a necessary stage in the breaking down of Marnie's defensive barriers, of all that prevents her being fully alive. Hitchcock emphasizes her rootlessness. Consider the opening of the film: we are shown first a yellow bag, which the camera follows in a tracking shot. The camera slows down, and the bag is given a context: a woman with long, black-dyed hair in a gray suit and high heels, walking stiffly and in a straight line. Then the camera stops altogether, and she in turn is given a context: a deserted station platform, empty trains, silence, no life anywhere. It is in this way that we see Marnie for the first time, and the image is immediately disturbingly evocative. The color assists this effect strongly: the yellow bag looks strikingly incongruous, adding to our sense of instability; apart from it, everything—platform, trains, station roofs, gasometer—is gray or gray-blue, steely and cold. Marnie is continually shown against or associated with these colors throughout the film: they are the colors of her mother's house, where all the rooms have gray or blue-gray wallpapers; of the ship at the end of the mother's street; of the office interiors that epitomize the business world; of the washroom and the cell-like lavatory in which she waits before the theft;

of other stations; of the exteriors of the ship on which Mark and Marnie spend their honeymoon; of stormy skies, and of the sea itself, whose desolation contrasts so movingly with the enclosed, flower-laden luxury of the cabin, the reality and the pretense of Marnie's life. The incongruous yellow becomes important later in the film, where it is frequently associated with the Rutland home: Mark's father's yellow waistcoast, his yellow cake (a foolish, trivial example? Look at the visual emphasis it gets, at its placing in the composition), the yellow chrysanthemums in the hall, yellow roses in Marnie's room, yellow-gold lampshades, etc. In that crucial scene where Mark sleeps with (or rapes?) Marnie, he wears yellow pajamas and yellow dressing gown—the dressing gown in which he encloses her as he lowers her to the bed (their cabin has yellow and grayish decor). Marnie herself wears yellow (but a pallid yellow) in the scene where Mark brings Forio to her, the moment that brings her for the first time close to him (look at their exchanged glances) if only in gratitude. In the Rutland house the yellow is always the focal point of the composition, in which the color range suggests natural surroundings, with a hint of the autumnal: browns, dark greens, occasional dull reds.

Marnie is continually traveling, by train, car, taxi, ship, on horseback, moving from one place to another but getting nowhere—a point that the dream-like quality given by the back-projection to the horse-riding sequence epitomizes. The Rutland world, on the other hand, is static, even stagnant: old Mr. Rutland never travels, it is "a nasty business." The two extremes throw into relief the movements of Mark, every one of which has a purpose and precipitates a new development; whereas Marnie's true progress is only incidentally related to her movements from place to place.

Though identification patterns in *Marnie* are more complex than in *Psycho* or the first half of *Vertigo*, it is broadly true that we are made to share Marnie's tensions throughout the film. Suspense is used always to convey the constant strain under which she lives, so that the extreme points of her tension are the extreme points of ours. We share, too, then, her first moment of genuine relaxation, when Mark brings her Forio; above all, we share her sense of release, at the image of the blood-soaked shirt that fills the whole screen, fulfilling and hence exorcising the intimations of unknown horror given by the red suffusions. But our suspense is not the simple thing it may at first appear: our tension derives from an unresolved contradiction within us: we want her to get away with things, yet we want her to be cured; we are curious to know what the red flashes mean, yet we dread finding out; we want to know the truth, and want to suppress it. All of this corresponds to the tensions in Marnie herself. The urge toward cure is there from the start. We see it in the beautiful image of release that first shows us Marnie's face: she is washing her assumed personality (literally) out of her hair. The release is partial and momentary, but clearly pleasurable: it epitomizes Marnie's need to find herself.

The constant general tension in which she lives—it is an existence from which all possibility of happiness or peace of mind is banished, a life of unrelieved precariousness—crystallizes into detail at a few key moments. We have, at the racetrack, the dialogue between Marnie and Mark about belief: dialogue casual and unconcerned, then plunging abruptly into intensity at a word that carries unexpected associations, builds up sudden emotional pressures: like the dialogue on the sand dunes in *The Birds*. Marnie (it is just after she has been recognized as "Peggy Nicholson," and has reacted with shock to the jockey's red-blotched shirt) says she doesn't believe in luck. Mark asks her what she *does* believe in. She replies, with a sudden intensity and bitterness, "Nothing," and the meaninglessness of her life as it is is brought home to us. It is significant, perhaps, in view of Hitchcock's supposed Catholic outlook, that what the ensuing remarks suggest she should believe in is relationships, not God.

It seems natural to link this with another moment where a similar particularizing of Marnie's tension occurs: the free association game. The scene is a superb example of Hitchcock's sureness of grasp, every point rendered with an exactness that by no means precludes complexity of attitude. We are not asked to take Mark as a profound psychologist; neither is he stupid. There is nothing intrinsically ridiculous in his reading psychological textbooks in order to explore his wife's condition more fully. Nor are we asked to believe that "Sexual Aberrations of the Criminal Female" gives him all—or any—of the answers. The whole point of the free association game is that it is Marnie's idea in the first place, and not only Marnie who initiates it, but Marnie who insists on prolonging it. All Mark has done is suggest she read some books and ask about her recurring dream. Certainly he wants to help her—wants to play amateur psychologist—but it is Marnie who insists on being helped. There is nothing abrupt or surprising about this. We have seen frequently in the film the possibility of a cure for Marnie. She is completely passive in Mark's arms, but at least she gives herself to them; in the beautiful sequence of three shots that closes Marnie's first visit to the Rutland home—the walk in long shot across to the table; the couple, still in long shot, moving among the stalls; the close-up of the kiss—we are made to feel the possibility for Marnie of integration into a balanced, tranquil existence; the cut straight from her troubled look as she turns away from Mark to the scene of the theft tells us that the crime, as committed, is an attempted flight from Mark—she feels her neurotic condition threatened by him. In the car, before he "proposes," he, and we, accept her statement that she "likes" him as perhaps more truthful than she knows. When she attempts suicide, it is in the ship's swimming pool, not the sea: though the attempt is genuine enough, she is careful to preserve the *possibility* of being rescued. These intimations of a desire to be helped crystallize in the "free association" scene.

The sequence opens with Marnie's dream, presenting the memory with greater immediacy and fidelity than hitherto. We see Marnie lying in a bed we haven't seen before, a cheap bed in a roughly furnished room, against a harshly blue pillow with "Aloha" painted across it. The image fills us at once with unease because of its inexplicability: we don't know that what we see is a dream, nor do we know that this is the bed Marnie slept in as a child. What we see is the grown woman: a beautifully simple and direct depiction of the past's grip on the present. A hand taps on a window behind the bed head; Marnie moans and tosses; the camera pans to the right and we pass from the childhood decor to the decor of Marnie's bedroom in the Rutland house (it was once Stella's, as the feminine decor and empty display cabinets have previously told us). Mark is now knocking on the door. He comes in, half arouses Marnie, who cringes away in terror: we get a subjective shot of his face, ominously dominating, very like the close-up of him as he overpowered her in the honeymoon sequence, his eyes boring into her. Then Lil comes in and succeeds in waking and calming her. After she goes, the idea of suicide is touched on (through the sleeping pills: "The world is full of alternatives"), then Mark begins to ask about the dream. Marnie, almost caught off her guard, stops herself, looks at him, says, "You Freud—me Jane?" We see Mark in his chair: the low angle makes him look powerful, potentially dominating, but his attitude and expression suggest un-

Rope. **Mr. Kentley (Sir Cedric Hardwicke), the film's touchstone of human decency, holds the books tied with the rope used to strangle his son; Philip's disturbance arouses Rupert's suspicions.**

Stage Fright. **Sybil Thorndyke with Richard Todd; Jane Wyman with Alistair Sim.**

Stage Fright. Marlene Dietrich.

Strangers on a Train. **Guy (Farley Granger), Bruno (Robert Walker), and the incriminating lighter.**

The murder of Miriam (Laura Elliott).

Rear Window. Lisa (Grace Kelly) invades Thorwald's apartment.

Lisa at the peak of poise, Jefferies at the peak of irony.

Jefferies involves Stella (Thelma Ritter) and Lisa in his theories.

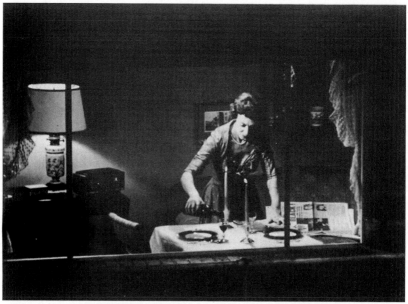

Secret lives: Thorwald (Raymond Burr) and Miss Lonelyhearts (Judith Evelyn).

The Man Who Knew Too Much. Hitchcock's most positive and celebratory mother/child relationship. (Doris Day with Christopher Olsen).

The Mckennas get acquainted with their alter egos in the Moroccan restaurant (Doris Day and James Stewart; Bernard Miles and Brenda de Banzie).

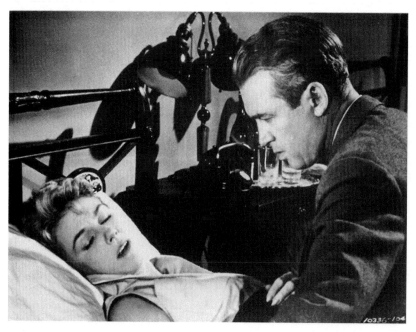

The sedation scene.

The man who didn't know enough visits the wrong "Ambrose Chap(p)e(1)l".

Hank between the father and his "shadow."

"Che sera, sera": the triumphant reconciliation of motherhood and performance.

Vertigo. Hitchcock's most literal enactment of "suspense."

Midge (Barbara Bel Geddes) supervises Scottie's unsuccessful attempt to overcome his vertigo.

Madeleine (Kim Novak) in Scottie's apartment.

Scottie and Madeleine about to "wander" together.

Scottie in the nursing home; Midge's defeat.

**Domination and resistance: Hitchcock and Kim Novak during the shooting of
Vertigo.**

North by Northwest. The flight of Thornhill (Cary Grant) and Eve (Eva Marie Saint) impeded by the "guardians of order."

certainty. He asks her to read some of his books. She tells him she
doesn't need to know how filthy men are, and adds, "In case you didn't
recognize it, that was a rejection." But we know it wasn't: know especially from her questioning glance at him, but also from the very over-
emphasis of her speech—she is being deliberately provocative. "Deliberately": but we have here a perfect example of that borderline between
conscious and subconscious intention, which makes "deliberately" not
quite the word. Using the same satirical tone, she suggests and then
insists on the free association: "Oh, doctor, I bet you're just dying to
free associate": taunting as it is, it becomes an invitation to more than
playing at psychology. He starts, awkwardly; she urges him on ("There.
I'm not holding back at all, am I, doctor?"). The word "sex" begins to
break down her defenses, although she still preserves the defensive-
satirical tone ("Jack and Jill—you keep your filthy hands off me, Jack").
Death brings simply the association "me," and a feeble attempt to break
off the game: we think of Marnie's declaration that she believes in
"nothing," and remember her body floating in the pool. But Mark,
encouraged, presses on with colors: "Black"—"White." Sudden low-
angled shot of Mark, ominous and accusing with pointing finger: "Red"
—and Marnie breaks down. The breakdown has been carefully prepared
—and prepared partly by herself. She repeats "White—white": at once
rejecting her own guilt and insisting on the whiteness—not redness—of
the sailor's shirt: then collapses in Mark's arms with a cry of, "Oh, help
me. Oh, God, somebody help me." It is the moment, in fact, toward
which the whole film has moved, from that first stiff walk along the
deserted platform.

Much of the film's significance, and much of its emotional impact, is
packed into the climactic cut of the flashback sequence from the child's
screaming in the past to Marnie's scream in the present. Child and
woman seem to face each other over the years, at the moment of experience and the moment of memory, and our awareness of the fragility and
precariousness of life, of the miseries of human waste, of the tyranny of
past over present, is most powerfully and movingly aroused. And after
it, Marnie's "There—there now," exact repetition of her words, expression, and intonation when she shot Forio, is clearly addressed to more
than the dead sailor: it is spoken to herself as child, to herself as woman;
it is a laying of ghosts.

Marnie cannot pretend to the formal perfection of *Vertigo*. Its narrative, though logical enough in that it follows through the stages essential to Marnie's cure, is comparatively rambling and episodic; not everything arises naturally, as in *Vertigo,* from a single situation. It is quite possible, for example—even probable—that Marnie would ride with the hunt; that she would see the kill; that she would rush off suicidally; that Forio would fail to take the wall; but the sequence of events lacks inevitability, for all the sense of continuity given by the slow lap-dissolve that gives us Marnie's face lingering on from the previous ("cat burglar") scene and suggests the continuance of her state of mind into the hunt episode, preparing us for her reactions. For all that, I am not sure that I prefer *Vertigo*'s compact perfection to *Marnie*'s relative looseness, which can be seen as reflecting a freedom new in Hitchcock. This is of all his films the one that most clearly formulates his moral position and most decisively, in a positive form, embodies his preoccupation with sexual relationships. With this freedom—to bring the argument of this chapter full circle—goes what has been condemned as carelessness or contempt for the audience, but is in fact merely a magnificent contempt for rules. The technical and formal freedom—the willingness to use any device, however conventionally dubious, to give each idea its most direct, most forceful, most economical expression—is but the outward manifestation of an ever freer creative flow, and *Marnie* is in many respects the satisfying culmination (to date: I do not wish to reject the possibility of further culminations beyond it) of the sequence begun by *Vertigo*.

Nineteen sixty-three brought us films from three major directors that offered, in their very distinct ways, interesting parallels. Fellini's *8½,* Bergman's *Winter Light,* and *The Birds* all brought their central characters to the point of development where limiting, obstructive immaturities had to be cast off and fully responsible, fully adult life begun. This seemed to imply that the directors in question had set themselves a challenge—a problem as much human as artistic—especially in the cases of Fellini and Bergman, whose films suggested a closer relationship of director to protagonist than did Hitchcock's. With regard to Fellini's new film, we must not assume that way-out fantasy and a return to Giulietta Masina necessarily indicates flight or evasion. *The Silence* reveals progress, certainly, but it is progress still further downward, a further ruthless demolition of humanist and religious assumptions that (for all the tentative gesture toward new life embodied in the child) leaves the positive work still to do. But with *Marnie* Hitchcock has responded to his own challenge magnificently, though in a devious, unexpected way. Perhaps the most disturbing and powerful factor in the effect of *Vertigo*, *Psycho*, and *The Birds* lay in the sense they communicated of a precarious order in constantly imminent danger of being undermined by terrible destructive upsurgings from an underlying chaos. It is not absurd to compare this with the overturning of a similarly precarious order, with the resulting freeing of an uncontrollable, destructive "under-nature" in the mature tragedies of Shakespeare. *Marnie* takes up again this assumption. Three varieties of order are set forth in the film: the neurotic order of Marnie's own life, rigidly held in place, constantly liable to irretrievable collapse; the order of the business world, materialistic, sterile, destructive of all human values; and the stagnant, over-tranquil order of Rutland Senior and his home—the tranquillity of a backwater. All three are exposed as inadequate, because all three are based on a rejection of the awareness of the underlying abysses, of human complexity and human needs, of the quicksands of identity. But in *Marnie* the underlying chaos finds an answer, and a logical one, in the film's endorsement of the implications of Mark Rutland's outlook and behavior. Through him, a true order is defined, an order very difficult and dangerous to achieve but, in the Hitchcock universe, the only order tenable: an order arrived at through empiricism, flexibility, a trust in instinct that has its source in a basic sympathetic flow, a rejection of all fixed rules, an acceptance of the necessary moral ambiguity of all positive action in an imperfect and bewildering world. Mark doesn't embody a positive force that can destroy the sense of precariousness and fragility —nothing can, and the film leaves us with the vulnerable children, potential Marnies, and their symbolic street game. But he *does* embody an attitude toward it. *Marnie* may lack, to some extent, the formal perfection of other Hitchcock films, but it certainly does not mark a retrograde step in his development. [24]

9
TORN CURTAIN

It is a pity that *Torn Curtain* is Hitchcock's fiftieth film: everyone expected a major landmark, a culmination. *The Birds,* despite weaknesses, was a culmination, and *Marnie* was another, beyond it. But *Torn Curtain* is no culmination, being unsatisfactory, episodic, lacking the really strong center we have come to expect. Yet, though more loosely constructed than any other recent Hitchcock, it is more coherent than may be immediately apparent. No doubt those who found evidence of failing powers in *Marnie* will find more here, but three things should make them pause before delivering a verdict of senility: 1) *Torn Curtain,* uneven in tone and in intensity as it is, contains sequences as fine as any in Hitchcock. 2) In certain respects which I shall go into, it continues the remarkably swift and consistent development traceable through Hitchcock's last half dozen films. 3) The denigrators should have had time by now to realize, in retrospect, how wrong they were about *Marnie.*

The movement of *Torn Curtain* follows the archetypal Hitchcock pattern: first, a world of superficial order (an international scientific conference) from which the protagonists (and the spectator) are plunged into a world of chaos through which they must struggle toward a new stability. But Hitchcock, deciding to return, after *Marnie,* to one of his favorite genres, needed a hero essentially different from those of any of his comparable earlier adventure films: a hero active and dynamic who plunges into dangers from choice (and a new actor to play him—not Grant or Stewart, but the more aggressive and self-assertive Paul Newman).

The simplifications of popular fiction can, by a process of heightening and intensification, merge imperceptibly into myth. Like many heroes of mythology, Newman here sets out on a quest for something of vital importance; to get it and bring it back he must undergo various tests and ordeals. Again as with certain mythological heroes, the quest involves a descent into an underworld from which the object of the quest must be retrieved. What we have to deal with here, it had better be insisted at the outset, is not an allegory worked out in consistent detail, but a drama whose significance is frequently heightened by certain suggestive undertones. The credit title sequence presents us with inferno images: to the left of the screen, flame; to the right, dense smoke, from which faces anxious, distraught, or tormented emerge and then disappear—faces we are to see later in the film. Only the faces of the lovers are calm and happy, and then only for the moment when they are shown together. In the penultimate sequence of the film the inferno idea recurs, the performance of *Francesca da Rimini* on stage being echoed in the auditorium, when Michael's cry of "Fire!" precipitates a mass panic that is the chaos world in miniature. The action in the theater parallels the action on stage: Paolo and Francesca menaced in hell by Guido; Michael and Sarah menaced in the seething hysterical mob by Gerhard. There are other hints in the film to support this view of it as a descent-and-quest myth. As the hero leaves on his quest, we are told (by the bookseller anxious about the condition of his religious section) to "pray for him"; Sarah accompanies Michael as a guardian angel ("I just knew I had to follow you, by instinct or to protect you . . ."); the members of Pi ("We are not a political organization") are his guides in the underworld. We cannot say that East Germany is hell (or what is nice Professor Lindt doing there?) but certainly it contains its lost souls, such as Gromek and the Countess Luchinska.

What is the object of the quest, what the nature of the underworld into which the hero descends, what (precisely) the dangers to which he exposes himself? Again, one must beware, with a film that strikingly lacks the extraordinary step-by-step logic of *Vertigo,* of suggesting that there is a symbolic or allegorical meaning that can be made to fit, point for point. No; but, again, there are overtones that make it clear we are dealing with something more than a simple thriller (if with something less than *Vertigo*). The answers to my questions can be approached through a further, related question: in what sense are Gromek and the Countess lost souls?—the Countess being entirely pathetic, Gromek more pathetic than sinister. They are lost because they belong nowhere; because they have no identity: both are displaced persons, Gromek with his constant nostalgia for America, the Countess with hers for Poland

and her social class. Yet this is precisely the condition into which Michael *appears* to be descending during the first half hour of the film, and in which Sarah hovers on the point of joining him. It is true that he is only pretending, and she draws back in time from the brink; but the pretense involves endangering their relationship and it draws her toward the false position of sacrificing her own integrity in order to remain beside him. The pretense also involves him, and the spectator, in moral impurities that give most of the suspense sequences in the film their peculiar character—"suspense" being here, as always in Hitchcock, essentially a matter of moral tensions. I shall return to this later.

The object of the quest? Ostensibly a formula in the head of a professor, a secret which will enable Michael to complete an "antimissile missile" that will render (he claims) nuclear war impossible. However, what gets the emphasis is not the political but the *personal* importance of this formula. Michael's failure to perfect the missile has lost him the position at Washington that he feels would complete him: deprived of it, he is sinking into a role he resents and feels unsuited to (teaching, instead of creating). The quest for the formula expresses, in a form almost diagrammatically neat, Michael's quest for that which will complete his sense of identity; and to gain it he must descend into a world where he exposes both himself and his fiancée to the most extreme dangers, moral as much as physical.

Closely connected with this, then, we find one of the clearest expressions of another recurrent Hitchcock theme: man's need to commit himself completely to a relationship with a woman, and not allow this relationship to be disrupted by doubts, secrets, concealments. At the opening of the film the hero's two basic needs are in direct conflict; the first half is concerned primarily with their reconciliation. Michael risks destroying his relationship with Sarah by refusing to be frank with her about what he is doing; it is only the strength of her fidelity that preserves it. The crucial development in the relationship—Michael's decision to tell her the truth—is precipitated by what is perhaps the one morally pure gesture in the film: her refusal during the preliminary interrogation to divulge, even for Michael's sake, what she knows about the missile. The fact that the characters are presented without much psychological detail is not a weakness: Hitchcock is giving us, in a pure and simplified form, all detail stripped away to give greater clarity to the essentials, a definition of fundamental human needs. For both, the relationship is crucial, yet for both it is necessarily subservient to something beyond it: for him the need to establish his identity finally through his work, for her, the need to preserve her personal integrity. Yet the relationship that appears at first sight to menace these higher needs is in fact vitally important to them. When the relationship is cemented by the removal of pretense and deceit, Sarah more than "protects": she saves Michael at exactly the moment when all seems lost, she proves herself indispensable to the success of his quest, for example, by agreeing to talk with Lindt, by dancing with Karl while Michael manipulates Lindt into arranging a private meeting, by persuading Michael to help the Countess Luchinska, by drawing him, in the theater, to the right door at the right moment. On the other hand, the spectator is made to feel that it is partly her ideal of Michael (which she thinks he has betrayed, yet to which he corresponds more closely than, at that time, she imagines) that gives her the strength to withstand her moment of trial at the interrogation. It is the love that made her waver that ultimately makes her stand firm.

The film, then, is built on strong foundations that have something of the essential simplicity of myth. But what gives it its particular pungent flavor—what acts as a veritable principle of composition, common to almost every episode—is Hitchcock's sense of the necessary moral impurity of action in an imperfect world. The private relationship can be protected, to some extent, from this impurity: at the start of the film the lovers hide themselves from the world under blankets, at the end they again draw a blanket over their heads to screen themselves from a photographer, and at the film's turning point, where Michael tells Sarah the truth, the kiss that seals their relationship is exchanged behind bushes. But as soon as there is involvement in the public world there is impurity. Sarah's act of moral integrity at the interrogation, by forcing Michael to reveal the truth to her, at once plunges her with him into the equivocal morality of his enterprise: she must begin lying, deceiving, tricking; and it is Sarah who persuade him to accept the Countess Luchinska's blackmail.

In some ways *Torn Curtain* refers us back to *Notorious* and *North by Northwest,* in both of which monstrous demands were made on the heroines in the name of political necessity. In *Torn Curtain* the morality of Michael's actions on the political level is called into question, though subtly and inexplicitly, throughout. He announces, at his first press conference, that he has defected in order to continue work on the anti-

missile missile that will make nuclear war impossible. We reflect at once
—and the presence of hostile reporters from the West encourages this—
that in fact all the invention will do is make it possible for East to bomb
West without fear of retaliation. When we learn the truth, this reflection
obviously still stands, not perhaps conscious in the spectator's mind but
there to trouble him just below the surface of consciousness: we have
merely to reverse the sides.

Throughout the first part of the film the hero's course of action places
him in a series of equivocal positions: especially, we watch his discomfiture at the press conference, under the questions from the reporters and,
more particularly, the incredulous and accusing gaze of Sarah. But it is
with the sequence of the killing of Gromek that the full bitter flavor of
the film is tasted. It is of great importance that Hitchcock leads us into
this sequence by revealing Michael's secret to us. We have spent the first
half hour of the film in unattached bewilderment, knowing too little to
identify with Paul Newman, yet too much to identify with Julie Andrews. At the moment when we learn the truth, our whole relationship
to the film changes, we seize gratefully on Michael as hero; here is
someone we can completely identify with. It is this involvement with a
character, hence with a course of action, that makes the killing of
Gromek the most disturbing murder in the whole of Hitchcock. The
murder of Marion Crane shocked us, certainly; but at least we were
taken by surprise, and had never *wanted* it. But here, as soon as Gromek
reveals his presence, we say, "He will have to be killed," and as the
moments pass and nothing is done, this merges into "Go on—kill him."
We are implicated—*we* are killing Gromek—and Hitchcock spares us
no discomfort for our complicity. So many factors contribute to the
effect of this rich and remarkable sequence. There is the sickening sense
throughout of enforced commitment to actions that are unspeakably
horrible—the presence of the farmer's wife is especially important in
this respect, the culmination of the scene being the symbolic passing of
blood from Michael's hand to hers as they try to wash it away. The
horror is intensified by the fact that it is Gromek himself who forces
them to kill him—he *wants* to die, placing himself in their power and
then insistently provoking them. Hitchcock and his actor (Wolfgang
Kieling, perhaps the finest performance in a film particularly rich in
marvelously created minor roles) here convey, with that economy so
characteristic of Hitchcock films, the essence of a human being, in this

case the sense of a man inwardly sickened by his own corruption. Hitchcock's method with Gromek (and it is repeated later with the Countess Luchinska) is to begin by arousing in the spectator a simple recoil of distaste (expressed on the screen for us in both cases by the reaction of Newman), and then, by making us feel the essential humanity of the character, to make us ashamed of our initial reaction. Finally, let me single out one other factor that contributes to the density of this sequence: the presence throughout it of the tax driver, which intensifies the horror of what is happening by placing it in the context of the everyday. The disturbing effect of the sequence is clinched when Newman walks out of the farm kitchen that, homely and reassuring in appearance, has become a world of nightmare, to find the taxi driver still standing waiting for him, an innocent and unaware bystander.

The later episodes, it is true, yield nothing quite as dense in significance: no doubt the somewhat unsatisfactory total effect of *Torn Curtain* is partly due to the fact that it reaches its point of maximum intensity about a third of the way through and never quite regains it. There is, nonetheless, a great deal that is of interest in these later sequences. One notes, for example, a certain difference in tone between these and comparable episodes in earlier films. Hitchcock's films abound in vividly realized small parts; but here, each of the subsidiary characters seems conceived specifically to intensify in one way or another our sense of moral complexity—of moral *discomfort*. Consider for instance Michael's duel of wits with Professor Lindt. This formula for which the hero undertakes his descent into the underworld has to be wrested, not from a devil, not even from a lost soul, a Gromek, but from a kindly, benign, delightful old gentleman. Hence, at the moment of Michael's triumph, when the professor exclaims: "You told me nothing!" our sympathies are at least as much with him as with the film's hero. Or consider another particularly rich sequence, the bus journey (where back-projection, elsewhere in the film sometimes crude and ugly, achieves a notable expressive effect, intensifying the spectator's sense of the bus as a small enclosed world sealed off from the surrounding normality). Here, the presence of Fraulein Mann provokes the moral tension that is the essence of Hitchcockian suspense. On a superficial suspense level, her objections to helping Michael and Sarah threaten to jeopardize their escape; on a deeper level, she brings closer to the surface our doubts about the morality of the whole enterprise. Fraulein Mann's objection is that this time they are helping, not their fellow East Germans, but two foreigners, and Americans at that; and the partial validity of her objection brings to our consciousness the remembrance of what these Americans are escaping *with*. The lives of the bus "passengers"—and they include, by the end of the trip, one genuine passenger, an entirely innocent old woman—are being endangered to enable Michael to take back to America a formula that may destroy them all. We are also very much aware of the personal nature of his quest: in effect, these lives are being endangered for one man's selfish ambitions. When the departing Fraulein says that she hopes they get caught, our sympathies are not entirely against her.

The encounter with the Countess Luchinska is one of the film's most complex sequences in terms of moral implications. Her calling out his name to Michael in the street clearly constitutes a veiled threat: it is never certain that, if they reject her offer, she will not expose them. Our first response is to share Michael's distaste; but gradually we are led to dissociate ourselves from it as the pathos of her predicament is revealed. *Should* he accept? She is a silly and useless old woman who will scarcely be an asset to America, nor is America (to her a dream world) likely to be of any use to *her:* she will be a displaced person anywhere, lost and wretched. But, as the scene progresses, we come to feel such compassion for her that we long for Michael to accept, and his hesitation seems priggish. He accepts, finally, for the wrong reason: not from compassion for a helpless and miserable old woman, but in order to be helped, and to remove the possibility that she will denounce them. Lila Kedrova is magnificent, with an extraordinary command of facial expression, gesture, and intonation. But Hitchcock indulges her rather more than enough: one has too much the sense of an actress being allowed to "do her piece," and occasionally she is permitted to over-make points, as in her last utterance.

The episode in the theater acts as an almost diagrammatically simple summing up of the whole film: Michael himself produces the chaos from which they must extricate themselves, with his cry of "Fire!"; torn apart, they are nearly lost in the seething anonymous crowds; finally, through their awareness of each other and thanks to Sarah's gaining the exit and drawing Michael to her, they escape, reunited. After which, the end is comparatively lightweight, a neatly executed Hitchcock suspense joke, rather disappointing after all that has gone before. But one notes that even here the protagonists' escape is due not to a heroic or altruistic action, but to the desire of the stagehand for payment—a motive scarcely more laudable than the petty vanity that causes the ballerina to denounce them. Our last glimpse of him is of a man alone, apart, greedily counting his money.

Torn Curtain is a remarkably rich film, yet one cannot escape, at the end, a certain sense of emptiness. This is partly due to what is in other ways so admirable—the undermining of the morality of what Michael is doing on a political level: we are left wondering what it has all been for, and not finding very much in the way of an answer. Worse, Hitchcock this time seems not greatly inspired by his principals—especially Julie Andrews, who is never more than adequate. The richness of the film lies, in fact, to a somewhat disproportionate degree in the vividness and complexity of the subsidiary characters and the use to which Hitchcock puts them: especially true of the latter half of the film, where the lovers occupy remarkably little of the spectators' attention, becoming, indeed, little more than pretexts for the various episodes, themselves uneven in complexity and interest. This leaves the film curiously without a firm center. An interview published in Sweden when *Torn Curtain* opened there reveals that commercial pressures led Hitchcock to modify his original conception, by wrenching the Newman character at the last minute into a conventional hero figure. The chief source of dissatisfaction with the film is, I think, our sense that we are being discouraged (unsuccessfully) from feeling the character to be as nasty as he in fact is. Although it contains much that one values, *Torn Curtain* as a whole is notably less successful than any other of Hitchcock's recent films.

10

RETROSPECTIVE (1977)

I wrote *Hitchcock's Films* somewhat more than ten years ago. Though my admiration for certain of Hitchcock's works is undiminished, and I would stand by much of what I wrote, the book now seems to me flawed by various excesses, imbalances, and distortions. Besides, my critical position—though it has not, I think, radically changed—has undergone some modification. The impetus behind the book sprang from two heterogeneous sources "yoked by violence together": Dr. Leavis and *Cahiers du Cinéma*; its originality is perhaps most readily explainable in terms of this fusion of apparent incompatibles. Ten years later, I feel more distanced from both (which is not to disown either as a continuing influence, especially Leavis). I do not believe in the revision of one's earlier work—not, at least, when the gap has widened beyond a certain extent. A book necessarily belongs to a particular phase in one's evolution and a particular phase in the development of the tradition within which it was written. Were I writing the book today, nothing in it would be quite the same—not because I wish totally to reject or retract what I wrote then, but because I would be writing under very different personal circumstances and within a very different phase in the development of film criticism. Rather than tamper with what I wrote, I prefer to offer a fresh statement of my position with regard to Hitchcock. (An earlier attempt to formulate this appeared in *Film Comment*, November/December 1972, under the title "Lost in the Wood" and the pseudonym "George Kaplan".)

One can usefully begin by considering the two major aesthetic influences on Hitchcock's work. In the early years of his career, when his creative personality was in the process of formation, he made two films (in fact, his first two completed films as director, *The Pleasure Garden* and *The*

Mountain Eagle) in German studios; the contact seems to have confirmed an interest in the potentialities of Expressionism that was already present (he speaks, in the Truffaut interview-book, of Lang's *Der mude Tod* as one of his first important cinematic experiences). A little later, he discovered the Soviet cinema, which confirmed for him the crucial importance of montage, its centrality to what he wanted to do. The Expressionist influence is already very plain in *The Lodger* (1926); the importance to Hitchcock of montage is also implicit there, waiting to be developed. The film was also Hitchcock's first suspense thriller, and first great commercial success: the coincidence of all these factors was obviously crucial in determining the development of his career.

"Expressionism" evades simple definition, but a central impulse was clearly the attempt to "express" emotional states through a distortion or deformation of objective reality, "expression" taking precedence over representation. The continuing dominance of such an aesthetic aim in Hitchcock could be suggested by innumerable examples, of varying degrees of subtlety, from any of the films; it is enough here to mention the most obvious, the red suffusions in *Marnie,* which have nothing to do with representing "reality" and everything to do with communicating the heroine's subjective experience.

The importance to Hitchcock of Soviet montage theory is if anything even more obvious. The affinities become plain if one begins to analyze the Odessa steps massacre in *Potemkin* as if it were a Hitchcockian suspense piece. Almost everything in the sequence works effectively in that way (and this partly accounts, of course, for its extraordinary emotional power): perhaps the most striking single example is the famous incident involving the baby's pram, where Eisenstein's fragmented editing is devoted to the buildup and release of tension on a basis of will-it-or-won't-it? All the techniques deployed in the Odessa steps sequence could be paralleled somewhere in Hitchcock, even the one potentially most disturbing to the audience's involvement on a "Realist" level, overlapping montage: in the sequence of the riding accident in *Marnie,* the camera covers (by a variety of technical means—both tracking and zooming) the same stretches of ground over and over again, to convey the effect of time agonizingly "stretched" at a moment of supreme fear and anguish.

A central characteristic of Expressionism (as a cinematic movement) is the distortion of the "reality" the camera records, or the creation of a world phenomenologically remote from the reality recognized by our senses; a central characteristic of montage theory is the creation of concepts that have no necessary phenomenological equivalents in what was actually presented before the camera. These two movements represent, in their very different ways, the two main lines of opposition to the notion of film as an inherently "realistic" medium: their emphasis is on artifice rather than representation. In Hitchcock's cinema, their "artificiality" is intensified by the fact that both techniques are divorced from their original ends. Expressionism was a "high art" movement rooted in a specific time and place, a specific "angst"; Soviet montage was associated with revolution and propaganda, with the task of making the principles underlying the revolution intelligible, cogent, and concrete. Hitchcock in a sense perverted both, employing their techniques (or his own modification of them) in the creation of popular bourgeois entertainment. Obviously, any innovation, its expressive possibilities established, becomes public property, a part of the complex apparatus of the cultural tradition, capable of being put to uses far beyond those that stimulated its evolution. Yet I find it significant—having in mind the whole Hitchcock oeuvre—that he should build the foundations of his style out of elements inherently "artificial," borrowed from cultures other than his own, and detached from the conditions that originally gave them their meaning.

Doubtless, scholars more intimate than I am with Hitchcock's British period will be able to trace the process of absorption into his style and method of these major influences. For my purposes, to illustrate their fusion in his work and the purposes to which he put them, his first sound film, *Blackmail* (1930), offers a convenient and striking example. Consider the famous scene—it is repeatedly cited in textbooks on film history with reference to the development of sound—where the heroine, who has stabbed to death a would-be rapist, is forced to listen to a gossipy woman talking garrulously about the murder. The scene unites a number of thematic and stylistic elements central to Hitchcock's work: the bourgeois family involved in daily routine (in this case, breakfast) contrasted with the extraordinary and disturbing, which exists nonetheless in their midst and for which one of them is responsible; the action presented through the consciousness (and to some extent the eyes) of the distraught heroine (who, like her successors through *Shadow of a Doubt* to *Psycho*, combines bourgeois "normality" with a romantic/dramatic

situation, hence is an ideal identification figure); the knife on the breakfast table, to which the camera (i.e., the heroine's consciousness) obsessively returns; closeups of the woman's lips moving as she chatters on;
the gradual distortion of her voice to an unintelligible gabble out of
which only the word "knife" emerges clearly, "cutting through" the
scrambled soundtrack [25]. Here montage combines with the Expressionist distortion of physical reality to communicate directly to the
spectator a character's subjective experience; to involve us in that experience; to confirm what is already encouraged by the construction of the
scenario, the empathic identification of spectator with character.

My use of the term "artificial" (intended as descriptive rather than
evaluative—though I shall argue that the particular artificiality of Hitchcock's cinema carries with it certain weaknesses and limitations) inevitably raises many of those questions about "Realism" that haunt contemporary film criticism; here I can only touch on them in a way that I
am aware leaves major theoretical issues unresolved. I will mention in
passing, however, that the Realism debate seems frequently clouded by
a failure to distinguish sufficiently two main ways in which the cinema
can be spoken of as a "Realist" art form—the two being neither incompatible nor necessarily, beyond a certain primitive point, interdependent.
The cinema derives from two major sources, the invention of photogra-
phy and the nineteenth-century novel. From the former comes the simple, basic notion of film "Realism": the camera records the reality in
front of it. From the latter comes a much more sophisticated and complex notion of "Realism," bound up not so much with literal visual
representation as with the audience's involvement in the movement of a
narrative, the illusion that we are experiencing "real life." The potentiality for confusion can be suggested by pointing out that the Odessa steps
massacre or the horse accident in *Marnie* is "Realist" in the former
sense only in the most barely literal way but intensely "Realist" in the
latter sense: the reality the camera records has very little to do with the
illusion the audience experiences. Hitchcock's cinema is either the least
or most "Realist," depending on which definition you are using.

    In order to define its artificiality more precisely, I want to draw on
certain key notions and motifs that recur almost obsessively in Hitchcock's interviews. His own statements about his work are—if one is
ready to make connections and read between the lines—more illuminat-

ing than I used to give them credit for: both for what they reveal and for what they conceal, the two aspects being significantly related.

First, one cannot leave the question of Hitchcock's debt to the Soviet cinema without considering the importance he attaches (from his point of view, quite rightly) to the famous Kuleshov experiment. A close-up of the actor Mosjoukin was intercut with various objects which the editing implied he was looking at (a baby, a corpse, a bowl of soup); the audience is supposed to have admired his expressive acting, although in fact the same close-up was used each time and when the shot was taken the actor didn't know what he was meant to be looking at. Both the alleged results and the theoretical validity of the experiment have been called into question (notably by V. F. Perkins in *Film as Film*); what concerns us here is not what the experiment actually proved but what lessons Hitchcock drew from it. He drew two which are absolutely central to the development of his art. First, the Kuleshov experiment suggests the possibilities of editing for deceiving the spectator, for playing tricks with time and space. It is a lesson he could have learned equally from Eisenstein: witness, again, the Odessa steps sequence, where the spacial relationships of the various characters are never clear (in fact, clearly didn't exist in terms of staged action), where the audience's sense of the length of the steps and the progress of the soldiers is consistently undermined, where the woman whose child falls *behind* her as they flee from the soldiers is subsequently shown going *down* the steps to retrieve his body. Spatial deception through editing is common practice in Hitchcock. For illustration, one needn't go to any of the famous set pieces. Consider the apparently simple moment in *Notorious* where Ingrid Bergman, having stolen Claude Rains' key from his key ring, is surprised by him as she holds it in one of her hands (we aren't allowed to be sure which). He, affectionate but gallant, wants to kiss her fingers; he uncurls one hand, and, after kissing it, makes for the other. She flings her arms round his neck, drops the key behind his back, and pushes it under a chair with her foot. Filmed by, say, Preminger, in a single-take long shot from across the room, this simple action would be ludicrously implausible: Bergman would have, first, to crane her neck over Rains' shoulder to see where the key had fallen (and, short as the actor was, this would involve some craning); she would then have to wrap one leg round his body to maneuver her foot into position, then move the foot several inches to conceal the key (which would not be very effectively concealed anyway)—and all this, of course, without Rains noticing. Hitchcock breaks down the incident into a characteristically detailed and fragmented montage, culminating in a close-up of the foot pushing the key, both bodies out of frame: it is doubtful, such is the tension and involvement generated by this admirable scene, whether any spectator at the time has questioned the plausibility of the action.

The other lesson is even more significant. The emotions Mosjoukin was felt to be expressing (tenderness, sorrow, hunger, or whatever) must obviously have been supplied by the spectator from his own fund of stock responses to babies, corpses, and bowls of soup: the principle of audience identification is already implicit in the Kuleshov experiment. Again, it is also implicit in Eisenstein, and a sequence such as the Odessa steps (which supplies the audience with a careful selection of identification figures) suggests the relationship between the two "lessons": it is the spectator's emotional involvement that carries him over the deceptions and the artifice, making him ready to accept as "real" an action that patently isn't, even in the limited sense of being performed in spatial and temporal continuity. The relationship is in fact even closer: the fragmentation of the Eisenstein sequence and the spatial temporal disorientation (as in certain of Hitchcock's tours-de-force—the shower murder in *Psycho,* where the blows are never seen actually to connect, the horse accident in *Marnie*) actually *increase* the spectator's sense of confusion and panic.

The relationship between identification and the ready acceptance of sleight-of-hand might be investigated through innumerable examples in Hitchcock's work. One general point emerges clearly: Hitchcock has grasped that the identification principle can work in this elemental/ elementary way only when very simple and basic feelings are involved— often, primitive feelings (especially terror) rooted in direct physical sensation. Otherwise, identification (empathy, as opposed to the kind of sympathy we may feel for the characters in, for example, a Renoir film) is a doubtful and complicated phenomenon that has to be built very subtly. There may be a reason beyond that of mere technical obviousness why many people are so alienated by the artificial devices of *Marnie:* that, in the very nature of the central character and her predicament, total identification is impossible. One can study the care with which Hitchcock builds identification, when he can't rely on "primitive" emotions, in the first scene of *Psycho,* where every stylistic decision and every step in the construction of the scenario can be seen as part of a process whereby Hitchcock prepares for that identification with Marion Crane on which the effect and essential meaning of the entire film depend (on whatever level of seriousness we feel it as working). The opening is not a single take (as my own treatment of it might seem to imply—an error perpetuated in Raymond Durgnat's interesting recent book, *The Strange Case of Alfred Hitchcock*) but a series of shots linked by almost imperceptible dissolves and one awkward cut (presumably from a location to the studio set) just before the camera moves in through the open window. The captions identifying place, date (but not the year), and time of day confirm the impression of "documentary" realism given by the location work; the dissolves subliminally convey the sense of covering a lot of territory, the progress toward the window seeming ambiguously arbitrary and purposive. The spectator (even if he missed the advance publicity) has been alerted to expect some kind of horror movie by the title and by Bernard Herrmann's opening music, but Hitchcock's insistence on the ordinary and "real" temporarily lulls him—under cover of which Hitchcock can begin at once to play on his voyeuristic tendencies. As the camera takes us in through the open window into the dark hotel bedroom, the lighting is subtly modified: the effect is of our eyes becoming adjusted to the dark after the sunshine outside. When Sam says, "You never did eat your lunch," Hitchcock cuts in a close-up of the sandwich lunch on the bedside table: the shot is obviously superfluous in terms of the conveying of information, but it corresponds closely to the movement of our consciousness: if we were in the room, and heard Sam say that, we would instinctively glance at the lunch. When the lovers lie down again on the bed, the camera moves in as though to lie down with them: from being invisible spectators actually in the room, we are led to become participants. Then, when Marion springs up in recoil, the camera abruptly recoils too, closely mirroring her movement: our participation begins to be given a clear bias, which is developed through the remainder of the scene. There are no shots that are strictly subjective, but the camera repeatedly favors Marion and her viewpoint. She is privileged with close-ups (notably on "I'll lick the stamps," where the music also endorses our romantic sympathy for her position and attitude) or shown in profile; we look at Sam, on the other hand, in medium long shot and *almost* as through her eyes (notably on his "Well, all *right,*" as he surrenders to her demand for "respectability" with a submissive gesture of the hands). In fact, the first clearly subjective shot in the film is withheld until the moment when Marion's car is stopped at the traffic lights and she sees her boss crossing in front of her—by which time the movement of the scenario, the editing, the placement of the camera, the music, have thoroughly but unobtrusively determined our relationship to her and to the action.

Hitchcock's attitude to actors—another, though seldom so explicit, recurrent theme of his interviews—follows logically from the centrality to his art of the Kuleshov experiment. One can make a broad distinction (and it is ultimately bound up with certain aspects of the "Realism" debate) between directors who work collaboratively with actors, and directors who use actors to execute a preconceived plan or idea: Renoir, Hawks, McCarey against von Sternberg, Antonioni, Hitchcock. To von Sternberg, actors were "puppets": he claimed that every detail of Dietrich's performances in their films was created by him, down to the smallest gesture or flicker of expression. Arthur Penn aptly described the actors in Antonioni's films as "beautiful statuary." Hitchcock has denied saying that "actors are cattle": what he said was that they should be *treated* like cattle. The former trio seek to discover what an actor can give and then encourage him to give it, within the limits of an overall conception which is relatively loose: one knows, for example, that some of McCarey's best scenes were improvised on the set, that *La Règle du Jeu* changed and grew during the course of shooting, that Hawks and his cast more or less made up *Hatari!* as they went along, within the loose framework of a hunting season. The spectator won't find in a Hitchcock film (or only very rarely) the continuous invention of detail, the spontaneous bits of business, that make *La Règle du Jeu, Rio Bravo, Once Upon a Honeymoon* so inexhaustibly alive; I find that Hitchcock's films go "dead" on me more easily. The broad distinction is between actor-centered cinema and image-centered cinema. The former implies a "humanist" philosophy and a certain form of "Realism." It also carries a logical thematic extension: the characters of Hawks, Renoir, McCarey experience and express at least a relative freedom (literally, of movements within the frame; spiritually, of moral choice); the films of these directors are centered on values of generosity and affection between people, on the possibility of contact and reciprocal relations. In contrast, the characters of von Sternberg, Antonioni, Hitchcock are, typically, trapped, isolated, unable to communicate; there is a strong emphasis on impotence (the word to be understood in its general sense, though its specifically sexual overtones are not inappropriate).

To define and exemplify Hitchcock's image-centered concept of cinema, one needn't adduce specimens of "Kuleshovian" editing: one needn't look beyond the first shot of *Marnie*. Its primary function is to arouse the spectator's curiosity/voyeurism, though it also introduces certain important thematic motifs; its method involves the virtual elimination of the actor or of acting. Each precisely calculated detail in the action, the decor and the camera movement conveys a precise idea or represents a strategy in the Hitchcockian game of audience manipulation (at this stage of the film taking the form of teasing). The close-up on the yellow bag tells us the bag is significant without giving us any clue as to why; as the camera slows and the figure walks on, our chief desire is to see her face—a desire Hitchcock systematically frustrates until, like Michelange in *Les Carabiniers*, we want to climb in through the frame and run ahead to take a look. She has black hair, so it can't be Tippi Hedren; except that it is so very black, and so glossy, that it may be dyed, so perhaps it *is* Tippi Hedren after all. We want the camera to catch up with her again so that we can get a better look: perhaps she will stop and turn. Hitchcock accordingly slows the camera down even more, eventually stopping it altogether; then, just as she turns and we might see her face (even at a distance) in profile, he cuts. Our curiosity is increased by other factors in the scene which are revealed as she moves further from the camera: the time of day (apparently very early morning), the station platform (completely deserted, without even a porter in sight, so she will have to wait a long time for a train), the way she is walking very straight and precariously along a yellow line, like a girl balancing on a tightrope. The "corridor" pattern of converging, receding lines (tracks, empty trains, the edges of the platform), familiar from *Vertigo* and taken up recurrently later in the film (the hotel corridor, the honeymoon ship, Mrs. Edgar's street), has an immediately expressive impact with its suggestion of a trajectory, introducing the "journey" motif on which the film is built. There is no purer example of the Hitchcock shot: the execution of a complex of ideas, with audience response a crucial determining concern.

The characteristics of Hitchcock's cinema so far described make logical another recurrent theme of his interviews: the repeated assertions that he is not really very interested in the actual shooting, because he knows, with the completion of the shooting script, shot by shot what the film will be like: the filming is merely the mechanical execution of a precise blueprint. One takes this with at least one pinch of salt. On the one hand, it helps to explain the unevenness of so many Hitchcock films, the process of shooting providing no compensation for a failure of interest at the planning stage. Were all those slack sequences in *Topaz*— that look as if they'd been shot and thrown together by a television crew during the director's absence—really planned shot by shot? Perhaps so; the slackness could be accounted for by assuming that Hitchcock wasn't interested in them at the planning stage and, because he isn't a McCarey, could instill no life into them during shooting. On the other hand, one needs to account for the numerous superb performances in certain films where the acting quite transcends any Kuleshovian trickery. Hitchcock might, of course, have anticipated Grant's performance in *North by Northwest,* and even Bergman's in *Notorious,* from prior knowledge of the players. But Joseph Cotten in *Shadow of a Doubt?* Robert Walker in *Strangers on a Train?* Anthony Perkins in *Psycho?* One might account for them by the hypothesis that, because Hitchcock isn't interested in acting, certain actors, left to their own devices, are able to seize their chances and create their own performances independently; there is more reason to deduce that there are certain performances—or, more exactly, certain *roles*—which arouse in Hitchcock a particular creative interest.

Minor reservations apart, however, the films convincingly bear out the notion of detailed preplanning—especially the set pieces of what Hitchcock calls "pure cinema," a concept that invariably turns out to be based on the possibilities of montage. This accounts for Bazin's famous disillusionment when he visited Hitchcock on location for *To Catch a Thief* and found the *metteur-en-scène* apparently very little concerned with what was currently being shot. It is also the ultimate confirmation of our sense of Hitchcock's conception of cinema as an artificial construct—the most artificial, perhaps, short of animation (which something like the horse accident in *Marnie* strikingly resembles). This goes some way toward explaining the paradox that Hitchcock's cinema, dedicated so singlemindedly to the total entrapment of the spectator in an emotional experience, is also the easiest mentally to deconstruct. It is a truism that works of art can give pleasure on different levels, depending on a variety of factors: familiarity with the work, familiarity with its background and context, familiarity with its conventions; personal temperament; degree of intellectual awareness; the mood of the moment. The sorts of pleasure afforded by Hitchcock's films are unusually disparate, even contradictory: one might assume they would be mutually exclusive. There is the pleasure derived from experiencing the films in a state of total submission, carried through step by step in the scenario, shot by shot in the montage, in intense emotional participation; there is the pleasure of total awareness of how everything is done, the pleasure usually termed "aesthetic," wherein one delights in the skills of Hitchcock's technical mastery (when it works). Happily, the complexity of the human organism and its responses is such that even such seemingly opposed experiences can operate simultaneously (though each will modify the other). This is in fact implicit in my parenthesis above on Hitchcock's mastery ("when it works"): our intellectual awareness that something "works" (on which that apparently purely "aesthetic" delight rests) inevitably refers to an emotional level of response, the only level on which (at least in a Hitchcock movie) the concept of "working" can be validated.

So far, this attempt at a more precise and concrete definition of the nature of Hitchcock's art than my book originally offered might seem to lead logically either to the traditional rejection or denigration of it as the work of a skillful technician and manipulator, or to the type of analysis favored by the semiological school of "materialist" critics which would bypass questions of individual creativity and personal response, seeing the films as part of a "social process." The latter, certainly, would produce its revelations: one looks forward (not without trepidation) to accounts of, say, *Vertigo* and *Psycho* along the lines of Stephen Heath's remarkable reading of *Touch of Evil* in the spring 1975 issue of *Screen*. But it is my contention that, however completely "coded" a work of art can be demonstrated to be, at its heart (if it is alive) is individual creativity, and it is with the nature of the creative impulses embodied in it that we must ultimately be concerned. This is not to talk naively about "genius" in a way that suggests that works of art spring spontaneously out of the artist's head via some process of immaculate conception. That Hitchcock's American period is in general richer than the British (a proposition I see no reason to retract or modify) can doubtless be attributed as much to a complex of interacting determinants as to personal development; similarly, a complete account of any one of the great

Hitchcock films would have to see it as the product of an intricate network of influences, circumstances of production, collaborations, happy confluences. But at the center of that network is—must be—a particular creative personality. The auteur theory, concerned to trace relationships between films and between different aspects (style, structure, theme) of the same film, exaggerated the degree of individual determination in the process of making it possible to define it; the current swing of the critical pendulum overcompensates for this by seeking to deny the individual altogether.

As soon as one begins to contemplate Hitchcock's work thematically, it becomes evident that its technical elaborations, the manifest desire to control audiences, have a thematic extension: they are determined, in other words, not simply by conscious commercial strategy but by powerful internal drives and pressures of the kind that never operate exclusively on a conscious level. The desire to control, the terror of losing control: such phrases describe not only Hitchcock's conscious relationship to technique and to his audiences, but also the thematic center of his films. The personal relationships that fascinate Hitchcock invariably involve the exercise of power, or its obverse, impotence; in many cases, a power drive that seeks to conceal or deny or compensate for a dreaded impotence, the perfect metaphor for which is provided by the "double" Norman Bates of *Psycho:* the young man terrified of women, and the exaggeratedly "potent" monster wielding the phallic knife. This relationship pattern, with its possible permutations and variations, links films as apparently diverse as *Notorious, Rope, Rear Window, Vertigo, Psycho,* and *Marnie:* on the whole, the more the plot structure allows it to dominate, the richer, more forceful, more fully achieved is the film. *Notorious*—one of Hitchcock's finest works, of which we still await an adequate critical account—derives its fascination from its complex shifting of power-and-impotence relationships, involving all four of the principal characters, and from certain suggestive Freudian overtones related to this: the key Ingrid Bergman steals from Claude Rains to give to Cary Grant; the bottle in the cellar which Grant discovers, and which contains Rains' secret "potency" (in the form of uranium ore).

The scene of the party in Rains' house suggests the central importance in Hitchcock of a motif peculiarly appropriate to the cinema, the "look," and its relation to the power/impotence obsession. It also suggests that the common simplistic association of subjective camera with audience identification (which parts of this book may have done something to encourage) needs careful qualification. During the early part of the scene, we are placed, in turn, in the positions of Bergman, Grant, and Rains as they watch each other across the room, through the throng of guests, each for his or her own reasons apprehensive; the spectator is led to participate in the tensions expressed through the pattern of interchanged looks rather than to identify with a particular character. The look expresses both dominance (the power of watching) and helplessness (the impotence of separation); by the use of subjective shots, Hitchcock at once makes the tension personal to himself (camera as the director's eyes) and transfers it to the audience (camera as eyes of the spectator).

The close connection between this and the voyeuristic tendencies so often noted in Hitchcock's cinema is obvious. Again, perhaps, the most vivid single instance is in *Psycho* (significantly, among the most intensely personal of all his films, and the one in which he was most singlemindedly dedicated to manipulating the audience): the close-up of Norman's eye as he watches through his peephole, and the cut to a subjective view of Marion undressing, so that the eye becomes both ours and Hitchcock's. The whole of *Rear Window* can be seen as an elaboration of this principle, the James Stewart character combining certain aspects of the roles of spectator and *metteur-en-scène*. The notion of impotence is concretely embodied in the broken leg; the people Stewart watches are at once dominated imaginatively by his consciousness (like Marion, they don't know they are being watched) and forever beyond his control.

To trace the creative drives behind Hitchcock's films to sources in psychopathology (possible, after all, to some degree with *any* artist) does not necessarily invalidate the emphasis placed in my book on their therapeutic impulses: indeed, it could logically be felt to strengthen the emphasis by giving the therapeutic impulses a particular focus or motivation. I still feel that the Hitchcock films I most admire are centered on a movement toward health via therapy and catharsis. I have, however, become much more keenly aware of a need to insist on sharp discriminations—a need to stress the limitations of Hitchcock's art and to distinguish the work (a small proportion of the total oeuvre) that succeeds in transcending them.

The limitations are of two kinds, though perhaps not entirely unconnected. There is, first, the somewhat equivocal relationship between Hitchcock the artist and Hitchcock the showman-entertainer. Obviously, the two can never be cleanly separated, nor would it be desirable that they could be, as their interrelationship is in many ways crucial to the robustness of Hitchcock's work. One can, nevertheless, set up fairly obvious polar opposites: the intensely involved personal art of *Vertigo*, say, as against the businessman who lends his name to anthologies of largely trivial horror stories or the comic fat man who introduces the Hitchcock half hour on television. Between the two, however, lie areas where the relationship becomes problematic. What concerns me here is the way in which some of Hitchcock's finest work is flawed by compromises that, in an artist free of "commercial" constraints, would appear neurotic, the result of a reluctance to allow certain disturbing implications to be fully explored, but which Hitchcock encourages us (sometimes, in interviews, explicitly) to regard as the result of external pressures, fears of alienating his audiences (the two motivations are not, of course, incompatible). There is a whole series of Hitchcock films which work magnificently up to a point, arousing complex and disturbing emotions, achieving a rich—and often very subversive—suggestiveness, and then evade their own implications by a sudden simplification. I have already touched in this book on the two most striking instances, *Strangers on a Train* and *Torn Curtain*. The former offers the neatest example of all, because one can point to the exact moment where the film goes wrong (which is also where it departs decisively from its source, Patricia Highsmith's novel)—the scene where Guy *doesn't* murder Bruno's father. Here and in *Torn Curtain* Hitchcock's reluctance to explore or acknowledge the disturbing implications of his hero's behavior results in a curious paralysis at the center of the film: neither one thing nor the other, the hero ends up nothing, and interest is displaced onto Bruno (in *Strangers*) and onto peripheral characters (in *Torn Curtain*). If in *Strangers* the simplification takes the form of trying to pass off Guy as a conventional hero, in *Shadow of a Doubt* it takes the opposite form of turning the film's most complex and ambivalently viewed figure (Uncle Charlie) into a mere monster for the last third. *Psycho* is much nearer being a masterpiece (the first half, up to the point where Marion's car sinks into the swamp, is certainly among the most extraordinary achievements of the American cinema). Yet even here one cannot but feel a lapse to a lower level of interest, with conventional detective story investigation, "flat" characters (Sam and Lila), and scenes (especially those involving Sheriff Chambers) that could easily come from one of the less distinguished of Hitchcock's TV shows. (The film picks up again, superbly, with Lila's exploration of Norman's home.)

The second limitation is more damaging: I would define it as the relative weakness in Hitchcock's art of the normative impulse. That great art strives—however implicitly—toward the realization of norms seems to me axiomatic, though the principle I am stating is frequently misunderstood or misrepresented. It is not a matter of whether a work is "optimistic" or "pessimistic," and certainly not a denial of the validity of a tragic vision of life. It is a matter of the nature of the creative impulse, which, to flourish, must be rooted in a sense of at least a *potential* normality to be striven for, values by which to live. "Normality" here must not be understood in terms of the reaffirmation of established values, least of all the norms of bourgeois society: Godard's *Tout va bien*, for example, answers perfectly to my concept of "normative" art, though its tone is not optimistic and it proposes no clearly definable solutions to the problems it raises; if I place beside it, as another essentially "normative" work, Bergman's *The Silence*, I shall perhaps sufficiently have safeguarded myself against simplification and parody.

It is not really paradoxical that Hitchcock's art is usually at its most creative when his material permits or encourages the most complete immersion in the abnormal. If creativity is, almost by definition, a striving toward norms, this implies a process, a *moving through*. The problem with Hitchcock is that the movement seems almost always blocked. His work typically equates "normality" with a bourgeois life in whose values the creative side of him totally disbelieves but to which it can provide no alternative. The couple in *Rich and Strange* pass through a series of disruptive experiences only to return, at the end of the film, to precisely the sterile existence of the beginning: all they have learned is to be afraid of the unfamiliar. The pattern established here is fundamental to Hitchcock's work: bourgeois "normality" is empty and unsatisfying, everything beyond it (or, more importantly, *within* it, secreted beneath its surface) terrifying. This explains why Hitchcock's most satisfying endings are those that express catharsis without reimposing a defined "normality"—at once, necessarily, the bleakest and most "open": the opening of the window and firing of the gun at the end of *Rope;* the car withdrawing from the swamp at the end of *Psycho;* above all, the end of *Vertigo*. And if this last remains, unchallengeably, Hitchcock's masterpiece, this is surely because there the attitude to the unknown and mysterious is not simply one of terror but retains, implicitly, a profound and disturbing ambivalence.

It is symptomatic that the most obvious legacy of Hitchcock's Jesuit education should be the lingering fascination with Hell and damnation, often concretized in the detail of the films. When Uncle Charlie arrives in Santa Rosa (*Shadow of a Doubt*), the whole image is darkened by the black smoke from the train, and the character is thereafter repeatedly shown with smoke hanging around him from his cigarette; when Bruno pursues Miriam through the Tunnel of Lover (*Strangers on a Train*) his boat is named Pluto; when Marion Crane tells Norman Bates that she "thought she must have gotten off the right road," he replies that "Nobody ever comes here unless they've done that." It is to these "damned" characters (ambiguously lost souls or devils) that Hitchcock's strongest interest gravitates, giving us some of the most vividly realized performances in his films; one looks in vain for any compensating intimation of Heaven. Hitchcock seems interested in the "normality" presented by the films only when he can treat it satirically, as with the "society" party of *Strangers on a Train*. *Shadow of a Doubt* is especially interesting here, as it is one film in which Hitchcock is supposed to create small town life affectionately. In fact, the family the film depicts consists of a collection of more-or-less caricatured individuals, each of whom inhabits a private, separate dream world, the mother nostalgic for her youth and her adored younger brother, the father living in a fantasy world of detective fiction and real-life crime, the younger daughter perpetually immersed in books. The film is rich in amusing detail, and the early scenes of Uncle Charlie's intrusion into the small town world are genuinely disturbing and subversive; but it would be difficult to claim either that the family life presented offers much in the way of affirmation or that the film suggests any possible alternative that isn't corrupt or "evil." Uncle Charlie, characteristically, brings life and excitement into an inert world, but proves to be a devil who must be destroyed: the sense of emptiness with which one is left at the end is closely bound up with the film's association of excitement with corruption, with Hitchcock's habitual distrust of the forces of the id.

If I were to undertake a revision of this book, the chapter that would call for the most modification would be that on *The Birds*, a film about which my feelings continue to be both mixed and fluctuating. It seems in some ways Hitchcock's most important, most "serious" film: the film in which he is most overtly concerned to elaborate a view of the universe. What is ultimately wrong with it is not that the eye too easily penetrates the technical trickery but that, for all the audacity of the conception and the consistent interest of the execution, the characters and their relationships are too slight to sustain the weight of significance implicitly imposed on them, too slight ever adequately to represent humanity and human potential; and there is no sign that Hitchcock can conceive of human potential positively in more adequate terms. The development the film appears to offer—the stripping away of the veneer of complacent superficiality—never really materializes: at least, not very impressively. One is left with a sense of discrepancy between the film's grand postulate—the threatened end of civilization and perhaps of humanity itself—and the actual created civilization and humanity presented in it. The weakness can be localized specifically in the perfunctory treatment of the children, in Hitchcock's notable failure to respond to the notion of renewed potential they and the school might have represented, his reduction of the concepts of education and childhood—the human future—to the automatic reiteration of an inane jingle. It is because the film fails to achieve the dimensions of tragedy (which depends on concepts of positive value) that it seems so perilously to border on the sadistic—the sadism directed ultimately, perhaps, at the audience. The film suggests, strongly, that the artificiality of Hitchcock's cinema, which I have attempted to define stylistically, has ramifications far beyond the "unnatural" surface of the films: he seems unable to create a "normal" life, whether actual or potential, of any richness or density, a point that holds whether one understands "normal" in the conventional, bourgeois sense or in my sense of "moving toward new norms."

The three films Hitchcock has made since the 1968 edition of this book —Topaz, Frenzy, and Family Plot—provide further confirmation and clarification of (to borrow Mr. Durgnat's title) "the strange case of Alfred Hitchcock." Topaz must surely be one of the most uneven films in the history of the cinema, in which something approaching Hitchcock's best rubs shoulders with his very worst: the relationship of good to bad in the film is very revealing. The unevenness, doubtless, can be partly accounted for by the fact that Topaz was a less personal project than the great majority of Hitchcock's films over the past two decades: Universal held the rights to the book before they offered him the subject, and the result suggests that he engaged with his material only intermittently. The film offers, therefore, a splendid opportunity for considering what Hitchcock responds to and what he doesn't. It contains three superb sequences. The opening defection in Copenhagen and the Hotel Teresa sequence are fully characteristic, meticulously articulated "suspense" set pieces, both built on the principle of the look—looks exchanged, looks unperceived, looks intercepted, as watchers and watched maneuver for power. The Hotel Teresa scene (in which power = possession of secret information locked inside a red case) is a remarkably complex and assured example of Hitchcock's use of point-of-view shots and spectator involvement. It is introduced by a quasi-subjective sequence shot through a telephoto lens as we watch with André Devereaux from across the street the pantomime of Juribe's rejection of, then surrender to, temptation: it has something of the tension and fascination of *Rear Window,* with Devereaux as spectator/*metteur-en-scène,* dominant yet impotent. During the main body of the scene, inside the hotel, we are passed from the viewpoint of the spy Dubois to that of Juribe to that of Rico Parra, the Cuban leader, so that, as with the party scenes of *Notorious,* we become involved in a complex of tensions rather than identified with a single character. Indeed, Hitchcock at times increases the tension by playing identification techniques *against* the natural gravitation of our sympathetic concern, so that (for example) we share in the process whereby Rico Parra discovers that the case is missing while our fears are for the safety of the men who have stolen it and are photographing its contents in another room.

The third fine sequence is that culminating in the death of Juanita (Karin Dor). The Cuban sequences generally—despite the utterly uninteresting performance of Frederick Stafford—represent a slight lift in interest over the film's more arid stretches. Without completely transcending a conventional Hollywood romanticism, they gain some intensity from the beauty and presence of Karin Dor, from the art direction, and from Hitchcock's characteristic response (compare *Notorious* and *North by Northwest*) to the interaction of love and espionage: I have in mind the scene where André unpacks his "gifts," the metallic objects cold and black against the soft white of the décor and of Juanita's negligee.

From the moment when Rico learns that Juanita herself is behind the counter-revolutionary espionage activities—a moment whose intensity is expressed by a sudden cut-in to Rico's hands arrested by shock on his knees as he is in the act of standing upright—the level of realization rises, as if Hitchcock were suddenly fully engaged by his material. The result is a notable specimen of "pure cinema," characterized by an intense and complex rhetoric of editing, camera movement, and angle. As she descends the stairs toward Rico, Juanita is privileged with that favorite Hitchcock device for special moments, the subjective forward tracking shot—in this case, the only one in the entire film. As Rico grabs her, there is a cut to a low-angled close shot of their tensed forearms. From the moment of physical contact, the erotic potentialities of the situation are vividly emphasized: the closely circling camera, seeming to bind the two bodies together as Rico decides to kill her (to spare her torture); the orgasmic jerk of the woman's body as the bullet is fired into it; the close-up of the gun in the man's hand "going limp," as it were. The scene's intensity—culminating in the extraordinary overhead shot as Juanita's body sinks to the floor, the purple dress spreading out like the petals of a flower—derives largely from its sexual overtones: from our sense of Rico's frustrated desire, which he can consummate only by killing its object: one of the supreme expressions in all Hitchcock of the power/impotence syndrome, and a precise enactment of his favorite Oscar Wilde quotation, "Yet each man kills the thing he loves . . ."

The badness of other parts of *Topaz*—badly written, badly acted, and shot any old way—can doubtless be attributed to the fact that the material doesn't lend itself easily to "pure cinema," only to "photographs of people talking." Yet this should prompt us to question the very basis of the familiar Hitchcockian opposition. "Pure cinema," if the term is to have any evaluative validity, must refer us not to fruitless questions about the cinematicness or otherwise of different sorts of material, but to the aliveness or otherwise of the film-maker's response. The point can be convincingly enforced by simply juxtaposing with the bad parts of *Topaz* two magnificently successful scenes from other films in which nothing "happens" except that people sit or stand around a table and talk: the kitchen scene from Welles' *The Magnificent Ambersons* (done mainly in a single static take), and the confrontation between husband, wife, and ex-lover in the restaurant near the start of Ray's *Bitter Victory* (where the suppressed emotional intensity is communicated largely through the rhythms of the fragmented editing).

The scenes in *Topaz* I have in mind are those involving Frederick

Stafford, Dany Robin, Claude Jade, and Michel Subor; I doubt whether their banality can be excused in terms of Hitchcock's possible awkwardness with French actors. They are the only scenes in the film where the material demands some constructive interest in the possibilities of a "normal" existence—here, in marital or familial relationships. Neither marriage relationship—the unhappy one of the older generation, the (supposedly) happy one of the younger—is created with any insight or density; to find this expressive of their emptiness is merely to confuse a *realized* sterility with banality of execution. As a result, what in structural terms is the center of a film whose unifying theme is the corruption of personal relationships by (in the broadest sense of the word) politics, barely exists. And with *Torn Curtain,* one treasures the richness of individual sequences while finding the whole disturbingly hollow.

Despite the expendability of the Billie Whitelaw scenes and a thinning of interest in its later stages, *Frenzy* is much the most satisfying, considered as a whole, of the three films Hitchcock has made between *Marnie* and *Family Plot*—perhaps because it is the most overtly cynical. One might be tempted to see it as a surreptitious attack (under cover of a "thriller" plot structure) on the institution of marriage itself—which would be by no means incompatible with "normativeness" were it accompanied by any corresponding movement toward the proposal of alternatives. In fact, its view of human relationships and human potential is almost uniformly sour, though not unsympathetic. The tensions in the Jon Finch/Barbara Leigh-Hunt relationship, for example, are realized with the sort of economy, precision, and vividness so lacking in the Stafford-Robin relationship in *Topaz.*

The film's crucial thematic opposition is between characters who never come together until the very end of the film; Inspector Oxford (Alec McCowen) and Bob Rusk (Barry Foster): an opposition that can stand as part paradigm, part parody, of the Hitchcock view of life. The hilarious scenes of the Oxfords' domestic life, beautifully played by McCowen and Vivien Merchant, are based on the notion that a "successful" marriage is built on the negative and repressive virtues of forbearance and endurance: a suggestion reinforced by the Finch/Leigh-Hunt scenes. Against this concept of "normality" is set, characteristically, the uncontrollable drive of a sexual psychopath. Oxford and Rusk are the two sides of the Hitchcock coin, archetypally confronting each other at the film's climax—Oxford's one remark to Rusk that he isn't wearing his necktie (it is around the neck of the latest victim) coming from a man who would never be seen without *his*. The Britishness of the film has been much noted: it offers a salutary reminder of the strength of Hitchcock's English middle-class roots in its constricted view of human potentiality (as well as in its saving grace of robust humor). The attitude of *Rich and Strange* has never really been abandoned.

Family Plot also—despite its cast and setting—testifies to the enduringness of certain strengths familiar from the British Hitchcock: meticulous craftsmanship and design, neatness and economy of execution, humor. The film has attracted an amount of attention and (slightly sentimental?) praise that seems to me disproportionate to its achievement, though I shall not quarrel with the view that it is the least seriously flawed of Hitchcock's late films (one might reasonably object to the callously dismissive treatment of the Karen Black character in its closing minutes). In its potential (partly that of its Ernest Lehman script, partly that of its splendid cast) it might well seem to challenge the view of Hitchcock I have presented here: indeed, it elicited from Roger Greenspun (*Film Comment*, May–June 1976) the following (to me) astonishing judgment: "Hitchcock's happens to be one of the great normative visions in the history of world cinema. To an astounding degree, men and women still have the option of loving one another and living together in sanity and happiness—under the aegis of Alfred Hitchcock." Greenspun's notions of sanity and happiness (not to mention love) would seem to differ radically from my own; even allowing for such personal divergence, I find it difficult to guess what films other than *Family Plot* he would adduce to support this view. *Family Plot* has two couples who enjoy each other's (sexual) company; even so, the relationships, though treated lightly, are both based, characteristically, on power—William Devane dominating Karen Black, Barbara Harris manipulating Bruce Dern. The film, though surprisingly pleasant after *Torn Curtain, Topaz,* and *Frenzy,* strikes me as altogether too lightweight to force any major reconsideration of Hitchcock: his involvement in it is predominantly on the level of a play with formal patterns, the pleasures the film affords arising mainly from its neat balances and symmetries. Indeed, one senses that Hitchcock deliberately avoided those aspects of the original material (Victor Canning's thriller *The Rainbird Pattern*) that might have engaged deeper levels of his creative personality. In the book, for example, the Barbara Harris character is abruptly and brutally murdered by the other couple: one can imagine a more centrally, intensely, and disturbingly Hitchcockian film that took that as its source of inspiration. The pleasantness of *Family Plot* is bought at the cost of suppressing (or carefully sidestepping) all that is most potent and subversive in the Hitchcock thematic; I cannot see it as more than a marginal note.

Auteur criticism has been too readily content to stop short at the identification of recurrent traits and the celebration of personal signature. If it is true that at the heart of every significant work of art is an individual creative talent, it follows neither that the success or failure of a given work is attributable solely to that talent nor that an artist's greatest works derive their quality from a particular freedom of self-expression. Hitchcock's finest films are all very much Hitchcock's—they would be unimaginable without him—but they are no *more* personal than *Frenzy* (and many others). Their greatness depends on the particular direction given to the individual talent by the material—and sometimes on the restraints the material imposes on certain personal tendencies. I am inclined, as time goes on, to talk less about great artists and more about great works. Of these, Hitchcock's cinema can boast an impressive list, even if its total represents only a small proportion of the whole output. No Hitchcock film—at least, since his earliest days—is without interest; *Notorious, Rope, Rear Window, Vertigo, North by Northwest,* the first half of *Psycho,* and *Marnie* stand up as major achievements.

ENDNOTES FOR EARLIER EDITIONS

1. Although the objection to the Chabrol/Rohmer formulation holds, this assertion (which owes far more to the American New Criticism than to Leavis) would now require a great deal of careful qualification. The significance of a work of art (or entertainment) is clearly inextricably involved in its cultural/ideological background; also, many works (including many of Hitchcock's) demand a psychoanalytical reading. My assertion here dangerously implies that a work can be accounted for in terms of a single "correct" reading, with neither work nor reading affected by its historical time and place.

2. It was at the beginning, too.

3. This is not quite accurate. The word she forms is "mudder"; Beaky (Nigel Bruce) points out that no such word exists and suggests the substitution of an "r." He then expresses a wish that he had an "er" to add on, and Fontaine immediately looks at Grant, associating the word "murderer" with him.

4. This still seems a fair enough (though obviously very sketchy) account of *Suspicion* "as we have it," but it is far from doing justice to the problems (both theoretical and practical) the film raises. The vexed question of the film's ending appears bewilderingly complicated and tangled, far from a simple matter of a studio imposing an ending contrary to the artist's intention. Hitchcock consistently claimed that he had always wished to adhere (at least in outline) to the ending of the original novel: Grant gives Fontaine poisoned milk, she drinks it knowing that she will die (and no longer wanting to live), and at the same time gives him a letter to mail for her which reveals the whole truth; the film was to end with Grant walking away whistling after dropping the letter in the mailbox. Donald Spoto, however (*The Dark Side of Genius*, pp. 253–257, claims documentary evidence that Hitchcock from the outset

"said that he . . . would revise the story by making the husband's deeds the fictions in the mind of a neurotically suspicious woman": the idea of following the original "cannot be found in the first treatment he submitted to RKO, and it is contradicted by memos in which he stated emphatically that he wanted to make a film about a woman's fantasy life." However, according to Fontaine (*Interview* magazine, February 1987) Grant went through the shooting believing that he was going to be allowed to kill her, and an ending built around her suicide was shot and previewed to an extremely hostile reception. Spoto claims that the entire film was shot without anyone knowing how it would end; the ending we have (starting, presumably, from the revelation that Fontaine has not drunk the milk) was a last-minute solution, though it appears to conform (in spirit if not in detail) with Hitchcock's original intention, in that first treatment.

All of this suggests that the film's insistence on identification with Fontaine was a matter as much of practical necessity as artistic strategy. If it is true that no one was sure whether Grant was guilty or innocent, the only way the film could possibly be shot was to deny all access to his consciousness, showing him exclusively through Fontaine's, sustaining his ambiguity until a decision about the ending was reached. Watching the film with this knowledge of its production can be a curious experience, rich in theoretical interest from the perspective opened up by recent structuralist/semiotic investigations (Barthes and his followers) into the workings of classical narrative. As one mentally "switches" from ending to ending, the significance of every scene changes, the apparent solidity of the narrative dissolves, the illusion of the fiction's "reality" disintegrates, the film becomes a "modernist" text in which the process of narrative is foregrounded.

5. This embarrassingly ignorant and supercilious dismissal of the first half of Hitchcock's career is perhaps the most obviously unacceptable passage in the book, from any critical standpoint. This is not totally to withdraw the relative valuation: I still consider at least half-a-dozen of the American films appreciably richer, more resonant, more deeply disturbing, more radical in their implications, than anything in the British period. If Hitchcock had made nothing after *Jamaica Inn* I don't think he would appear to us today more than a very interesting and distinctive figure who produced fascinatingly idiosyncratic interventions within a generally conservative, unadventurous, and imaginatively impoverished

national cinema. But that doesn't excuse a sweeping rejection of a body of work that includes numerous admirable and fully realized films and that at once establishes the thematic and structural bases of the work to come and suggests other paths that were not followed. It also needs to be said here that there are valid reasons for examining a given body of work (from a filmmaker, a genre, a period, a national cinema) quite apart from one's sense of its artistic value— consideration that did not occur to the author of *Hitchcock's Films*.

I think now that a personal motivation lay behind my reluctance to look seriously at the British films: the British middle-class milieu in which most of them are set is simply too close to the one in which I grew up, and I recoiled from having to reenter its atmosphere and ethos, constricting and cramping from every viewpoint, moral, emotional, intellectual, psychological. The films themselves suffer to the extent that they belong to the milieu they depict, though Hitchcock was never at any stage of his career a comfortable conformist.

6. Even were it correct the objection would be trivial; in fact, it is Hitchcock's camera that tracks in, not Maxim de Winter's.

7. A callow and inept account of an extremely rich and difficult film. It testifies most strikingly to the limitations of auteurism in its naive heyday: a film is evaluated in strict and exclusive relation to the discernible presence of its director, rather than as a complex text in which the director's presence is one determining factor among many possible ones. A case might certainly be argued that *Rebecca* belongs to the Selznick canon as much as to the Hitchcock; that need in no way diminish its interest. A concern with transgressive female sexuality in common to *Gone With the Wind, Duel in the Sun,* and *The Paradine Case,* all of which were to varying degrees dominated by Selznick as his own projects. It is also common, of course, to much of Hitchcock and to many Hollywood melodramas, and must finally be seen as a preoccupation— an anxiety—of our culture, which the individual artist inflects in specific ways.

Although there are precedents in the British period, it is Hitchcock's first Hollywood film that establishes definitively two of the major bases of his later work: the identification with the woman's position, and the preoccupation with male sexual anxiety in the face of an actual or potential autonomous female sexuality: the central structuring tension of many of his greatest films. Maxim de Winter, having killed Rebecca (we must I think accept the logic of the narrative against the "evidence" of an accident imposed on it to pacify the censor), can relate only to a child-wife who unquestioningly adores him and over whom he can exert total control. The film implies (in direct contradiction to the generically guaranteed and generally taken-for granted "happy ending") that he stops loving her when she loses her innocence and grows up. The heroine's opening and closing voice-over narrative nowhere suggests present happiness (though Manderley is burned, Mrs. Danvers dead, and Rebecca's ghost officially laid to rest): indeed, it fails even to establish that the couple are still together.

What was Rebecca's crime? Apart from minor mental cruelty to a harmless lunatic, simply that she resisted male definition, asserting her right to define herself and her sexual desires (including an at least implicit lesbian attachment to Mrs. Danvers). The logic of the film would have Rebecca its heroine, a project made impossible by Selznick's well-documented commitment to a faithful rendering of du Maurier's novel, but realized magnificently a few years later by him and Hitchcock as *The Paradine Case*.

(This note owes a great deal to a lecture delivered at York University, Canada, by Andrew Britton in 1984.)

8. The problems of *Spellbound* are far deeper and more complex, and more central to the Hitchcock thematic, than this account suggests. They are dealt with thoroughly and brilliantly in an article by Andrew Britton in *CineAction!* ³/₄.

9. This account of *Lifeboat* perhaps just merits a B + : it seems to me one of the stronger sections of this skimpy and uneven introduction. I would now wish to offer a more political reading, examining the film's very subversive critique of capitalist values: the way in which, by paralleling the Nazi captain and the American self-made millionaire, it suggests that fascism is an extension rather than an opposite of capitalist democracy. That is again, however, too simple a formula for this extremely complex work, one of the guiding principles of which seems to be that every position, once established, is elsewhere qualified or contradicted. The Nazi is also paralleled, even more explicitly, with the Communist stoker. Andrew Britton once again (*Cary Grant: Comedy and Male Desire, CineAction!* 7) has a remarkably suggestive aside on the film: "Three years before *Notorious*, in *Lifeboat*, Hitchcock had argued

that fascism rises to power with the connivance, and on the basis of the deadlocked class antagonisms, of bourgeois democracy . . ." Much has been made of the technical tour de force of shooting virtually an entire film in a severely restricted space, but the real tour de force, unique in Hitchcock's work, lies in the continuous shifting—hence continuous qualifying—of identification positions, often within a single shot.

One may add here a note on *Saboteur*—clearly not among Hitchcock's great films, but a very interesting one in relation to his attitude to the fascism/democracy opposition. Here, all the sympathetic minor characters (generally credited with an "intuitive" grasp of the hero's innocence) are either working class (the truck driver who gives him a lift), social outcasts (the circus freaks), or social outsiders (the blind musician). As a corollary, the American rich and/or powerful—from the ranch-owner Tobin and the "benevolent" society hostess Mrs. Sutton down to members of the law enforcement authorities—are systematically revealed to be complicit with fascism. No "established" American authority is clearly vindicated.

10. In chapter 15 I attempt a more adequate account of this extraordinary film—one of Hitchcock's finest achievements—which has elicited such contradictory readings.

11. Before this was written an excellent article on *Rope* by V. F. Perkins had been published in *Movie 7,* to which I should have paid closer attention. It deals (as if in anticipation) with the second of these two "weaknesses" in some detail. Both Perkins and I resolutely ignore, in our readings of the film, what now seems its main source of fascination, the homosexual subtext, a topic that, in the England of the early '60s, was still virtually "unspeakable." See chapter 16 of the present book.

12. This "revelation" appears to have taken place entirely in my imagination.

13. Here, at the end of the book's first detailed analysis, seems a suitable point to spell out the difference between my approach to the films twenty-five years ago and my approach today. By and large, the perceptions about *Strangers on a Train* still stand, and so does my final evaluation. What changes is not the perceptions but the uses to which they are put, the cultural/ideological position they are made to serve. So much for the notion of unbiased "objective" criticism or interpretation: there is simply no such thing. The reading I offered in 1965 is every bit

as ideologically weighted as the reading I would offer today; I just wasn't aware of this then.

The problem I now have with the reading of *Strangers* (and this applies equally to subsequent readings in *Hitchcock's Films*) is the way it essentializes everything. The film's dominant oppositions (light/dark, good/evil, order/disorder, surface world/under-world) are treated as if they represent some kind of eternal or universal principle, unrelated to any specific cultural situation (whether that the film describes or that within which it was produced). If the account invokes Freudian theory (the superego/id reference), it is only to incorporate it in this essentializing strategy. In fact, the film responds superbly to Freudian notions of repression as they are enacted within our highly specific, surplus-repressive culture, the patriarchal order of The Law (the world of politics in Hitchcock never embodies the positive values with which I endow it here, albeit somewhat uneasily and ambiguously) threatened by the return of all that it represses, become perverted and monstrous as a result of the repression.

The film's partial failure can be partly explained (as my 1968 note hints) in terms of a conflict between the impulse toward the "art" movie (for want of a better word—my readers will scarcely need reminding that I do not use it evaluatively) and the requirements of popular cinema. The "art" movie and the "entertainment" movie have each their own rules, practices, and conventions. Masterpieces and worthless idiocies can equally be produced within either format, but there are inevitably intermediate instances, awkward areas of overlap, where the two sets of rules come into conflict. It would be interesting to know (I have found no documentation) at precisely what stage in the elaboration of the scenario the crucial decision was made: the decision to depart drastically from the narrative line of Patricia Highsmith's novel, wherein Guy does murder Bruno's father. This seems to me absolutely demanded by the narrative logic and characterization, but it obviously conflicts with certain major requirements of the classical Hollywood film: no "hero," no construction of the heterosexual couple, no happy end.

14. In fact, Jefferies does not save "Miss Lonelyhearts" from suicide: he forgets all about her in his morbid preoccupation with Thorwald. She is saved when she hears the composer's new song issuing from his apartment on the piano.

15. A failure of memory here: "Miss Lonelyhearts" ends up in the apartment of the songwriter, whose tune saved her from suicide.

16. Many continue to assert that what Scottie sees is merely the view from Midge's window; numerous recheckings assure me that the account given here is correct.

17. Given that this supposedly farfetched and pretentious literary comparison provoked much amusement when the book was first published, I was interested to learn (from Donald Spoto's often useful *The Dark Side of Genius*) that an early draft of the *Vertigo* screenplay (by Maxwell Anderson) was entitled "Darkling I Listen."

18. In fact "sempervirens," always green: the word combines the idea of "ever living" with the color associated with Madeleine (and Judy) throughout the film.

19. I now see this as one of the book's major critical blunders. Whatever Hitchcock's original casting choices (he wanted Vera Miles for the role), *Vertigo* as we have come to know it is unimaginable without Novak. One can even assert that on a non-diegetic level the film is *about* her: Judy Barton left Salina, Kansas, three years earlier, a clear enough reference to the end of *Picnic*. When *Hitchcock's Films* was written there was really no serious access to the study of stars and how they function in filmic texts. For a detailed account of Novak as star, including an analysis of how she functions in *Vertigo,* see Richard Lippe's exemplary article in *CineAction! 7,* in which he argues, from a feminist viewpoint, that Novak's star persona is centered upon an uncertainty as to her identity, a resistance to being confined to any of the available Hollywood stereotypes of women.

20. This sentence was written by a gay male who at that time was desperately trying to reject and disown his own homosexuality. It is not, I think, an inaccurate description of the effect of the film at this point, but I am deeply ashamed of its tone and implicit attitude.

21. The effect now seems to me far more equivocal and ironic. Mount Rushmore becomes (as Andrew Britton points out in the essay on Cary Grant in *CineAction! 7* cited earlier) the final obstacle to Thornhill's rescue of Eve, connected to the film's two monstrous though opposed authority figures, Vandamm and the professor.

22. See the 1977 "Retrospective," pp. 211-212.

23. Lila does, in fact, open it. Some claim that she looks shocked,

and that the book "obviously" contains pornographic pictures. I find her expression unreadable, and now see the moment as a very knowing Hitchcockian variant on the "Kuleshov experiment."

24. *Marnie* now seems to me—looked at retrospectively from the positions made available by the subsequent development of feminism— a more problematic work than this account suggests: it is no longer so easy to see Mark unambiguously as a "positive hero," and my efforts to do so led me to downplay (though never quite ignore) the character's massive male presumption and the film's own evident uneasiness about him. Does Mark want to cure Marnie (as a neurotic) or tame her (as a human variant of the jaguarundi)? While I still regard the film as among Hitchcock's richest, I would now want to discuss it more in terms of inner tension, contradiction, and ambivalence than in terms of an achieved coherence.

25. This (written from memory) outdoes even the most outrageous effusions of Raymond Durgnat in its accumulation of errors. None of the action is presented through the heroine's eyes; the camera moves down to the knife on the table from a close-up of her face, without a cut, only when she picks it up to slice the bread; there is not a single close-up of the woman's lips. This doesn't invalidate the general point I was making about the evolution of Hitchcock's style. A far more convincing example from *Blackmail* of the merging of Expressionist and Soviet montage influences would have been the heroine's walk through the London streets after the killing of Crewe.

BOOK TWO
HITCHCOCK'S FILMS REVISITED

I I
PLOT FORMATIONS

One of the clearest ways to demonstrate, simultaneously, the validity of the auteur theory and the necessary qualifications to it, is to examine the relationship between Hitchcock's British and American films, a relationship of both rupture and continuity. When one passes from the British films to *Rebecca,* one feels at once in—on certain levels—a different cinematic world: the film, quite simply, *looks* different. The reasons for this are obvious enough: the availability of a higher budget; the dominating presence of Selznick (a rival auteur), his preoccupation with prestige, expensiveness, "finish," but also his own authorial inclinations and obsessions; the availability not only of Hollywood technicians with their highly developed and sophisticated professionalism, but of "the Hollywood way of doing things." My sense of the tangible difference is impressionistic: I have not gone into the laborious statistics of shot counts, shot lengths, number of times the camera moves, types of camera movement, ratio of close-ups to long shots, etc., regarding statistics with a certain suspicion. My impression is, then, of far greater technical fluency or fluidity (which is not to be taken as necessarily an evaluative judgment), and of greater (or more pervasive) depth to the images. The lean economy and wry humor of the British films have gone, replaced by Hollywood's luxury and Selznick's melodramatic romanticism. One caveat is instantly necessary: this cannot be taken, without heavy qualification, as a straight Britain/Hollywood opposition. Selznick's presence is clearly crucial: the shooting/editing practices of many of Hitchcock's later masterpieces are actually closer to the austerity of the British films than to the luxuriance of *Rebecca (The Paradine Case,* to which Selznick can again lay some authorial claim, can be taken as confirmatory evidence). Hitchcock was able, after *Rebecca,* to make movies in Hollywood that are "British" not only in setting but in "look" *(Suspicion).*

And the stylistic discontinuity of *Rebecca* on one level is counterpointed by its stylistic continuity on another: Hitchcock was able to develop his interest in point-of-view editing and spectator-identification techniques. Most strikingly, that Hitchcock "signature" so familiar from the later films—the forward point-of-view tracking shot—appears here for, I believe, the first time (a perception originally of Michael Walker's which I have found no evidence to refute). This must be seen, I think, as a logical continuation and refinement of Hitchcock's earlier techniques, rather than as a phenomenon somehow dependent upon the move to America. The point-of-view montage techniques that reach their ulti-mate mastery and elaboration in films like *Rear Window, Vertigo, Psycho,* are already highly developed in the British period.

It is clear that Hitchcock approached the plunge into American cul-ture with caution. The first "American" films are either set in England *(Rebecca, Suspicion)* or are picaresque adventure films *(Foreign Correspondent, Saboteur)* in which the Americanness of the leading characters is more incidental than essential: the fact that *Saboteur* can be seen as a loose remake of *The 39 Steps* confirms this. (One may note here that no less than seven of the films of the American period are set in England—in whole or in part—plus one shot in England and set in Australia). In the midst of the first five Hollywood films is *Mr. and Mrs. Smith:* here, direct contact with American culture is mediated by the presence of a genre (screwball comedy) with already highly developed and clearly defined conventions. It is only with *Shadow of a Doubt* and *Lifeboat* (the sixth and seventh Hollywood films) that Hitchcock begins to grap-ple with the realities and mythologies (material, cultural, spiritual, ideo-logical) of "America." I hope I shall not be taken as suggesting that these films lack generic mediation, that American life and values are somehow present in them as unqualified "reality"; but it seems clear that here Hitchcock confronts American capitalism in a way that the insulated stylization of screwball comedy enabled him to evade.

Again, the discontinuity on one level is countered by the continuity on another. If all the major elements of Hitchcock's mature style are already present in the British work, the same is true of the films' basic plot formations. It is here—in the continual recurrence and variation of a number of simple embryonic structures, separately and in combination —that the essential unity of the oeuvre is most evident. I list here what seem to me the basic formations (without claiming that the list is exhaustive or that it accounts for all the films), giving what appears to be the work in which the formation is first clearly established (a British film in every case), followed by a list of its major successors, British and American.

1. THE STORY ABOUT THE FALSELY ACCUSED MAN. *The Lodger; The 39 Steps, Young and Innocent; Suspicion, Saboteur, Spellbound, Strangers on a Train, To Catch a Thief, The Wrong Man, North by Northwest, Frenzy.*

2. THE STORY ABOUT THE GUILTY WOMAN. *Blackmail; Sabotage; Rebecca, Notorious, The Paradine Case, Under Capricorn, Stage Fright, Vertigo, Psycho, The Birds* (arguably), *Marnie.*

3. THE STORY ABOUT A PSYCHOPATH. *The Lodger; Murder!; Shadow of a Doubt, Rope, Strangers on a Train, Psycho, Frenzy.*

4. THE STORY ABOUT ESPIONAGE/POLITICAL INTRIGUE. *The Man Who Knew Too Much* (1934); *The 39 Steps, The Secret Agent, Sabotage, The Lady Vanishes; Foreign Correspondent, Notorious, The Man Who Knew Too Much* (1956), *North by Northwest, Torn Curtain, Topaz;* also *The Long Night,* the film Hitchcock was planning when he died, and of which a draft screenplay has been published.

5. THE STORY ABOUT A MARRIAGE. *Rich and Strange; Sabotage; Rebecca, Mr. and Mrs. Smith, Suspicion, Under Capricorn, The Man Who Knew Too Much* (1956—which I see as being *about* a marriage in a sense in which the British version is not), *Marnie;* to which I would add *Rear Window* and *Frenzy,* neither centered exactly on *a* marriage, but in both of which "marriage" is a pervasive preoccupation. *Family Plot* also has its relevance here.

The "falsely accused man" films typically take the form of what Andrew Britton has termed the "double chase" plot structure: the hero, pursued by the police, pursues the real villain(s). He is always innocent of the crime of which he is accused but (perhaps ambiguously) guilty of something else: at the least, egoism and irresponsibility *(North by Northwest),* at the most of a *desire* that the crime be committed *(Strangers on a Train).* Somewhere in between lies the attribution of *sexual* guilt, a concept that has undergone such transformation during our century that a proper understanding of (at least) some of the earlier films has become problematic: today's audiences may have difficulty in grasping that, say, Richard Hannay (in *The 39 Steps*) is to be regarded as "guilty" because he anticipated a night of "illicit" sex with a woman who (after all) picked *him* up, not the other way around, but the apprehension is crucial to a reading of the film's narrative progress.

The falsely accused man films move unanimously toward the protagonist's rehabilitation/restoration to society (often, as in *Strangers on a Train,* disturbingly, as he remains essentially unregenerate). One can make a general (not absolute) distinction here between the British films and the American: in the latter the implicit critique of the hero tends to be carried further, and his redemption (when he is felt to *be* redeemed) accordingly requires a more radical transformation. Unlike Thornhill in *North by Northwest,* the male protagonists of *The 39 Steps* and *Young and Innocent* do not have to undergo any major evolution (such as learning to defy patriarchal authority in order to express their identification with and commitment to a woman). On the whole, the British films fit into the patriarchal order more comfortably, with less sense of constraint and dissonance (which is not to say that such qualities are absent). A comparison of the two versions of *The Man Who Knew Too Much* confirms this.

The "guilty woman," on the contrary, is *always* guilty: whether we know this from the outset *(Blackmail, Marnie)* or learn it subsequently *(The Paradine Case, Vertigo),* she *did* commit the crime of which she is (initially or later) accused.[1] This sexist imbalance (which tells us more about our culture in general than about Hitchcock in particular) is partly rectified by the sympathy the films extend to their transgressive women: if Rebecca *should* have been the heroine of the film that bears her name, Mrs. Paradine is certainly the heroine of *The Paradine Case,* and the final effect of *Vertigo* is that of a denunciation of male egoism, presumption, and intransigence. Far more than the falsely accused man films, the guilty woman films belong predominantly to the American period. Mrs. Verloc *(Sabotage)* is not by any means a fully characteristic example, her guilt being dubious, her crime more a matter of intention than execution, the feelings that give rise to it morally justified even from the most conventional standpoint. That leaves, among the British works, the extraordinary *Blackmail,* in many respects the most strikingly anticipatory film of the entire British period. *Blackmail,* one might say, is Hitchcock's

---

[1] The figure of the guilty woman occurs already—if not very interestingly—in *Easy Virtue,* but the film's plot structure scarcely anticipates that of the later guilty women movies, and it seems reasonable to claim *Blackmail* as the film that established the pattern.

Stagecoach: the (relatively) early major work in which all the tensions and contradictions that structure the later films are clearly articulated, manifesting themselves as uncontainable within a coherent traditional value system or a "satisfying" resolution. A glance at the list of titles will suggest—justifiably I think—that the guilty woman category represents the richest vein in the Hitchcock mine, the area of greatest disturbance and tension, from which his most profoundly troubling and subversive films have been worked.

If the falsely accused man's destiny is to be restored (perhaps with some improvement) to the social order, the case of the guilty woman is inevitably more problematic, the resolution depending on the degree of her guilt and having more to do, perhaps, with the constraints of the Motion Picture Code than with Hitchcock's or the spectator's sympathies or moral judgment. Those guilty of, or complicit in, murder (Mrs. Paradine, the Judy Barton of *Vertigo*) must die; others can be restored to "normality" (a normality that Hitchcock's work in general discredits) only after more or less severe punishment and suffering; others still suffer fates that even the most conventionally moral and judgmental viewer must see as disproportionate (Marion Crane in *Psycho,* Melanie Daniels in *The Birds*). In no single case, I think, does the film invite us to view the punishment with complacence or satisfaction: typically, we are left with a sense of unresolved dissonance that relates, at bottom, to the fundamental strains produced by our culture's organization of sexuality and gender.

Obviously, the falsely accused man films and the guilty woman films exist in an intricately dialectic relationship of complementarity/opposition, a relationship that is surely the lynchpin of the entire Hitchcock oeuvre. One can examine it further by considering the role of women in the falsely accused man films and of men in the guilty women films. In the former, the woman characteristically occupies a subordinate position; she is initially antagonistic to the hero (accepting automatically the social assumption of his guilt), then learns (usually by intuition) to be assured of his innocence, to trust and support him. *The 39 Steps, Young and Innocent* and *Saboteur* are the purest instances, but many other films work variations on this pattern. *Spellbound* is complicated by the fact that Dr. Peterson falls in love with Ballantyne at first sight, and by the more determining fact that Ingrid Bergman has star precedence over Gregory Peck; *Strangers on a Train* is complicated by the fact that Ruth

Roman is already (if unofficially) engaged to Farley Granger before she suspects him of murdering his inconvenient wife; *North by Northwest* is complicated by the fact that Eva Marine Saint knows that Cary Grant is innocent before she meets him, as well as by the fact that she is herself a "guilty woman"; *The Wrong Man* is complicated by the fact that the protagonist's wife, far from being supportive, goes insane under the stress.

The role of the male in the guilty woman films is subject to even greater variation, in which the one constant appears to be that the man is never cleanly exonerated or endorsed. There are two major functions, the split depending on the question of whether the woman can be "saved" (the notion of salvation becoming here itself somewhat problematic, since it depends in its turn on her relationship to the patriarchal order which the films in general tend to undermine or discredit):

a) If the woman, because of the degree of her guilt, has to die, the man is effectively responsible for her death. There is no Hitchcock film in which he literally despatches her himself (the death of Juanita in *Topaz* might be considered an exception), although the logic of *Rebecca* is clearly that he *did,* and we know that the change from the novel was dictated by the Motion Picture Code, not anyone's actual desire. In *The Paradine Case,* Mrs. Paradine's desperate climactic confession is directly provoked by her defense barrister's intransigence in insisting on her innocence (because he is madly in love with her); in *Vertigo,* we have little doubt that Scottie would rather have a dead Judy than a live one, if she really isn't (or can't be transformed into) Madeleine.

b) If the woman's guilt is not such as to put her beyond the pale of the law, the hero's function is to guide her back, suitably chastized for her transgressions, within the bounds of patriarchal "normality." This is of course, put like that, a commonplace enough version of the "happy ending"; except that in Hitchcock's films it typically acquires disturbing and dissonant undertones. The hero's "love" for the woman, his desire to save her, is characterized above all as a desire for power over her, and his saving of her develops connotations of an alternative form of entrapment: Marnie's "I don't want to go to prison, Mark,' I'd rather stay with you" conveys the effect precisely, not only of the end of *Marnie,* but of that of *Blackmail. Under Capricorn* provides a fascinating variation and partial exception: its happy ending, one of the most unambiguous in all of Hitchcock, is achieved because the woman's "savior" *loses* her.

It remains to note a few exceptions to the general rules of these two categories. Uncle Charlie in *Shadow of a Doubt* is a *rightly* accused man, and so (it transpires) is the Jonathan of *Stage Fright;* the Ivor Novello of *The Lodger* and the Cary Grant of *Suspicion* would have been too if Hitchcock had been allowed to shoot the endings he claims he wanted. Conversely, Grace Kelly in *Dial M for Murder* is, like the falsely accused men, innocent of the crime of murder but guilty of a sexual "crime," adultery. Marlene Dietrich in *Stage Fright* is not directly guilty of the murder of her husband, but guilty of setting up Jonathan to commit it for her.

The "psychopath story" sometimes combines with the falsely accused man story: *The Lodger, Strangers on a Train, Frenzy.* It should be clear that I am thinking here in quite superficial terms of those films in which the character's psychopathic nature is made explicit and in which he is the "villain" (if often the character toward whom the energies of the film seem drawn as to a magnet);[2] I am not thinking of the blatant psychopathology of many of Hitchcock's ostensible heroes *(Rebecca, Notorious, Vertigo).* As with the guilty woman films, the psychopath is often the center of fascination, at the hero's expense—though never, like some of the guilty women, a primary identification figure. He also functions at times as the hero's "double" in the celebrated "exchange of guilt" theme traced throughout Hitchcock's work by Rohmer and Chabrol: *Strangers on a Train* and *Frenzy* are the two most developed examples.

The "espionage story," though it recurs fairly frequently, is the least essential to the overall structure of meaning in the Hitchcock oeuvre— often closer to a McGuffin than a plot formation. But from the films listed in this category one can extract a coherent group in which espionage/political intrigue is a central concern and develops a particular thematic resonance: *The Secret Agent, Notorious, North by Northwest, Torn Curtain, Topaz.* Two factors distinguish this group (occurring either separately or in combination): the sense of the inevitable corrup-

[2] One may well question whether "psychopath" is an appropriate term for the Handel Fane of *Murder!,* which I included in my list; but the whole point about Fane is his deviance from social/sexual norms, and in terms of his *function* he belongs with the psychopaths.

tion and contamination of political intrigue, expressed especially in the souring or poisoning of human relationships (the pervasive, unifying theme of the apparently diffuse *Topaz*); and the victimization of women within the domain of masculinist politics. In *Notorious, North by Northwest*, and *Topaz*, the struggle for power between two opposing patriarchal authority structures (nominally the Good Law and the Bad Law, but both are discredited by the film) crystallizes itself as the struggle to possess, manipulate, or dominate a woman. The ultimate, emblematic expression of this is the death of Juanita in *Topaz*, provoked by her French lover, carried out by her Cuban lover.

If "stories about a marriage" are relatively rare, their implications are far more pervasive. From *Rich and Strange* through to *Frenzy*, the attitude to marriage is remarkably (given the very high value placed on that institution within patriarchal ideology in general and the Motion Picture Code in particular) bleak and skeptical. This may account for the perfunctory, strictly "conventional" nature of so many Hitchcock happy endings: the expected construction or reconstruction of the heterosexual couple is presented without much evidence of engagement or conviction (e.g, *Shadow of a Doubt, Stage Fright, The Paradine Case, Strangers on a Train*) or with overt skepticism *(Rear Window)*. The films centered on a marriage are scarcely more encouraging. Leaving aside the unresolvably problematic *Suspicion*, consider the following:

Rich and Strange. The couple try to escape from the boredom and staleness of their marriage by seeking adventure, then, finding adventure even worse, sink back into boredom and staleness with a sigh of relief.

Sabotage. Mrs. Verloc has married her unappealing and self-preoccupied husband to provide security for her younger brother; discovering that Verloc has been responsible for the boy's death, she "accidentally murders" him.

Rebecca. Maxim de Winter marries the (unnamed) heroine because he sees her as a helpless child, his "little girl," whom he can mold and dominate; in the course of the film she grows up, and romance abruptly evaporates.

Rear Window. The Thorwald marriage—wherein the husband murders and dismembers his wife—is presented consistently in relation to the central projected marriage between Jefferies and Lisa, carrying the tensions in their relationship to their logical culmination.

Marnie. Mark forces Marnie into marriage, ostensibly to save her from the clutches of "some other sexual blackmailer," in reality to dominate and tame her by curing her neurosis. The film is reticent about what will happen after she is cured (compare *Rebecca*).

Frenzy. The film's central structural opposition is that between the Blaney's marriage and the Oxfords' marriage, the former disordered, violent, and broken, the latter ordered and permanent, built upon a willed mutual forbearance ironically counterpointed by pervasive signs that the husband and wife unconsciously detest each other. In *Frenzy,* marriage is treated as purely a social institution, devoid of emotional validation; significantly, the ending is striking for the absence of any attempt to construct a new heterosexual couple.

There are two marriage films in which the couple's union carries somewhat more positive connotations. But *The Man Who Knew Too Much* (1956 version) in fact stresses the tension between husband and wife far more strongly and convincingly than their solidarity, and the ending offers no guarantee that those tensions have been permanently resolved. *Under Capricorn* is another matter: for all the author-ity of the mise-en-scène, the film belongs as much to the woman-centered melodrama (and to Ingrid Bergman) as it does to Hitchcock. But even here there is an anomaly that slightly disturbs the resolution. The narrative logic demands, here, the restitution and celebration of the marriage, yet Hitchcock denies us the satisfaction of its logical culmination, a convincingly realized scene of marital reconciliation.

This leaves *Mr. and Mrs. Smith.* Even the most dedicated auteurist is unlikely to claim it as among Hitchcock's successful, fully realized works, but in the present context it takes on an interest out of proportion to its achievement. An almost painfully unfunny screwball comedy, the film's peculiar character—its thin and crabbed distinctiveness—develops out of a direct conflict between auteur and genre. The obvious and very telling comparison is with *The Awful Truth,* McCarey's genius being as compatible with the genre as Hitchcock's is alien to it. The two films share a number of structural features, the parallels being close enough to suggest a direct connection: both open with the dissolution of a marriage and end with its reaffirmation; most of the intervening narrative movement is activated by the couple's experiments with alternative partners. Both films contain a scene in a nightclub where the husband feels humiliated when his wife sees him in the company of an "inappropriate" other woman, and both culminate in a movement away from the city for a denouement in a country lodge where the obstacles to reunion are dismantled. In *The Awful Truth* we don't doubt for a moment that the couple will and should be reconciled, not only because this is demanded by the generic conventions but because, under McCarey's direction, Cary Grant and Irene Dunne communicate a constant and incorrigible affection for and delight in each other. Even the scene of Grant's ultimate humiliation—when Dunne, masquerading as his fictitious, irrepressibly vulgar sister, invades a society gathering in the home of his snooty new fiancée—is colored by the glances of reluctant admiration he can't help casting at her. The inner movement of the film—like that of all the finest examples of the genre—is a progress toward liberation (however qualified), especially liberation from restrictive social and gender roles and norms.

Nothing of this transpires in *Mr. and Mrs. Smith*. Here the final reconciliation seems motivated entirely by the exigencies of the genre. Robert Montgomery seems to want Carole Lombard back solely because her leaving him is an affront to his male ego. There is no sense at the end that the marriage has been radically transformed or that "male presumption" has been "chastised" (Andrew Britton's felicitous formula for *The Awful Truth*) into anything new or positive. We are, as in *Rich and Strange,* back to square one, to a marriage characterized by loveless bickerings and artificially contrived reconciliations.

Hitchcock's films cannot of course produce an alternative to marriage as our culture knows it. What they *do* provide is a thoroughgoing and radical analysis of the difficulties placed on successful heterosexual union by the social structures and sexual organization of patriarchal capitalism. A connective thread running through the studies that follow—studies for which this examination of plot formations forms a basis—will be the analysis of the films' complex dramatizations of sexual politics.

12

SYMMETRY, CLOSURE, DISRUPTION: THE AMBIGUITY OF *BLACKMAIL*

The extensive and intensive investigation into the operations and function of classical realist narrative over the past two decades has stressed two basic premises:

1. The function of classical narrative has been, overall, to reinforce and appear to validate the patriarchal order and its subordination of women.
2. The fundamental principles that govern the structuring of classical narrative include symmetry (especially of the beginning and end—"the end answers the beginning") and closure (the resolution of all the narrative threads and moral issues, the restoration of order, the reaffirmation of a set of values, embodied in a system of rewards and punishments of which marriage and death are, respectively, the privileged instances).

One need not argue with this, provided it is understood as the kind of crude generalization that can offer a useful starting point for critical inquiry into particular works—and provided the inquiry is prepared to find exceptions to the rules as well as examples that prove them. Where the line of argument becomes very dubious is in its tendency to collapse the two premises together, so that symmetry and closure are seen as indissolubly tied to the reaffirmation of patriarchy. There are strong reasons why this might be expected to be the case within our classical cinema (itself a patriarchal capitalist institution with its stake in preserving the status quo) but no convincing ones why it should be held to apply absolutely. Consider a simple imaginary scenario: at the beginning of the film a housewife arrives home from the daily shopping; during the ensuing ninety minutes of screen time she comes to learn that she is oppressed, subordinated, trapped in her domestic role; at the end of the film she packs her suitcases and leaves. There you have a very precise example of symmetry (arriving home/leaving home, opening the door/ closing the door, carrying shopping bags/carrying suitcases) and a permissible type of closure (the end of a marriage which also marks "a new beginning"). One need not be surprised that such a scenario has not formed the basis for a great many classical Hollywood films (the two versions of Ibsen's *A Doll's House* were both produced outside the mainstream), but its possibility surely challenges any notion of a necessary and indissoluble connection between symmetry/closure and the restoration of patriarchy. Or imagine a more extreme instance, a sequel to the above. The film starts where the original ended, with the woman walking out of the house with her suitcases. In the course of the action she develops a sense of solidarity with other working women, joins a revolutionary Marxist/feminist organization, sells everything from her past to make an entirely new start. The film ends with her entering a lesbian commune. Here we have a scenario that is unthinkable within the terms of classical Hollywood but perfectly thinkable within the rules of classical narrative. I might add that the middle section (and main body) of the Mulvey/Wollen *Riddles of the Sphinx,* "Louise's Story Told in Thirteen Shots" (to which my second scenario bears certain resemblances), is a classical narrative filmed in an avant-garde manner, its action situated entirely within the bounds of "realist" plausibility.

The function of symmetry and closure can in fact be theorized quite differently. One may even question whether "closure" is not a misleading term: the sense of closure in my two imaginary examples is dependent entirely upon the "classical" symmetry ("the end answers the beginning"). For the character, the ending in each case marks simply a crucial decision she has made which points forward to new problems, new developments, new struggles. If the function of the symmetry is to "close," this operates on a purely formal level and is contradicted on other levels. What the symmetry marks most obviously and strongly is neither finality nor the restoration of an earlier order, but *difference.* For the spectator this opens up rather than closes the narrative, inviting us to reflect back on how far the character has traveled and to speculate ahead on what may be in store for her. Many actual classical narratives can be argued to work in this way. Many more, in which the closure (*en*closure might be better) appears complete, are characterized by an irony or dissonance that makes possible for the spectator a critical distance: if the characters are seen to be definitively trapped, the spectator is set free to become aware of the entrapment and of the social conditions that produce it (*Blonde Venus* and *The Reckless Moment* are exceptionally fine examples).

Blackmail provides an admirable opportunity for the exploration of these issues. One of the most obsessively symmetrical classical narrative films ever produced, it is also profoundly ambiguous (conservative, radical) in its overall significance, the ambiguity—the possibility offered of diametrically opposed readings—being central to the entire Hitchcockian oeuvre, British or American. The film is of course celebrated in the history books as Hitchcock's first (and the first British) sound film: it is unnecessary here to recapitulate the eulogies (thoroughly deserved) of Hitchcock's inventiveness within the new medium. (At the same time, a comparison of the two versions—the sound version and the silent version it superceded—is beyond my scope, the silent version being inaccessible. Readers are directed to Charles Barr's fascinating article in *Sight and Sound,* which strongly suggests that Hitchcock's mature POV shooting/editing style was more fully developed in the silent version and was actually retarded by the arrival of sound). What concerns me here is *Blackmail*'s privileged status as the first of Hitchcock's guilty woman films, a narrative pattern not taken up again until the move to Hollywood, where it becomes so central to his work. The pattern—and its characterizing ambiguities—is established in *Blackmail* with extraordinary completeness, Annie Ondra's performance at moments strikingly anticipating those much later ones of Grace Kelly and Tippi Hedren.

I shall concentrate on what is usually (but erroneously, the error testifying to the sexism of our culture) referred to as the "murder" scene, but I want first to place it within an overview of the film's wider, all-embracing symmetry. One can analyze the use of symmetry at all levels (and this is applicable to classical cinema generally, *Blackmail* being simply an extreme example): symmetry of overall construction, symmetry within the larger segment (by which I mean a *series* of sequences linked together by continuity of action), symmetry within the individual sequence, symmetry within the construction of the individual shot, symmetry of composition within the individual frame. Since my interest here is in narrative structure this last will not concern me greatly: it is basically determined by the principle (practically ubiquitous in classical cinema) of centering, whereby the character(s) or object(s) on which our attention is to be focused is/are placed in the middle of the image with roughly equal space on either side. It is a principle that can of course be used dramatically (either by emphasis or negation), and *Blackmail* provides plenty of examples, of which I note two: 1) The use of the screen in Crewe's apartment during the "murder" scene to separate Crewe (at the piano) from Alice (changing her clothes), symbolizing the barrier that Crewe will try to breach; 2) The strongly symmetrical triangular compositions during the scene between Alice, Frank and the blackmailer in the back room behind the Whites' store, in which Alice (seated, compelled to silence by her lover) is placed centrally in the foreground of the image while the two men struggle for domination (of her, of each other) behind the sofa.

The principle of construction that dominates the smallest unit, the frame, also dominates the largest, the film as a whole. The encompassing symmetry of *Blackmail* is particularly strongly marked by the repeated close-up of the revolving wheel of the speeding police car, which introduces a whole series of repetitions: the quasi-documentary shots describing the mechanics of a police chase. Hitchcock's account of the ending he originally planned suggests that the symmetry was to have been even more rigorous:

After the chase and the death of the blackmailer the girl would have been arrested and the young man would have had to do the same things to her that we saw at the beginning: handcuffs, booking at the police station, and so on. Then he would meet his older partner in the men's room, and the other man, unaware of what had taken place, would say, "Are you going out with your girl tonight?" And he would have answered, "No, I'm going straight home." (Truffaut, pp. 63–4)

As the film stands, the parallel between beginning and end is still strong: (a) the pursuit and arrest (actual or attempted) of a male criminal; (b) a scene at the police station involving Alice's visit and culminating in a three-way conversation and shared laughter between Alice, Frank, and the constable on duty. I shall examine in detail the effects produced by this complex symmetry—the significance that arises from the play of sameness and difference.

THE PURSUITS

I suppose one might describe Hitchcock's presentation of the police as ambiguous. The criminals they pursue are not presented positively, and Frank is, after all, in terms of the conventions of classical narrative (i.e., the story, as distinct from the way in which Hitchcock tells it), the film's hero. It is a question, perhaps, of which is more powerful, the conventions or Hitchcock's use of them, a use that produces Frank as the most unsympathetic character in the film. One must assume that the narrative conventions (essentially, the mapping of "good" and "evil" in terms of the dominant social norms) were strong enough to preserve an appearance of respectability and the endorsement of the law, and they are supported by the most superficial of the film's signifiers (handsome detective, ugly criminal). What is remarkable is the thoroughness with which they and their very strong class bias are simultaneously undermined, in a film produced primarily (though not exclusively) for the bourgeois audience. Before Frank has been established as an individualized character, the activities and nature of the police have already been described with a harsh hostility that undercuts the ostensible documentary objectivity of the whole opening sequence. They are characterized from the outset in terms of aggression, domination, intrusion, penetration: the forward-moving POV shots from inside the police van, the breaching of the archway that marks off the private world of the working class, the forced entry through the front door, the penetration of the bedroom. The private world through the arch is colored for us by a whole cluster of signifiers that carry positive connotations: children playing tag (albeit somewhat violently, but their spontaneous violence is set against the willed and impassive violence of the police); washing hanging on lines, a window being cleaned (in contradiction of bourgeois myths of working-class squalor); a white horse, that archetypal emblem of purity and nobility.

The sequence in the criminal's bedroom is marked most powerfully by his first awareness of the intrusion of the police detectives (it is also the first time we are allowed to see their faces clearly, so it is *our* introduction to them as well—one of them is Frank): the shot of their faces reflected in a mirror, criminal's point of view, the faces immobile, stonily expressionless, "the Law" at its most impersonal and implacable, the dehumanization underlined by the fact that this is an image on a glass surface. The anticipation (by about forty years!) of the opening shot of *Topaz* is very striking: the stony face of the surveillance officer caught (again within a complicated camera movement) in the mirror at the entrance to the Soviet embassy. The negative attitude to institutionalized authority (no matter what its ideological sanction) encapsulated in those two moments runs right through Hitchcock's work, ranging from uneasiness through resentment to outright denunciation. The ambivalence already established (coldly impersonal authority, shifty-eyed criminal) crystallizes in the ensuing incident of the struggle for the gun by the man's bed: it activates one of the basic principles of Hitchcock identification practice—his frequently reiterated assertion that we identify with the character who is being threatened, irrespective of moral norms—but it is very difficult to say who, here, *is* being threatened, the police (who may get shot) or the criminal (who may get arrested). Accordingly, embryonic point-of-view technique is used to dramatize *both* sides: the glances, directed toward the gun, of both the police and the criminal. The editing suggests, in fact, that the detectives see the gun and at first make no move for it, waiting for (perhaps willing) the criminal to grab it so that he will incriminate himself: our sense of threat is, if anything, weighted in favor of the criminal. The bedroom sequence culminates in the smashing of a windowpane: one of the outside bystanders has hurled a stone, as a gesture of protest and working-class solidarity. Do we identify with the discomfiture of the detectives, or with the sardonic laughter of the criminal?

Not all of the film was reshot for sound. The absence, throughout this entire opening segment, of a dialogue track was presumably motivated by a desire to tease the audience by withholding the promised "miracle" of spoken dialogue: we see the characters' lips moving, but can only guess at what is being said. The strategy presupposes a kind of growing baffled frustration ("I thought this was supposed to be a *talking* picture" which will be relieved just in time to prevent the spectators demanding their money back. However, the decision has an interesting side effect: it represses any possible information we might have received as to the man's crime—its nature, motivation, the degree of certainty of his guilt. Dialogue is withheld, uncertainty maintained, right through to the moment of his incarceration: it is only after the door to the cells closes that we are at last allowed to hear the detectives' voices, as they walk away to go off duty. We watch the criminal being worn down by interrogation (its length suggested by the elliptical dissolve that shows an initially empty ashtray subsequently filled with cigarette butts), three authority figures (two of them standing over him) apparently browbeating him for a confession, but it is not clear that he confesses (if he did, then the ensuing identification parade[1] would be superfluous). The only evidence of his guilt we are given is (a) his possession of a gun and (b) the recognition of one woman during the identification session.[2] What is inescapably striking is the entire sequence's often point-for-point anticipation of the opening movement of *The Wrong Man,* and the connection (unless we take the criminal's guilt as a generic "given") might make us reflect that the circumstantial evidence against the wrongly accused Henry Fonda is incomparably stronger, more detailed, more convincing. (Behind both sequences, of course, though their significance is scarcely reducible to it, lies Hitchcock's personal dread of incarceration as embodied in his familiar story—whether fact or fantasy—of his own arranged incarceration as a childhood punishment).

With no information as to what crime the man has committed, and only the most minimal evidence that he is guilty of it, we are free to speculate—on the clear evidence the film *does* offer—that his *real* crime is to be working class and perhaps socialist (he is introduced reading the *Daily Herald,* the newspaper associated with the British Labour Party). The police are presented from the outset as the defenders and preservers of a specifically bourgeois order—the order that produces, as its representative citizens, Frank, Crewe, the blackmailer Tracy, and Alice White, and the impossible contradictions that compromise the positions (moral, legal, ideological) of all four. At this point in the film (the moment of incarceration, the moment when the picture begins to talk) the class issue is dropped, to be replaced almost immediately by issues of sexuality and gender. But the opening of *Blackmail* must not be dismissed as irrelevant to what follows (its relevance, indeed, is guaranteed by the symmetry). The opening establishes the police as the representatives of a repressive (male) bourgeois order, its agents of control, and what they control or contain here (very precariously) is but the first link in a chain

1. This brief scene is missing from some prints, but it is present in the readily available commercial video.
2. The silent version has a shot of the criminal's record sheet, which categorizes his crime as "breaking and entering." It would be interesting to learn why this was cut from the sound version—especially as this is not one of the sequences that was reshot.

traversing the entire film: the working class—criminality—sexuality—art—women.

The function of the symmetry of the two pursuits is twofold: to underline the parallel between the criminal of the opening and the blackmailer (together with their common positions as victims of the system which the police enforce and uphold); and to underline the contrast between the locations (working-class yard and room, the British Museum). On one level, the blackmailer appears as a "resurrection" of the criminal within the narrative: he has a criminal record. On the level of class, his accent and manner suggest a fallen middle-class gentility rather than a proletarian background. Presented initially as mysterious, sinister, and threatening, the character is rapidly demystified, revealed as a pathetic failure and victim rather than a hardened and malevolent criminal. The protracted scene of confrontation between Frank and Tracy, over a silenced Alice, in the living room behind the Whites' store, crystallizes the theme of the film, a central Hitchcockian concern here receiving its most complete and complex statement in his work to date (and arguably in all his pre-Hollywood period): life in patriarchal capitalist society as an incessant struggle for domination. The entire Frank/Tracy battle of wills, with its shifting balance of power, might be seen as an elaborate extension of the struggle for the gun in the opening segment, the film evoking in the audience a similar ambivalence, a split or uncertain identification. It has become something of a critical commonplace that the "blackmail" of the title is practiced by Frank as much as by Tracy. That is, I think, inexact—Frank blackmails Tracy only in the loosest sense. What can be accurately asserted—and it is central to the film's presentation of authority—is that Frank's behavior is, both legally and morally, far more reprehensible than the blackmailer's. He withholds evidence (Alice's glove), and attempts to coerce a man into accepting the blame for a "murder" Frank knows he didn't commit. If he blackmails him in the strict sense of the word, it is in forcing him to try to escape, the editing here strongly echoing that of the moment when the detectives *will* the criminal to grab for the gun: it is in Frank's interest that Tracy should incriminate himself by fleeing (the wish accompanied perhaps by a hope that he might get killed trying to escape?). Frank stands with his back against the door to the shop, through which we heard the noises of the police's arrival. He stares at Tracy, then looks significantly to his right (screen left) in the direction of the window. He then makes no move to stop Tracy until the police are at the door behind him; when he *does* dash to the window after Tracy, he awkwardly stands back to let another policeman go through first. By this time Tracy —because of his weakness, his vulnerability, his "underdog" mentality —has drawn to himself a great degree of audience sympathy (divided here between him and Alice, with Frank the only character quite beyond it). Indeed, this triangular character structure in *Blackmail* anticipates that of *Notorious* (Frank/Alice/Tracy parallel Devlin/Alicia/Sebastian) with the villain destroyed by the joint action (in Alice's case *in*action) of hero and heroine, the sympathy attracted by the villain coloring our response to the "happy ending." The crucial difference is that Frank, unlike Devlin, remains totally unregenerate: where Devlin openly defies authority in order to identify himself with, and rescue, Alicia, Frank surreptitiously perverts police authority while remaining one of its representatives. It is possible to read Frank's motivation as not so much the desire to save Alice as to maintain and reinforce his personal authority over her. A recurrent—indeed pervasive—motif of the last third of the film is his refusal to allow her a voice, hence any personal autonomy. From this viewpoint, the version of the ending that Hitchcock originally projected—Alice's arrest—is, ironically, much closer to a "happy ending" that the version we have: Alice would have been removed from Frank's oppressive domination and, imprisoned, would have been set free to speak at last for herself.

The oblique echoes of the opening sequence in the scene in the Whites' living room anticipate the literal repetition of shots (revolving wheel, "documentary" details of police procedure) that initiate the climactic chase, culminating in Tracy's death. The ambivalence of the opening (with whom do we identify, police or criminal?) is here developed and dramatized much more fully. Do we want Tracy to escape or do we (with Frank) wish him dead? Do we want Frank to "save" Alice, knowing the kind of personal terrorism this implies as the future of their relationship? It is probably easier to answer the latter question negatively today (in retrospect from the feminist insights of the past twenty years) than it was in 1930, but it also seems unlikely that the affirmative answer could have been given without discomfort and disturbance, Alice being the spectator's primary identification figure throughout most of the film. The ambivalence takes on tangible form in the crosscutting between Alice and the chase, which expresses (or perhaps fails effectively to suppress) the ambiguity to which many instances of parallel montage are prone, the question of the precise relationship between the two terms. The dominant reading is clearly that Alice is experiencing guilt and contrition—which eventually crystallize in the letter she writes declaring her decision to confess. But the crosscutting—close-ups of Alice, shots of the pursuit in the British Museum—can also be read as implying a closer relation between the two actions, one of cause and effect: that Alice on some level *wills* Tracy's death as the convenient answer to her quandary (she writes the letter only *after* his fall). This possible but by no means necessary secondary reading does not significantly detract from the sense that Alice, here, clearly represents the film's conscience— the conscience that Frank completely lacks.

The British Museum climax—the first of three Hitchcock climaxes to take place in or on a national monument—acquires some of its significance from its symmetrical relationship (here a relationship of opposites) to the working-class courtyard of the opening. It lacks the overt political reference of the Statue of Liberty *(Saboteur)* and Mount Rushmore *(North by Northwest),* but one might argue that the symmetry/opposition confers political connotations upon it: an oppressed and hostile proletariat "answered" at the film's close by the grandeur of a national institution with strong imperialist overtones (the "British" museum contains treasures hoarded from all over the world). The use of these monuments is consistent throughout Hitchcock's career, on either side of the Atlantic, corresponding to his attitude to authority in general. Just as there is a frequent conflict between narrative conventions and the Hitchcock tone, so here the cultural code and the authorial code collide, producing further ambivalence or discord within the text. The grandeur of the monuments is in each case qualified by their attributes of stoniness, heartlessness, implacability, derived from the dramatic situations and the mise-en-scène. The discord is perhaps most extreme in the case of *Saboteur:* the film's wartime patriotic rhetoric produces the Statue of Liberty as the ideal image of symbolic retribution, yet no one wants Fry to fall from it, and our anguish for him vastly outweighs any sense of satisfaction at the triumph of democracy over fascism—a democracy all confidence in which has been effectively undermined earlier in the film. I was quite correct, in the analysis of *North by Northwest* in *Hitchcock's Films,* to describe the Mount Rushmore presidential heads as the "guardians of order"; what I failed to add (and at that time quite failed to grasp, privileging cultural over authorial code) is that it is an order the overall narrative context of the film discredits. As Andrew Britton has argued, the stone heads (guardians of the patriarchal order represented within the fiction by the callous, unscrupulous, and opportunistic professor) "impede" the escape of Thornhill and Eve: they are not the solution to the hero's problems but the final obstacle he must overcome.

The most memorable image of the British Museum sequence is also that of a statue: the colossal head of an Egyptian god, "its gaze blank and pitiless as the sun," which dwarfs the figure of Tracy as he slithers down a rope beside it in his desperate flight from the police. Its cold impassivity remotely echoes the mirror reflection of the police detectives in the opening segment; it is also, in the film's system of images, the opposite of Crewe's painting of the laughing jester, the symbol of heartless authority against the figure that ridicules *all* authority, the latter the most vital and animated "character" in the film just as the statue is its most stonily expressionless. Its implacable indifference to human pain and terror marks a kind of preface to Tracy's death, when he falls through the museum's glass dome as the police, Frank in the lead, trap him on the roof. Frank here occupies a position (characteristic of the film's ambivalence) midway between the hero of *Saboteur* (who actively tries to save Fry) and the villain Leonard of *North by Northwest* (who actively tries to kill Eve and Thornhill by pressing his foot on the latter's hand): Frank neither deliberately precipitates Tracy's fall nor makes any attempt to prevent it.

An examination of the film's other element of embracing symmetry — Alice's two incursions into Scotland Yard — must be delayed pending the analysis of the film's major central segment, to which I now pass.

I have already suggested that the fact that this segment (which occupies almost a third of the film's running time) is habitually referred to as the "murder" scene testifies to the pervasive sexism of our culture. Alice does not murder Crewe. He is attempting to rape her, and she defends herself with the only weapon to hand. It might be claimed that she overdoes it (the struggle behind the bed curtains suggests that she stabs him a number of times), but she is clearly overwhelmed by terror and panic; the most of which she could possibly be found guilty is manslaughter. Underlying the label "murder scene" is the common masculinist myth that women *want* to be raped. If it is true that Alice's behavior has provoked Crewe's assault, it is equally clear that, far from welcoming it, she is appalled by it. On a conscious level, what she wants is the fun and excitement of a "daring" flirtation, with some but not too much danger. One might reasonably argue that her behavior suggests that, on an unconscious level, she would like a sexual experience (*not* rape) but is also afraid of it. The film is deeply embedded in the middle-class British culture of its day, and the modern viewer ("modern," as Peter Ustinov remarks in the American release version of *Le Plaisir,* is what we all like to call ourselves while we are alive) may need some imagination to bridge a certain gulf (which is not to suggest that our own world has severed itself cleanly).

Blackmail was made a year before I was born and is set in a milieu thoroughly and depressingly familiar to me. My parents were antique dealers, hence a few rungs higher in the social scale than tobacconists, to whom they would have condescended, but in terms of sexual mores the differences would be minimal. In the environment in which I grew up all bodily functions were regarded as shameful. I was made to feel deeply ashamed of pissing and shitting, and these simple natural functions had to be referred to (if at all, in cases of direst necessity) in whispers, using absurd euphemisms (I first heard the words "piss" and "shit" when I was in my teens). I never heard the word "sex" spoken within my family, either by my parents or by any of my four older brothers and sisters: I developed a vague sense that it was an obscenity, a "dirty word" that must not be uttered and that presumably referred to something even dirtier. When I was about eleven, a friend of my sister's had an illegitimate child. I am not sure how I deduced this, as it was alluded to only in muffled and obscure hints even when I was supposed *not* to be listening. Certainly I was not supposed to know about it, and I was actually afraid I might inadvertently reveal my knowledge to my family, who would have been shocked and angry. (In retrospect, it seems to me that the typical British middle-class upbringing was dedicated mainly, both at school and in the home, to the task of stifling the child's natural desire to learn. Much of what we continue to call "education" today appears to have the same ambition, though the taboos now are more likely to be political than sexual.) My sister, a woman in her early thirties, never, as far as I know, met or spoke to her "friend" again. As for myself, I knew by that time (without ever being told) that babies somehow grew in women's bodies; I had absolutely no idea how they got there, so had only the vaguest notion of why my sister's friend's misfortune was so unspeakable.

My case may have been extreme (though I have every reason to believe the contrary). But one can safely assume that the essentials of the kind of cultural/sexual situation I have described (which "modern" people today may find so alien in its details but so disturbingly familiar in its underlying principles) were taken for granted by the audiences for whom *Blackmail* was made, and by the people who made it. (Donald Spoto's account of Hitchcock's childhood in *The Dark Side of Genius* is useful here.) Alice is certainly a virgin: Frank would never dream of suggesting premarital intercourse, and if he did she would repudiate the suggestion with horror. The entire manslaughter sequence can only be understood if, at the very least, we have in mind that a family like the Whites would have regarded the use of contraceptives (if they had ever heard of such a thing) as an unspeakable abomination, and abortion as unthinkable. Alice is caught in a particular cultural moment: a moment when everything in popular fashion encourages permissiveness, "naughtiness," rebellion (epitomized in the song Crewe sings for her at the piano), and everything in one's home and educational environment repudiates such licence. She is also caught between two men, who are much more than two individual characters. They represent two divergent, antagonistic, yet curiously complementary masculinist attitudes to women and sexuality, and the film treats them both with uncompromising harshness: Frank, who wishes to dominate, enclose, and contain Alice within the horror of bourgeois respectability; Crewe, the "nippy cock-" of the half-seen menu in the restaurant, who wants to use her for his casual gratification. Both indeed want to *use* her, whether for sex or for the bolstering of the male ego: for ends that are in effect socially sanctioned (officially or unofficially) within a masculinist culture. The sexuality that Alice consistently expresses has no worthy responder: Frank wants to control and contain it, Crewe to exploit it. What the film —like so much of Hitchcock's work—reveals is not the personal wrongness of this or that individual so much as the wrongness of an entire social/sexual/ideological system.

Bearing all this in mind, it becomes clear that Alice's behavior throughout the manslaughter segment (throughout the film) is very precisely described, with all of Hitchcock's characteristic empathy for the feelings and responses of women trapped in the impossible situations the patriarchal system creates. The irony of the neon gin advertisement ("White Purity") that Alice sees in her wanderings after the "crime" is complex. On one level she has killed to defend her "purity"; on another, that purity is at once a mere technicality and a factor of desperate importance. She goes off with Crewe as an act of rebellion against Frank's masculinist domination and his unquestioning assumption of its rightness. Her behavior in Crewe's apartment continuously suggests a desire for erotic pleasure (the "purity" is an illusion, an imposition), but a desire she cannot even *think* might be voluntarily fulfilled: the absence of a means of birth control, the terror of pregnancy, the stigma of illegitimacy, are but the surface manifestations of a wider terror of sexuality itself instilled by the culture and particularly emphasized in relation to the female, whose "purity" must at all costs be preserved for monogamous marriage. Crewe, precisely because all he is after is a moment of pleasure (the "poor benefit of a bewildering minute"), could respond to this only by renunciation or rape. The blame for what happens is neither his nor Alice's so much as the system's: the film makes it clear that Crewe's "dishonorable" intentions are really no more oppressive than Frank's "honorable" ones.

It is against this background that I want to examine the manslaughter segment—and particularly its symmetry—in detail. It is necessary to begin with a complete shot breakdown. The segment, though continuous in action, divides into five sequences according to location.

<u>Blackmail</u>: The Manslaughter Sequence: Shot Breakdown

A. <u>Exterior</u>

1. LS, static. No dialogue. Blackmailer, then Crewe and Alice.
2. Medium 2-shot, Crewe and Alice.
3. Insert: Mr. White's shop.
4. As 2.
5. Insert: the blackmailer. CU.
6. As 2 and 4: Motor horn.
7. As 5.
8. As 2, 4, 6.
9. Up step to door. Voice off. Motor horn. Crewe exits from and subsequently reenters frame.

B. Interior of house

1. Hall. Crewe and Alice. Pan left.
2. LA. POV. The stairs.
3. As 1. The note.
4. Split screen effect: Alice to stairs R, Crewe along hall L.
5. Crewe and landlady. 2-shot.
6. Crewe to stairs.
7. Crane shot up stairs. Crewe and Alice in LS.
8. To Crewe's door.

C. Inside Crewe's apartment

1. Inside door. Crewe and Alice enter (medium 2-shot). Light switched on. The mask.
2. Room. POV.
3. As 1. Crewe to light fire.
4. Crewe draws curtain over bed.
5. LS. They move about the room.
6. MS. Alice. Looks L.
7. LS. HA. POV. Policeman along street, R-L.
8. As 6. Alice looks ahead.
9. The pointing jester. LA. Rapid track out. POV with licence.
10. As 6 and 8, but more LS. Alice points and laughs. Pan R with her. Whistling begins.
11. MS. Alice. Piano L, dress in b.g., empty canvas R. Alice picks up easel.
12. LS. Crewe startled, wipes hands with handkerchief.
13. Alice's drawing. Long take (2 minutes, 22 seconds).
14. Alice and the dress. Closer MS.
15. Repeat of 12. Crewe with drinks.
16. Alice, Crewe, dress. Pan L when he goes to piano. Split screen effect: partition.
17. Crewe by window. Repeats composition of Alice in 6, 8, 10. Alice's movement at R.
18. Split screen effect. Alice changes. The song. Long take (2 minutes, 22 seconds).
19. Doing up dress.
20. Straps lowered; seduction attempt.

21. Close shot: the kiss.
22. As 20. Crewe repulsed.
23. Alice behind screen.
24. MS. Crewe. Shadows over face. Steals Alice's dress.
25. Split screen effect. Piano. Dress thrown off screen L. Alice dragged by wrists.
26. The policeman. As 7, but movement L-R. Alice's cries.
27. The bed (curtain). Alice's hand. Track in on knife.
28. The curtain. Struggle. Crewe's hand. Then Alice with knife. Look into camera. Composition echoes 17, with curtain replacing screen.
29. Closer MS. Alice shivering. Pan L with her to window. Then she looks up and R.
30. The black dress over the picture.
31. Alice to picture.
32. CU picture. Dress pulled away. The jester.
33. CU Alice. Strikes at picture.
34. The torn picture. Alice turns and walks into camera. Dissolve to
35. LS. Alice in the room. Like 2, but no longer POV. Static long take: dressing, coat, to door, light switched off, back for handbag, look L.
36. The name on picture blacked out.
37. As 35. Second light switched off. The empty room.

D. Interior of house

1. Alice outside Crewe's door.
2. Overhead LS. Alice descends stairs. Dissolve to
3. CU: Alice's feet. Camera moves back to LS (hall).
4. Closer shot. Alice by door. Dissolve to

E. Exterior

1. Alice outside door.
2. LS. Alice walks off R out of frame, shadow of blackmailer enters frame.

Abbreviations: LS: long shot; CU: close-up; LA: low angle; POV: point of view; MS: medium shot; HA: high angle.

It will be apparent at once that the entire segment is symmetically constructed, the five sequences forming an ABCBA arch in which A is the exterior of the house, B the interior (hall, staircase), C the interior of Crewe's apartment. The symmetry is underlined by the fact that, according to Metz's categories, the sequences given above as A, C, and E are "scenes" (i.e., sequences with no lapses of temporal continuity) while B and D are "ordinary sequences" (containing time ellipses), though in practice Metz's distinction seems often merely academic. In accordance with the usual practice of classical cinema, the symmetry is never perfect, countered here by the common principle of condensation: the first interior sequence (B) consists of eight shots, the balancing sequence (D) of only four; sequence (A) (outside the house), with nine shots, is answered by E, containing only two. The primary function of symmetry that I began by describing—the emphasizing of difference—is established here with exemplary clarity. Consider two pairs of "answering" shots: 1. The first (A1) and last (E2) of the entire segment. The camera position is identical, both shots being static long shots of the house front; both are marked by the intrusion of the blackmailer. In A1 he is a small, insignificant figure, unidentified, who could be taken for an irrelevant passerby were it not for his suspiciously furtive movements; in E2 he is present as a large, ominous shadow that looms up over the front door as Alice hurries out of frame into the darkness. 2. The only two obtrusively "striking" shots of the entire segment—striking, that is, in terms of a cinematographic virtuosity that attracts attention to itself: the elaborate upward crane shot (B7) that accompanies Crewe's and Alice's progress up the stairs—it is obtrusive also in its revelation that the studio set lacks a wall—"answered" by the overhead shot of the stairwell (D2) that passively and distantly records Alice's solitary descent. The differences the symmetry marks are in both cases determined by the events that intervene.

One may note here, parenthetically, the one instance in the whole segment of a major disruption of symmetry: the appearance of the landlady in sequence B, which has no equivalent in sequence D. But this is not so much the exception to a rule as the demonstration of another of its principles: that the patterns of symmetry within a classical movie continually overlap, forming a complex network. The landlady's appearance here is a component of another formation within the overall structure that is an instance of virtually perfect symmetry. She appears three times. The middle occasion is very strongly marked by the use of non-realist cinematic devices: Alice's scream when she sees the extended arm of the derelict in the street becomes the landlady's scream when she finds Crewe's body (one of the familiar textbook examples of Hitchcock's inventive use of sound); and this is followed by the use of split screen to show her phone call to the police. This occurs at almost exactly the film's midpoint, and her two other appearances are grouped almost equidistantly around it: the conversation with Crewe (approximately twenty minutes from the film's beginning), her interrogation in the police station (approximately twenty minutes from the end).

As preface to a detailed discussion of sequence C, I want to demonstrate briefly another aspect of classical symmetry, the symmetrical construction of a sequence, and sequence A, in its relative simplicity and conciseness, offers a convenient instance. The sequence is framed by two shots that mark, respectively, the couple's entrance into and exit from the scene, and link them within a single take with the blackmailer, who appears in A1 as a hovering figure and in A9 as an offscreen voice. Between these two framing shots we have a simple alternating pattern, of which the basic element—the anchor of the sequence—is established in A2 (the two-shot of Crewe and Alice) and repeated in 4, 6, and 8. The three inserts that interrupt what could have been a single take, producing the sequence's alternating symmetry, are all marked by the fact that they are not located spatially in relation to the couple: Mr. White's shop is "around the corner," so the insert shot of it (A3) cannot be point of view, and we don't know where or how far "the corner" is; Tracy is shown listening to the couple's conversation in close-up (A5, 7), but exactly where he is standing is never made clear (beyond the fact that it is somewhere offscreen left). The inserts epitomize—at the very moment when Alice and Crewe are negotiating the terms of her visit to his apartment/studio, when she is hesitating between two worlds, two sets of values—the two opposite potential threats: the parental authority (the shop prominently bears her father's name) which she is about to flout by entering a strange man's apartment (and an artist to boot); the sinister potentialities of the uncertain world of dubious morals to which she is attracted. The inserts in fact complete a chain started by the last shot of the previous sequence which, through a dissolve, becomes the transition to the present one: a close-up of Frank against a dark background as he finds himself abandoned, very similar to the two inserts of

Tracy. (The symmetry of a given sequence is seldom closed or perfect. The end of the segment provides another example: D3, the close-up of Alice's feet as she completes her descent of the stairs, introduces a new series that will be developed throughout the *next* segment, the "episodic sequence" of Alice's walk through the nocturnal streets.) Frank, father, blackmailer: diverse faces of the male-constructed moral order by which Alice is oppressed, the blackmailer dependent upon precisely the patriarchal morality that Frank upholds and embodies.

THE MANSLAUGHTER SCENE

Inevitably, given the duration and complexity of the action, the symmetry of the sequence is less precise and schematic than that of A, its patterning correspondingly more intricate. This intricacy—essentially a play with paired images, the pairing often overlapping so that a single motif operates within more than one pair—is however contained within a clearly marked symmetry of beginning and end such as we have seen functioning over the entire film, over the larger segment, and within that segment's component sequences. And again the symmetry marks difference: here, the change wrought in Alice's life by the events the scene dramatizes, a change one might describe as the loss of innocence, or perhaps more accurately as the loss of her *belief* in her innocence. The scene opens with Alice's entry into the apartment with Crewe and ends with her exit from it, alone. Shot C2 is answered by C35 and 37. The camera position is similar, but C2 is offered as Alice's point of view, shared by the viewer, while C35 gives us Alice in the room, in long shot, now looked at rather than looking, and C37 gives us the darkened room, now empty save for Crewe's body. (Precise analysis here is rendered problematic by the fact that Hitchcock plays havoc with spatial relations throughout the sequence. It is quite impossible to make sense of the layout of Crewe's apartment—where, for instance, is the bed supposed to be in relation to the other objects? What passes for a POV shot as Alice enters at the start of the sequence cannot possibly be taken from the doorway by which she leaves at the end, although she emerges on to the same staircase.) Further, the first and last shots of the sequence are marked by the switching on and off of a light, respectively. C4 (Crewe concealing the too suggestive presence of the bed by drawing the curtains over it, revealing that his dishonorable intentions are already at least partly conscious) is answered by the sequence's dramatic climax (C27, 28), the struggle and stabbing behind the same curtains.

The sequence's pattern of pairings is organized within this symmetrical framework and around the turning point, the close-up of the kiss (C21), almost the central shot of the sequence and the moment when Alice realizes that things are "going too far" and begins to reverse her behavior and actions. (The sequence is as intricately composed as a piece of serial music, and I am reminded here of the central orchestral episode in Berg's *Lulu* where the music *literally* goes into reverse after it reaches its midpoint.) I begin by examining three overlapping pairings: policeman/jester, jester/nude, the two dresses.

Policeman/Jester

The two male figures (occupying opposite poles of the film's authority/ subversion system) are introduced in very close proximity (C7, C9) in shots from Alice's point of view, the high angle shot of the policeman answered by the low angle shot of the painted jester. Although the interval is longer, the pattern is repeated (same angles) in shot C26 (the policeman's direction reversed) and shot C32. By shot 26, however, the safety apparently represented earlier by the policeman (Alice looks reassured, C8) is no longer accessible: the shot is no longer POV, and the policeman doesn't hear her screams. And by shot 32 she is no longer able to laugh, even hesitantly, at the jester, instead tearing the canvas with her fingernails in an attempt to destroy the image she associates with her surrender to moral laxity, and which now seems to be ridiculing her in her terrifying predicament.

Initially, Alice feels reassured by the policeman and alarmed by the jester. The policeman stands in for Frank and the security the patriarchal order offers to helpless females. The jester transcends all the characters in the film, including the one who painted him: the object of his laughter is too nonspecific, its significance cannot be reduced to a projection of Crewe's social attitude (the latter being firmly within the patriarchal ideology, although seemingly nonconformist). One might suggest that he is ridiculing, among other things, the private life of his creator, as is not uncommon with works of art (including many of Hitchcock's own). The traditional court jester was licensed to ridicule authority; Alice here nervously misinterprets him as ridiculing simply the narrowly circum-scribed morality she is tempted to flout. Hence her tentative identifica-tion with him: she points her finger, imitating his gesture, momentarily constructing herself as his mirror image (C10); Crewe's whistling begins offscreen at this point, marking his growing confidence in being able to seduce her. Yet the jester is laughing here *at* Alice, not *with* her, just as in the later scene of the police investigation he will laugh at Frank. Finally, his silent laughter will dominate the film's conclusion as Alice's laughter dies, the "restoration of order" colored by a whole complex of dissonances. In the last resort he can be seen (given the repeated use of POV shots) as laughing at the audience, who are as much entangled in the web of ideological contradictions as the characters.

The Two Pictures

Crewe's painting of the jester, Alice's sketch of the female nude, are similarly integrated in the scene's "serial" patterning of symmetry, op-position, repetition, inversion. The formal parallel in this case is very precise: the first POV shot of the jester (C9) is followed four shots later (C13) by Alice's execution of her drawing (Crewe guiding her hand); the second POV shot of the jester (C32) is followed four shots later (C36) by Alice's act of blacking out her name under the sketch. It might be argued that the sketch is Crewe's rather than Alice's: she has no artistic ability (as her outline of a face demonstrates), he skillfully completes the "masterpiece" by guiding her in the construction of the nude she would never have dared to draw (her response is "Ooh, you *are* awful!," at once shocked and complicit). Yet she promptly expresses her acceptance of the sketch as her own by signing her name under it. What is more, the "signing" is deeply ambiguous: she prints her name in block capitals, so that it looks less like the artist's signature than like the picture's title. It is easy to interpret the incident as expressing an unconscious wish: Alice would like to be naked in Crewe's apartment.

The Dresses

At the center of the scene, organized around the pivotal kiss, is the complicated play with dresses: the dress Alice has worn for what was initially to be a "respectable" evening out with Frank (who wanted to take her to a movie about Scotland Yard), the dress Crewe persuades her to put on by offering to paint her portrait. The connotations of the latter dress have been widely misperceived: it is not necessarily a dress from classical ballet, but equally the dress worn by women in the traditional British seaside pierrot shows, hence evoking risqué songs and anecdotes, loose morals, promiscuity. It is the perfect complement to Crewe's song, a eulogy of the "modern" (i.e., permissive, emancipated) young woman. Alice's willingness to put on the pierrot costume confirms, therefore, the implications of her name on the nude sketch; it also links her, by association, with the jester, whose costume also signifies "license," albeit of a somewhat different order. The changes of dress are organized around the central kiss: Alice changes into the pierrot costume in C18; the kiss occurs three shots later, C21; Alice attempts to change back (Crewe steals her own dress) in C23-24. When Crewe flings aside Alice's respectable black dress, it falls over the image of the jester; when Alice finally retrieves it (C32), she can no longer identify with the jester's mockery, because she is now irrevocably a part of what is being mocked. The moment draws together two of the scene's major motifs: the jester, whom Alice now tries to destroy, ripping the canvas; the black dress, which she now resumes, attempting to reassert a persona, a social role, the reality of which the scene has effectively undermined.

The patterning of motifs in the scene can be summed up in a chart (though this cannot at all convey the complexity of effect):

ENTRY	C1
curtain	C4
policeman	C7
jester	C9
sketch	C13
dresses	C18
KISS	C21
dresses	C23–24
policeman	C26
curtain	C28
jester/dress	C32
sketch	C36
EXIT	C37

This analysis of the structuring of symmetry brings us finally to the question of identification. It seems that the editing of the silent version of *Blackmail* was at a number of points far more fragmented, far more congruent with the fully developed editing style of Hitchcock's maturity, with its characteristic use of point-of-view shots; the long takes, in particular (e.g., C13, C18), were forced on Hitchcock by the initial technical problems arising from the direct recording of dialogue. What this goes to prove, however, is that POV editing technique, though it may be used to reinforce identification, is not essential to its construction. Alice is our primary identification figure throughout the scene. The audience at which the film was directed consisted far more of Alices and Franks than of Crewes: Crewe is the alien figure who has to be "figured out" (by Alice, by the spectator). And, although she finally kills Crewe, it is Alice throughout who is perceived as threatened. This accounts for the fact that she remains our identification figure even when we are shown things she is not aware of: Crewe surreptitiously drawing the bed curtains (C4), Crewe, just before the assault, suddenly endowed by shadows with the traditional mustachios of the villain of melodrama (C24). In both instances it is Alice that we care about and, such brief moments apart, it is everywhere Alice's experiences that we share. One tiny, eccentric detail of editing exemplifies this: the dissolve that links C34 and 35. The most familiar "textbook" use of the dissolve is to indicate a time lapse (and frequently a change of locale), but here there is none: shot 35 takes up precisely Alice's movement in the preceding shot, and there is no disruption of the temporal continuity that makes this extended scene a "scene" in the strict Metzian sense. What the false indication of a time lapse achieves is to convey to us Alice's sense at that point of the dreamlike protraction of time. Paradoxical as it may be, this identification with Alice is not seriously undermined by the fact that, from the killing of Crewe on, Hitchcock uses a number of devices to distance us from her: the direct look into camera (C28), the walk into camera (C34), and in the next sequence the overhead stairwell shot (D2). The whole business of identification in the cinema is enormously complex (far more so than the author of *Hitchcock's Films* recognized), and I shall take up this issue in a later chapter. For present purposes it is sufficient to assert that, given the complexities of human perception and human sympathy, it is not impossible to identify with and be detached from a character simultaneously.

Above all, our identification with Alice is constructed by the patterning of symmetry and its marking of difference. From the pivotal kiss—the point where the action and some of the motifs go, as it were, into reserve—the major motifs (policeman, jester, sketch, dresses) are transformed, take on new meanings, and this transformation is centered securely in Alice's consciousness; the meaning even of what must logically be beyond her consciousness (the policeman passing outside, C26) is comprehensible only in relation to it. Identification with/detachment from: we share Alice's consciousness but are by no means restricted to it. It is the fact that we are not restricted to it that makes it possible to assert that, if the film offers its audience another identification figure, one who knows more than Alice knows, it is the jester.

A possible reading of *Blackmail* would reveal it as deeply sexist and misogynist (a charge that has of course been leveled at numerous Hitchcock films: see, as among the more distinguished and intelligent examples, Michael Renov's reading of *Notorious,* which I discuss in chapter 15). According to this reading, the opening establishes the "man's world," the world of crime and the law, as the serious and important one. This the woman disrupts, with her frivolousness, selfishness, and triviality: Alice is annoyed because Frank has kept her waiting, then irresponsibly dumps him in favor of Crewe. Her subsequent behavior provokes the deaths of two men, Crewe (who, while not blameless, is sexually aroused by her flirtatiousness) and Tracy, who dies for the crime she committed. She is also responsible (her ultimate guilt, perhaps) for compromising the integrity of Frank, the hitherto upright and irreproachable policeman, by placing him in a position where he feels compelled to betray his moral principles and civic duty by covering for her. Alice gets the suffering she deserves, and the satisfaction the film offers the spectator (always constructed, of course, as male, although women might be able to derive a certain masochistic pleasure from Alice's punishment) is that of seeing a silly, irresponsible young woman chastised for her weaknesses, so that at the end she is ready to accept her "correct" place subordinated to Frank's authority as his wife.

What is to prevent one from extracting such a reading from *Blackmail?* Nothing: the film makes such a reading available. Nothing, that is, so long as we reduce the film to its narrative structure. Like all fully coherent readings (by which I mean readings that resist the awareness of complexity and contradiction), its elaboration would be dependent upon multiple suppressions and evasions. There is a higher coherence possible, the coherence that strives to hold in balance and tension the alternative readings the film makes available. I hope I can claim without immodesty that the analysis I have developed so far exposes the superficiality and inadequacy of a reading of the type I have just outlined. It is available in the film because its attitudes are inherent, even dominant, in the culture that produced it; its coherence is shattered by the film's detail, and by the structures it develops that transcend linear narrative.

It remains to examine the film's ending—the precise nature of its "closure." First, however, it is illuminating to glance briefly at Hitchcock's personal appearance, his most elaborate "cameo" in all of his films, for the attitude to authority and rebellion that it encapsulates. Hitchcock appears as a passenger on the train on which Alice and Frank travel for their date; a small boy leans over from the seat behind him and repeatedly pushes off the pompous fat man's hat; Hitchcock responds with impotent exasperation. Even in this brief, limited instance we may raise the issue of identification: with whom do we, with whom does Hitchcock, identify here? Clearly with *both* characters. We have all been bothered, at some point in our lives, by obstreperous children, and we all know how aggravating it can be to have our sense of dignity challenged; at the same time, a part of us loves to ridicule Hitchcock— both in his character as the pompous commuter, and as that even more powerful and intimidating figure the Great Film Director. And Hitchcock delights in this (self-)ridicule too: that is the whole point and substance of the joke, and why it is so charming. We can confidently assert, in fact, that "Hitchcock" is not only the fat commuter: he is also, in spirit, the small boy, the rebellious child. We should also note that this brief sequence shot anticipates (by inversion) the closely ensuing incident where Frank (the film's major embodiment of authority) flouts the authority of the young boy attendant in the restaurant: even authority figures resist the system on which their authority depends.

The primary function of the symmetry of Alice's two visits to Scotland Yard—to meet Frank for their date at the beginning, to confess to killing Crewe at the end—is clearly to dramatize her chastisement. What is in question is not the resolution of the narrative but the attitude to that resolution defined by both the immediate dramatic realization and the wider context of the film as a whole. Our continued identification with

Alice—as, by this point, the film's conscience, a conscience that is denied
a voice by the male authority figures, the constable who won't take her
seriously, the commissioner who doesn't want to listen, Frank who
wants to silence her—is decisive here: it is precisely this identification
that enables us to experience the film's dominant male figures as oppressive and invalidated. The most precise point of symmetry is the repeated
motif of the joke: the joke (which we don't hear) whispered in Alice's
ear by the police constable, at which she laughs; the same constable's
final joke ("Well, did you tell them who did it?") at which she *tries* to
laugh. The symmetry is compounded by the fact that, at moments in
both scenes, the framing places Alice between the two men, a composi-
tional device we have already noted in the symmetrical framings of the
triangle in the Whites' living room, Frank/Alice/Tracy: the woman denied the voice between the two men who possess it. The joke at the
beginning is presumably quite trivial; that at the end expresses a kind of
amiable, unconscious contempt for women (what could Alice possibly
know about something as serious as a murder?). Alice's attempted laughter is frozen when she is confronted, once again, by the film's only
authentic laugher: the jester, as Crewe's painting is carried past, appropriately now back to back with Alice's sketch. What do the jester's
laughter and Alice's inability to return it now signify, at the film's final
moment? Again, different readings are possible. Alice, chastened (rendered chaste), cannot face the laughter which she interpreted as ridicule
of conventional morality, and which helped seduce her in her fall from
"innocence." Alternatively, she sees the jester as laughing at her as she is
now, finally trapped within the male order, subordinated to Frank by
the role she has played in his own corruption. Once again, it could be
argued that the former is the reading implied by the conventions of
classical narrative, the latter by Hitchcock's intervention, the particularities and peculiarities of his "inscription." From a Hitchcockian viewpoint, the jester (the film's final image) is laughing at the entire social
order, with its monstrously oppressive (dis-)organization of gender and
sexuality and at the people (all the film's characters) who remain trapped
within its contradictions.

13

NORMS AND VARIATIONS: *THE 39 STEPS* AND *YOUNG AND INNOCENT*

The 39 Steps established definitively both the stucture and thematic of the "double chase" movie. Two superficial, closely interrelated characteristics have proved deceptive. First, genre. The film belongs to the "picaresque": an apparently inconsequential assemblage of episodes (the train, the crofter's cottage, the professor's mansion, the political meeting, etc.) whose common link is simply that each constitutes a further "adventure" for the protagonist. In fact, the film's structure is neither loose nor merely linear: each episode proves on closer inspection to be a component in a coherent scheme, each acquiring a deeper resonance when seen in relation to the others.

Second, the espionage plot: typically, with Hitchcock, a cover for the film's real concerns with gender relations and sexuality. One way of putting this would be to say that, with the death of Annabella Smith/ Lucie Mannheim, the sexual theme introduced in the film's opening section is deflected on to, disguised as, the espionage plot. But the concern with sexual relations and arrangements never entirely disappears from the film's surface: the traveling salesmen, the crofter and his wife, the professor and his family, the developing relationship between Hannay/Robert Donat and Pamela/Madeleine Carroll, amount to a remarkably comprehensive survey of the possibilities of heterosexual relationship under patriarchy (including, it can be argued, the possibility of transcending it). Hanging over all of these, like the finger of fate, is the film's privileged signifier: the little finger with its missing top joint, the sign of castration (actual or threatened). The strength and coherence of this become even clearer if we compare the film to its apparent loose remake, *Saboteur:* the fact that the latter was made in wartime guarantees its anti-fascist espionage theme a dominance beside which that of *The 39 Steps*—like that of *North by Northwest*—dwindles to a "Mc-Guffin." The sexual concern in *Saboteur* flickers spasmodically; in its finer, more interesting predecessor and successor, it generates the entire structure.

That structure is, again, strongly symmetrical, the picaresque episodes held together not only by the thematic scheme but by a corresponding, supportive formal scheme. If one works from the beginning and end inward to the center, one finds:

1. A particularly clear, classical instance of "the end answering the beginning": the film opens in an (unnamed) music hall and ends in the London Palladium; both segments are centered upon the interrogation of Mr. Memory by members of the audience, both of his performances culminating in the firing of a gun.

2. The second segment, the negotiation of a relationship between Hannay and Annabella in Hannay's rented apartment, is balanced by the extended sequence in the Scottish inn, the negotiation of a relationship between Hannay and Pamela, Hannay's decision to help Annabella answered by Pamela's decision to help Hannay.

3. More loosely, the comic episode on the train (the traveling salesmen, the interested clergyman) is balanced by the comic (but also suddenly serious) episode of the political meeting: both include a search for Hannay (in the first instance by the police, in the second by the agents masquerading as police); both are marked by the introduction/reintroduction of Pamela and her denunciation of Hannay to the authorities; both culminate in Hannay's escape (each escape underlining his initiative, improvisatory spontaneity, and courage).

4. The film's central sequence, the confrontation between Hannay and Professor Jordan/Godfrey Tearle, central both in its position and its thematic significance, is framed between the two appearances of the crofter (James Laurie) and his wife (Peggy Ashcroft): the night Hannay spends in their house, the wife's punishment for giving him the crofter's overcoat.

Most importantly, the film's symmetry (underlined by the use of a specific device, the insert close-up) confirms my description of the mutilated little finger as its "privileged signifier." The motif occurs three times. There is the central moment (on which the whole film obviously pivots, whether one reads it as a simple "action thriller" or, in Leavis' felicitous phrase, as a "dramatic poem" on the theme of sexual constructions) where the professor, informed by Hannay that the head of the enemy organization has the top joint of his little finger missing, holds up his right hand in the foreground of the image to reveal his true identity. Around this are organized the two insert close-ups: that when Annabella (shortly after the film's beginning) holds up Hannay's little finger to demonstrate and underline what she is telling him; that when Hannay (shortly before the end) borrows opera glasses to get a closer look at the shadowy figure in the London Palladium box, and sees the telltale mutilated hand gripping the upholstery.

Hitchcock's detailed and complex presentation of the British music hall —a strictly national, and now virtually obsolete, institution—emphasizes a number of features of the social/moral milieu that provides the film's starting point and an essential component of its symbolic structure. The music hall was primarily a working-class institution, providing entertainment for an urban proletariat—the only appearance of this social group in the film. It has something in common with the London Palladium of the final climax: the onstage entertainment in both instances consists of a series of unrelated variety acts (comic turns, songs, specialty acts like Mr. Memory's—it is not implausible that he can pass from one location to the other). But the Palladium is an altogether more grandiose, more respectable, middle-class version of the music hall. Despite the invitation to test Mr. Memory with questions, the separation of audience from spectacle is far more complete, the interaction between spectators and performers that characterizes the music hall minimized. In the music hall the entertainment is not only the stage show: Hitchcock shows us a bar at one side of the auditorium, where the spectators can drink beer as they watch and participate. The questions addressed to Mr. Memory offer a fairly comprehensive coverage of the interests which capitalism foists on to the workers to fill their leisure: sports, gambling, murder ("When was Crippen hanged?"), gender and marital antagonisms expressed as humor ("Who was the last British heavyweight champion of the world?"/"My old woman"). Hitchcock presents all of this with affection and good humor, but also with a kind of potential unease: there is the sense that everything may fall apart at any moment into violence and disorder (as indeed it does): the chaos world here has definite class connotations. We may note that the disruption in the music hall arises spontaneously among the audience, while that in the more respectable world of the Palladium is provoked by Professor Jordan's shooting of Mr. Memory.

Within this world, Hannay is doubly alien: not only from Canada but (as Mr. Memory immediately recognizes) a "gentleman." What the music hall provides for this stranger in class and nationality is an atmosphere in which he can feel that "anything goes," so that when a woman approaches him amid the chaos and says "May I come home with you?," he seems scarcely surprised, and accepts her without hesitation.

The film (within the constraints of contemporary "decency") makes it abundantly clear that Hannay expects a night of illicit sex, a "one night stand" with a woman who gives her name as "Smith" (offered with an implicit question mark: "Will that do?"). He guesses first that she is an "actress" ("Not in the way you mean"), then that she is "in the chorus." Subsequently, when she tells Hannay that *she* fired the shots in the music hall and that "there were two men there who wanted to kill me," his reply is a laconic "You should be more careful in choosing your gentlemen friends." And indeed Annabella *is* a kind of prostitute, the exact nature of her "prostitution" marking the film's replacement of sexual transgression by espionage: she is a spy for "any country that pays me." The episode, then, has a dual function: it launches the espionage plot, and it provides the first of the film's models of sexual/gender organization.

The opposite pole to the casual and anonymous one night stand is represented by the relationship between the crofter and his wife—among the most touching and beautifully realized episodes in all Hitchcock's British period. The two episodes are linked, their oppositeness stressed, by one detail: Hannay serves Annabella haddock, the crofter's wife serves Hannay herring. Against moral laxity is posed extreme puritanical repressiveness; against mutual gratification without commitment, the worst aspects of traditional marriage, the woman owned, dominated, tyrannized, and eventually beaten by the husband. If Hitchcock's attitude to Hannay's readiness to profit from a woman's (apparently) sexual offer of herself seems half critical, half indulgent, there can be no doubt that the attitude to its polar opposite is defined with uncompromising firmness. Here, our identification is entirely with the oppressed woman, who is characterized by intelligence and, above all, generosity, and with her hopeless dream of escape from an intolerable situation. It is for her spontaneous and unreflecting generosity that Margaret is punished—her readiness to help Hannay (prompted by an instinctive sympathy for the victimized), her gift of her husband's coat, with the lifesaving hymnbook in its pocket. When she reassures Hannay that, when her husband discovers the coat's disappearance, "He'll pray at me but no more," she is plainly lying: she knows what to expect.

John the crofter, at the opposite end of the social scale from Professor Jordan, anticipates him as the film's first monstrous father figure: when Hannay first sees Margaret he assumes she is John's daughter. Much has been made of Hitchcock's treatment of mothers; in fact, his attitude to fathers (or, more generally, father figures) is just as hostile and more consistent, the "montrous mother" not making her appearance until the American period. This is of course fully compatible with—indeed, the logical extension of—Hitchcock's attitude to authority throughout his career. In general, fathers and father figures in his films can be divided into two main types: ineffectual, (symbolically) castrated, predominantly comic (Alice's father in *Blackmail,* Basil Radford in *Young and Innocent,* Nigel Bruce in *Suspicion,* Henry Travers in *Shadow of a Doubt,* Cecil Parker in *Under Capricorn*); or variously oppressive, sinister, dominating—whether they embody the "Good Law" or the "Bad Law," legality or criminality, democracy or fascism. The range here is much greater: it encompasses not only the villains of *The 39 Steps* and *Saboteur* (very close counterparts, seemingly benign, wealthy "family men" who also happen to be the heads of fascist spy rings) but also the Charles Laughton characters of both *Jamaica Inn* and *The Paradine Case;* the Leo G. Carroll of *Spellbound* and *North by Northwest;* his counterpart the Louis Calhern of *Notorious;* General McLaidlaw of *Suspicion* (especially when he is "reduced" to a portrait); the coroner of *Vertigo;* and certain husbands whose age or title gives them father figure status (John of *The 39 Steps,* Colonel Paradine of *The Paradine Case,* Claude Rains in *Notorious*). One may note that the dichotomy corresponds fairly precisely to Hitchcock's presentation of the police: either coldly impersonal or oppressive (*Blackmail, The Wrong Man*) or ineffectual/comic and misguided in their assumptions (pervasive throughout Hitchcock's career—the *reductio ad absurdum* is in *The Birds*). It is also interesting that the Godfrey Tearle character of *The 39 Steps* and the Leo G. Carroll character of *North by Northwest* (ostensibly at opposite poles of the moral spectrum, representing "Evil" and "Good" respectively) are both designated "The Professor": the coincidence should remind us that for Hitchcock the Good Law and the Bad Law are still the Law.

John and the professor—the primitive and the super-civilized, super-suave—are both presented as oppressive patriarchal figures. The professor's role is to embody solid upper-class respectability (he is a "pillar of the community") and "family values": a role the film goes on to reveal as a facade, a masquerade. Yet, at the same time, not *just* a masquerade: the professor *has* a wife and daughter, they appear to form a close-knit family unit, the wife (at least) knows of his activities. Hitchcock colors our perception of what appears to be the bourgeois ideal of the nuclear family by characterizing the professor as a fascist spy. And what is the price for entering into this "ideal" social/familial arrangement, for achieving this respectability, this status, this power? Clearly, to complete the oedipal trajectory, to accept symbolic castration, the final means of entry into the patriarchal order, of becoming in the fullest sense "the Father." And where exactly does this leave Hannay, who holds up the little finger of his *left* hand as the precise mirror reflection of the mutilated little finger of the professor's right?

In the course of the film, Hannay traverses Britain, from London to the highlands of Scotland; more importantly, he traverses Britain's entire class and gender structures. Out of this trajectory develops the relationship with Pamela, at once the most engaging and most problematic aspect of the film. Clearly, we are to find the relationship significantly different from the film's other "couple" relationships—Hannay/Annabella, John/Margaret, the professor and his wife: different, that is, from the established norms which the film variously but systematically discredits. The problem arises from Hitchcock's inability (at this stage of his development) fully and convincingly to define the nature of the difference; it arises, in the last resort, from his failure clearly to define Hannay, who remains something of a blank, albeit a blank filled in by the charm and grace of Robert Donat. This surely explains why Hannay had to be Canadian, rather than British or American, the Canadian identity being generally seen in terms of negatives (*neither* British *nor* American), the difficulty of its self-definition being a commonplace even in Canadian culture itself. The obvious comparison is with Cary Grant in *North by Northwest,* where the definition is from the outset detailed and thorough: Roger Thornhill can undergo transformation precisely because there is a character there to transform. Hannay seems to require no transformation: it is difficult, even if one thinks oneself back historically into the moral codes of '30s middle-class England, to find his treatment of Annabella Smith more than minimally reprehensible. He is responsible for Margaret's suffering, but only inadvertently—we are not invited to feel that he deliberately exploits her—and if his treatment of Pamela is pretty rough at times, it is always adequately motivated by the demands of the moment. What *partly* defines the difference of the Hannay/Pamela relationship from the others is its tentative progress toward both commitment and (somewhat dubious) equality, but the definition remains essentially negative: the relationship is to take the form *neither* of a one-night stand *nor* of brutal domination *nor* of traditional marriage/family. Perhaps it is unreasonable to ask the film to tell us more about *how* it will differ from these. The limitations of '30s British cinema (and of the culture that produced it and for which it was produced) make it possible for us to see no more in the relationship than a certain bourgeois ideal of decency and mutual caring (I have already suggested that the falsely accused man films, on both sides of the Atlantic, never carry quite the subversive charge of the guilty woman films). The film's psychoanalytically accessible subtext *does,* however, tell us something positive and hopeful about Hannay's particular version of masculinity: on the one hand he escapes the threat of castration and identification with "the Father" (i.e., final entry into the patriarchal order), and is saved (by Margaret's inadvertent gift of the hymnbook) from the professor's bullet; on the other, the "gun" with which he threatens Pamela turns out to be only a pipe. To adopt (and adapt) Freud's celebrated remark that "sometimes a cigar is just a cigar," one might take this as suggesting that sometimes "the phallus" can be just a penis. The other relevant motif here is that of the handcuffs, used by the professor's agents (masquerading as policemen) to bind Hannay and Pamela together, subsequently used by Hannay to prevent Pamela from autonomous action. It is Pamela's initiative that enables her to extricate herself while Hannay sleeps, an action followed by (a) her acceptance of his innocence and (b) his acceptance of her freedom.

If the film's most obvious "core" moment is the professor's raising of his mutilated finger—a moment crucial to both the surface narrative and the sexual subtext—it has one rival: a moment strongly marked and privileged by cinematic rhetoric (emphatic editing, close shots, low angles): Hannay's speech to the political meeting, an incident apparently quite irrelevant to the narrative development, which makes its cinematic underlining the more incongruous. Hannay, sparked off by a question about "the idle rich," swings into what is essentially a description of an ideal international socialist society: ". . . a world where no nation plots against nation, where no neighbor plots against neighbor, where everybody gets a fair deal and a sporting chance, a world from which suspicion, cruelty, and fear have been forever banished." (His final "Is that the world you want?" is followed by unanimous and rapturous applause.)

The speech is curious, almost incongruous, coming from Hannay who, scarcely a character, never develops the characteristics that would give it credibility as issuing from his mouth. Perhaps the film itself is uncomfortable with it, which is why its force—its almost exaggerated "sincerity"—is partially undermined by its being given to Hannay. This uncertainty, or hesitancy, might be related to the film's uncertainty as to what the Hannay/Pamela relationship actually amounts to: the two instances are linked by the notion of a possible human equality, based on international politics (the speech) and on gender (the relationship). That the film is able to connect the two, however tentatively and obliquely (it clearly is not aware that it is doing so, simply by placing both within the same classical text wherein everything must respond to everything) seems quite remarkable. There is, in fact, one *almost* explicit connection: Hannay's wish for "a world from which suspicion, cruelty, and fear have been forever banished" can scarcely, within the context of the film, fail to make us think of John and Margaret.

The entire film moves (with a logic, underlined by the structuring symmetry, that is not without its ambiguities) to its final shot: Mr. Memory, fatally wounded by the professor's bullet, dies after repeating for Hannay the secret formula he has learned by heart for the professor, relieved to get it off his chest at last; the foreground of the image has Hannay, screen left, and Pamela, screen right; in the background, in soft focus, on stage, is the line of chorus girls kicking up their legs. The camera then moves down and in to close-up to show Hannay and Pamela clasping hands. "The End." The image literalizes the idea that the world of the music hall (the chorus line) is now pushed to the back of the memory (though still present) and dramatizes with exemplary clarity and precision that favorite culmination of classical cinema, the construction of the heterosexual couple. But are they the same old couple all over again or a new version somehow freed from the oppressive constraints of patriarchy? In a sense, Mr. Memory is passing on to Hannay the source of the professor's power (possession of the secret formula); yet to Hannay that formula is meaningless and irrelevant gibberish (beyond the simple plot necessity of finally establishing his innocence by confirming his account of the espionage activity). To me the ending seems unresolvably ambiguous (neither will the ambiguity be resolved in *North by Northwest:* what exactly *is* to be the relationship between the protagonist and the new "Mrs. Roger Thornhill"?). Perhaps it cannot be resolved within the terms of classical cinema, which can suggest the possibility of new possibilities but cannot tell us what those possibilities might be, beyond a few tentative hints. As the hands of Hannay and Pamela meet, we are reminded that, although the handcuffs no longer bind the couple, they are still dangling from Hannay's wrist.

Young and Innocent—two years and three films later—provides a charming and playful set of variations not only on the narrative structure of *The 39 Steps* ("double chase" combined with romantic love story) but also on its interlocking themes of class and sexuality. Again the hero's trajectory constitutes a traversal of the British class structure, from upper bourgeoisie (Aunt Margaret and Uncle Basil, and their daughter's birthday party) to workers, tramps, and derelicts. And again the value of the central relationship is defined in comparison to other couple, or family, arrangements: the aberrant, warring couple of the opening, Margaret and Basil, the motherless family of the heroine Erica/ Nova Pilbeam, within which she assumes the mother's role, presiding over meals with her five younger brothers, sitting at the head of the table opposite her father. An important difference is that here the story is told as much from the woman's viewpoint as the man's: Hitchcock is careful to equalize the relationship in terms of narrative weighting, balancing an episode in which Erica takes the initiative (the "Tom's Hat" truckdrivers' cafe sequence, for example) with an "answering" episode in which Robert/Derrick de Marney is the active force (the dosshouse).

Also as in *The 39 Steps,* the apparently episodic, picaresque nature of the narrative is qualified by a very strong formal symmetry of which the pivot is an episode widely regarded as so irrelevant that (according to Hitchcock) it was cut entirely from the original American release prints:

the birthday party. Its structural centrality can be easily established in relation to the film's other major episodes. On either side of it come sequences of investigation (the young couple's attempts to trace the missing raincoat) in working-class or sub-proletarian milieux: it is preceded by the episode in "Tom's Hat" and followed by the episode in the dosshouse. Moving outward in both directions, one finds these in turn framed by episodes in which the couple hide out in derelict edifices: the old mill, the abandoned mine. Their symmetrical relationship is underlined by the fact that each culminates in a police chase in which the couple's escape is jeopardized by Erica's refusal to abandon her dog (in the later episode she is captured). These again are framed by the establishment of the film's narrative premise (the murder, Robert's arrest) and its resolution (the unmasking of the real murderer, Robert's release). True, the birthday party sequence adds nothing to the development of the plot, from which viewpoint it is indeed just an "episode," an interruption, a Hitchcockian jeu d'esprit. We should, however, be alerted to its importance in the *thematic* structure by the emphasis conferred upon it by its position in the film's formal organization.

It is not merely a link in the chain of the film's depiction of contrasting domestic arrangements; it constitutes the closest it offers to a depiction of the bourgeois social norm, a children's party presided over by the parents of the birthday girl, the upper-class nuclear family in all its stability and affluence. What the sequence does is to carry this version of "normality" (based upon the division of labor) to its logical conclusion: the mother, deprived of any power or authority outside the home, compensated by her role of monstrous matriarch within it (while no Mrs. Bates or Mrs. Anthony, she is the closest figure in the British films to the monstrous mothers of the American period); the father, with no discernible function within the domestic realm, reduced to redundancy and emasculation (his party hat is of the type associated with Dutch peasant girls). Aunt Margaret/Mary Clare, in fact, is the film's supreme, extreme embodiment of a repressive morality: she has fully internalized the "Law of the Father," the "Thou shalt not" of bourgeois respectability. Assuming automatically that Robert and Erica are engaged in an illicit liaison, she interrogates them, spies on them, and finally intervenes by phoning Erica's father. We may note that the domestic arrangements within Erica's family put her in danger of a similar destiny: her father, Colonel Burgoyne/Percy Marmont, the local chief of police, appears to play no role in the upbringing of his sons, this task becoming the exclusive responsibility of Erica as surrogate mother and "boss," a role in which her intuitive sympathy, vivacity, and inventiveness have to be suppressed.

The film's pivotal sequence—the normally abnormal upper-bourgeois home presided over by a patriarchal matriarch—is set between the two visits to working-class or sub-proletarian environments, "Tom's Hat" and the dosshouse, presided over by males and, indeed, exclusively male locations, characterized predominantly by the continuously imminent eruption of violence. If Hitchcock's presentation of the bourgeoisie (upper and lower) is scathingly critical, and consistently so throughout his career, he also never sentimentalizes the working class: if one can deduce from his films a general statement about class structures, it is that their very existence contaminates all the strata. It is characteristic that, in *Young and Innocent,* the figure who proves most supportive and beneficent is not so much working class as outcast: a tramp and down-and-out, a self-employed itinerant.

The film produces no fewer than four father figures, the two who are helpful and supportive being the most oppressed, whether within the home (Uncle Basil/Basil Radford) or within the social order (Old Will/Edward Rigby, tramp and china mender). The other two are Erica's father, well-intentioned but consistently wrong in his judgments because, from his position of patriarchal authority and responsibility to the Law, he lacks the gift of intuitive perception, his intuition inhibited by his commitment to abstract principles and rules; and the murderer, Clay, himself. Burgoyne and Clay represent the film's opposite but complementary poles of patriarchal domination, the former too completely in control, the latter too out of it, but both applying the same moral law of punishment for deviancy, whether through the "justice" system or through murder.

It is a consistent principle of the double chase movies that those who help the hero either belong to socially oppressed groups (women, workers) or are for some reason (personal affliction, social position) outsiders or outcasts. In the former category we have the innkeeper's wife and the crofter's wife of *The 39 Steps,* the truck driver of *Saboteur,* and (after initial hesitation) the heroines of both those films and of *Young and Innocent;* in the latter, Old Will, and *Saboteur*'s circus freaks (or most of them) and blind musician. The films credit them—presumably as a

by-product of their subordinate or oppressed position, or of their rele-
gation to the role of outsider/spectator—with an intuitive knowledge
and sympathy which have become atrophied or repressed in those who
have authority (who are of course almost invariably male), the latter
being either actively malevolent (the "villains") or obtusely obstructive
(the police, and legal authorities in general).

Three of the four father figures converge for the film's denouement. It
is appropriate that Old Will is a china mender: it is he who finally "puts
the pieces together," the character who lacks all social status being the
only one in a position to restore order to the narrative. The official
investigator, Burgoyne, is pushed into the background. The highlight of
the sequence is one of Hitchcock's most celebrated tours de force: the
long traveling crane shot that opens on a general view of the Grand
Hotel restaurant/ballroom and moves to a big close-up of the murderer's
telltale twitching eye. The shot is from no character's physical or mental
viewpoint: the revelation at this stage is for the audience only, the
remaining suspense being built on the question of how and when Erica
and Old Will will catch us up. The exposure of Clay is merciless. Already
in a position of humiliation (the band are all in blackface under the
direction of a "white" leader), Clay is highlighted by the musical number
itself ("No one can/Like the drummer-man"), and the camera's inexorable and undeviating progress seems to adopt an active role in wearing
on his nerves and breaking him down, the convulsive twitch erupting in
direct response to its stare. It becomes clear also that Clay *wants* to be
exposed: his frantic out-of-rhythm drumming goes far beyond a mere
expression of nervousness, obsessively attracting attention to itself,
amounting almost to a public confession. Clay's character throughout—
but especially here—exposes the impossible strain and tension involved
in male dominance and its assumed right of sexual regulation.

As in *The 39 Steps*, the value of the film's central relationship has to
be assessed in comparison with the various relationships against which
it is constructed, and this inevitably reproduces the same problem: the
question of how exactly we are to see the Robert/Erica relationship as
differing from those contrasted with it. Its relative equality (as against
the imbalances of the Clay marriage and the Basil/Margaret marriage) is
guaranteed (as I suggested earlier) by the narrative structure and to an
extent is dramatically realized in the course of the action, through the
engaging freshness of the two principals. Yet the film cannot test it in

relation to the actual social structures: we are left, again, with a promise that cannot achieve realization within the available social conventions. We are left, in fact, with the fairly precise indications of the film's last line ("Don't you think we ought to invite Mr. Tisdale to dinner?") and the film's last shot: a close-up of Erica as she transfers her gaze from her father to Robert. Domestic/familial arrangements, we are led to believe, will go on pretty much as before.

14

IDEOLOGY, GENRE, AUTEUR (1976)

The truth lies not in one dream but in many.—Pasolini, *Arabian Nights*

Each theory of film so far has insisted on its own particular polarization. Montage theory enthrones editing as the essential creative act at the expense of other aspects of film; Bazin's Realist theory, seeking to right the balance, merely substitutes its own imbalance, downgrading montage and artifice; semiotic theory rejects—or at any rate seeks to "deconstruct"—Realist art in favor of the so-called "open text." Auteur theory, in its heyday, concentrated attention exclusively on the fingerprints, thematic or stylistic, of the individual artist; recent attempts to discuss the complete "filmic text" have tended to throw out ideas of personal authorship altogether. Each theory has, given its underlying position, its own validity—the validity being dependent upon, and restricted by, the position. Each can offer insights into different areas of cinema and different aspects of a single film.

I want to stress here the desirability for the critic—whose aim should always be to see the work, as wholly as possible, as it is—to be able to draw on the discoveries and particular perceptions of each theory, each position, without committing himself exclusively to any one. The ideal will not be easy to attain, and even the attempt raises all kinds of problems, the chief of which is the validity of evaluative criteria that are not supported by a particular system. From what, then, do they receive support? No critic, obviously, can be free from a structure of values, nor can he afford to withdraw from the struggles and tensions of living to some position of "aesthetic" contemplation. Every critic who is worth reading has been, on the contrary, very much caught up in the effort to define values beyond purely aesthetic ones (if indeed such things exist). Yet to "live historically" need not entail commitment to a system or a cause; it can involve, rather, being alive to the opposing pulls, the tensions, of one's world.

The past three decades have seen a number of advances in terms of the opening up of critical possibilities, of areas of relevance, especially with regard to Hollywood: the elaboration of auteur theory in its various manifestations; the interest in genre; the interest in ideology. I want here tentatively to explore some of the ways in which these disparate approaches to Hollywood movies might interpenetrate, producing the kind of synthetic criticism I have suggested might now be practicable.

My concern here is to suggest something of the complex interaction of ideology, genre, and personal authorship that determines the richness, the density of meaning, of the great Hollywood masterpieces; I cannot, therefore, restrict the discussion to Hitchcock. In the introduction to this book I juxtaposed *Shadow of a Doubt* to *Blue Velvet* in order to raise certain issues of evaluation. To juxtapose it, here, with a film of comparable stature but of very different authorial and generic determination— Capra's *It's a Wonderful Life*—is to raise other and wider issues. In order to create a context within which to discuss the two films, I want to attempt (at risk of obviousness) some definition of what we mean by American capitalist ideology—or, more specifically, the values and assumptions so insistently embodied in and reinforced by the classical Hollywood cinema. The following list of components is not intended to be exhaustive or profound, but simply to make conscious, and present to a discussion of the films, concepts with which we are all perfectly familiar.

1. Capitalism: the right of ownership, private enterprise, personal initiative; the settling of the land.

2. The work ethic: the notion that "honest toil" is in itself and for itself morally admirable, this and (1) both validating and reinforcing each other. The moral excellence of work is also bound up with the necessary subjugation or sublimation of the libido: "the Devil finds work for idle hands." The relationship is beautifully epitomized in the zoo cleaner's song in Tourneur's *Cat People:*

Nothing else to do,
Nothing else to do,
I strayed, went a -courting
'cause I'd nothing else to do.

3. Marriage (legalized heterosexual monogamy) and family: At once the further validation of (1) and (2)—the homestead is built for the Woman, whose function is to embody civilized values and guarantee their continuance through her children—and an extension of the ownership principle to personal relationships ("My house, my wife, my children") in a male-dominated society.

4a. Nature as agrarianism; the virgin land as Garden of Eden: A concept into which, in the Western, (3) tends to become curiously assimilated (ideology's function being to "naturalize" cultural assumptions): e.g., the treatment of the family in *Drums Along the Mohawk*.

4b. Nature as the wilderness, the Indians, on whose subjugation civilization is built; hence by extension the libido, of which in many Westerns the Indians seem an extension or embodiment *(The Searchers)*.

5. Progress, technology, the city ("New York, New York, it's a wonderful town," etc.).

6. Success/wealth: A value of which Hollywood ideology is also deeply ashamed, so that, while hundreds of films play on its allure, very few can allow themselves openly to extol it. Thus its ideological "shadow" is produced.

7. The Rosebud syndrome: Money isn't everything; money corrupts; the poor are happier. A very convenient assumption for capitalist ideology: the more oppressed you are, the happier you are (e.g., the singing "darkies" of *A Day at the Races*, etc.).

8. America as the land where everyone actually is/can be happy; hence the land where all problems are solvable within the existing system (which may need a bit of reform here and there but no radical change). Subversive systems are assimilated wherever possible to serve the dominant ideology. Andrew Britton, in a characteristically brilliant article on *Spellbound*, argues that there even Freudian psychoanalysis becomes an instrument of ideological repression. Above all, this assumption gives us that most striking and persistent of all classical Hollywood phenomena, the happy ending: often a mere "emergency exit" (Sirk's phrase) for the spectator, a barely plausible pretense that the problems the film has

Psycho. Identification with the person threatened (production still).

Marion tempted (Janet Leigh, Frank Albertson).

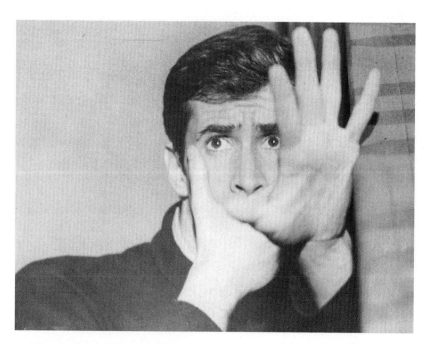

Anthony Perkins as Norman Bates.

Conversations with Norman (Martin Balsam as Arbogast).

The Birds. The attack during Cathy's birthday party.

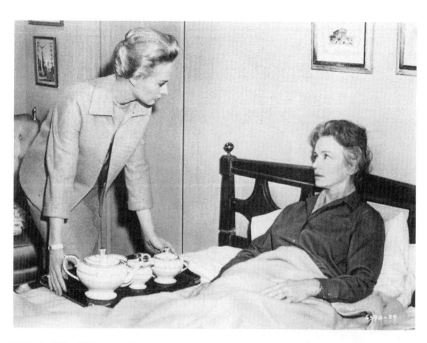

Melanie (Tippi Hedren) brings Lydia (Jessica Tandy) tea after the traumatic visit to Dan Fawcett.

The home-as-refuge becomes home-as-cage.

With the eruption of chaos, the concept of "hero" becomes untenable (Rod Taylor).

Marnie. The honeymoon (Sean Connery, Tippi Hedren).

The gift of Forio.

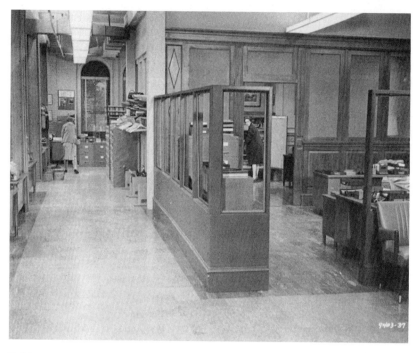

Robbing the Rutland safe: Marnie and the deaf cleaning-woman.

The "cat" paces its cage, under the angry eye of its tamer.

Torn Curtain. The murder of Gromek and its aftermath (Paul Newman with Wolfgang Kieling and with Carolyn Conwell).

Michael Armstrong with Professor Lindt (Ludwig Donath).

"Fire!"

Topaz. Philippe Dubois (Roscoe Lee Browne) flees from the Hotel Teresa.

Mounting suspicions (John Vernon and Karin Dor).

The death of Juanita is precipitated by her involvement with her French lover (Frederick Stafford, left) and executed by her Cuban lover.

Frenzy. Images of the "double" (Jon Finch as Richard Blaney).

The rape and murder of Brenda Blaney (Barry Foster, Barbara Leigh-Hunt).

Family Plot: **Karen Black.**

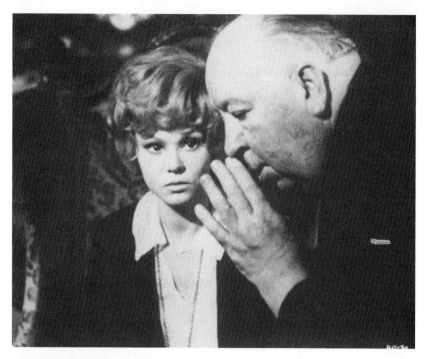

Hitchcock directs Barbara Harris.

Hitchcock's last personal appearance.

raised are now resolved. (*Hilda Crane* offers a suitably blatant example among the hundreds possible.)

Out of this list emerge logically two ideal figures, giving us:

9. The Ideal Male: the virile adventurer, potent, untrammelled man of action.

10. The Ideal Female: wife and mother, perfect companion, endlessly dependable, mainstay of hearth and home.

Since these combine into an Ideal Couple of quite staggering incompatibility, each has his or her shadow, giving us:

11. The settled husband/father, dependable but dull.

12. The erotic woman (adventuress, gambling lady, saloon "entertainer"), fascinating but dangerous, liable to betray the hero or turn into a black panther.

The most striking fact about this list is that it presents an ideology that, far from being monolothic, is inherently riddled with hopeless contradictions and unresolvable tensions. The work that has been done so far on genre has tended to take the various genres as given and discrete, and seeks to explicate them, define them, in terms of motifs, etc.; what we need to ask, if genre theory is ever to be productive, is less what? than why? We are so used to the genres that the peculiarity of the phenomenon itself has been too little noted. The idea I wish to put forward is that the development of the genres is rooted in the sort of ideological contradictions my brief list suggests. One impulse may be the attempt to deny such contradictions by eliminating one of the opposed terms, or at least by a process of simplification.

Robert Warshow's seminal essays on the gangster hero and the Westerner (still fruitfully suggestive, despite the obvious objection that he took too little into account) might be adduced here. The opposition of gangster film and Western is only one of many possibilities. All the genres can be profitably examined in terms of ideological oppositions, forming a complex interlocking pattern: small-town family comedy/ sophisticated city comedy; city comedy/film noir; film noir/small-town comedy, etc. It is probable that a genre is ideologically "pure" (i.e., safe) only in its simplest, most archetypal, most aesthetically deprived and intellectually contemptible form: Hopalong Cassidy, the Andy Hardy comedies.

The Hopalong Cassidy films (from which Indians, always a potentially disruptive force in ideological as well as dramatic terms, are, in general, significantly absent), for example, seem to depend on two strategies for their perfect ideological security: (a) the strict division of characters into good and evil, with no grays; (b) Hoppy's sexlessness (he never becomes emotionally entangled); hence the possibility of evading all the wandering/settling tensions on which aesthetically interesting Westerns are generally structured. (An intriguing alternative: the Ideal American Family of Roy Rogers/Dale Evans/Trigger.) *Shane* is especially interesting in this connection. A deliberate attempt to create an "archetypal" Western, it also represents an effort to resolve the major ideological tensions harmoniously.

One of the greatest obstacles to any fruitful theory of genre has been the tendency to treat the genres as discrete. An ideological approach might suggest why they can't be, however, hard they may appear to try: at best, they represent different strategies for dealing with the same ideological tensions. For example, the small-town movie with a contemporary setting should never be divorced from its historical correlative, the Western. In the classical Hollywood cinema motifs cross repeatedly from genre to genre, as can be made clear by a few examples. The home/ wandering opposition that Peter Wollen rightly sees as central to Ford is not central only to Ford or even to the Western; it structures a remarkably large number of American films covering all genres, from *Out of the Past* to *There's No Business Like Show Business*. The explicit comparison of women to cats connects screwball comedy (*Bringing Up Baby),* horror film *(Cat People),* melodrama *(Rampage),* and psychological thriller *(Marnie).* An example that brings us to my present topic: notice the way in which the Potent Male Adventurer, when he enters the family circle, immediately displaces his "shadow," the settled husband/ father, in both *The Searchers* and *Shadow of a Doubt,* enacted in both cases by his usurpation of the father's chair.

Before we attempt to apply these ideas to specific films, however, one more point needs to be especially emphasized: the presence of ideological tensions in a movie, though it may give it an interest beyond Hopalong Cassidy, is not in itself a reliable evaluative criterion. Artistic value has always been dependent on the presence—somewhere, at some stage— of an individual artist, whatever the function of art in the particular society, and even when (as with Chartres cathedral) one no longer knows who the individual artists were. It is only through the medium of the individual that ideological tensions come to particular focus, hence become of aesthetic as well as sociological interest. It can perhaps be argued that works are of especial interest when (a) the defined particularities of an auteur interact with specific ideological tensions and (b) the film is fed from more than one generic source.

The same basic ideological tensions operate in both *It's a Wonderful Life* and *Shadow of a Doubt:* they furnish further reminders that the home/wandering antinomy is by no means the exclusive preserve of the Western. Bedford Falls and Santa Rosa can be seen as the frontier town seventy or so years on; they embody the development of the civilization whose establishment was celebrated around the same time by Ford in *My Darling Clementine.* With this relationship to the Western in the background (but in Capra's film made succinctly explicit), the central tension in both films can be described in terms of genre: the disturbing influx of film noir into the world of small-town domestic comedy. (It is a tension clearly present in *Clementine* as well: the opposition between the daytime and nighttime Tombstones.)

The strong contrast the two films present testifies to the decisive effect of the intervention of a clearly defined artistic personality in an ideological generic structure. Both films have as a central ideological project the reaffirmation of family and small-town values which the action has called into question. In Capra's film this reaffirmation is magnificently convincing (but with full acknowledgment of the suppressions on which it depends and, consequently, of its precariousness); in Hitchcock's it is completely hollow. The very different emotional effect of the films—the satisfying catharsis and emotional fullness of the Capra, the "bitter taste" (on which so many have commented) of the Hitchcock—is very deeply rooted not only in our response to two opposed directorial personalities but in our own ideological structuring.

One of the main ideological and thematic tensions of *It's a Wonderful Life* is beautifully encapsulated in the scene in which George Bailey (James Stewart) and Mary (Donna Reed) smash windows in a derelict house as a preface to making wishes. George's wish is that he shall get the money to leave Bedford Falls, which he sees as humdrum and constricting, and travel about the world; Mary's (not expressed in words, but in its subsequent fulfillment—confirming her belief that wishes don't come true if you speak them) is that she and George will marry, settle down, and raise a family, in the same derelict house, a ruined shell which marriage-and-family restores to life.

This tension is developed through the extended sequence in which George is manipulated into marrying Mary. His brother's return home with a wife and a new job traps George into staying in Bedford Falls to take over the family business. With the homecoming celebrations continuing inside the house in the background, George sits disconsolately on the front porch: we hear a train whistle, off-screen, to which he reacts. His mother (the indispensable Beulah Bondi) comes out and begins "suggesting" that he visit Mary; he appears to make off toward her, screen right, physically pointed in her direction by his mother, then reappears and walks away past Beulah Bondi in the opposite direction.

This leads him, with perfect ideological/generic logic, to Violet (Gloria Grahame). The Violet/Mary opposition is an archetypally clear rendering of that central Hollywood female opposition that crosses all generic boundaries—as with Susan (Katharine Hepburn) and Alice (Virginia Walker) in *Bringing Up Baby*, Irena (Simone Simon) and Alice (Jane Randolph) in *Cat People*, Chihuahua (Linda Darnell) and Clementine (Cathy Downs) in *My Darling Clementine*, Debby (Gloria Grahame) and Katie (Jocelyn Brando) in *The Big Heat*. But Violet (in front of an amused audience) rejects his poetic invitation to a barefoot ramble over the hills in the moonlight; the goodtime gal offers no more solution to the hero's wanderlust than the wife-mother figure.

So back to Mary, whom he brings to the window by beating a stick aggressively against the fence of the neat, enclosed front garden—a beautifully precise expression of his ambivalent state of mind, desire to attract Mary's attention warring with bitter resentment of his growing entrapment in domesticity. Mary was expecting him; his mother phoned her, knowing that George would end up at her house. Two ideological premises combine here: the notion that the "good" mother always knows, precisely and with absolute certitude, the working of her son's mind; and the notion that the female principle is central to the continuity of civilization, that the "weaker sex" is compensated with a sacred rightness.

Indoors, Mary shows George a cartoon she has drawn: George, in cowboy denims, lassoing the moon. The moment is rich in contradictory connotations. It explicitly evokes the Western, and the figure of the adventurer-hero to which George aspires. Earlier, it was for Mary that George wanted to "lasso the moon," the adventurer's exploits motivated by a desire to make happy the woman who will finally entrap him in

domesticity. From Mary's point of view, the picture is at once affectionate (acknowledging the hero's aspirations), mocking (reducing them to
caricature), and possessive (reducing George to an image she creates and
holds within her hands).

The most overtly presented of the film's structural oppositions is that
between the two faces of capitalism, benign and malignant: on the one
hand, the Baileys (father and son) and their Building and Loan Company, its business practice based on a sense of human needs and a belief
in human goodness; on the other, Potter (Lionel Barrymore), described
explicitly as a spider, motivated by greed, egotism, and miserliness, with
no faith in human nature. Potter belongs to a very deeply rooted tradition. He derives most obviously from Dickens' Scrooge (the film is set at
Christmas)—a Scrooge disturbingly unrepentant and irredeemable—
but his more distant antecedents are in the ogres of fairy tales.

The opposition gives us not only two attitudes to money and property
but two father images (Bailey Sr. and Potter), each of whom gives his
name to the land (Bailey Park, in small-town Bedford Falls, and Pottersville, the town's dark alternative). Most interestingly, the two figures
(American choices, American tendencies) find their vivid ideological extensions in Hollywood genres: the happy, sunny world of small-town
comedy (Bedford Falls is seen mostly in the daytime), the world of film
noir, the dark underside of Hollywood ideology.

Pottersville—the vision of the town as it would have been if George
had never existed, shown him by his guardian angel (Henry Travers)—
is just as "real" (or no more stylized) than Bedford Falls. The iconography of small-town comedy is exchanged, unmistakably, for that of film
noir, with police sirens, shooting in the streets, darkness, vicious dives,
alcoholism, burlesque shows, strip clubs, the glitter and shadows of noir
lighting. George's mother, embittered and malevolent, runs a seedy
boardinghouse; the good-time gal/wife-mother opposition, translated
into noir terms, becomes an opposition of prostitute and repressed spinster-
librarian. The towns emerge as equally valid images of America—validated by their generic familiarity.

Beside *Shadow of a Doubt*, *It's a Wonderful Life* manages a convincing and moving affirmation of the values (and value) of bourgeois family
life. Yet what is revealed, when disaster releases George's suppressed
tensions, is the intensity of his resentment of the family and desire to
destroy it—and with it, in significant relationship, his work (his culmi-

nating action is furiously to overthrow the drawing board with his plans
for more small-town houses). The film recognizes explicitly that behind
every Bedford Falls lurks a Pottersville, and implicitly that within every
George Bailey lurks *The Searchers'* Ethan Edwards. Potter, tempting
George, is given the devil's insights into his suppressed desires. His
remark, "You once called me a warped, frustrated old man—now you're
a warped, frustrated young man," is amply supported by the evidence
the film supplies. What is finally striking about the film's affirmation is
the extreme precariousness of its basis and the consequent hysteria
necessary to its expression. Potter survives, without remorse, his crime
unexposed and unpunished. It may well be Capra's masterpiece, but it is
more than that. Like all the greatest American films—fed by a complex
generic tradition and, beyond that, by the fears and aspirations of a
whole culture—it at once transcends its director and would be inconceivable without him.

Shadow of a Doubt has always been among the most popular of Hitchcock's middle-period films, with critics and public alike, but it has been
perceived in very different, almost diametrically opposed ways. On its
appearance it was greeted by British critics as the film marking Hitchcock's coming to terms with America; his British films were praised for
their humor and "social criticism" as much as for their suspense, and
the early American films (notably *Rebecca* and *Suspicion*) seemed like
attempts artificially to reconstruct England in Hollywood. In *Shadow*,
Hitchcock (with the aid of Thornton Wilder and Sally Benson) at last
brought to American middle-class society the shrewd, satirical, affectionate gaze previously bestowed on the British. A later generation of French
critics (notably Rohmer and Chabrol in their Hitchcock book) praised
the film for very different reasons, establishing its strict formalism (Truffaut's "un film fondé sur le chiffre 2") and seeing it as one of the keys to
a consistent Catholic interpretation of Hitchcock, a rigorous working out
of themes of original sin, the loss of innocence, the fallen world, the exchange (or interchangeability) of guilt. The French noted the family comedy beloved of British critics, if at all, as a mildly annoying distraction.
     That both these views correspond to important elements in the film
and throw light on certain aspects of it is beyond doubt; both, however,
now appear false and partial, dependent upon the abstracting of elements from the whole. If the film is, in a sense, completely dominated by

Hitchcock (nothing in it is unmarked by his artistic personality), a complete reading would need to see the small-town family elements and the Catholic elements as threads weaving through a complex fabric in which, again, ideological and generic determinants are crucial.

The kind of "synthetic" analysis I have suggested (going beyond an interest in the individual auteur) reveals *It's A Wonderful Life* as a far more potentially subversive film than has been generally recognized, but its subversive elements are, in the end, successfully contained. In *Shadow of a Doubt* the Hollywood ideology I have sketched is shattered beyond convincing recuperation. One can, however, trace through the film its attempts to impose itself and render things "safe." What is in jeopardy is above all the family—but, given the family's central ideological significance, once that is in jeopardy, everything is. The small town (still rooted in the agrarian dream, in ideals of the virgin land as a garden of innocence) and the united happy family are regarded as the real sound heart of American civilization; the ideological project is to acknowledge the existence of sickness and evil but preserve the family from their contamination.

A number of strategies can be discerned here: the attempt to insist on a separation of Uncle Charlie from Santa Rosa; his death at the end of the film, as the definitive purging of evil; the production of the young detective (the healthy, wholesome, smalltown male) as a marriage partner for young Charlie, that the family may be perpetuated; above all, the attribution of Uncle Charlie's sexual pathology to a childhood accident, as a means of exonerating the family of the charge of producing a monster (a possibility the American popular cinema, with the contemporary overturning of traditional values, could dramatize explicitly in the horror films of the seventies, e.g., *It's Alive*).

The famous opening, with its parallel introductions of Uncle Charlie and Young Charlie, insists on the city and the small town as opposed, sickness and evil being of the city. As with Bedford Falls/Pottersville, the film draws lavishly on the iconography of usually discrete genres. Six shots (with all movement and direction—the bridges, the panning, the editing—consistently rightward) leading up to the first interior of Uncle Charlie's room give us urban technology, wreckage both human (the down-and-outs) and material (the dumped cars by the sign "No Dumping Allowed"), children playing in the street, the number 13 on the lodging house door. Six shots (movement and direction consistently left) leading to the first interior of Young Charlie's room give us sunny streets with no street games (Santa Rosa evidently has parks), an orderly town with a smiling, paternal policeman presiding over traffic and pedestrians.

In Catholic terms, this is the fallen world against a world of apparent prelapsarian innocence; but it seems more valid to interpret the images, as in *It's A Wonderful Life,* in terms of the two faces of American capitalism. Uncle Charlie has money (the fruits of his crimes and his aberrant sexuality) littered in disorder over table and floor; the Santa Rosa policeman has behind him the Bank of America. The detailed paralleling of uncle and niece can of course be read as comparison as much as contrast, and the opposition that of two sides of the same coin. The point is clearest in that crucial, profoundly disturbing scene where film noir erupts into Santa Rosa itself: the visit to the "Til Two" bar, where Young Charlie is confronted with her alter ego Louise the waitress, her former classmate. The scene equally invites Catholic and Marxist commentaries; its force arises from the revelation of the fallen-World/capitalist-corruption-and-deprivation at the heart of the American small town. The close juxtaposition of genres has implications that reach out through the whole generic structure of the classical Hollywood cinema.

The subversion of ideology within the film is everywhere traceable to Hitchcock's presence, to the skepticism and nihilism that lurk just behind the jocular facade of his public image. His Catholicism is in reality the lingering on in his work of the darker aspects of Catholic mythology: Hell without Heaven. The traces are clear enough. Young Charlie wants a "miracle"; she thinks of her uncle as the "one who can save us" (and her mother immediately asks, "What do you mean, *save* us?"); when she finds his telegram, in the very act of sending hers, her reaction is an ecstatic "He heard me, he heard me!" Hitchcock cuts at once to a low-angle shot of Uncle Charlie's train rushing toward Santa Rosa, underlining the effect with an ominous crashing chord on the sound track.

Uncle Charlie is one of the supreme embodiments of the key Hitchcock figure: ambiguously devil and lost soul. When his train reaches Santa Rosa, the image is blackened by its smoke. From his first appearance, Charlie is associated consistently with a cigar (its phallic connotations evident from the outset, in the scene with the landlady) and repeatedly shown with a wreath of smoke curling around his head (no one else in the film smokes except Joe, the displaced father, who has a paternal pipe, usually unlit). Several incidents (the escape from the policemen at the beginning, the garage door slammed as by remoted control) invest him with a quasi-supernatural power. Rather than restrict the film to a Catholic reading, it seems logical to connect these marks with others: the thread of superstition that runs through the film (the number 13; the hat on the bed; "Sing at table and you'll marry a crazy husband"; the irrational dread of the utterance, however innocent, of the forbidden words "Merry Widow"); and the telepathy motif (the telegram, the tune "jumping from head to head")—the whole Hitchcockian sense of life at the mercy of terrible, unpredictable forces that have to be kept down.

I suggested, in the introduction to this book, that Hitchcock is identified, on different levels and in different ways, with both young Charlie and her uncle; and in a subsequent chapter I discuss the complexities of identification structures in films (especially Hitchcock's) and the possibilities of split identification. Here, it seems worth noting that Hitchcock establishes his (partial, and very complicated) identification with his "villain" through his obligatory "personal appearance." On the train, in the interests of secrecy, Uncle Charlie pretends to be sick and has to be helped from his berth. He is led past a table at which Hitchcock, his back to the camera, is playing bridge. One of his fellow players comments: "You look sick, too," and we cut to Hitchcock's bridge hand, which consists of the entire suit of spades. Like Uncle Charlie (through most of the film), Hitchcock "holds all the cards"; but they are the cards that signify death. Charlie's "sickness," though feigned, is of course, as psychopathology, real, manifesting itself in the power/impotence obsession that we know to be central to Hitchcock's auteurist concerns and methodology.

The Hitchcockian dread of repressed forces is characteristically accompanied by a sense of the emptiness of the surface world that represses them, and this crucially affects the presentation in *Shadow of a Doubt* of the American small-town family. The warmth and togetherness, the mutual responsiveness and affection, that Capra so beautifully creates in the Bailey families, senior and junior, of *It's a Wonderful Life*, are here almost entirely lacking—and this despite the fact, in itself of great ideological interest, that the treatment of the family in *Shadow of a Doubt* has generally been perceived (even, one guesses, by Hitchcock himself) as affectionate.

The most striking characteristic of the Spencers is the separateness of each member; the recurring point of the celebrated overlapping dialogue is that no one ever listens to what anyone else is saying. Each is locked in a separate fantasy world: Emmy in the past, Joe in crime, Anne in books read, apparently, less for pleasure than as a means of amassing knowledge with which she has little emotional contact (though she also believes that everything she reads is "true"). The parents are trapped in a petty materialism (both respond to Young Charlie's dissatisfaction with the assumption that she's talking about money) and reliance on "honest toil" as the means of using up energies. In *Shadow of a Doubt* the ideological image of the small-town happy family becomes the flimsiest facade. That so many are nonetheless deceived by it testifies only to the strength of the ideology—one of whose functions is to inhibit the imagining of radical alternatives.

I have argued elsewhere that the key to Hitchcock's films is less suspense than sexuality (or, alternatively, that his "suspense" always carries a sexual charge in ways sometimes obvious, sometimes esoteric); and that sexual relationships in his work are inevitably based on power, the obsession-with-power/dread-of-impotence being as central to his method as to his thematic. In *Shadow of a Doubt* it is above all sexuality that cracks apart the family facade. As far as the Hays code permitted, a double incest theme runs through the film: Uncle Charlie and Emmy, Uncle Charlie and Young Charlie. Necessarily, this is expressed through images and motifs, never becoming verbally explicit; certain of the images depend on a suppressed verbal play for their significance.

For the reunion of brother and sister, Hitchcock gives us an image (Emmy poised left of screen, arrested in mid-movement, Charlie right, under trees and sunshine) that iconographically evokes the reunion of lovers (Charlie wants to see Emmy again as she was when she was "the prettiest girl on the block"). And Emmy's breakdown, in front of her embarrassed friends and neighbors, at the news of Charlie's imminent departure, is eloquent. As for uncle and niece, they are introduced symmetrically lying on beds, Uncle Charlie fondling his phallic cigar, Young Charlie prone, hands behind head. When Uncle Charlie gets off the train he is bent over a stick, pretending to be ill; as soon as he sees Young Charlie he "comes erect," flourishing the stick. One of his first actions on taking over her bedroom is to pluck a rose for his buttonhole ("deflowering"). More obviously, there is the business with the ring, which not only, as a symbolic token of engagement, links Charlie sexually with her uncle, but also links her, through its previous ownership, to his succession of merry widows. The film shows sexual pathology at the heart of the American family, the necessary product of its repressions and sublimations.

What exactly happens to Young Charlie in the course of the film? The superficial ideological project tries to insist upon the preservation of her innocence, in association with the restoration of "small-town" values: hence her final reassurance, outside the church, when she asks her detective lover how to account for a world that produces people like her uncle, that it "just goes a little crazy sometimes" and has to be "watched." Yet the film has made clear that Uncle Charlie's "sickness" cannot be dissociated from the values and assumptions of capitalist ideology, and is in fact their extreme product: the ideology that implicitly acknowledges the complementarity of its oppositions (city/small town, film noir/ family comedy) even while it seeks to assert their discreteness. Young Charlie's experience in the film must be seen, in fact, as a form of psychic violation from which (while it has rendered her older and wiser) her "innocence" will never recover. When Uncle Charlie falls in front of the oncoming train, his death is ambiguously accident and "killing in self-defence": it is staged and shot in a way that exonerates Young Charlie from all moral responsibility. Yet the film, in a single disturbing image whose implications are virtually subliminal, has already suggested that she wills it. She has told her uncle earlier that if he ever touches her mother again, she will kill him (the extremeness of the statement is very suggestive in relation to the "double incest" theme). At the station, he takes Emmy's hands in his. Hitchcock cuts to a close shot of Young Charlie glowering at him; in the background of the image (literalizing the phrase "at the back of her mind") a train enters the frame.

As for the "accident"—that old critical stumbling block—it presents no problem at all, provided one is ready to acknowledge the validity of a psychoanalytical reading of movies. Indeed, it provides a rather beautiful example of the way in which ideology, in seeking to impose itself, succeeds merely in confirming its own subversion. The "accident" (Charlie was "riding a bicycle" for the first time, which resulted in a "collision") can be read as elementary Freudian metaphor for the trauma of premature sexual awakening (after which Charlie was "never the same again"). The smothering sexual/possessive devotion of a doting older sister may be felt to provide a clue to the sexual motivation behind the merry widow murders: Charlie isn't interested in money. Indeed, Emmy is connected to the merry widows by an associative chain in which important links are her own practical widowhood (her ineffectual husband is largely ignored), her ladies' club, and its leading light Mrs. Potter, Uncle Charlie's potential next in line.

A fuller analysis would need to dwell on the limitations of Hitchcock's vision, nearer the nihilistic than the tragic; on his inability to conceive of repressed energies as other than evil, and the surface world that represses them as other than shallow and unfulfilling. This explains why there can be no Heaven corresponding to Hitchcock's Hell, for every vision of Heaven that is not merely negative is rooted in a concept of the liberation of the instincts, the Resurrection of the Body, which Hitchcock must always deny. But my final stress is less on the evaluation of a particular film or director than on the implications for a criticism of the Hollywood cinema of the notions of interaction and multiple determinacy I have been employing. It is its rootedness in the Hollywood genres, and in the very ideological structure it so disturbingly subverts, that makes *Shadow of a Doubt* so much more suggestive and significant a work than Hitchcock the bourgeois entertainer could ever have guessed.

Note: I am indebted to Deborah Thomas for certain insights into *Shadow of a Doubt*.

15

STAR AND AUTEUR: HITCHCOCK'S FILMS WITH BERGMAN

Arguably the most important recent development in film theory/criticism has been the radical opening up of discussion of stars: the construction of the star image/persona, the intricate interrelationship of acting/presence/image, the ways in which a star functions, and the complex of meanings she or he generates, within a given filmic text. I draw here upon the pioneer work of Richard Dyer *(Stars, Heavenly Bodies)* and, especially, Andrew Britton in his brilliant *Katharine Hepburn: The Thirties and After* (to my mind among the finest books on the Hollywood cinema so far produced), in examining the interaction between the Hitchcock thematic and the Ingrid Bergman thematic in the films they made together (particularly *Notorious* and *Under Capricorn,* which are among both Hitchcock's and Bergman's highest achievements).

This chapter also has a secondary ambition (and the two will interrelate): to challenge the continuing hegemony of a certain psychoanalytical approach to Hitchcock that, deriving from the theories of Lacan, can be exemplified at its most influential by the work of Laura Mulvey and Raymond Bellour. This will not, of course, constitute an attack on the use of psychoanalytical theory to analyze films *in principle;* it will rather register a sense that the particular approach, in its tendency to exclusivity and its claims to the definitive and comprehensive, has proven constricting and reductive, obliterating or marginalizing considerations that are in fact of the first importance in determining a film's meaning. I begin by summarizing an intelligent and distinguished (it deserves to be far more widely known and should certainly be anthologized) but ultimately inadequate article by Michael Renov on *Notorious* that situates

itself explicitly within this tradition; I then offer an account of Ingrid
Bergman as Hollywood star; finally, I examine the films, in the analysis
of which these two discrete approaches will converge.

The full title of Renov's article (*Wide Angle,* vol. 4, no. 1) tells all:
"From Identification to Ideology: The Male System of *Notorious.*" Although he offers Bellour as his starting point, it is evident that Laura
Mulvey's seminal feminist/psychoanalytical article "Visual Pleasure and
Narrative Cinema" (*Screen,* autumn 1975) is lurking in the background,
with its thesis that mainstream cinema constructs the spectator as male
and that, within the film, it is the man who looks, the woman who is
looked at: *Notorious* carries us from "identification" with the male gaze
to the "ideology" that subordinates women by constructing or reinforcing patriarchal myths and gender roles. According to Renov, the male
gaze at the "notorious" woman (whose notoriety it will be the film's
purpose to chastise and reform) is established at the very outset in the
flash cameras of the reporters: with them, we seek to probe the woman
Alicia Huberman whose face is half-concealed by the shadow of a wide-
brimmed hat. The second sequence (the party in a Miami bungalow)
identifies this gaze (already *our* gaze) with that of Devlin/Cary Grant as,
silent and impassive, he watches Alicia as she tries to get a response from
him. At first we see only the back of his head: shadowy, unidentified, in
the foreground of the image, he could almost be another (male) spectator
sitting a few rows ahead of us in the movie theater. Before him/us, Alicia
displays herself as spectacle, tipsy, cynical, promiscuous, the very image
of the "loose" woman.

Subsequently (Renov argues) identification is split between Devlin and
Alex Sebastian/Claude Rains: respectively, they embody the "Good Law"
and the "Bad Law," but the Law of patriarchy is always the Law, and
Alex gains our sympathy because of the precariousness of his position
and because he is presented throughout as a potential victim (victimized
by, among others, his domineering mother). This split identification
enables the film to perform a complex, intricate, and insidious ideological operation: the negotiation of two apparently opposed and irreconcilable patriarchal myths of Woman, fusing them within a single character
(and, at the end of the film, a single moment): woman as the "good
object" (tamed, domesticated, subordinated, submissive, the future wife)
and woman as betrayer/deceiver. Alicia becomes, in the progress of the

narrative, simultaneously Devlin's good object and Sebastian's betrayer, the whole film moving toward the moment of her smile as Devlin, driving her to safety, locks the car door against Sebastian, the smile expressing at once her submission to Devlin and final betrayal of Sebastian (who will return to the house and to his death).

Renov's argument is plausible, closely argued, up to a point convincing; and it has behind it the weight of a formidable intellectual tradition. Yes, we may agree, there *is* a "male system" operating in *Notorious,* and this is broadly how it functions. I wish, then, not so much to refute Renov's reading as to question its adequacy. For the time being, I suggest that the model of identification he is employing is far too simple, its insufficiency deriving from the strategy, inherent in the very premises of the semiotic tradition, of reducing the complexities of signification within a text to those aspects that are "scientifically" demonstrable, but which are not necessarily the most important determinants of its meaning and effect.

The construction of identification within a film is a delicate and complex matter that can never be reduced simply to the mechanics of "the look" (the look of characters, of spectator, of the camera). It must be said at the outset that the term "identification" is itself problematic —far more so than Renov and others find it convenient to acknowledge. I use it here in its widest sense to cover the whole spectrum of spectator response from feelings of sympathy through empathy to total involvement, because I believe these experiences exist on a continuum and are not cleanly distinguishable from one another. At least six factors in the construction of identification (also not always cleanly distinguishable) can be listed:

1. Identification with the Male Gaze. Yes, mainstream cinema has been predominantly sexist and patriarchal: I don't wish to reject the Mulvey thesis as a useful starting point for the exploration of filmic texts, the purpose of that exploration being to see how specific works differ from the norm. The problem is that the thesis has been taken (and indeed was explicitly offered) as much more: as a comprehensive overview of mainstream cinematic practice. The inadequacy (to put it politely) of Mulvey's accounts of films by Hawks, Sternberg, and Hitchcock in what is put forward as a demonstration of the correctness of the thesis should (one would have thought) have stood as the opposite: an eloquent warning against swallowing the thesis whole. The warning has not been much heeded, and students still frequently find it sufficient to quote Mulvey on the Sternberg/Dietrich films, for example, in order to save themselves the bother of exploring their complex and profoundly subversive implications. We may concede, nonetheless, that this level of identification exists, and that in *Notorious* it produces an identification with the gazes of Grant and Rains, as Renov asserts. Indeed, much of the tension the film generates is dependent upon the existence of this level.

2. Identification With the Threatened or Victimized. A recurrent motif of Hitchcock interviews: there is a "natural" (read: endemic to our culture) tendency to identify with the character who is threatened. In *Notorious* this is primarily Alicia, secondarily Sebastian, never (until the film's final sequence) Devlin. In that first scene, our identification with the male gaze (the reporters with their flashbulbs) is countered by our much stronger identification with Alicia as the object of aggression. Indeed, with Hitchcock's characteristic directness and economy, this immediately establishes the film's dominant principle of construction (and that of other Hitchcock films earlier and later—think of *Blackmail* and the last third of *Vertigo*): the creation of tension through a conflict between different levels or modes of identification.

3. Degrees of Sympathy. Irrespective of the mechanics of point of view, we identify with characters to the degree to which we are able (are encouraged) to sympathize, or, better still, empathize with them. This is of course quite "unscientific," hence beyond the limited grasp of semiotics, but it is of central importance to our experience of any fictional narrative. To a certain degree it is personal and subjective (presumably, a sadist in the audience might identify with a sadist on the screen, despite all the efforts of the filmmakers to prevent such an identification). But, even if it eludes rigorously "scientific" demonstration, it is not beyond rational discussion and analysis: an examination of the construction of the scenario, the dialogue, the use of cinematic devices (both visual and aural) as "pointers," should take us a long way toward an understanding of the degrees of sympathy a film *wishes* us to feel for its various characters. In *Notorious* it seems, again, clear that Alicia is from a very early point (arguably from her first appearance) its emotional center, the magnet that draws our sympathy the most powerfully. Again also, Sebastian is a secondary potential identification figure, but *only* because he is a victim: we are *positively* drawn to Alicia, only negatively to Sebastian, who can never be more to us than an object of compassion (we are never allowed to forget that he is also a monster). As victims, he and Alicia are explicitly paralleled: I am thinking of the paired shots (both extreme high angle) looking down on the chessboardlike hall of the Sebastian mansion, in the first of which Sebastian crosses to the staircase after discovering the fact of his betrayal, in the second of which Alicia collapses in her attempt to reach the staircase (and a telephone) after she realizes that she is being poisoned. But as usual, the symmetry is there to mark difference as much as to suggest resemblance. As for Devlin, a limited and partial identification with him on grounds of sympathy is not ruled out altogether, especially in scenes from which Alicia is absent (I shall argue later that Andrew Britton, in his admirable monograph on Cary Grant in *CineAction! 7,* is wrong in seeing Devlin as totally beyond sympathy). On the one hand such an identification is obviously facilitated by the casting; on the other, it is consistently obstructed by the character's relentlessly unpleasant treatment of Alicia, even though we are permitted occasional glimpses of the pain and vulnerability that motivate it.

4. The Sharing of a Consciousness. We might label this "intellectual identification," to distinguish it from the forms of emotional identification described above. What I have in mind here is less the use of point-of-view techniques (they may of course operate in close conjunction with it, and in Hitchcock usually do) than the construction of the scenario to limit our knowledge to what a character knows: Hawks achieves this very thoroughly in *The Big Sleep* without recourse to POV shooting/editing. This produces a significantly different form of identification from those discussed so far: in theory at least it would be possible to restrict us to the consciousness of a thoroughly unpleasant character for whom we could feel neither pity, concern, nor sympathy. Hitchcock sometimes adopts a variation on this possibility: he involves us intimately with a character whose drives are neurotic and potentially destructive but are not readily perceived as such because they are so pervasive within our culture and so central to our "normal" conditioning, in order to effect an abrupt disequilibrium and rethinking when the

sharing of the consciousness is ruptured (*Vertigo* is of course the supreme example, wherein we are forced to reassess the nature of our own
identification with Scotty's obsessive romantic love). In *Notorious* this
form of identification works again, overall, to involve us with Alicia,
both Devlin and Sebastian being, for certain crucial stretches of the film,
ignorant of information that she possesses. The sequence of the first
dinner party in the Sebastians' home, for example, is constructed rigorously on the principle of our sharing Alicia's perceptions, from her
entrance into the house to her aroused suspicions about the wine
bottle.

5. The Use of Cinematic Devices.   One thinks especially, of course,
of those point-of-view techniques of shooting and editing with which
Hitchcock has been particularly associated, but there are many other
ways in which our responses to characters can be conditioned: the use
of close-up against mid- or long-shot, of lyrical music against harsh
music, low angle against high angle. The power of the POV shot in
constructing identification has been greatly exaggerated (by myself, among
others): it is simply not true that to stick in a shot from a given character's point of view automatically identifies the spectator with that character, beyond the obvious enforced identification with a physical position (we see what the character sees). In general, Hitchcock uses POV
editing to clinch an identification that has already been solidly built: the
opening of *Psycho,* as I tried to show in chapter 10, is exemplary,
Marion's first strict POV shot withheld until more than ten minutes into
the film. "Scientific" analysis notwithstanding, the efficacy of POV to
construct identification can only be validly argued in conjunction with
other factors. Nevertheless, it is worth pointing out that the overwhelming majority of POV shots in *Notorious* belong to Alicia, not to
the men: in the magnificent party scene, with its intricate orchestration
of point of view divided among the three principals, the number of shots
from Alicia's point of view more than doubles the total of those accorded Devlin and Sebastian.

The skill and precision with which Hitchcock uses point-of-view
techniques to clinch identification, and their relation to the presentation
of the consciousness with which we are invited to identify, can be
exemplified by an analysis of the sequence in which Alicia comes to
understand that she is being systematically poisoned by Sebastian and

his mother. At the beginning of the scene we are in possession of knowledge that Alicia does not yet have (that the Sebastians know she is working for the Americans; that they are poisoning her). The first part of the scene (shot "objectively") recounts the process whereby she catches us up; the second part involves us more and more intimately in her experience. There are four stages, each marked by the use of a specific cinematic mode or device:

1. "Objective" (but not exactly neutral) camera. The sequence opens with one of Hitchcock's virtuoso long takes, beginning with a general view of the room and its occupants (Alicia and the Sebastians, with the "innocent" Dr. Anderson) and moving to a traveling close-up of the poisoned cup of coffee in Madame Sebastian's hand as she carries it to Alicia. The sequence then develops through a series of non-POV shots showing us Alicia's attempts to gain information as to where Dr. Anderson is going (i.e., the location of the uranium ore) and the Sebastians' growing concern to prevent his giving away their secrets—a concern that at last arouses Alicia's suspicions. This—the moment when she begins to "catch on"—precipitates

2. The first POV shot of the sequence: the Sebastians' spontaneous cry of warning when Dr. Anderson picks up Alicia's cup by mistake motivates her look at the cup; the POV shot registers her recognition of what is happening. This leads immediately to

3. The pair of "subjective" POV shots as, from Alicia's point of view, the camera rapidly tracks in on the obtrusively unconcerned faces of Madame Sebastian and her son, the movement departing from strict physical POV (obviously Alicia is not flying across the room toward them) to give us her mental shock of awareness: from sharing her vision we now share her consciousness. This in turn leads to

4. The use of fully subjective, "expressionist" camera, involving visual distortion: the terrifying images, from Alicia's point of view, of the Sebastians and their merging, imprisoning shadows, as Alicia struggles to get to the door. It is at this moment of the film that our identification with Alicia, and with her experience of oppression, exploitation, and victimization, becomes complete.

6. Identification With the Star. It has always been a commonplace of theories about Hollywood that stars function as fantasy identification figures for the spectator (one need not invoke the Lacanian mirror phase with its misrecognition of the coherent ideal self to grasp the provisional validity of this). What needs to be asserted here, as far as *Notorious* is concerned, is that essentially it is Bergman's film: if Grant is more than a stooge he is less than a full partner, the film's most dramatic, intense, and involving scenes being centered on Bergman as both their magnet of sympathy and dominant consciousness. In the scenes they share it is always Bergman who is privileged, partly because we are aware, from sharing her viewpoint, of the monstrousness of Grant's treatment of her. (The corollary of this is that it is only in scenes from which she is absent that Grant becomes sympathetic enough to function as a primary identification figure).

I draw from all this two conclusions: (a) That identification in the cinema is an extremely complex, multilayered, intricate phenomenon which absolutely prohibits reduction to a simple formula such as the "male gaze" or the use of POV shots. Identification may not be total or nontransferable; it can flicker sporadically and partially in the play of sympathies, shift from character to character, operate in relation to two different (and perhaps antagonistic) characters at once, be encouraged, qualified, or denied altogether. Most important, it can function on different levels simultaneously, developing tensions and contradictions in a complex dialectic.

(b) That in *Notorious,* only the first of the six (overlapping, interactive) forms I have somewhat artificially distinguished privileges the male characters as primary identification figures; all the other five privilege Alicia/Bergman.

BERGMAN AS STAR

Bergman's cinematic career divides neatly into four parts: the Swedish period (1934–40); the first Hollywood period, from *Intermezzo* to *Under Capricorn* (1939–49—the slight overlap in dates is accounted for by her return, after *Intermezzo,* to make one more film in Sweden); the Rossellini period (1950–55); the final period, marked by her rehabilitation in America (*Anastasia* and an Oscar), but far more heterogeneous than any of the previous periods, both in roles and countries, with films in Europe for Renoir and Ingmar Bergman, and appearances in TV movies (1956 until her death in 1982). My concern here is with the second period, within which all her work for Hitchcock is situated, and I shall refer to the others only incidentally.

Nineteen thirty-nine, the year of Bergman's Hollywood entrance, marked the nadir of the careers of her two major predecessors (as female European imports), Garbo and Dietrich, both recently certified as "box-office poison." (It was also, of course, the year of their box-office reha-bilitation, with their careers drastically reactivated by the expedient of casting them in comedy for the first time—*Ninotchka* and *Destry Rides Again.*) Bergman was introduced as a replacement: at oonce the "new Garbo" and the anti-Garbo. Despite the actual complexities of their personas, Dietrich and Garbo were popularly defined in terms of "glamor," representing different inflections of the concept of "screen goddess": the Garbo mythology emphasized her aloofness ("I want to be alone"), the Dietrich mythology her exoticism. Both mythologies developed a femi-nine mystique, woman as inaccessible, mysterious, irreducibly "other" while irresistibly desirable: the mystique essential to our culture's partic-ular inflection of romantic love, of which *Vertigo* was to be the supreme critique. The mythology relates obviously enough to Garbo's and Dietrich's actual roles and performances, while defusing the force of their subver-sive implications: in fact, its function now appears in retrospect to have been to mystify and recuperate. Despite the mystification, one may surmise that the loss of popularity was due to the sense that the two stars represented a threat to dominant male sexuality and its patriarchal norms. This is especially clear in the case of Dietrich, at her most overtly threatening in the two films that did most to destroy her appeal at the box office, *The Scarlet Empress* and *The Devil Is a Woman*. Both Garbo and Dietrich raise in a particularly acute form a perennial problem of the Hollywood star system that will resurface, despite all attempts to suppress it, with Bergman: how can a female star of sufficient force and charisma to dominate the films in which she appears *fail* to become threatening in one way or another within the structures of patriarchal culture?

The persona Bergman developed (or which Hollywood constructed around her) during the first Hollywood period has four major compo-nents: nature and health; niceness; the lady; the actress. I shall discuss each in turn.

Connotations of the "natural" and the "healthy" (both physical and psychological) were central to the promotion of Bergman as the new

Hollywood star, in contrast to the connotations of decadence and artificiality the Dietrich image had accumulated, or to the soulfulness and languor associated with Garbo. Interestingly, from the viewpoint of image construction, this seems not to have been the case in Sweden, or at least not nearly so predominantly: John Kobal's collection of publicity photographs suggests that the Swedish period emphasized glamor, the pictures he reproduces being more like typical Hollywood star portraits than those actually used to promote Bergman in America. Two of the early Hollywood publicity stills epitomize Selznick's concept of the Bergman image. One shows her with baby ducks; the other shows her holding a sheaf of corn, the caption alerting us to the fact that she is "unadorned by the artifices of makeup and glamorous hairdos" (the artifice of the photographs is of course quite blatant—what Nancy Allen in De Palma's *Blow Out* refers to as the "no makeup look," the most difficult of all to fabricate). Much was made in press handouts of Selznick's decision *not* to remold her features or glamorize her (and of her own resistance to such a process); and another handout revealed the secret of how she maintained her wonderfully "natural" complexion— by going for walks in the rain.

Clearly the "natural" is as much a construction as the "glamorous," the difference being that the latter foregrounds the notion of construction where the former suppresses it. What is not in itself a construction (though much was constructed upon it, and whole films constructed around it) was the supreme evidence of "naturalness" and "health," the famous Bergman smile. Among other things, this was what constructed Bergman (at least implicitly) as the "anti-Garbo": the myth of Garbo's romantic moroseness was so pervasive and so familiar that an entire advertising campaign for *Ninotchka* could be mounted around the slogan "Garbo laughs." If Garbo was aloof, Bergman was accessible: the radiance of the smile betokened an openness and generosity that dispelled any overt sense of a "feminine mystique." Superficially, by depriving her of the aura of mystery, it also made her unthreatening. Yet the radiance, the naturalness, the health carry a problematic corollary. Our culture has habitually confused (in order to mystify) the terms "natural" and "normal," conflating both with "healthy" ("Please God, make me a normal, healthy girl"): the "normal" woman (the woman who conforms to the norms and repressive demands of the patriarchal organization) is by no means "natural," and the prayer, offered to the supreme patriarch, should logically run "Please God, make me a normal, *un*healthy girl." The threat that the attribution of naturalness is intended to repress returns through the very agent of repression: naturalness inevitably entails sexuality—for a woman, the untrammeled female sexuality upon the subjugation and regulation of which patriarchy is built. More: if we acccept Freud's "discovery" of constitutional bisexuality (and how, today, can we not?), it entails the expression of the woman's "masculinity," her active, assertive, energetic side that patriarchal culture has long striven definitively (but unsuccessfully) to deny. Activity, assertiveness, energy: Bergman's smile, and all the characteristics that go with it (appearance, stance, body language, speech), are the signs of precisely these qualities. The "natural" woman can become, within the patriarchal organization and the male anxieties generated by its demands on men, more strongly (if less obviously) threatening than the "glamorous." (Similarly, the "sexual" is more threatening than the "sexy." The latter —as embodied in, for example, Lana Turner—is perceived on some level as a set of constructed signifiers and can be relished in safety; the "sexual" is the real thing.)

The "nice" and the "ladylike" provided means of containing Bergman's energy and activeness. They also immediately introduce into the persona the possibilities for tension and contradiction: she becomes the "natural" woman who can also function as a potential society hostess. In traditional Hollywood terms, the "nice" woman (rancher's daughter or schoolmarm in the Western, actual or potential wife/mother in all the genres) is habitually opposed to the sexual woman (the saloon entertainer, the *femme fatale*). In Bergman we have the "nice" woman who is also irreducibly and palpably sexual, the "natural" woman who is also somehow a "lady." The niceness, like the naturalness, is very much a component of the image emphasized and developed during the Hollywood period: she never played a "bad" woman, and it is virtually impossible to imagine the Hollywood Bergman playing the Joan Crawford role in *A Woman's Face,* despite the fact that she did precisely that in the earlier Gustav Molander version of that film in Sweden. (I have not been able to see any of the films from the Swedish period, but plot synopses suggest that her roles were considerably more diversified than was generally the case in America.) This emphasis on Bergman as the "nice," "good" woman surely accounts for the extraordinary intensity of the animus against her over her involvement with Rossellini: the roughly contemporaneous case of Rita Hayworth and Ali Khan (which, as it encompassed miscegenation, might reasonably have been expected to be perceived as even more scandalous) provoked little beyond a raised eyebrow (what would you expect of Gilda, after all?).

These seemingly contradictory components of the image are not beyond ideological resolution: the *nicest* thing a *lady* can do is behave *naturally*, without pretension or condescension, naturalness in this context being the most sophisticated attainment of lady-icity. But the potential for tension and rupture is always there, its source always in the threat of an active female sexuality, especially when, in the case of a movie star, the components will be variously inflected, emphasized, and developed from role to role. The typical early Hollywood roles can in fact be seen as attempts to reconcile the opposites by casting Bergman as an essentially nice woman in a morally ambiguous position. In *Intermezzo* she is the "other woman" who threatens Leslie Howard's marriage and family precisely because of her irresistible niceness; in *Rage in Heaven* her paranoically jealous husband (Robert Montgomery) believes she is unfaithful to him, his jealousy eventually driving her into the arms of another man; in *Casablanca* she is caught in a romantic love vs. duty quandary; all three films derive their (varying degrees of) energy from her sexuality while finally containing it in the promise of bourgeois marriage (to George Sanders in *Rage in Heaven*) or renunciation. Hollywood was swiftly to find another, more drastic, way of dealing with it, to which I shall return presently.

The notion of the "actress" is another important component of the Bergman image, manifested not only in her performances but in publicity and her own reiterated aspirations. What is at issue here is the traditional, naive opposition star/actor: the actor works hard, is dedicated, reveals extraordinary skills, expresses depth and commitment; the star is a kind of lucky parasite who, after arbitrary "discovery," just lazily gets by on personality and charisma: Wayne and Grant are stars, Olivier and De Niro are actors. Bergman-the-person was never satisfied with being just a star: she wanted to be an actor as well. "Acting," in this sense, is clearly an ideological category (like naturalness, niceness, lady-ness, etc.). It appears to have three possible embodiments, all of which are relevant to Bergman:

1. The "great role." Bergman always wanted to play Joan of Arc, and did so twice, once for Victor Fleming and once for Rossellini; her

rehabilitation in Hollywood was ratified appropriately enough by the title role of *Anastasia*.

2. Versatility. The "star" is always the same, the actor is a kind of histrionic chameleon, with excellence measured by the ability to play roles so varied that she or he becomes virtually unrecognizable. Bergman (wisely) never carried this principle very far; it manifested itself mainly in her understandable rebellion against typecasting. We have this to thank for her remarkable performance in *Dr. Jekyll and Mr. Hyde:* Lana Turner was originally cast as Hyde's cockney barmaid mistress, Bergman as Jekyll's high society fiancee, and it was Bergman who persuaded Turner to join her in a demand that they switch roles. This gave Bergman by far the meatier part, and also the chance to display her sensuality unconstrainedly: her Ivy, despite the peculiarity of the accent, is a marvelous creation, at once active, sexual, vulnerable, pathetic (predictably, the critics almost unanimously protested that she was hopelessly miscast).

3. Emotional authenticity. Again, it needs to be stressed that one is speaking of a construction rather than a reality—of something that is *acted* but which gives the impression of transcending "mere" acting. One variation on this is the "Method" school, with its emphasis on entering into, "becoming," the character. More generally, it is manifested in the acting of emotional extremes, "tearing a passion to tatters." One thinks at once of Anna Magnani, and recalls that it was Magnani's performance in *Rome, Open City* that first inspired Bergman to seek a (professional) relationship with Rossellini. Magnani filmed Cocteau's *La Voix Humaine* for Rossellini; Bergman subsequently recorded it. Doubtless she expected to give Magnaniesque performances for Rossellini, and her disappointment at finding that he wanted exactly the opposite is understandable. If for Selznick Bergman was the anti-Garbo, for Rossellini she was the anti-Magnani: where Magnani acts out every emotion her character is experiencing, Bergman in the Rossellini films seems (apart from rare eruptions) constantly to be holding her emotions in. Paradoxically, if such a thing as *genuine* emotional authenticity, beyond the acted or the signified, is possible in a filmed performance, one might claim it as a characteristic of her roles for Rossellini; but for Bergman the films did not make any demands on her as an actress—she "just walked through" them.

By the mid-'40s Hollywood had found a logical way of dealing with the threat posed by Bergman's health, naturalness, energy, sexuality: to burden her with illness (whether mental or physical). The importance of this strategy—its expressive potential, its tendency to intensify and foreground rather than suppress the persona's ideological contradictions—can be gauged from the fact that it operates in all four of her finest Hollywood films (both the best films per se and the ones one would single out to represent the Hollywood-period Bergman persona at its most fully developed, the films that most beautifully use and express her *meaning*): in *The Bells of St. Mary's* she has tuberculosis; in *Gaslight* her husband (almost successfully) attempts to drive her insane; in *Notorious* she is near-alcoholic in the first part and systematically poisoned in the second; in *Under Capricorn* she is both alcoholic and driven close to insanity. The essential Bergman thematic, however complex its realization in specific texts, might be summed up in a simple formula: the attempt (usually by men) to destroy Ingrid Bergman's smile, and its final, triumphant restoration. Before considering the Hitchcock films I want briefly to discuss the ways in which Bergman functions in *The Bells of St. Mary's* and *Gaslight*—the ways in which her presence contributes to their meaning.

It is precisely Bergman's unrepressed "masculinity" that McCarey, with his customary sensitivity to the particular qualities of his actors, draws upon throughout *The Bells of St. Mary's:* there is the reminiscence of skiing in her Minnesota childhood, Bergman's body involuntarily mimicking the movements; the boxing lesson; the baseball game. In every instance the confinement of the nun's habit (and the nun's decorum) actually enhances our sense of Bergman's natural energy and athleticism by constricting or inhibiting her movements. The ambiguity of gender is summed up in her combination of a female title with a male name: Sister Benedict. Out of it McCarey develops one of the Hollywood cinema's most beautiful and complex enquiries into gender roles and the possibility of undermining their rigidity. Father O'Malley/Bing Crosby retains to the end the authority of his position, using it to get Sister Benedict transferred (for her own good but against her will). On the personal level, however, the couple move toward a relationship of equality based on an exchange of gender characteristics: Sister Benedict teaches a boy to box; O'Malley helps a girl to write an English essay. This dovetails with a constant McCarey preoccupation that runs from the Laurel and Hardy shorts of the '20s, through *Make Way for Tomorrow*, to *Rally 'Round the Flag, Boys:* the critique of domesticity and the structures of bourgeois marriage/family/home. Precisely because they are a priest and a nun, hence necessarily outside the deadening constrictions of the biological family of our present culture, O'Malley and Benedict are able to construct an alternative form of family, fluid, free from the demands of patriarchal gender positions and familial roles: witness the marvelous scene of the rehearsal for the Christmas play, which develops out of the undermining of O'Malley's authority and the freeing of the children to improvise, a freedom accepted and endorsed by the parent figures. The ending of the film offers perhaps the most beautiful rendering in Bergman's career of the restoration of her smile: her response to O'Malley's revelation that she has tuberculosis, which also registers her understanding that he loves her.

Gaslight offers a quite different development of the potentialities of the Bergman persona. Her natural "masculine" energy and vigor make her victimization infinitely more unendurable than is the case with the frail and "feminine" Diana Wynyard of the British version. Cukor's film, and Bergman's performance, continuously suggest that Paula is ready—against her very nature—to believe that she is insane because there is no other way of denying the unbearable alternative: the recognition that her husband Gregory/Charles Boyer is trying to *drive* her insane. From this viewpoint the film becomes a critique of romantic love, of the pressures society has placed on women to commit themselves to men without hesitation or question, if necessary suppressing their own innate intelligence when it conflicts with this romantic commitment. Paula's partial complicity in her husband's systematic undermining of her confidence in her own perceptions gives added force to the film's climax, where she uses her (alleged, imposed) insanity as a weapon against him, and where Bergman's strength and energy are fully restored to her.

One sequence, around the middle of the film, is worth examining in detail, because of the intelligence with which Cukor's mise-en-scène mobilizes the various facets of the Bergman persona, a sequence built around the man's extinction of her smile and, finally, her very presence: the sequence in which Gregory pursues his destruction of her by first reviving then drowning her hopes of happiness, a happiness dependent upon her ability to win his approval. He announces that, as a surprise for her, they are going to the theater. The Bergman smile is restored in all its radiance, the energy, long pent-up in anxiety, is released in her vigorous dance around the room, humming "Tales from the Vienna Woods." He then produces his trump card: a little picture is missing again from the wall. He proceeds to humiliate her by interrogating housekeeper and parlor maid in her presence, making them swear on the Bible that they haven't stolen it. Paula then passionately swears the same herself, whereupon he coerces her into complicity with his assault on her own certitude: she demonstrates that she "knows" where the picture has been hidden (in the same place where it was found when it disappeared before). The sequence ends with a series of shots, as Gregory leads her upstairs, the theater visit abandoned, dramatizing Paula's obliteration: (a) Bergman's face, already deprived of its smile, the shadow of her husband's head falling over it as he dominates her from a higher step; (b) Bergman, thrust into her room, reduced to a shadow on the open door; (c) Gregory closing the door on her, the shadow vanishing.

More interesting, however, than the critique of female romantic love is the critique the film develops of its corollary, male sexual anxiety as the source of the man's persecution of the woman. Gregory's sole motivation throughout the film is his quest for the jewels of the woman he has murdered (Paula's aunt). We learn that the jewels could be of no possible use or monetary value to him (they are far too famous to be marketable), and at the end of the film he admits that he doesn't know why he has been single-mindedly obsessed with their possession. The aunt, Alice Almquist, was a woman of power, a great opera singer; Gregory was the mere accompanist for her vocal practice. It was Alice, then, who possessed the "jewels" (the colloquial and psychoanalytical connotations of the term are inescapable): it turns out that she even displayed her possession of them brazenly to the public, by having them sewn into her robe for the role of (appropriately enough) the Empress Theodora. Paula resembles her aunt so closely that she can be mistaken for her ghost. The sexual subtext so central to Cukor's film (the man persecuting the woman because he perceives her as the possessor of the "jewels" whose lack humiliates and torments him) is entirely absent from the British version (and from Patrick Hamilton's original play). The crucial plot change was that of making Paula Alice's niece and resurrected image (in the British version they are unrelated and bear no physical resemblance; the husband, much less interestingly, is only after his wife's money, in order to buy the house where the jewels lie hidden).

But even more telling is Bergman's presense as Paula: no film has used more powerfully her own possession of the "jewels" of female energy and potency. It is this, and its corollary in male sexual anxiety, that Hitchcock takes up and develops in the three films they made together.

I want to argue that Hitchcock understood the complexities and potentialities of the Bergman persona more fully than any other director. (Rossellini's exploration seems to have been directed more at Bergman-as-person than as persona, at a certain phase of her emotional development, though the films draw clearly enough on elements of the image, reminding us that "person" and "persona" are not as cleanly separable categories as film theory would find convenient.) Though I shall concentrate initially on *Notorious,* the confession scene from *Under Capricorn* provides an ideal starting point.

The scene in which Henrietta confesses to Charles Adare/Michael Wilding that it was she and not her husband who shot her brother Dermot is done in a single take, over eight minutes long—the longest in the film. Within this unbroken sequence shot, Hitchcock plays with, and variously combines, all the components of the Bergman persona outlined above. We have first, and dominantly, the "actress": this, surely the most stylized of all Hitchcock's films, especially on the level of performance, consistently foregrounds Bergman's acting. We may call this "theatrical" provided we don't dismiss it for being so: this is no mere "filmed theater." The constant reframings create an entirely different relationship between audience and action from anything possible on the stage. One can see this, for example, in the continuously shifting (though always subordinate) status of Adare throughout the take, from active interrogator to mute witness to participant in Henrietta's reconstruction of the past (he is inadvertently placed in Sam's position as she describes how the latter rode five paces behind her) to nonexistence (when Henrietta forgets his presence, her monologue becoming less confession than self-catharsis, he disappears from the frame altogether). The film—and in particular the performances of Bergman and Margaret Leighton—draw upon a specific tradition of theatricality, the melodrama, with its roots in the nineteenth century.

Then there is the "lady": *Lady* Henrietta, still in the dress she has worn for the Governor's Ball. The "lady" of the present evokes and reanimates the "naturalness" remembered from the distant past: the

Irish countryside, Galway Bay, freedom of movement. This is linked at once to "health" and "energy" (riding with Sam the groom) and counterpointed explicitly with the realities of the less distant past (her degraded condition during the first years in Australia) and, implicitly, with the realities of her present condition (sickness, alcoholism, potential insanity). It also leads, by the most natural of extensions, to the erotic: the mutual declaration of love, the furious ride through the darkness to Gretna Green. The intimations of degradation serve to enhance the connection between health and sexuality by juxtaposing them with their perversion: there is no moment in Bergman's career where her sensuality is more overtly expressed than the moment when, recalling her life among derelicts in a Sydney slum (with hints of recourse to prostitution), she touches her bared throat with her hand and speaks of the temptation to sink beyond possible redemption into squalor.

I shall return to *Under Capicorn* at the end of this chapter. Before I turn to *Notorious, Spellbound* demands brief consideration. Superficially, Bergman's role corresponds to the most banal Hollywood formula for dealing with active and powerful women: at the beginning of the film Dr. Constance Petersen is presented as masculinized and desexualized, more iceberg than "woman"; attracted instantly to Ballantine/Gregory Peck, she falls in love, and her femininity miraculously resurfaces. This suggests one use that could clearly be made of the Bergman persona: the first movement of the film recounts the restoration of her "naturalness" (the country walk, the wind dishevelling her hair) at the expense of her "masculinity" (for a woman, to be "natural" is to be "feminine"). But that is not at all the use Hitchcock makes of her. In *Spellbound* her "masculinity" (force, activeness, energy, strength) is never sacrificed, Constance remaining throughout the protagonist who drives forward the narrative, Ballantine remaining helpless and passive, not even present at the denouement, where Constance has to expose and confront the murderer singlehanded. It is not so much femininity that is released with the restoration of naturalness, as sexuality, and the threat it poses to the male. Andrew Britton's detailed reading of the film in *CineAction!* 3/4 ("*Spellbound:* Text and Subtext") seems to me definitive. He argues that, while Ballantine's neurotic outbursts and breakdowns appear to be sufficiently accounted for by the film's overt "Freudian" explanation (the reactivation of repressed memories of childhood trauma), the film's almost equally consistent subtext suggests an alternative analysis: the anxiety aroused by the threat of an active female sexuality. If one accepts this reading (which seems confirmed not merely by Britton's meticulous commentary but by its centrality to the Hitchcock thematic), then the casting of Bergman becomes particularly felicitous.

FROM IDENTIFICATION TO (THE EXPOSURE OF) IDEOLOGY: THE FEMALE SYSTEM OF *NOTORIOUS*

The opening movement of *Notorious* closely parallels that of *Spellbound:* we are introduced to an "unnatural" Bergman (albeit of a very different kind from the icy and "masculinized" Constance), and the film then proceeds to restore her "naturalness" through contact with a man with whom she swiftly falls in love. I have argued that we identify with Alicia from her first appearance—because she is theatened, and because she is Ingrid Bergman. This identification survives the ensuing sequences in Miami, despite obvious obstacles: this cynical and promiscuous heavy drinker is not the Bergman we expect to see, but—simply because she is, irreducibly, Bergman—we trust her. It is clear to us that her behavior is more willed than real, a response to immediate narrative circumstances, and we are confident that it will not be finally definitive of the character. Further, her behavior, although it represents a violation of Bergman's emotional depth and sincerity (the essence of her "niceness"), is in some ways very attractive: if it denies some aspects of the persona, it foregrounds others—energy, activeness, rebelliousness, defiance of male control and authority (particularly *police* authority, which always carries especial resonance in a Hitchcock movie). In contrast, any identification we may make with Devlin must be at best perfunctory, and built solely on the grounds that he is played by Cary Grant: aloof, enigmatic, ungiving, judgmental, he caps all the strokes against him by knocking Alicia out with a brisk punch on the jaw.

The process of restoring the "natural" Bergman initiates a major strategy of the film, the use of objects to carry forward the narrative. The most obvious instance here, and the beginning of a chain that runs through the film, is the transition from the alcohol of Alicia's party to the (what I take to be) orange juice that Devlin brings her in bed the next morning (the subjective camera, humorously viewing Devlin upside down from Alicia's position in the bed, confirming our identification with *her* and objectification of *him*). A subtler process involves Alicia's hair. One can distinguish four stages: (a) At the party, her hair style (neat, chic) goes with the other accoutrements of her "loose woman" persona (a persona we know Alicia is acting just as surely as we know that Bergman is acting Alicia): the bare midriff, tight-fitting sweater, etc. (b) During the frenetic car drive, the composure of her hair is disturbed by the wind, which loosens it and blows it around her face (underlined by another POV shot—Alicia thinks it is fog). (c) When she wakes up the morning-after, Alicia's first action is to grope for the false hairpiece that has come unfixed during the night. (d) She emerges from the bedroom, as Devlin plays the record that documents her fierce opposition to her father's Nazism, combing her hair, finally restoring its "natural" look. The sequence ends (as Devlin leaves) with her holding the comb against the flimsy scarf he has tied around her bare waist to "keep her warm" (I shall return to the scarf later).

As in *Spellbound*, the restoration of Bergman's "naturalness" coincides with the release of her sexuality. This may appear at first sight a perverse reading, given that the entire Miami sequence is posited on Alicia's persona of "loose woman." I want to recall here my earlier distinction between the "sexy" and the "sexual": in Miami Alicia is playing sexy, in Rio she becomes sexual. All personas are of course constructions, but in the Miami scenes we *perceive* Alicia's persona as such, and wait in the confident expectation for the emergence of the "real" Bergman. The difference is that between Alicia's flirtatious, "loose" behavior at her own "perfectly dreadful" party, and the authentic sensuality of the famous kissing scene on her Rio balcony. It does not seem to me a contradiction or even a paradox to claim that Bergman's persona is constructed upon an authentic sexuality. I am aware that, since Foucault, we are expected to agree that sexuality is always constructed, but this is true only in a specific sense and in another sense it is non-sense. It is impossible to imagine a culture *without* sexuality. What is constructed, then, is not sexuality itself but the *form it* takes within specific cultures and historical periods. It may well be impossible to define exactly what sexuality is per se, because it never *is* per se: we can study only its culturally/historically specific forms. This offers no grounds whatever for denying its existence. I am not suggesting that Alicia's (Bergman's) sexuality is the expression of some eternally unchangeable essence (it is culturally specific enough to be evoked by Cary Grant within a Hollywood movie as a monogamous heterosexual attraction). The distinction is between a sexiness Alicia assumes (because she *wants* to feel degraded) and a sexuality that is authentic *for her,* that expresses her lived desire.

It is much easier for men within patriarchy to deal with the sexy than the sexual: the former can be named, placed, and simultaneously exploited and despised. As in *Spellbound,* the release of an active female sexuality is experienced by the man as a threat. Why does Devlin treat Alicia so monstrously? The answer is not simple. For a start, Hitchcock is clearly wrong (misled, perhaps, by his own personal and idiosyncratic identification pattern?) when he suggests that Sebastian is the more sympathetic of the male characters because he is the one who "really" loves Alicia (implying that Devlin doesn't). Given that "love" is a profoundly difficult concept (like sexuality, its form is always culturally constructed), we are never in doubt that Devlin loves Alicia in his way. If that way is problematic, then what are we to say of Sebastian's? Devlin merely tries to destroy Alicia emotionally and morally, Sebastian actually tries to murder her. Like so many other Hitchcock films, *Notorious* is clear in its perception that, within the patriarchal organization, a man's "love" for a woman will not be cleanly distinguishable from his desire to control and possess her (and, if he finds he can't, destroy her). But the film also makes a clear enough distinction between the two male characters, again dramatized by means of objects. The scarf that Devlin ties around Alicia's bare midriff in Miami inaugurates another chain of objects running through the film, in this case denoting male possession. The scarf is first replaced by the necklace fastened around Alicia's neck by Prescott/Louis Calhern, Devlin's immediate superior and the film's supreme embodiment of patriarchal authority (the "Good Law"), when she is sent off on her first date with Sebastian: a necklace "rented for the occasion" (like Alicia herself). If Devlin's scarf signifies male possession, it is at least associated with playfulness, humor, and affection: it is a piece of soft fabric, a mere large handkerchief, loosely tied, that won't even keep her warm. The necklace, in contrast, carries connotations of exploitation and prostitution.

The transition established here is repeated, more tellingly, toward the end of the film. Alicia meets Devlin for what she believes to be the last time (she has heard that he has been transferred to Spain, at his own request) and returns the scarf. This is immediately followed by the scene in which Alicia realizes that she is being poisoned. She is wearing a

very tight "choker" necklace, its presence literally highlighted by Ted
Tetzlaff's cinematography, the camera catching the glint of one of its
stones. We assume (as the previous necklace had to be "rented for the
occasion") that it is one of Sebastian's "love" gifts. If Devlin's drive to
possess can express itself in playfulness, Sebastian's is a stranglehold.

The emphasis within patriarchal cultures on the necessity for the
woman's chastity has been generally explained (logically enough) in
terms of the need to protect and guarantee the patriarchal lineage.
Within the "advanced" capitalist cultures with their (however compromised) notions of sexual emancipation, there may be a related but
deeper, more obstinately enduring, cause: given the enormous value
placed upon potency and sexual prowess (even, at its crudest and ugliest,
on cock size) as evidence of the "real man," the fear of competition, the
fear that the woman may discover that another man is "better." This is
surely the root of male possessiveness in our own culture; it explains
Devlin's and Sebastian's mutual fear of each other as Alicia's sexual
partners (given an extra edge in Sebastian's case by Rains' shortness of
stature, which Hitchcock plays upon repeatedly). With Sebastian the
drive takes a relatively straightforward form, the obsession with possessing Alicia exclusively. In the case of Devlin, the response is more perverse, more tortuous—paradoxical and ultimately self-defeating.
Threatened by Alicia's awakened sexuality, he tries to force her back
into precisely what he cannot bear—promiscuity, prostitution—so that
he can feel morally justified in rejecting her.

The parallel between Devlin and Sebastian is underlined by the wider
parallel between the masculinist political organizations within which
both function and within which both are trapped. As with Hitchcock's
other espionage movies, Notorious is forced to pay lip service to patriotism and the "democratic" cause. The systematic paralleling of American
authority and Nazi authority, however, goes a long way in undermining
the simplistic Good Law/Bad Law opposition. Especially striking are the
twinned scenes of round-table discussion: the after-dinner conference of
the Nazis, which results in the death of Emil Hrubka; the conference of
the Americans, which results in the cynical exploitation (and eventual
near death) of Alicia. From both, women are entirely absent: even
Madame Sebastian, for all her cultivation of an aggressive and brutal
masculinism, is excluded from the male ruminations and decision making.
As usual in Hitchcock, both organizations are effectively discredited,

and from a viewpoint one can without absurdity call "feminist": war, imperialism, the arms race, are all logical extensions of "masculinity" as our culture constructs it, in terms of aggression, domination, and competition. The political theme of *Notorious* is inextricably linked to— indeed, functions as an extension of—the sexual theme: the drive to control Alicia, the drive to control uranium ore have the same psychic source.

I must at this point take issue with Andrew Britton's reading of Devlin in his monograph on Cary Grant in *CineAction! 7*. Britton sees Devlin ("the most detestable leading man in the American popular cinema") purely in terms of "cynical emotional detachment and exploitativeness"; he "can only accept the heroine when she has been reduced to a state of complete emotional and physical prostration." The ending of the film, it follows, must be seen as characterized by a "bleak, ironic dissonance." It seems to me impossible to experience the ending like that while actually watching the film, and impossible to see Devlin in terms of emotional *detachment* anywhere. Certainly, the ending is not without its characteristic dissonance, but that arises exclusively from the compassion we continue for feel for Sebastian (a compassion that can, however, be overrated: anyone who almost murders Ingrid Bergman and destroys her smile—until its restoration by Devlin—can at best gain only a heavily qualified pity). Britton's misreading depends upon the ignoring of certain scenes—those from which Alicia is absent, wherein he passionately defends her, jeopardizing his own position by verbally assaulting his superiors, making clear to the audience the love he is neurotically incapable of expressing in her presence. It also involves at least one curious and perverse distortion, his reference to "Devlin's staging, for Sebastian's gaze, of the embrace which leads to the discovery that Alicia has been working for the Americans": Sebastian has already seen them outside the wine cellar, and the explicit intention of the embrace is to *prevent* his discovery of the truth about Alicia by distracting him and offering an alternative reason for their clandestine meeting. It is also clear that the staged embrace swiftly becomes a genuine one, Devlin involuntarily manifesting his continued love for Alicia.

Sebastian cannot rebel against the masculinist organization of which he is a member; Devlin can and does. His refusal to save Sebastian, sending him back into the house to face death, like Emil before him, at the hands of his fellow Nazis, therefore has its appropriate poetic justice.

When Devlin rescues Alicia, he is knowingly violating the explicit orders
of his immediate superior, Prescott, who has told him that if he goes to
the Sebastian house he must do nothing that might jeopardize the plan
to round up the entire spy ring by prematurely revealing the Americans'
knowledge of their activities. The ending anticipates very fully that of
North by Northwest a decade later: the hero redeems himself by rejecting his involvement in patriarchal authority, even in its "patriotic" guise,
and rescues the heroine through an emotional identification with her
situation. The bedroom scene clearly reprises the famous kissing scene
on the balcony, but here with the difference that Bergman's passionate
sensual tenderness is unambiguously reciprocated. Rohmer and Chabrol
described *Notorious* as "the magnificent story of a woman saved by
love"; it would have been equally, perhaps more, felicitous to describe it
as the story of a *man* saved by love. It is not at all that Devlin can accept
Alicia only "when she has been reduced to a state of complete emotional
and physical prostration." What we actually see is a thoroughly contrite
and chastened Devlin reawakening Alicia/Bergman to health, energy,
and sexuality, all implicit in the restoration of her smile. The scene's full
meaning is, again, dependent upon the Bergman persona, its implications
and potential.

Against the "male system" of *Notorious* must be set its female system,
firmly built upon Bergman-as-star, that turns the male system on its head
and subjects it to astringent criticism. It is not a film that reinforces
patterns of male aggression, but a film that identifies us, and finally
Devlin, with the woman's experience of that aggression, the mechanics
and motivation of which are uncompromisingly exposed.

UNDER CAPRICORN: BERGMAN, GENDER, AND CLASS

The particular richness of *Under Capricorn* derives partly from the
multiplicity of its influences, determinants, and anticipations. First, there
is its intertextual relationship (despite the obvious superficial differences
—period film, woman's melodrama, long take technique) with other
Hitchcock films past and future. I shall argue (taking a hint from Truffaut)
that it relates interestingly to Hitchcock's last silent film *The Manxman,*
made twenty years previously. Like *The Manxman,* and with *Rebecca,*

The Paradine Case, I Confess, and *Vertigo,* it is one of the Hitchcock films that hinge on a confession (in *Vertigo* albeit a *suppressed* confession). It bears a particular relationship to *Rebecca,* not only in the centrality of its confession scene and its theme of the persecuted wife, but in the relationship of Milly/Margaret Leighton to Mrs. Danvers/ Judith Anderson, two very different variants of the sinister housekeeper, and through that in its debt to the tradition of the Gothic melodrama, both Manderley and Minyago Ugilla functioning as the Terrible House, the opulent prison within which the heroine suffers and guilty secrets are hidden. As I shall argue later, in one respect it also strikingly anticipates *Vertigo,* both in theme and structural strategy.

Second, there is the equally important intertextual relationship with other Bergman films. I have already argued that the confession scene represents one of the most comprehensive expressions of the Bergman persona in all its complexity. In the immediate background to *Under Capricorn* are *Gaslight* and *Notorious:* in the former, Bergman is being deliberately driven insane, in the latter she is driven toward alcoholism, then systematically poisoned. *Under Capricorn* combines these strategies for dealing with her energy, her smile. That this is the film in which (short of being burned at the stake) Bergman's punishment for transgression is most excessive is perhaps accounted for by the fact that it is also the most explicit about her appropriation of "masculinity": it was she, not Sam, who grabbed the "big horse pistol" and shot her brother dead.

But what contributes most to the textual richness of *Under Capricorn* is precisely what seems to have turned so many people away from the film: its complex involvement in the long tradition of the woman-centered melodrama. It is far from being the *only* woman's melodrama in Hitchcock's work (that misapprehension is encouraged purely by the film's Gothic elements and period setting): *Blackmail, Rebecca, Suspicion, Notorious, Marnie,* all clearly either belong to the genre or relate closely to it, and *The Paradine Case* and *Vertigo* might be read as women's melodramas narrated from a male viewpoint. What is distinctive about *Under Capricorn* is that it relates to virtually every form of the woman's melodrama. The exception is the "mother love" variation, and one might posit that even that is present by default, the childlessness of the Flusky marriage (explicitly foregrounded during the confession scene) being crucial to our sense of its present sterility, our sense of its being blocked and poisoned. Otherwise, all the sub-categories are represented: the domestic melodrama (the story about a marriage, a home, and the woman's entrapment), the triangle melodrama (the story about adultery, actual or potential, about romantic love vs. marriage), the Gothic melodrama (the story about the persecuted woman).

Under Capricorn is of particular interest in relation to the question of identification, since the stylistic decision to build the film predominantly on complex and elaborate long takes virtually precludes the use of strict POV shots. Our initial identification figure is clearly Charles Adare. He, like us, is a stranger trying to understand an unfamiliar culture; we learn with him about Australian society and its customs; with him we are introduced to Sam Flusky/Joseph Cotten. Flusky is immediately associated with mystery: his name is familiar to both Adare and his cousin the new Governor (Cecil Parker), though neither can quite place it; Flusky is an "emancipist" and his crime cannot be mentioned—except perhaps by the irate purveyor of shrunken human heads, who calls him "murderer" but may just be expressing his anger. Adare, then, who swiftly (against advice and orders) accepts an invitation to Flusky's home, is to be our access to the solution of the film's enigmas. The first part of his visit to Minyago Ugilla (the house's name, he is informed by the cabby, means "Why weepest thou?," which encapsulates the dominant enigma) is the one scene in the film that conforms fairly closely to Hitchcock's characteristic deployment of POV identification techniques: the film's two most striking POV shots (striking because forward-tracking—the already familiar Hitchcock fingerprint) occur as he approaches the house, and the long take that accompanies him as he moves from window to window, his back to the camera, while not strictly POV, allows us to share his discoveries (Milly, her intimacy with her "master," her brutal treatment of the other servants, her power within the household). Identification with Adare is further strengthened by the fact that, prior to the introduction of Lady Henrietta, he is clearly (if only by default) the most attractive figure in the film. The society we discover with him has three main components, all variously unappealing: the stuffy and pompous world of the British administration (embodied mainly in the Governor himself, with his rigid adherence to "rules" and "orders"); the nouveau riche bourgeoisie, crass, complacent, and uncultivated; the brutalized lower orders—convicted felons leased out as servants as long as they preserve a semblance of good behavior. Adare's charm resides partly in his placing himself outside all three, and in his healthy contempt for the regulations and etiquette that motivate and hamper his cousin, though we are aware that the contempt is a prerogative of class privilege.

This identification is subtly undermined shortly before Lady Henrietta's first appearance, in preparation for the transference crucial to our experience of the film: Adare, in the background of the shot engaged in conversation with Flusky's male guests, cannot possibly overhear the dialogue about Henrietta between Flusky and Milly ("Don't let her come down"), the first event in the film that occurs outside his consciousness, which hence ceases to be our sole mode of access to the solution of the film's enigmas. Henrietta's entrance is a classic instance of the introduction of "the star," so long awaited (we are about twenty minutes into the film). Preceded by a long buildup, a complex hermeneutic chain involving enigmas about Flusky, enigmas about his wife, enigmas about their social position (why do all the men's wives fail to turn up for the dinner?), it also comes at the end of one of the film's longest and most complicated takes (which appears even longer than it actually is, as the preceding cut—on Adare's entrance into the house—is cunningly concealed by the closing of the door): the cut itself, so long withheld, adds to the moment's privileged status. The men's heads, one by one, turn left, to where we know the dining room doorway to be; conversation falters, then stops altogether. The tracking camera finally frames Flusky, who, alarmed, also turns toward the door. Cut to a close-up of a woman's incongruously bare feet, beneath an ornate but faded dress whose somewhat battered artificial flowers are revealed as the camera rises to show us, at last, the face of the star. What we first see (as in *Spellbound* and *Notorious*) is a perversion/denial of the Bergman persona, weak where she should be strong, the smile a mere feeble ghost of its familiar self, the "lady" patently drunk, the energy buried beneath a pathetic, would-be disarming assumption of "femininity." Yet she remains Bergman and here more indisputably "the star" than in the two previous films, neither Joseph Cotten nor Michael Wilding having the status, prestige, or charisma of Gregory Peck and Cary Grant: *Under Capricorn* is unambiguously a Bergman movie, a "vehicle," as we recognize even before we enter the theater.

Obviously, the transference of identification cannot yet be complete: Henrietta is distanced from us by the enigmas surrounding her, Bergman is not yet Bergman, and Adare appears to be the character most capable of solving the puzzles and effecting the necessary transformation. At this stage of the film, in fact, a probable scenario (based jointly on our knowledge of Bergman and our knowledge of the conventions of melodrama) seems to be taking shape, and the immediately ensuing scenes will confirm its probability: Adare will save Henrietta, who will fall in love with him; Flusky, the inconvenient husband, will conveniently get killed (accidentally? in a struggle? by Adare in self-defence?); Adare and Henrietta will sail for Ireland, where she will be restored to her "correct" social position and the promise of conjugal bliss. (Such expectations are in no way impeded by the star system: there is no reason, in 1949, to assume that Joseph Cotten will take precedence over Michael Wilding.) The central movement of *Under Capricorn* (up to the confession scene) hence plays upon a split identification: with Henrietta, because the film is "about" her (because Bergman is the star); with Adare, because he will be Henrietta's savior and the restorer of the Bergman persona and the Bergman smile.

But this is still too simple an account of the film's play with identification. The adoption of the long take as the major stylistic device makes possible a continuous shifting of perspective in which our interest and sympathy can move, moment by moment, from one character to another, rendering problematic the very notion of "identification." From the rupture of our initial single identification with Adare by the introduction of Bergman, there arises the possibility that the film's apparent endorsement of the male position Adare represents may shift into a critique of it. The play of interest and sympathy is guided partly by technical factors: who is or is not in the frame at a given moment, who is given centrality within the composition, who is in close-up and who in mid- or long-shot, who is observer or listener, what takes place outside the observer/listener's consciousness, to which only we as audience have access. Consider the sequence that immediately follows the dinner party —the conversation between Adare and Flusky after the departure of the other guests. In the film's overall structure it balances Henrietta's confession scene, being Sam Flusky's confession, his partial account of past events that Henrietta's confession will correct and complete. It is also strongly symmetrical in itself, comprising two long takes of roughly equal length, each of which ends with the camera craning up to Henrietta's bedroom window. In the first, the camera tracks the two men, moving left to right, walking in the darkness outside the house; in the second, the movement (of actors, of camera) is reversed. Adare throughout is the listener/questioner, hence he remains our means of access to the solution of enigmas (here incomplete, the full truth being reserved for Henrietta's "answering" confession later). But any simple identification with him on the emotional level is disturbed by two factors: Flusky is revealed as a far more sympathetic character than he has hitherto appeared (it is probably around this point in the film that we begin to think of him as "Sam"); and he is progressively favored by the camera as the scene continues, Adare at key moments actually disappearing from the frame altogether (as will also be the case in the scene of Henrietta's confession). We may even find distasteful his (facial) expression of repugnance when Sam talks of Henrietta's love for him. Identification is further complicated by the fact that the "twin" crane movements that end both takes have as their function the disclosure of events and information outside the consciousness of either of the men. The first shows us Henrietta on her balcony, distressed (we take it that she has overheard enough of the conversation for her own memories of the past to be revived) but closer to the familiar (the "authentic") Bergman persona than we have seen her so far: dressed in a relatively simple white nightgown, her hair blown by the night wind. The second crane-up shows us Milly pouring her a drink—the film's first clear intimation that Henrietta's condition may have causes outside herself, that she is the victim of the machinations of others. Both crane movements work, then, to strengthen our identification with Henrietta, now more recognizably "Bergman," but a Bergman who is once again threatened and victimized.

By and large, however, Hitchcock plays (and plays most craftily) on the plausibility of the scenario I have outlined, in order finally to shatter it in the confession scene—the precise point where the transference of identification is completed, the film's structural pivot as well as the Hollywood cinema's most complete expression of "Bergman." Hitchcock's mise-en-scène thoroughly marginalizes Adare, reducing him to little more than a prop; Henrietta's passionate declaration of her enduring and impregnable love for Sam instantly deprives Adare of his assumed (by the audience, by himself) status as "romantic hero." All that is left him is the noble gesture of renunciation, the nobility of which, while genuine enough, is slightly undercut by the fact that, recognizing that he will never gain Henrietta for himself, he really has nothing to sacrifice.

The process I have described—the construction of identification with the male hero and the undermining of that identification in the scene of a woman's confession—recurs, much more drastically, in *Vertigo,* where it is more clearly the film's central structuring principle. The anticipation of formal procedure is accompanied by an anticipation, in the Adare/Henrietta relationship, of *Vertigo*'s central theme: the man's love for the woman expressing itself in the drive to (re-)construct her in the image that he desires. For Adare, Henrietta must be again "Lady Hattie," and Hitchcock dramatizes his attempt to realize this project as, precisely, the construction of an image: the famous moment when Adare persuades Henrietta to look at herself in the "mirror" he improvizes by holding his coat behind a pane of glass. It is swiftly followed by his gift of a real mirror, asking her whom she sees in it, and answering for her "Lady Henrietta Considine," thereby eliminating Flusky and the marriage. The image is "the first work of art I've ever done." What is especially interesting is that the very different ways in which Adare and Flusky relate to Henrietta are defined in terms of different and contradictory aspects of the Bergman persona. For Adare she must be, exclusively, "the lady." One could say that he has failed to understand Henrietta; one could equally say that he has failed to understand Ingrid Bergman, "the lady" representing, as I argued earlier, one of Hollywood's strategies for containing and defusing the threat of Bergman's energy, sexuality, "masculinity." Sam's image of her is quite opposite, and amounts to a celebration of everything "the lady" neutralizes: recalling Henrietta's past, he tells Adare that "She'd go at a fence like it had the kingdom of heaven on the other side of it," a comparison that beautifully connects horse-riding and jouissance. It is crucial to the film that Adare can't ride, and that his attempts to do so (in the past and in the film) end in disaster —in the *laming* of a horse.

Under Capricorn is the only film of Hitchcock's Hollywood period, prior to *Frenzy,* in which class becomes a central issue. In this it invites brief comparison with another important and generally neglected work, *The Manxman.* The relationship is a complex one, of both parallel and inversion. Both are triangle melodramas, in which the woman, married to a man of a lower social caste, is loved by a man from a higher class.

Both set up expectations as to how the scenario will develop and be resolved, but the expectations are exactly opposite: it seems as certain in *The Manxman* that the marriage will be reaffirmed as it seems in *Under Capricorn* that Henrietta will end up with Adare. In both cases the expectation is thoroughly baffled. The strategy works more satisfyingly in *Under Capricorn*, where, as soon as we are taught to resist the pull of generic conventions, the logic of the narrative becomes irresistible: the marriage *must* be reaffirmed. In both films the tensions in the relationships have their source in class and social status. in *The Manxman* the future judge is warned by his aunt against marrying the woman he loves because, as a publican's daughter, she would jeopardize his respectability, hence his career; the publican, for his part, refuses to accept her other suitor as a potential son-in-law because, as a fisherman, he is penniless. Despite the two narratives' directly inverse resolutions, the attitude to class remains firm and consistent. Both films move toward climactic confession scenes. That of *The Manxman* owes a clear debt to *The Scarlet Letter* (of which Sjöström's version with Lilian Gish was still fresh in the memory): even the judge's Manx title ("Deemster") subtly evokes the name Dimmesdale. The point here is that his public disgrace, his forfeiture of his position as class superior and patriarchal authority figure, is a necessary precondition for his being found worthy of the heroine's love. The confession in *Under Capricorn* goes much further: it becomes a virtual celebration (in defiance of the agonies inflicted by patriarchal regulation) of the couple's transgression against the social conventions of gender and class, Bergman's "masculine" activeness expressing itself in her declaration of love for her father's groom, their elopement on horseback, her killing of her own brother to save Sam's life. The rigorousness of the attitude accounts for our sense of the film's necessary inner logic, contrary to generic expectations: if Henrietta and Sam must end up together it is precisely because their love for each other transgresses society's artificial boundaries of gender and class.

Adare, in fact, far from evolving into the film's romantic hero, becomes (for all his attractiveness and generosity, and despite the fact that in certain respects he *does* help Henrietta, provoking Bergman's first spontaneous smile in the film) a close counterpart of Milly in the structure of character relations. One can show this in a simple chart:

UPPER CLASS   LOWER ClASS

Henrietta   =   Sam

Adare   Milly

Once we realize the logic and authenticity of the union of Sam and Henrietta, we also realize that Adare and Milly (representing the extremes of class and gender positions among the major characters) both act to pull the couple apart by playing upon their class prejudices. Leaving aside the question of intentions, Adare's reconstruction of "Lady Henrietta Considine" corresponds closely to Milly's deliberate attempts to play on Sam's sense of social inferiority, to nurture his resentment of the upper class and his feeling that he can never really share their world and their rules, or lack of them. ("They're gentry, you see. They don't have the same rules as us.") It is the confluence of class and gender oppression that largely explains Milly's twistedness (rather than any claptrap about diabolism and original sin): she is twisted because, as woman and working class, she is doubly a victim. Conversely, Adare's strength (far from unambiguously a virtue) derives from the confidence (read arrogance) nourished by his class and gender privileges. Between the two are Sam and Henrietta, the one oppressed because he was a groom, the latter because she is a woman.

It is likely that the popular undervaluation of *Under Capricorn* will continue; it may be incorrigible. Its particular mode of stylization—the theatrical, the melodramatic—is quite out of favor with the type of modern spectator who prides herself or himself on a totally illusory "sophistication," and it withholds the pleasures of humor and suspense expected from "the Hitchcock touch." One must concede that the film is weakened by one of the rare serious errors of casting in Hitchcock's work. Joseph Cotten's screen persona of genteel decency and impotence, so memorably inflected in *Shadow of a Doubt,* is strikingly at odds with his role here. I find his accent an insuperable obstacle in itself, in a film where class definition through accent is so important. (Bergman, on the contrary, constitutes no real problem in this respect: having established a creditable Irish accent on her first appearance, she is wisely permitted not to burden herself with it for the rest of the film, given the role's extreme demands, and her Swedish accent never seriously compromises the character's class status). Hitchcock himself suggests, aptly enough, that Burt Lancaster would have been ideal for the Cotten role; personally, I think of James Mason, who, in the very same year, played a lower-class criminal Irishman in *The Reckless Moment.*

But anyone willing to accept that terms such as "slow-moving," "melodramatic," "devoid of humor" are descriptive, not evaluative, should be capable of recognizing the centrality of *Under Capricorn,* both to the Hitchcock canon and the Bergman canon.

16

THE MURDEROUS GAYS: HITCHCOCK'S HOMOPHOBIA

It has been often noted that the figure of the psychopath that recurs throughout Hitchcock's work is sometimes coded (with more or less explicitness) as gay (or in one case lesbian). There is the "half-caste" transvestite of *Murder!;* the two young murderers of *Rope;* Mrs. Danvers, of whose (presumably late) husband we learn nothing, in *Rebecca;* Bruno Anthony in *Strangers on a Train.* Some have sought, with far less incontrovertible evidence, to extend the list to include the Uncle Charlie of *Shadow of a Doubt* and Norman Bates; in which case we may as well add the Bob Rusk of *Frenzy.* These latter instances seem to rest upon little except popular (and generally discredited) heterosexist mythology: one is probably gay if one shows traces of effeminacy, had a close relationship with one's mother, or hates and murders women. However, in questioning whether the term "gay" is applicable to all of these characters, I don't wish to suggest that they are not all closely inter-linked, or that they don't relate to some permanent component of the Hitchcock psyche (as embodied in the films), of which both repressed homosexuality and its inevitable corollary homophobia may form a significant part.

It is necessary at this point to make explicit certain assumptions (which, deriving from the Freudian psychoanalytical tradition, are not unarguable or universally accepted, though I personally find them convincing) which will form the basis of the argument I wish to build. They will already be familiar to my readers (notably from the essay on *Raging Bull* in *Hollywood from Vietnam to Reagan*); I apologize for the repetition, but cannot take the familiarity for granted. What is at issue here is not simply the meaning and nature of Hitchcock's homophobia, but its relationship to the treatment of heterosexual relations in his films. These, then, are the principles on which the ensuing speculations are based:

1. **Constitutional Bisexuality.** According to Freud, the human infant is already a sexual being, but the sexuality is at this stage indeterminate, both in its means (the various erogenous zones) and its ends (object choice). Freud used the term "polymorphous perversity" to describe this (it seems to many of us) highly desirable and enviable state of being. It is not a felicitous choice of words: surely, if the infant's "polymorphous" eroticism is natural and innate, it is the "normal" (i.e., socialized) adult who is "perverse" (literally "turned aside"). For practical, social/political purposes in relation to our culture in its current phase of evolution, the crucial implication of this is that we are all, innately, bisexual, at least in potential. This potential is, of course, very infrequently realized in our adult lives, greatly to our psychic impoverishment and to the detriment of relations between the sexes.

2. **Masculinity/Femininity.** Not identical with, but closely related to and paralleling, Freud's discovery of constitutional bisexuality, is his perception that, in the infant, the characteristics our culture labels "masculine" and "feminine" are by no means the exclusive property of male and female respectively: little girls have as much claim to "masculinity" (activeness, forcefulness, assertiveness, aggression, dominance, etc.) as little boys, and little boys exhibit the "feminine" traits (passivity, gentleness, submissiveness, sensitivity, emotional expression, etc.) as part of their natural human legacy. There is, that is to say, no reason whatever to suppose that these apparently—culturally—opposed characteristics are in any way "naturally" tied to the facts of anatomical difference or develop organically out of it. The relationship of this to bisexuality is not entirely clear (though one can scarcely doubt that there *is* one): it is a readily observable fact of our culture that heterosexual men can exhibit markedly "feminine" qualities, and that gay men can be aggressively "masculine." We can, however, assert that a complete human being would be one capable of expressing both trans-genderic and bisexual tendencies: our society would become one within which infinite variation, infinite choices, were possible.

3. Repression. If not nature, then culture: there has to be *some* way of accounting, not only for the sorting out of human beings into heterosexual/homosexual, masculine/feminine, but also for the disappearance, from most people's conscious lives, of even the traces of tendencies regarded as inappropriate to their socialized makeup. Patriarchy cannot endure ambiguity (or infinite possibilities of variation): it requires "real men" and "real women" for the maintenance of its power and of the central social unit through which its power is transmitted and perpetuated, the family. This hatred of ambiguity applies equally to sexuality and gender, uniting the two streams of development (or, more precisely, *arrested* development). But of course it is not enough to say to the infant "Don't be bisexual" or "Don't be masculine (or feminine)": even if she or he obeyed, the threat of conscious desire and conscious choice would remain. Hence patriarchal cultures have evolved (with innumerable local variations, the terrain of anthropologists) those social and psychic processes which Freud described so brilliantly (if not always accurately, and with his regrettable tendency to universalize the culturally specific): the Oedipus and castration complexes and their resolution, the "oedipal trajectory" that guides the boy to his identification with the father (actual and symbolic) and the girl to her identification with the mother. If it is "successful" (a word that, in this context, becomes painfully ironic), the completion of the trajectory involves the repression of the individual's homosexual tendencies, which become *literally* unthinkable. For men, it also involves the repression of "femininity," that collection of human attributes (often morally admirable) that is henceforth associated with the "weaker" sex and despised as inferior and "unmanly." It is very dangerous to regard evolution as natural, inevitable, unchangeable, and irreversible. True, it embodies a response to human needs, but those needs are always culturally and historically specific, not an irreducible and immutable "fact of life." Often, the needs change or disappear altogether, and we are left with an evolved response to them that is archaic, culturally useless, or actively harmful in its regressiveness. One can certainly argue that this is now the case with the whole bag and baggage of repression, the oedipal trajectory, castration complexes, "traditional" family structures, gender construction, homophobia. It is amazing that it has taken civilization so long explicitly and consciously to challenge this entire process of social/psychic structuration, and very exciting to be alive in an age when the challenge has at last been uttered (by women, by gays, and, increasingly, by heterosexual men).

4. Homophobia. What is repressed is never annihilated: it survives in the unconscious as a constant potential threat, capable of resurfacing in response to changing circumstances or particular stimuli. Hence the explanation of that otherwise inexplicable malady homophobia. In every homophobe, the repressed homosexual tendencies are dangerously close to the surface of the unconscious, yet their existence must never be acknowledged. The homophobe's fear and hatred of homosexuals is essentially a projection outward of his fear and hatred of tendencies within himself of which he dare not permit himself to become aware. Every expression of homophobia is therefore revealing: one may look in confident expectation for the traces of homosexuality.

5. Men's Hatred of Women. Again, the parallel holds. There is always a close relationship between the heterosexual male's attitude to gays and his attitude to women: to put it simply, one will expect a homophobe to treat women very badly. As with bisexuality, so with the man's femininity: what is repressed is not destroyed but constantly threatens to return, and must be disowned and repudiated. The word "love" is always problematic, because it means so many different things (in different cultures, and to different individuals within the same culture). One might suggest, however, that authentic love must always have as a major component the ability to identify. Only a man who freely accepts and expresses his own femininity can truly love a woman: otherwise, "love" becomes perverted into the drive to dominate, possess, and if necessary destroy. In extreme cases, the psychic violence—the acts of repression demanded by the oedipal trajectory—that males in our culture are conditioned to inflict upon themselves in the interests of socialization and "normality," will find their external manifestation in acts of physical violence against women.

The above is offered as a (provisional) blueprint for the exploration of Hitchcock's films and, through them, of our civilization in its contemporary phase of evolution. It is not intended completely to *explain* the films: if it did so, they could not be considered great or particularly significant works (beyond the significance necessarily inherent in any cultural artifact). The films—and the "Hitchcock" they embody, related to but not necessarily identical with Alfred Hitchcock the human individual—relate very intimately to the blueprint but do not neatly fit it: therein, precisely, lie their greatness and fascination. Their importance resides in the intensity and complexity with which they dramatize the impossible strains, tensions, and conflicts inherent in my psychoanalytical outline. It is this that gives them their cultural centrality.

In every case history that he explored, Freud discovered, at some level of the analysis, the traces—the scars—of repressed homosexuality, and it seems clearer to us than it was to him that the repression (not the homosexuality itself) was intimately related to the sources of the disorder—in many instances *was* the source. To explore Hitchcock's films is to explore issues that are of crucial and increasingly urgent importance to the future of our civilization; the films *demand* a resolution that they themselves can never reach, leaving us with that often noted "nasty taste" in the form of unresolved tensions.

THE DARK SIDE OF GENDER CONSTRUCTION

Donald Spoto's *The Dark Side of Genius: The Life of Alfred Hitchcock* is an extremely unpleasant book but is a very useful one: far more useful, to my mind, than its predecessor, *The Art of Alfred Hitchcock*. The project embodied in the two books (considered together) seems somewhat perverse (though only "normally" so, within the terms of our culture): the idolization of the "art" of Hitchcock followed by the thoroughgoing denigration of the man who created it. To borrow a title from Molly Haskell, Spoto moves abruptly "from reverence to rape," illustrating yet again the very close psychic proximity of those two apparently opposed human activities. Spoto's book is undoubtedly ungenerous to the point of the meanminded: he certainly sees to it that "the evil that men do lives after them, /The good is oft interred with their bones." He acknowledges the nice things that Hitchcock did, but perfunctorily, glossing over them in a sentence or two; the nasty things are lingered over, described in detail and with relish. If one refuses to be alienated by this (and it takes a degree of conscious determination and resistance), then the biographical material Spoto presents becomes quite fascinating in its resonances (in relation to the films, to the culture, and to the relationship between the two).* The book's central problem lies in Spoto's failure to provide a theoretical and psychoanalytical framework adequate to *explain* the material: there is plenty of "pop" psychologizing, always at the level of the individual, but no attempt at a psychoanalytical theory of culture which would encompass both the life and the films.

Before attempting to reread some aspects of the material Spoto presents, I need to add one further psychoanalytic observation to the schema set forth above, one that, while not without a general relevance, is more obviously specific to the Hitchcock "case." When I wrote *Hitchcock's Films* I suggested that the sense of precariousness and unpredictability, that something terrible, uncontrollable, and perhaps inexplicable may erupt at any moment within the most seemingly normal and secure environment and circumstances—the phenomenon that achieves its most explicit embodiment in *The Birds*—is central to the Hitchcockian world view. I did not recognize at that time that what I was describing was the paranoid mentality (my own, perhaps, at that period of my life, when my personal identification with the Hitchcock world view—as I perceived it—was at its most intense and least distanced). I wrote at length on the implications of paranoia, using Freud's account of the Schreber case, in the essay on *Raging Bull* cited above, and I don't wish to reiterate my points here in detail. All that requires to be reiterated is Freud's finding (confirmed by both Jung and Ferenczi) that *in all cases* "a defence against a homosexual wish was clearly recognizable at the very centre of the conflict which underlay the disease, and that it was in an attempt to master an unconsciously reinforced current of homosexuality that they had all of them come to grief." It seems logical, in fact, to interpret male paranoia in terms of a *double* bind, its source not only in the repression of homosexuality but in the repression of femininity, its consequence the hatred, fear, and distrust not only of other men (as potential, hence threatening, love objects) but of women also (as the embodiments of the femininity that must be disowned), the consequence of that consequence the possible eruption of violence against both sexes. *Raging Bull* perhaps offers the cinema's most radical and comprehensive examination of this, but Hitchcock's work as a whole (and his life,

---

* Like all biographical data, Spoto's "facts" and his interpretation of them doubtless can and will be challenged. I accept them here as a working hypothesis.

insofar as it is relevant to the work) seems richly suggestive in relation to these ideas.

The testimonies and biographical data that Spoto presents, with reference to Hitchcock's attitude to homosexuality and homosexuals, add up to evidence that is characteristically complex and contradictory: the attitude certainly was not simple, the available (admittedly rather meager) evidence suggesting an ambivalence that parallels and is closely related to the ambivalence toward women, exactly as the repression of homosexuality parallels the repression of femininity. On the one hand we are told that Hitchcock was at ease with gay people: Spoto's source, identified only as "an actress who knew him well," is quoted as saying "Some people might be surprised by this. . . . but Hitchcock was always quite comfortable with homosexual or bisexual people. He always told his actors that they really had to be part masculine and part feminine in order to get inside any other character. Subjectivity, he felt, and feeling, transcended gender." The remarks take on a particular resonance, not only in relation to the films themselves, but in relation to the whole complex controversy about spectator identification that has raged in film theory since Laura Mulvey's "Visual Pleasure and Narrative Cinema" was published in 1975. Spoto also conjectures, reasonably enough, that, with his sexually repressive childhood as background, Hitchcock was intrigued by all forms of deviancy. There is also Spoto's account of the meeting with Murnau, with Hitchcock "not even comfortable in the presence of women, let alone homosexual men." Being at ease and being intrigued are not exactly synonymous, and being uncomfortable is congruent with neither: one can already discern, in the incompatible but not necessarily inaccurate descriptions, the characteristic tension between identification and distance. The ambivalence is confirmed by Spoto's accounts of Hitchcock's methods of dealing with, and attitudes toward, the gay men with whom he inevitably shared a prolonged proximity: gay actors.

During 1925–27 Hitchcock directed two films starring Ivor Novello, *The Lodger* and *Downhill:* Novello was noted publicly for his extreme, somewhat "feminine," good looks, and privately for his relative openness about being actively gay. During the same period, two things occurred that proved of great significance both in Hitchcock's personal and professional development, the significance having as much to do with the construction, and exploitation, of a public image as with a private life style: (a) he put on a great deal of weight; (b) he married Alma Reville. One does not wish to reduce the complexities of such occurrences to a single motivation: obviously, one can have ten different, perhaps contradictory, motivations (conscious and unconscious) for getting married. But one contributing psychoanalytical explanation is tempting and plausible (if purely conjectural): that, on some level, they can be interpreted as defenses against the feelings aroused by Novello. Why, in fact, *did* Hitchcock put on so much weight? No clear medical evidence has been produced, as far as I know. There seems to be abundant testimony that Hitchcock, throughout his life, longed to be attractive to women and experienced agonies of frustration over his fatness. The psychoanalytical evidence seems to point in the opposite direction, to a hysterical resistance to being physically attractive to *anyone*.

In 1952 Hitchcock directed *I Confess*, starring Montgomery Clift. There are perfectly plausible ways of rationalizing Hitchcock's consistent hostility to Clift: the "Method" acting, the neuroticism, the heavy drinking. More than plausible, they are clearly *sufficient*, if one wishes to look no further. Yet one wonders. Novello and Clift were certainly not the only homosexual men with whom Hitchcock worked, but they were certainly the two most physically attractive.

It is at this point that my present theme—Hitchcock's reactions to gay actors—bleeds inevitably into my next: his notorious practical jokes. All of these were clearly acts of aggression; they appear to have been distributed roughly equally, against women (including Hitchcock's own daughter) and against men, though it seems plain that men were the victims of the two ugliest. One may invoke here—it is central to my thesis, sketchy as that thesis admittedly is—Michael Kaufmann's essay in *Beyond Patriarchy*, "The Triad of Male Violence"—against women, against other men, against oneself. Kaufmann's theme is precisely that this triad of violence *characterizes* what we in our culture call masculinity: it is not the exception but the rule, if not necessarily on the physical level then on the psychic.

Novello and Clift were both the objects of Hitchcock's "jokes"—the essential seriousness of which one scarcely needs Freud to illuminate: Novello in a very mild way, Clift arousing Hitchcock's "sense of humor" at its most vicious. With Novello the joke took the form of photographing him (in *The Lodger*) with a flowerpot behind him, so that it appeared that the flowerpot was on his head, making him look ridiculous: it is easy to read this as a defense against Novello's beauty. With Clift the "joke" consisted in daring him, already very drunk, to drink a whole beaker of brandy in one gulp: Spoto tells us that the actor "fell to the floor, face down, in a perilous alcoholic stupor." A somewhat extreme revenge for the crime of "Method" acting.

The cruelest of all Hitchcock's practical jokes had for its victim a property man. Spoto is tantalizingly unspecific about this—presumably no more precise information is available. The man is nameless, and no offense that could even remotely justify the joke is presented; it is also not clear when the incident occurred, though it was somewhere in the late twenties. Hitchcock bet the property man a week's salary "that he would be too frightened to spend a whole night chained to a camera in a deserted and darkened studio." Before departing Hitchcock offered him a beaker of brandy (the link with the Clift "joke," across a period of about twenty-five years, is obvious), which the man eagerly accepted. It was "laced . . . with the strongest available laxative." What one most wants to know, of course, is whether the unfortunate victim was gay, sexually attractive, or both.

Yet together with these displays of aggression against gay men goes a tendency to identify with them. I shall return to this in discussing certain characters in the films, but certain casting choices are also intriguing. There is a continual sense that Hitchcock identified masochistically with his villain victims, and two instances are supported by specific hints. There is the sacristan murderer (O. E. Hasse) of *I Confess:* Hitchcock, at the last minute, gave his wife the name "Alma" and wrote in dialogue that has startlingly personal overtones ("Where is my Alma?"—he has just killed her! — "I loved her. It made me cry to see her work so hard"). And there is the case of Alexander Sebastian in *Notorious* who, Hitchcock says, was the one who really loved Ingrid Bergman (as, according to Spoto, did Hitchcock himself). Spoto suggests that O. E. Hasse was gay; he also reveals that the actor Hitchcock originally wanted for Sebastian was Clifton Webb.

Many of the victims of the practical jokes were women, and one must connect these relatively harmless (though frequently unkind, embarrassing, and malicious) acts of aggression with the violence (physical and psychic) against women enacted in the films, and with the *real* ordeal inflicted upon Tippi Hedren during the filming of *The Birds* (an ordeal that, as Spoto describes it, evinces a powerful obsessional drive on

Hitchcock's part). That there is another side to this—an ambivalence of which the tension merely carries to its extreme a predominant characterizing feature of our culture—will I hope already have been suggested by my accounts of *Blackmail* and *Notorious:* in the films, at least—and it is the films, not the private life, that should be our concern—Hitchcock manages frequently to dramatize an identification with his female characters that must deny all but the most singlemindedly sadistic male viewer any simple pleasure in the violences to which they are subjected. The repression of men's femininity is scarcely less damaging than the repression of their homosexuality (and I have posited a strong if not entirely clear connection between the two). Hitchcock's greatness as an artist may ultimately be found to reside in the fact that both of these parallel repressions were in his case—from the point of view of "normality" and "socialization"—only partially "successful."

In the shower murder sequence of *Psycho*, with what/whom does Hitchcock—hence, through the communicative processes of cinema, the compliant spectator—identify, the hacking, stabbing, phallic knife or the terrified woman? I think the answer must be "both"—with the addendum that the latter identification is, by virtue of the terms the film has set up, by far the more powerful, making terror rather than sadistic pleasure the dominant impression. (One could extend this, clearly enough, to the most impressive, and most profoundly disturbing, scene in *Frenzy*, the rape and murder of Brenda Blaney/Barbara Leigh-Hunt). The "triad of male violence," as reproduced in Hitchcock's work, is never simple: hence its fascination and distinction. The violence against women and the homophobia must be seen as the products of a terror and panic that are the logical response, within the terms of our culture, to its construction of gender, of one of its "unsuccessful" graduates. Against these phenomena must be set Hitchcock's frequently passionate identification with his female characters, and his more troubled and ambivalent, partial identification with his gay characters.

But which, in fact, *are* Hitchcock's gay characters? It seems to me a matter far harder to determine than has often precipitously been claimed. I suggested earlier that the claims largely rest upon heterosexist myths about homosexuals (which Hitchcock may of course have shared). What immensely compounds the problem is the fact that, prior to the '6os, it was impossible openly to acknowledge even the existence of homosexuality in a Hollywood movie; consequently, homosexuality had to be coded, and discreetly, and coding, even when indiscreet, is notoriously likely to produce ambiguities and uncertainties.

Is Louis Jourdan in *The Paradine Case* supposed to be gay? He has none of the iconography of "gayicity," but gayicity has always been a heterosexual construction, in one way or another. Despite the passionate erotic commitment of Alida Valli, he has remained totally faithful to his "master," Colonel Paradine, his commitment seeming as passionate as hers, leading to his suicide when accused of murdering him. As a gay man, I find it far easier to accept him, on this evidence, as gay or bisexual than, for example, Joseph Cotten in *Shadow of a Doubt* or Anthony Perkins in *Psycho*. But if this reading is correct (or at least plausible), he is certainly the only gay character in Hitchcock who is neither neurotic nor villainous, a reason, perhaps, not so much for denying that the character is gay as for assuming that it didn't occur to Hitchcock that he might be. Such a reading seems clearly to be outside Hitchcock's understanding of the film: he wanted Robert Newton for the role, and compares the plot to *Lady Chatterley's Lover*, which he appears to understand as little as he understands his own film, seeing Mrs. Paradine as a "nymphomaniac" who degrades herself. But he is here talking somewhat obsessively about his original concept, which seems totally at odds with, and much less interesting than, the film he and Selznick actually made. The attribution of gayness doesn't seriously alter the film's central tragic irony—that a strong and passionate woman has rebelled against patriarchal subservience to the extent of murdering her husband because of her love for a man who can't possibly reciprocate it—but it would certainly intensify it. There can be no doubt that Valli and Jourdan (gay or not) constitute the (hopelessly split) moral center of the film, highlighting the emptiness of the "normality" represented by Gregory Peck and Ann Todd and presided over by the monstrous patriarchal figure of Charles Laughton.

Mrs. Danvers appears to be the only lesbian in the Hitchcock canon. There was to have been a lesbian couple in *The Long Night*, the project on which Hitchcock was working when he died, and his screenwriter, David Freeman, tells us that Hitchcock had qualms about making them villains. The qualms were not shared by Mr. Freeman, who remarks that today "the love that dared not speak its name has become the love that won't shut up." One must take this as his sophisticated and enlightened response to two thousand years of systematic oppression, persecution, and, in certain periods, mass slaughter of gays by the heterosexual power hierarchy, of which the oppression at least continues; or perhaps just as another uneasy giveaway manifestation of homophobia. In any case, Hitchcock's attitude seems to have been more sensitive than his screen-writer's, even though we have it only in the latter's description.

As for "Danny" herself, she is of course both neurotic and a villainess: one cannot gloss over the fact that she tries to drive Joan Fontaine to suicide. Yet how we read her depends to a degree on how we read the film as a whole: is it about the construction of the "good wife" and the ideologically correct heterosexual couple? Or is it about the male's fear of an adult and autonomous female sexuality, which makes it impossible for him to relate to any woman who resists definition as his "little girl"? If the latter, then Rebecca becomes—implicitly—the film's real heroine (and victim), and Mrs. Danvers' devotion to her takes on rather more complex connotations. At the end of the film generic conventions, and their inherited meaning accumulated through a long tradition, become so powerful as virtually to supersede questions of personal authorship (Hitchcock, Selznick). Throughout the literature and cinema of melo-drama, women victimized within patriarchy have, recurrently, two re-courses: passive—the retreat from patriarchal rationality into madness; and active—fire, as supreme symbol of revolt (Brunnhilde burns down Valhalla). At the end of *Rebecca* (as in *Jane Eyre*) they are magnificently combined: Mrs. Danvers goes insane and burns down Manderley, the symbol of the patriarchal order within which Maxim tried to contain the first Mrs. de Winter and now hopes to live with the second (suitably subordinated if regrettably adult).

It seems to be generally accepted that Bruno Anthony in *Strangers on a Train* is supposed to be gay. "Supposed to be" strikes me as the appropriate way of putting it, because once again the attribution seems to rest more on popular heterosexual myths about gay men than on any actual evidence the film (caught in the constraints of censorship) can provide: he hates his father, is overindulged by his silly mother, seems rather to enjoy murdering women, and dresses flamboyantly. It is prob-able that Hitchcock thought he was gay. What must be said is that Bruno forms a link in a chain of fascinating, insidiously attractive Hitch-cock villains who constantly threaten to "take over" the films in which they appear, not only as the center of interest but even, for all their monstrous actions, as the center of sympathy: Uncle Charlie in *Shadow of a Doubt*, Willy, the U-boat commander, in *Lifeboat*, Brandon in *Rope*, Norman Bates in *Psycho*, the Bob Rusk of *Frenzy*. Only one of these (Brandon) is defined, as unambiguously as censorship allowed, as gay, and no one, as far as I know, has yet attributed homosexuality to Willy. Gayness, that is to say, is by no means an *essential* attribute of the Hitchcock villain. What connects the various links in the chain is either a form of fascism (whether political or personal), or psychopathology, or both: Willy is a Nazi, Charlie and Brandon both subscribe to what one might call pop-Nietscheanism, and all but Willy are presented as, to varying degrees, psychologically disturbed. All these characters strike me as very personal to Hitchcock, as partial identification figures who must also be repudiated. They enact that obsession with power/domination/control and the dread of its loss (impotence) that pervades his work at every level, from the thematic to the methodological; they also dramatize his sense of horror at this syndrome, his awareness of its harm, both to the self and to others. As for the threat of these characters unbalancing their respective films, it seems to me to be effectively and convincingly countered in all but *Strangers on a Train* (and perhaps *Frenzy*), which remains as a result one of the least satisfying films of Hitchcock's maturity (if also one of the most "brilliant"). Hitchcock clearly has no interest whatever in the characters played by Farley Granger and Ruth Roman, and this lack is inevitably communicated to the audience; their relationship has no emotional weight, their aspirations no moral value. Everything gravitates toward Bruno as the film's magnetic center of attraction: he becomes not only its most complex and detailed character but also its most vulnerable, in his struggle for control and the escalation of his failure to maintain it. I find it difficult to decide exactly how much this has to do with Hitchcock's fascination with sexual/gender ambiguity and how much with the failure of the scenario to provide opportunities to develop an effective counterweight or counter-identification (such as Young Charlie in *Shadow of a Doubt*, the various subsidiary characters and alternative ideological positions of *Lifeboat*, the force of James Stewart's horror and self-horror in *Rope*).

WHO KILLED DAVID KENTLEY?

Rope seems to me both generally underrated and in certain crucial aspects widely misperceived. Although it is now universally acknowledged that its two murderers are characterized as gay, very little work has been done on the implications of this: it is treated as if it were a mere incidental. Behind this neglect I suspect lies an overt hostility on the part of gay critics and a "liberal" queasiness on the part of heterosexual ones: no one is likely to praise the film for its promotion of "positive" images of gayness, and on certain obvious levels it can clearly be read as reinforcing harmful derogatory myths of homosexuality (the tendency to associate it with neurosis on the one hand and fascism on the other). It seems to me important, however, to make careful distinctions between a film's (presumed) immediate social effect (i.e., how we deduce, forty years after the event, that it was received by that ill-defined and ultimately indefinable body the general audience), and what we can learn from it now if we attend to it carefully. It is possible to deplore it from the former point of view while finding it immensely valuable from the latter, though we should also be aware that the opposition is a very dangerous one: it may rest on gross bourgeois-intellectual snobbishness as to the nature of the general audience and its responses.

As I want to begin by making a point about the film's famous technique, I must first correct a common erroneous assumption. (I am not the first to correct it, but as the error persists it seems worth correcting again.) Repeatedly, one hears that *Rope* was shot entirely in ten-minute takes.[1] As the film is approximately eighty minutes long, this entails the presumption that it consists of eight shots. Including the credit shot (roughly three minutes; it has to be included because it is clearly "within the diegesis," establishing the environment and culminating in the camera's pan left to show the closed curtains from behind which issues David Kentley's death scream), there are eleven shots. Only three of these (Nos. 2, 6, and 9) are over nine minutes long; one (No. 10, culminating in the flinging open of the chest lid by Rupert Cadell/James Stewart) is under five minutes; the last is under six. The remainder are all between seven and eight minutes.

This does not of course detract in the least from the film's technical tour de force; it is the nature of that tour de force that I want to examine.

1. See, for example, page 78 of the present book!

One can define it by saying that *Rope* is the film that most strikingly justifies the antipathy to Hitchcock's work evident in the writings of that most eloquent exponent and theorist of the long take, André Bazin. For *Rope* represents the thorough refusal of all those potentialities of long take/camera movement style that Bazin celebrated in the work of Welles and Wyler. For Bazin, the long take, absence of editing, and use of depth of field played a key role in the cinema's potential objectively to "reveal" reality (see the remarks on Flaherty and Stroheim in "The Evolution of Film Language"), and to realize itself as the ideal "democratic" art: the spectator is left free to choose which aspect of the image he will concentrate on, his response no longer dictated by the manipulations of Eisensteinian (or Hitchcockian) montage. For Hitchcock, the experimentation of *Rope* is never in the least conceived as in *opposition* to his already highly developed montage technique, but as a possible alternative to and equivalent for it, another means of exerting a total control over the gaze and the emotional response of the viewer. The spectator of *Rope* has no more freedom of choice than the spectator of *Psycho* (who has in any case more freedom than this somewhat simplistic opposition allows for: Hitchcock does not reduce his audiences to mindless zombies). I shall return to this when discussing Hitchcock's relation to Brandon/John Dall.

Rope can be read as associating homosexuality with the unnatural, the sick, the perverse—with "evil" and fascism. Nothing prohibits such a reading; Hitchcock and/or his writers may have thought that was what the film was saying. But what Hitchcock thought the film was saying is of little relevance: *Rope* belongs to a certain point in the evolution of homosexuals as social beings, of societal attitudes to them, of the material and social realities of homosexual existence, and it must now be read within a complicated cultural/historical context.

We may take as a starting point the famous disparaging remark attributed to Renoir, that Hitchcock made a film about two homosexuals and never showed them kissing. The remark is puzzling: Renoir, who had worked at that time in the Hollywood cinema, could scarcely have been unaware of the constraints of censorship. But even beyond that, the remark may miss the point: *Do* Brandon and Philip kiss (offscreen)? *Could* they? They are gay and they live together, but are they technically lovers? Today, everyone seems ready to answer in the affirmative, and to regard as very naive people who didn't "get" this in

1948. The affirmative answer is quite possibly the correct one: I am not saying that it is wrong, only that we can't be so certain and may be thinking unhistorically.

The problem doubtless derives from the fact that a Hollywood movie made in the late '40s could not possibly answer a question which it couldn't even raise. Even the matter of the apartment's sleeping accommodation is kept carefully ambiguous: at one point we are told that the telephone is "in the bedroom," which seems to imply that there is only one (and Janet/Joan Chandler's response, "How cozy," can certainly be taken as the film's most loaded comment on the issue); later, however, we hear of a *second* bedroom (neither is ever shown). It's not simply that *Rope* cannot tell us that the two men sleep together; it also cannot tell us clearly that they *don't*, since that would imply that they might. A parallel instance: five years after *Rope*, Preminger made *The Moon Is Blue*, and ran into massive censorship problems centered on the film's use of the word "virgin." It is not of course that the word itself was ever regarded as obscene (surely not by the Catholic Legion of Decency!); it is rather that for an unmarried young woman to assert that she is a virgin is instantly to imply the possibility that she might not be.

I offer here another excursion into personal history as (I hope) the most vivid way of reconstructing, for *Rope*'s modern audience, something of the social context within which it was made and received. When *Rope* was released in England in 1948 I was seventeen. I had been having elaborate erotic fantasies about men for at least seven years, and at the age of fifteen I had discovered the word "homosexual" (in a book about Tchaikovsky), and suddenly realized with amazement that there must be other people in the world like myself. I grasped this intellectually; it didn't occur to me that I might ever meet (or perhaps already know) such people. Homosexuality then was not only "the love that dare not speak its name," it was the love whose name could not be spoken, because to speak it would be to acknowledge its existence. *Rope* completely fascinated—even obsessed—me: I went to see it at least three times, which was not common for me in those days. Although I was vaguely aware of the long takes (they had received a lot of publicity), I don't think it was only its technique that fascinated me. I identified almost obsessively, and somewhat morbidly, with Brandon. I had better be careful with the word "identified" here: I have never wanted to strangle anyone (at least not without a strong motive). The identification was superficially provoked, no doubt, by the fact that at that time I stuttered very badly (and I found the performance of John Dall, whom I had never seen before, so convincing that I remember believing, until the point in the film where Rupert comments that Brandon "always stutters when he's excited," that it was the *actor,* not the character, who had the speech defect and had heroically controlled it sufficiently to become a movie star). But, deeper than that, the source of the identification was a combination of Brandon's surface assurance and my own awareness of his extreme vulnerability (of which the stutter is of course a betraying symptom)—the arrogant assumption of control and power continuously undermined by the impossibility of maintaining it. On the simplest level I was perfectly aware that, in a Hollywood movie, no one can get away with murder, that Brandon would inevitably be exposed, caught, and punished: within such a context, his arrogance and assurance cease to be alienating and become perversely touching, because one has recognized the illusoriness of their foundations. But the vulnerability is also fully dramatized, in the constant tension of Brandon himself and, more importantly, within his relationship with Philip.

I think it is significant that, despite the fact that I knew I was gay myself, it never occurred to me for a moment that the characters in the film might be: it was, at that time, literally *unthinkable.* If I couldn't believe, emotionally, in the existence of other homosexuals in real life, how could I believe in their existence within a Hollywood film? Yet I am quite certain now that my *unconscious* understanding that Brandon was gay strongly underlined the identification with him, and that it explains the fascination the film held for me. That the identification was largely masochistic, and tended to reinforce all my negative attitudes toward myself, is probably true. Yet no other film had ever given me a character with whom I could identify in quite that way, certainly not a *leading* character. Was I also aware, on some even more deeply unconscious level, that Hitchcock partly identified with Brandon? I could never have formulated it like that at the time, but I don't see how I could *not* have been: the whole film is structured on it.

Rope could not possibly "deal with" the subject of homosexuality, but it seems to me to offer a very precise account of its status and the mental "set" that would logically accompany it at that stage of our history. Of course, Brandon and Philip's milieu is far more sophisticated than was mine. Even allowing for this, however, it is certainly not a milieu in which homosexuality would be acknowledged, let alone accepted. Do Brandon and Philip acknowledge (offscreen) that they are homosexual? Again, the film cannot tell us. Ultimately, perhaps, it doesn't matter. Brandon and Philip may or may not be "lovers" in the technical sense. What the film conveys so impressively, and so accurately, is the intensity with which they hate each other. Doubtless in 1948 there were homosexuals who were able to love: given the social conditions, one might see it as a heroic achievement, a triumph of the human spirit over almost insuperable ideological odds. For, brought up and conditioned to detest ourselves, how could we love each other—each seeing in the other a reflection and constant reminder of his own sickness and evil?

Hence the fascism, hence the murder. Brandon has to see himself as a superior being because he knows that, however intelligent he might be, as a homosexual he is by definition an inferior one. Is the film about homosexuality as a perversion, or about society's perversion of homosexuality? As Brandon and Philip cannot love each other, and must be deeply ashamed of any sexual activities they have performed together, and hate each other for precisely the experiences that should have brought them most intimately together, they commit a sexual act that society, if it forbids and punishes it, at least condones to the extent that it can be represented on the cinema screen before a mass audience: the murder of David Kentley. In 1948 we could not watch Brandon and Philip kiss, or even be told that they ever did so, but we could watch them share the intimate experience of jointly strangling another young man. If the nature of the murder as sexual act (whether as projection of their hatred for the pleasure they share or substitute for the pleasure they dare not) is not clear from the outset, it becomes so from their reminiscence of it as Brandon tries to open the champagne bottle later in the same take. Philip asks him how he felt; Brandon, his hands struggling with the cork in a manner that evokes at once strangulation, masturbation, and impotence (Philip eventually has to open the bottle for him), replies that his real excitement came at the moment when David's body "went limp"— i.e., at the "evidence" of orgasm. The image of the champagne bottle can be read as the clearest—though heavily coded—information as to what Brandon and Philip actually "do": self-masturbation rather than intercourse. The action vividly suggests the inherent shame and frustration that characterize the relationship—a kind of socially imposed impotence. Ultimately, it was society that was responsible for David Kentley's

death, and if the film does not and cannot say this, it can, however
inadvertently, supply the evidence that enables *us* to say it.

METTEURS-EN-SCÈNE

Rope shares with a number of subsequent Hitchcock films (*Under Capricorn* and *Vertigo*, for example) the structural strategy of a transference
of identification whereby we are led to identify with a position that is
later undermined and subjected to criticism and, to varying degrees,
condemnation; the difference being that here, because we know that
Brandon is a murderer, the identification is rendered problematic, qualified by a partial revulsion, from the outset. In each case the initial
identification is with a character seeking power and domination over
others (which distinguishes these films from *Psycho*, which employs a
similar strategy to different ends: the difference depends on whether the
first identification figure is male or female). I have already tried to
suggest that my own identification with Brandon was not merely personal: I identified with him because Hitchcock did, and because he
constructed the film around that. Brandon, though extreme, is a "typical" Hitchcock identification figure because he exemplifies the desire-
for-power/fear-of-impotence syndrome that characterizes so many other
male Hitchcock identification figures, be they nominally "heroes" (Peck
in *The Paradine Case*, Wilding in *Under Capricorn*, Stewart in *Vertigo*)
or "villains" (Uncle Charlie, Bruno Anthony). But in Brandon's case
there is a unique factor not shared by his fellows: as with Hitchcock, the
particular form through which his drive to dominate expresses itself is
mise-en-scène.

Consistently, Brandon sees the murder and the ensuing party as a
"work of art"; it is crucial to the film—and to Hitchcock—that from
the outset he is aware of its limitations and imperfections. Almost his
first remark is that it's a pity they had to draw the curtains: the murder
should have taken place in broad daylight. If he is readier than Hitchcock to improvize (his sudden inspiration of shifting the meal to the
chest containing David's body, turning it, with the twin candelabra, into
an altar), the Hitchcockian distrust in such rashness is immediately
dramatized in Philip's response. The murder also, necessarily, lacked the

essential component that gives works of art (and in a very special way Hitchcock's films) their meaning: an audience. The party guests perform a dual function: they are both actors to be manipulated and the audience Brandon desired—unfortunately, an audience who missed the premise and are therefore frustratingly unable to appreciate the full artistry. Brandon is motivated throughout (and, significantly, it is the cause of his downfall) by that desire for acknowledgment that William Rothman argues is central to Hitchcock's work (see *The Murderous Gaze*). In its way, *Rope* is as much a "testament" movie as *Rear Window*. For Hitchcock as for Brandon, acknowledgment inevitably entails exposure: the audience can only acknowledge Hitchcock's art by becoming aware of precisely those things of which they are supposed to remain unconscious, the extent to which they have been manipulated, whether by montage or by *Rope*'s continuous reframings.

I do not wish to assert that Hitchcock identifies with Brandon *because* the latter is gay—although I have argued that this is central to the character's psychology and the source of his Hitchcockian obsession with domination. The point is rather that the gayness is no impediment: Hitchcock was able, with apparent ease, to identify with gay characters, just as he was able to identify with female characters, his "unsuccessful" socialization making it possible for him to cross boundaries that must remain closed to males who "successfully" complete the oedipal trajectory. Another way of saying this is to argue for the positive nature of the self-evident neuroticism that characterizes—that *drives*—Hitchcock's work (and which also defines its limitations). Neurosis, by definition, damages the psyche, stunting its free growth, its blossoming; yet it must also be read as an instinctual rebellion against the sexual and generic regulation of our culture. One can certainly question whether to be non-neurotic (i.e., to complete the oedipal trajectory unproblematically) would be any less disqualifying: it would be very unlikely to produce art of any interest or distinction.

As I said above, identification with Brandon (ours, Hitchcock's) must from the outset be heavily qualified: he is a murderer and a fascist, and we are in 1948, only a few years after the full revelation of the appalling social consequences of his philosophy. In other words, the identification brings with it, automatically, feelings of resistance and disturbance, shame and guilt. The film provides the necessary corrective, countering the potential morbidity and masochism, in a number of ways and through a number of subordinate characters of whom Mr. Kentley (not unlike Hitchcock in age and build) is clearly the most important. What is crucial to this process, though, is the film's systematic transference of identification from Brandon to Rupert Cadell. Inaugurated by the functioning of the star system (James Stewart must take immediate precedence over John Dall), this is completed, it seems to me, precisely at the moment when Rupert (with the connivance of Hitchcock's camera) usurps the role of *metteur-en-scène*—his reconstruction (take No. 9) of how David was murdered, in which the camera effectively comes under his control, illustrating by its movements every step in his discourse.

It is important that Rupert is a very imperfect character who needs to learn about himself as much as he needs to learn about his pupils. As with all too many learned academics, there is a marked discrepancy between what he teaches and how he lives; now Brandon has lived what Rupert has taught, and Professor Cadell must face the consequences, in the form of David Kentley's body in the chest. Rupert's complicity is intricate and complex: he has espoused and professed theories which he himself (and we believe him in this) would never have been capable of putting into practice. Is this because Brandon and Philip are gay and he is not? He tells them, in his impassioned denunciation, that they are incapable of loving, and this is surely true. Again, the film's unresolvable, even undiscussable ambiguity: Is it saying that homosexuals are "really" like this, or that this is what society makes of them? In fact, however, the film is notably reticent on the subject of Rupert's own sexuality (he is a bachelor). If it cannot tell us explicitly that Brandon and Philip are homosexual, it conspicuously abstains from telling us that Rupert isn't—apart from the fact that he is played by James Stewart, which of course carries its weight (Hitchcock originally wanted Cary Grant for the role).

It is Rupert's complicity—the fact that his horrific recoil must also be a *self*-recoil—that makes his exposure and denunciation of the crime so powerful and ratifies the film's moral authority. It corresponds to our (and Hitchcock's) fascinated, horrified involvement with Brandon, and the necessity to cast off and repudiate that involvement. The film never lets Rupert, or ourselves, off the hook: as Victor Perkins demonstrated (in *The Movie Reader*), it moves toward the completion of the figure of the triangle, with Rupert finally taking his appropriate position at its apex. Nevertheless, the moment when he flings open the window and fires the shots is among the most liberating in all of Hitchcock's work: the fresh air, after the moral, psychic, and physical claustrophobia of the preceding narrative, seems almost tangible.

17

THE MEN WHO KNEW TOO MUCH (AND THE WOMEN WHO KNEW MUCH BETTER)

Andrew Sarris has described my recent work on Hitchcock, with cautious disapproval, as "revisionist"; it is true that I no longer view the films with the naive and frequently uncritical enthusiasm that characterized the original *Hitchcock's Films*. Yet my estimate of Hitchcock's importance has if anything risen over the past few years, since I have at last (I think) begun to understand his work. Unless one is a great original thinker one's work is inevitably limited by the theoretical and ideological context within which one operates, and the context that determined the nature of *Hitchcock's Films* was severely circumscribed. The description of me (by one of the editorial board of *Screen* magazine) as an "unreconstructed humanist" was largely correct (I now aspire to be a reconstructed humanist): as a good (if troubled) bourgeois I habitually mistook ideology for truth and was unable to perceive the real issues—the conflicts—of our culture, conflicts that our films inevitably dramatize in a wide variety of ways whether their auteurs are conscious of them or not. Hence the emphasis in my early work on coherence rather than on contradiction, and the failure to perceive Hitchcock's work as the site of an ideological battleground.

Neither version of *The Man Who Knew Too Much* receives more than a passing mention in *Hitchcock's Films,* so I begin with the question of evaluation: where do they stand in the Hitchcock canon? I cannot do much here to make amends for the ludicrous dismissal in the book of the entire British period: the 1934 version seems to me a pleasant minor entertainment, one of the least interesting of the films of Hitchcock's first (British) maturity. The lingering belief that it is superior to the

American version is incomprehensible outside the most flagrant chauvinism. Yet I cannot place the 1956 version quite in the front rank of Hitchcock's movies: the material does not permit the radical critique of patriarchal structures that Hitchcock undertook (whether he knew it or not) in, for example, *Notorious, Rear Window,* and *Vertigo,* which is what gives those films their profundity, their sense of being at once both profoundly disturbed and profoundly disturbing. They resist all attempts at containment within the ideological status quo; *The Man Who Knew Too Much* does not. Its project is epitomized in the contrast between its opening and final images: first shot, the couple (James Stewart, Doris Day) separated by their child; last shot, the couple united by their child. In between, Mr. Drayton's sermon (delivered hypocritically, but God can put the truth into the mouth of the devil) tells us that adversities make us better people. But we should not allow recognition of the film's overall project to blind us to the tensions that continuously threaten it.

I wish to approach the film obliquely, through a number of different channels most of which reflect current critical/theoretical preoccupations: Hitchcock and politics; Hitchcock and mothers; the complex question of identification in his films, especially as it affects the spectator's relationship to male/female relations within them; the question of genre; Hitchcock's use (in his American period) of established stars and star images. These will lead to a brief comparison of the film to its British original. I hope these various forays from different angles will gradually define the nature of the film's achievement and justify a high evaluation: in general, it has been seriously underestimated.

HITCHCOCK AND POLITICS

We don't go to Hitchcock (or to the Hollywood cinema in general) for helpful or enlightened statements about the practical realities of international politics: as F. R. Leavis once remarked, we don't go to D. H. Lawrence to learn whom we should vote for. The surface level is inevitably dominated by conventional Hollywood (read: popular American) attitudes, evasive, banal, or both: bad Nazis, good Americans, the free world vs. duplicitous and torturing Communists, etc.. Hitchcock developed intermittent strategies for qualifying these (in *Topaz,* all the energy is attributed to the Cubans), but he couldn't effectively undermine them (even supposing that he had wanted to). In the British version of *The Man Who Knew Too Much*, we learn that the assassination, explicitly compared to that at Sarajevo, could start a world war; in the American version even this elementary political statement is suppressed, and the assassination becomes a matter of internal politics and personal ambition.

Below this surface, however, the treatment of politics becomes really interesting (and truly Hitchcockian)—in that area where politics and sexual politics converge and interact. For Hitchcock, politics is a male-dominated—indeed, exclusively male—world within which women, insofar as they are allowed admittance at all, are pawns to be manipulated, used, exploited, and often destroyed. It is on this level that the bad Nazis/good Americans (etc.) dichotomy becomes thoroughly subverted: the nominal commitment to America, democracy, the free world, demanded by Hollywood, is revealed as a mere facade for a far more sweeping denunciation of masculinist politics in general. Two examples will suffice: (a) *Notorious*: the recurrent round-table discussions of the all-male American authorities which result in the cynical exploitation and eventual near death of Alicia/Ingrid Bergman are exactly mirrored by the Nazis' after-dinner round-table discussion (again all-male—even that dedicated Nazi Mrs. Sebastian is excluded) that results in the death of Emil Hrupka. It is scarcely coincidental that Cary Grant and Claude Rains are competing for control both of Ingrid Bergman and of the materials with which to build atomic bombs. (b) *Topaz*. Juanita/Karin Dor is actually executed (in the film's most emotionally agonizing scene) by her Cuban lover, but the murder is directly precipitated by her French lover (working for the Americans) and the use he makes of her. We should also note the corollary of this motif of the masculinist exploitation of women: in the two Cary Grant espionage films (*Notorious* and *North by Northwest*), the hero fully redeems himself only when he directly violates the orders of his American superiors, thereby expressing his rejection of masculinist politics altogether in favor of identifying himself with a woman and rescuing her from victimization and death.

Domination—power/impotence as two sides of the same coin—is clearly the central concern (one might say the driving obsession) of Hitchcock's work on all levels, methodological, stylistic, thematic; the distinction of that work—its importance for us today—lies in the ways in which that obsession is pursued to the point where its mechanisms, its motivations, its monstrousness, are thoroughly exposed. The political level of the films—superficially so trite and uninteresting—in fact represents a logical extension of the films' obsessive sexual concerns (the drive of men to dominate women) into the structures of power politics that men have constructed. The two great liberating screams of *The Man Who Knew Too Much* (Doris Day's in the Albert Hall, Brenda de Banzie's "answering" scream in the embassy) must be read on one level as the protests of women against masculinist politics and the cruelty and violence that issue from it. Allowing for the differences between popular entertainment and "serious" art works—the differences between what they can explicitly say—we might compare those screams to Liv Ullmann's cowering from the televised Vietnam newsreel and the Warsaw ghetto photograph in *Persona*. They are also, of course, the screams of mothers: real mother, surrogate mother.

HITCHCOCK AND MOTHERS

It is something of an understatement to say that, in Hitchcock's American films, mothers are generally not presented in a very favorable light. There are three mothers of psychopathic killers (Mrs. Anthony, Mrs. Bates, Mrs. Rusk); the neurotically clinging mother of *The Birds;* the love-withholding, guilt-ridden mother of *Marnie*. Other mothers are presented somewhat more sympathetically: the nervous, pathetic, well-meaning Emma of *Shadow of a Doubt,* the caustic and skeptical mother of Cary Grant in *North by Northwest;* but the former may be partly responsible for her younger brother's psychopathic condition by "mothering" him too much when he was young, and the latter obstructs rather than assists her son's efforts to avoid getting killed. This preoccupation with the darker side of motherhood may be a consequence of Hitchcock's experience of America rather than of personal psychology (there are surprisingly few mothers in the British films, and not a single monstrous one). What is clear is that the one unambiguously and actively positive mother in Hitchcock's American work is Jo McKenna—or rather, and importantly, Jo Conway. I mean that shift to her stage (maiden?) name to signify the essential difference between Jo and Hitchcock's other American mothers: the rest are *just* mothers, in a culture that has (disastrously) effected a division of labor which makes nurturing almost exclusively the mother's responsibility: the whole meaning of their lives has been bound up with their children, and the suggestion of the films is that motherhood can turn sour and twisted when it becomes an exclusive vocation. Jo, along with her male name (a point underlined in the film—Louis Bernard at first assumes that "Jo" is the name of her son), possesses traits that our culture commonly defines as "masculine": she is assertive, active, dynamic, she makes autonomous decisions and takes independent action. She has also had—and wishes she still had— a career, and with it a degree of personal autonomy: she is a good mother because, emotionally at least, she is not *just* a mother. In this she complements rather than contradicts Hitchcock's characterizations of mothers elsewhere: if she is the exception to the rule, she is also its proof.

IDENTIFICATION AND GENDER

Questions of spectatorship, identification, and gender difference have become a major preoccupation of much contemporary theoretical writing on film, and Hitchcock has often been used as a central focus for this. It can be argued (because it *has* been) that Hitchcock's films imply a male spectatorship, and that the only position they offer women is that of accepting the subordination of female desire to male desire (construction of the "good object") or that of a more overtly masochistic complicity in guilt and punishment. Raymond Bellour, very influentially, has attempted to demonstrate this quasi-scientifically in his extraordinarily detailed and meticulously accurate analyses of narrative movement and the technical apparatus of point of view. Personally, I am at best only half convinced—I think such analyses reveal only one side of a much more complex story. There seem to be two problems here. One is that such approaches tend to ignore the existence of innate bisexuality (however repressed), hence the possibilities of transsexual identification; the other is that, like so many attempts to approach art "scientifically," they privilege what can be proven and ignore or at least play down factors that are less tangible, less amenable to scientific demonstration, yet nonetheless palpably there, such as the ways in which stars function in movies or the ways in which our sympathy for a character's position in the narrative may cut against the technical apparatus of identification (POV shots, etc.) to produce fruitful tensions and disturbances.

What I am suggesting is that films can—and Hitchcock's often do—play on a tension between technically constructed identification and emotional identification. I offer two examples:

1. *Vertigo*, arguably the locus classicus of this strategy. Throughout the first part, Hitchcock uses the technical apparatus of point-of-view shooting/editing systematically to enforce identification with the male viewpoint. The very first sequence after the credits employs this more emphatically than any other Hitchcock opening; thereafter, we see through Scottie's eyes and we are prevented from seeing virtually everything that is beyond his consciousness. Hitchcock's revelation of the truth via Judy's flashback and letter (to neither of which Scottie has access) shatters this identification beyond possible repair—we now know the crucial facts that Scottie doesn't, and the entire intrigue is transformed, it is no longer the romantic drama we have been sharing with him. Yet Hitchcock continues to shoot the film essentially from Scottie's viewpoint, even though he is fully aware that our emotional identification must now be with Judy. The effect is ruthlessly to expose the entire apparatus of male domination and the anxiety that motivates it.

2. The whole of *Notorious* provides another sustained example. Our identification with the film's "female system" turns the male system on its head: it becomes a characteristic Hitchcockian study in male anxiety, in which both men, knowing well that Alicia is no virgin, are absolutely terrified that they may not measure up (so to speak) to the competition, and therefore feel driven to torment, punish, and destroy the woman who produces in them such terrible feelings of insecurity. Central to Hitchcock's work (especially the American films, though it's already fully there in, e.g., *Blackmail*) is the culture's investment in masculinity, potency, the phallus, and the dread that actual men may not be able to fulfill the demands that masculinist ideology makes on them. Also central is the corollary to this: the effect of this anxiety on heterosexual relations, the revenge of men on women for arousing these fears, and the monstrous irrationality of that revenge. The methodological strategy—the identification that is enforced on one level is contradicted on another—seems to me crucial to the effect of much of Hitchcock's finest work: it accounts for that extraordinary fusion of fascination and disturbance, with its resultant tension and anguish, the ultimate manifestation of

"suspense," that is the dominant factor in most people's experience of the films.

The Man Who Knew Too Much (1956) appears initially to offer us two identification figures of equal status, a married couple, then swiftly problematizes identification by developing tensions between them. The tension is resolved by making our primary identification figure the woman, then doubling her with another woman, Mrs. Drayton: both have husbands who attempt to dominate them, and our identification with the female position exposes the domination drive's very mechanisms.

GENRE

I have argued elsewhere that the Hollywood genres represent different ways of resolving—or seeming to resolve—basically similar ideological tensions/contradictions, and that films that cross genres, or are generically impure, are often of particular interest in the way the contradictions become foregrounded. The British version of The Man Who Knew Too Much is generically quite unproblematic. To raise the issue of genre is to suggest one of the ways in which the American version is so enriched: the simple action thriller is complicated by the intrusion of a genre that in the '50s reached one of its peaks of significance and expressiveness, the domestic melodrama. The Man Who Knew Too Much belongs (and not merely in terms of chronology) to the ten years that produced The Reckless Moment; Madame Bovary, and Home from the Hill; There's Always Tomorrow, Written on the Wind, and Imitation of Life; Rebel Without a Cause and Bigger Than Life. It takes up certain of the domestic melodrama's characteristic concerns—the oppression of women within the family, marriage vs. career, motherhood—and with them its disturbance about gender roles and social positions. No such disturbance is present in the British version.

STARS

Cary Grant and James Stewart appear in four Hitchcock films each; I want to comment briefly on how they function within their respective texts, because I think they are used quite differently. For Hitchcock,

Stewart became the epitome of the masculine power/impotence syndrome that both structures and disturbs so many of his films. If invited to picture Stewart in a Hitchcock film, doesn't one (unless one thinks of *Rear Window!*) see him shot from a low angle, towering over someone (usually a woman), looking at once dominating and helpless, out of control, near hysteria? *Vertigo* offers of course the supreme instances: Kim Novak seated, Stewart standing over her, the scenes where Stewart forces Judy to dress as Madeleine. But the entire protracted sequence in *The Man Who Knew Too Much* in which Stewart sedates Doris Day unknown to her and against her assumed wishes (when she realizes what is happening she violently repudiates the action) is in its way equally striking. Cary Grant is never used by Hitchcock in quite this way: he may lie to and manipulate women (*Suspicion*), but he doesn't try directly to dominate them. When he is given something like the Stewart domination image, Hitchcock plays the effect for comedy, as in the celebrated inverted shot near the beginning of *Notorious* where he is seen from Ingrid Bergman's point of view as she lies in bed. As Andrew Britton has suggested in his marvelous monograph on Grant, the image typically carries connotations of gender-role ambiguity (so that he becomes, among other things, the perfect medium for Hawks's play on sexual role reversal). The Hitchcock films with Grant move toward an equalized male/female relationship (a reading that stressed star persona over directorial authorship might go some way toward justifying the "happy ending" of *Suspicion*). Stewart, on the other hand, embodies for Hitchcock the desperate and hopeless drive to dominate—to assert an ideologically constructed "masculinity" that always sits uneasily on the Stewart persona and, in *Vertigo*, provokes the film's catastrophe. *Rear Window,* of course, is built entirely on Stewart's physical inability to assume the position of domination, and his desperate drive to compensate for this via the potency of the "look."

THE TWO VERSIONS

The most obvious difference between the British and American versions is their respective lengths, the American remake being half as long again as the original. This follows a general pattern of directors remaking their own early films late in life: Ozu (*Story of Floating Weeds/Floating*

Weeds) and McCarey (*Love Affair/An Affair to Remember*) provide striking parallels. There is doubtless some correlation between a director's age and his desire, through the adoption of a more leisurely style, to elaborate. The basic narrative structure of the two versions is very similar. Its main features:

a. Family abroad (Switzerland, Morocco): exposition.
b. Police investigation.
c. Father goes to investigate (dentist, taxidermist).
d. Chapel sequence (the closest to a direct remake—some of the original dialogue is repeated).
e. Albert Hall sequence.
f. Final climax and resolution (siege of Sydney Street, embassy).

Yet this structure is very differently realized in the two films, the differences relating to far more than the auteurist notion that an individual artist called Alfred Hitchcock had developed, deepened, and matured (though I do not wish to discount that as one factor). Cultural difference, the difference in period, greater generic complexity, the Hollywood star system, all make their contributions.

I think the crux of difference is the relative stability of sexual ideology, as between Britain in 1934 and America in 1956. From our present perspective we can see that the structure of the patriarchal nuclear family, and the supposedly monogamous marriage (in effect, monogamous for the woman) that guarantees it, has always been an institution for the subordination of women (whatever else). The hegemony that upholds it, however, has been subject to a whole series of fluctuations and challenges in different times and different places. In middle-class Britain in 1934 (which represents the audience toward which the original version was primarily directed, Hitchcock not being, at that stage, internationally celebrated), the hegemony was very strong (I know—I grew up in that time and class, and was three years old when the film came out). This does not mean of course that British middle-class families in the '30s were any happier than American ones in the '50s—simply that they had less incentive to question whether they were happy or not; all the members of my own family were variously miserable, but none of us ever explicitly doubted that we were the ideal happy family. Between 1934 and the remake, two changes occur, the change of place and the change of time. The notion of the "career woman" seems strongly

American: it's already there as an established theme in much pre-World War II American cinema, far more than in the British, which has no real equivalents for *Stage Door, Christopher Strong, The Miracle Woman.* The Second World War saw the release of women from the home and the subsequent efforts to force them back into it. These factors provide a context in which the differences between the two versions begin to make sense. What follows is an attempt to deal with the major ones systematically.

1. Switzerland/Marrakesh. The British version shows us a conventional holiday resort where the family seems quite at ease, as untroubled by external pressures as by internal tensions, with no sense of alienation. The American version gives us a family in a world whose alienness is stressed at every point (see, for example, the elaborate comic detail of the restaurant scene). One feature of that world receives special emphasis in that it provides the starting point for the entire action: the position of Moslem women, epitomized in the compulsory wearing of the veil which Hank accidentally tears off, thereby giving Louis Bernard the pretext he needs for questioning the McKennas. The Moslem veil is clearly a signifier of the husband's total possession of his wife: no other man must even see her face, "possessing" her via the look. Jo, we recall, has had a triumphant stage career, gazed at by thousands; she has now been compelled by circumstances (in effect by her husband) to give up that career and be gazed at only by Ben. The climax of the film comes when he permits her to return to the public gaze, temporarily at least suspending his sole ownership of her. (We don't know of course what will happen after the film's closure, but we are at liberty to speculate that the internal tensions of the marriage, far from being resolved, may prove to have been exacerbated by Jo's reexperience of recognition as an autonomous person outside the confines of the marriage.) As a footnote, one may add that the point about Moslem women and the look is underlined by Hitchcock in the unobtrusive little visual joke of the woman at the market wearing glasses over her veil.

2. The expositions. Much of the extra running time of the American version is accounted for by its enormously more elaborate exposition. Up to the return to England, the British version contains, by my reckoning, six sequences, 109 shots, and lasts about 15 minutes; the American version contains 11 sequences, 351 shots, and lasts 46 minutes. This is scarcely necessitated by any greater complexity in the espionage plot; it

seems necessitated almost exclusively by the critical concern with marriage, family, and the position of women that simply isn't there in the British version. Related to this of course is the development of the Draytons as a kind of childless mirror to the McKennas (the equivalent couple in the British version offers no substantial parallel to this).

3. The stability of the marriage in the British version and its instability in the American can be pinpointed in one detail: Mrs. Lawrence's teasing of her husband by humorously flirting with Louis Bernard. This testifies to the absolutely solid base of the Lawrences' marriage; contrariwise, the fact that we absolutely cannot imagine Jo Conway behaving in that way testifies, perhaps paradoxically, to the precariousness of the Conways' marital arrangements: the marriage patently could not sustain such a flirtation, and it wouldn't be funny. Similarly, Jill is able to joke about not wanting children, referring to Betty as "it," in her daughter's presence (and to her enjoyment)—the strength of family ideology could scarcely be more eloquently confirmed. The thinness of the British version, in fact, is the result of its not being about anything very much beyond its McGuffin.

4. Superficially, because it is regarded as a "masculine" activity, one might see the woman's sharpshooting as more "positive"—i.e., dynamic, aggressive, "possessing the phallus"—than singing "Che sera, sera."But what is far more decisive here is the distinction between a hobby and a career: Jill has a hobby, which her marriage can easily accommodate; Jo had a career, and her marriage has depended upon its renunciation.

5. One may consider briefly here the most obvious change between the two versions: Why does Betty change sex to become Hank? Tentatively, I think we may invoke Freud's theory that the woman who is denied the phallus sees her child as substitute/compensation, and that this is especially the case when the child is male. The narrative, one might suggest, provides Jo with a son as compensation for renouncing her career, her autonomy, her power outside the home; Jill, presented as totally contented with her position, has apparently renounced nothing. We should also note that since she relinquished her career Jo has been taking too many pills, has become nervous, and now wants another child: the compensation has not worked very successfully.

6. The American version's privileging of Jo over Ben is strongly underlined by the one step in the basic structure I outlined (c) from

which she is absent: the substitution for Bob's visit to the dentist of Ben's visit to the taxidermist. In the remake, the tracking of Ambrose Chappell to his taxidermy studio represents the husband's one solo undertaking. The visit to Barbor the dentist in the British version is a necessary link in the proairetic/hermeneutic chain; it also underlines Bob's phlegmatic, very British heroism. He discovers important facts, he is endangered, he gets the upper hand. Ben's visit to the wrong Ambrose Cha(p)pe(l)l, on the other hand, is a complete fiasco: he learns nothing (except that he was wrong), he loses all control of the situation, and he is reduced to humiliating buffoonery.

7. In fact, despite her famous Albert Hall scream and her sharpshooting expertise, Jill's function in the British version is far more restricted than Jo's in the American. (It is striking that in the British version Bob is accompanied to the chapel by a male friend, not by his wife.) It is true that as the American male Ben plays the more obviously active role (that he prefers his wife to be passive is the point of the sedation scene): he fights, rings bells, bursts in on assassins, and finally rescues Hank. But the recurring motif of the film is that it is Jo who has the right instincts and perceptions and who makes the right decisions: it is she who becomes suspicious of Louis Bernard's questions, she who realizes that Ambrose Chapel is a place not a person; her scream saves the prime minister, her song saves Hank (and redeems Mrs. Drayton).

The film raises very strikingly one of the major features of gender division in our culture, the notion that men are rational while women are emotional/intuitive. Men have laid claim to rationality as justification for their power, patronizingly granting women "female intuition" as compensation. The film suggests that it is men who are the more impoverished by this division. It is Ben's rationality that leads him to sedate Jo before telling her what has happened, subjugating her emotional response to the kidnapping of her son; the film is quite unambiguous, I think, as to the monstrousness of this, and it colors our reading of the character throughout. One might suggest that the "rational" is what the conscious mind works out for itself without assistance, while the "intuitive" is what the conscious mind comes to realize when it allows itself close contact with the subconscious. It is a structuring motif of the film, established in its first sequences, that Jo knows better than Ben. Her insights and decisions—suspicion of Louis Bernard, sense that the police should be told what has happened, realization that Ambrose

Chapel is a place, her scream in the Albert Hall—can all be justified rationally, but they are reached "intuitively." Ben, limited to the purely rational, understands very little, though he can ring bells and burst open doors when required.

Most seem agreed that the ending of the British version is an anticlimax after the Albert Hall sequence, so I want to conclude by celebrating the real climax of the American version, Jo's song in the embassy. Middle-aged academics are not supposed to admit that they burst into tears every time Doris Day begins "Che sera, sera," but in my case it is a fact. What makes that moment so moving is its magical resolution of apparent oppositions. Eric Rohmer (in the book on Hitchcock he coauthored with Claude Chabrol) grandly implies that it resolves the eternal theological quandary of predestination vs. free will: "Che sera, sera," but "the Lord helps those who help themselves." Less metaphysically, I see it as resolving the more practical and prosaic opposition of motherhood vs. career: it represents Jo's triumph simultaneously as mother and performer (and we can admire the power of her voice even if the embassy audience is a trifle taken aback). The shots of Doris Day's voice traveling up the stairs (so to speak) are among the most moving in the whole of Hitchcock. They lead to Hank's whistling and to Mrs. Drayton's scream, which, as I suggested earlier, answers Jo's scream in Albert Hall: the screams of women who know better. Mr. Drayton's rationality, which reflects Ben's as its darker shadow, tells him that Hank must be murdered; his wife's emotional/intuitive understanding knows that Hank must be saved. Her scream is directly produced by the sound of approaching footsteps which she believes to be her husband's but are in fact Ben's: the parallel between the two couples, introduced in the exposition, is sustained right to the denouement.

Within the safe framework of the reconstruction of an American family, *The Man Who Knew Too Much* has some very important things to tell us about our culture and the strains and tensions upon the suppression of which the family's precarious stability depends.*

---

* Since this chapter was written, an extremely interesting article by Deborah Thomas has appeared in *CineAction!* 13/14 ("Film Noir: How Hollywood Deals with the Deviant Male"), in which Thomas relates *The Man Who Knew Too Much* to the *films noirs* of the 1940s and '50.

18

MALE DESIRE, MALE ANXIETY: THE ESSENTIAL HITCHCOCK

THE PERSONAL IS POLITICAL

Hitchcock's Films opened with the question, "Why should we take Hitchcock seriously?" At that stage in the evolution of film criticism, the meaning would not have been significantly different if I had written *"Should* we take Hitchcock seriously?" Twenty-five years later, one can confidently assume general agreement that the latter version of the question is no longer at issue. Many conflicting answers have been proposed, and still have currency, to the former version (Raymond Bellour's, for example, is very different from William Rothman's), and negative, hostile answers are still possible (e.g., we should take Hitchcock seriously because his films express and encourage misogyny, often in very violent forms).

Had I decided to open the present book with a question, it might well have been, "Can Hitchcock be saved for feminism?"—the question that haunts contemporary Hitchcock criticism, explicitly or implicitly, in article after article, especially those belonging to what we might loosely call "the Bellour school." It also sums up (it seems to me—the author would not entirely agree) the central concern of Tania Modleski's splendid recent book *The Women Who Knew Too Much,* to which I shall return presently. My own answer to the question has, I hope, been very thoroughly defined by this point. I want here to make explicit some of the issues involved.

First, there is the question of my own status as self-professed feminist —the question of my right to the title. I have been told many times, often by women in my classes, that men (even gay men) can't call themselves feminists because they can't possibly understand what it feels like to be a woman within patriarchal culture: they haven't experienced the horrors—from rape and battering down to the minutiae of casual daily oppression—for themselves. If this argument is accepted, one would also, presumably, have to insist that an American black, for example, cannot validly declare himself to be anti-apartheid: he will have experienced oppression and discrimination in many forms, but never quite the particular, extreme, institutionalized and legally sanctioned forms those take in South Africa. No, I have not been raped (not, at least, in the sense that that term popularly evokes—I have had experiences that might now stand up in the courts), but I think I am capable of the necessary imaginative leap. As a child I was repeatedly victimized, both by individual boys older and stronger than myself, and by gangs. For one extended period of my life I was subjected to systematic daily persecution, tormented both physically and psychologically. The aim was to reduce me to a state of abject hysteria in which all I could do was close my eyes and scream as loudly as I could, and the aim was always realized, my persecutors (there were about six of them, and although this was nearly fifty years ago I can still remember their faces vividly) achieving great satisfaction from my display. This was not rape, but I certainly experienced it as a form of violation: I was deprived of all dignity and self-respect and made to feel what is surely one of the ultimate and least desirable of all possible human sensations, that of utter helplessness. (I could not, of course, tell any of the teachers what was happening to me: that would have been "sneaking," the worst crime you can commit within the ethos of a British boys' private school, and it never occurred to me, at the age of ten, that such an august law might be challenged or broken). I see now that this experience constitutes one of the roots of my feminism.

Another involves my last meeting, very many years later, with my mother—in 1977, just before I left England for Canada. She was ninety years old and had had to be placed in a nursing home. I visited her there knowing that I would probably never see her again. I must explain that I am not only the youngest of five children but the youngest by twelve years: my parents were both middle-aged when I was born, and it is quite obvious that I was an "accident." During that last meeting she couldn't remember me at all, although she remembered my four brothers and sisters: she had literally repressed the fact of my birth. I accepted this after a few minutes, and was content that she thought she was being visited by some kindly stranger. The reason for the repression soon became clear. She repeatedly pulled out from under her bed a tattered folder I had never seen before in which were faded newspaper clippings —advertisements for and reviews of an antique exhibition she had organized in Chicago one year before I was born. We must have gone over the collection at least three times during the hour I spent with her. This had been the first time in her life that she had been permitted to undertake such a project on her own—her children were at last old enough to be left in the care of others, and she had insisted, for once, on doing something outside her husband's jurisdiction. It was also the last time: I put an end to all that. I found the implications of all this immensely moving and illuminating: as that old, part-senile woman moved toward death, the one memory she clung to tenaciously, to feel that her life had some meaning, was of the only moment when she had achieved something autonomously, when she had experienced that sense of self-respect to which every human being should be entitled. That is one of the reasons I call myself a feminist: it establishes a kind of posthumous link between us, and is my way of paying tribute. It is also one of the reasons why I am firmly pro-choice.

I could recount other experiences that have contributed to my feeling entitled to claim the capacity for the "imaginative leap" that many women believe men cannot make. This is not at all to say that my feminism is perfect: I am guilty of theoretical gaps and some dreadful personal lapses. But it has been my experience that not all women who call themselves feminists are infallible either.

Some important questions arise. What kinds of concern—and consequently of discourse—should feminism embrace? What particular concerns and insights might men bring to feminist discourses? A gay man has of course particular advantages here: he is at least partially liberated from those pressures our culture exerts on men to dominate, subordinate, and possess women, and he will have experienced forms of oppression not identical with but parallel to those that women experience. Yet it seems vitally important, at this stage of cultural evolution, that more and more heterosexual men should begin to define themselves as feminists and bring their own experiences of oppression (since what we call "normality" oppresses all of us, to varying degrees and in different ways) to such a commitment. In fact, the traditional concerns of feminism—

protest against and analysis of women's oppression, the drive to construct positive images of women outside the constraints of male determination and male fantasy—have begun to be complemented in recent years by the feminist research (conducted, appropriately, in many cases by men) into "masculinity" as a social construction, its foundations, its characteristics, its consequences.

I hope that everyone who reads this book will also read Tania Modleski's (if she or he has not already done so): despite many important differences of position and emphasis, the two seem to me more complementary than oppositional. Modleski deals very impressively with certain films that I neglect (the chapter on *Murder!*, especially, relates very interestingly to the work on Hitchcock's treatment of sexuality that I have attempted), and what are perhaps the two strongest chapters provide useful correctives of emphasis to my readings of *Rear Window* and *Vertigo*. It is one of those books (very rare among critical works) that one wishes were twice the length: especially, given the project (the subtitle is *Hitchcock and Feminist Theory*), one regrets the absence of chapters on *Shadow of a Doubt*, *Under Capricorn*, and *Marnie*.

I first encountered Modleski's work on Hitchcock at an academic conference in Boston. She was reading a paper on *Frenzy* (now incorporated in her book). Before the lecture, she asked me whether I were writing a chapter on this film for *my* book. I said I wasn't yet sure. After the lecture I approached her to say "Now I'm sure": it was evident to me that anything I might wish to say in defense of *Frenzy* had now been said, and most eloquently. Modleski's book appeared just as I was completing the final (i.e., last-to-be-written) chapter of the present work (chapter 16). I deliberately refrained from reading it until I had finished (and have refrained from rewriting anything in response to it, the present section excepted): not, I know, the "correct" scholarly attitude, but I have never been a "correct" scholar, and I knew that the intricate network of correspondences and differences, together with Modleski's strength and penetration, would confuse and inhibit me, and probably undermine my confidence in my own "voice." I am sure my decision was the right one. The two books work best as a kind of inadvertent dialogue characterized by a constant give-and-take of "This is so, isn't it?" and "Yes, but . . ." (Intriguingly, Modleski actually uses the latter phrase on the page of her book open before me—page 3 of the introduction—though not with explicitly Leavisian reference).

On that same page, Modleski takes me to task for employing the question "Can Hitchcock be saved for feminism?", in the article on *Vertigo* (it first appeared in *American Film,* November 1982) that constitutes the main body of this chapter. I must quote her at some length:

his very language, implying the necessity of rescuing a favorite auteur from feminist obloquy, suggests that the question is fundamentally a rhetorical one . . .

It may be symptomatic that in contrast to the female critics I have mentioned, the stated goal of the one male critic concerned with feminism is to reestablish the authority of the artist—to "save" Hitchcock. For Wood, political "progressiveness" has come to replace moral complexity as the criterion by which to judge Hitchcock's art, but the point remains the same—to justify the ways of the auteur to the filmgoing public. The feminist critics I have mentioned, by contrast, use Hitchcock's works as a means to elucidate issues and problems relevant to women in patriarchy. In so doing these critics implicitly challenge and decenter directorial authority by considering Hitchcock's work as the expression of cultural attitudes and practices existing to some extent outside the artist's control . . .

My response to this is somewhat complex. On the one hand I certainly do not wish to dissociate myself entirely from notions of personal authorship. I *could,* in formulating my question, have employed the Wollenesque distinction of placing Hitchcock's name within quotation marks (the sense would not have been different), to signify the body of work rather than the human individual; but I have already argued in the introduction to this book that such a distinction is neither satisfactory nor helpful. It was, however, the films, not the person, to which my question referred. I might further point out that (whether here or in the article as originally published in *American Film*), I have not introduced the question merely as my own, but as "the central question that haunts contemporary Hitchcock criticism" (in which I would now include Modleski's); I do not see it as "fundamentally rhetorical," as it has received many different answers.

Modleski's attitude to personal authorship seems to me shot through with a disingenuousness that is by no means personal to her but endemic to the entire semiotic/structuralist school: if one is not concerned with the personal nature of the work (which does not at all preclude a concern with its representativeness, as a product of the culture)—with the individual stamp that distinguishes it from other Hollywood movies—then why write a book on *Hitchcock's* films at all? Why *this* grouping of films rather than other groupings (films made in the same period, within the

same genre, on similar subjects, etc.)? And in fact Modleski uses Hitchcock's name precisely as I do: I see no epistemological difference between my use of it and hers, in a sentence later on the same page: "But
what I want to argue is *neither* that Hitchcock is utterly misogynistic *nor*
that he is largely sympathetic to women and their plight in patriarchy,
but that his work is characterized by a thoroughgoing ambivalence
about femininity." (That is precisely what *I* want to argue, too.) The
corollary of this is that I as much as she am concerned to "consider
Hitchcock's work as the expression of cultural attitudes and practices
existing to some extent outside the artist's control," and to "use Hitchcock's works as a means to elucidate issues and problems relevant to
women in patriarchy." I explicitly relate *Vertigo,* for example, to "the
nature of desire and how it is constituted within patriarchal culture." In
fact, I think Modleski here is a victim of those "false oppositions" I
noted in my introduction (author/cultural production, personal expres-
sion/signification) and the confusions that inevitably arise from them.

Modleski tells us, in a footnote (page 134), that in her opinion the
discussion of *Vertigo* that follows this preamble "is not . . . ultimately as
useful for feminism as [my] earlier discussion of the film in [my] book."
I am puzzled by this judgment, and she doesn't elaborate. Now that the
two readings of the film are appearing within the same covers, readers
will have a good opportunity to make up their own minds. I claim the
following analysis of *Vertigo* as a feminist reading, not because it sees
the film as offering "positive" images of women, but because it sees it as
exposing and subjecting to criticism certain compulsive drives of the
male ego as constructed within our culture. That, it seems to me, is a
valid and necessary feminist concern: the education of men (which is
likely to be a long and very painful process, generating intense resistance
on both conscious and unconscious levels) must be a very high priority
if we are ever to achieve a culture characterized by liberation and equality. It is an undertaking in which Hitchcock's films might play a very
significant part.

A NOTE ON *REAR WINDOW*

My prime concern here is a rethinking of *Vertigo.* Rereading the original
attempt to interpret the film in my book, I find many of the perceptions

valid but am greatly dissatisfied with their formulation. Especially, the chapter is shot through with a subtle and insidious sexism (at that time I had no awareness whatever of the oppression of women within our culture), and (closely related to this) it strikingly lacks any psychoanalytical account of the nature of "romantic love," accepting it as some eternal and unchangeable "given" of "the human condition." I want, however, to preface this with a few sketchy remarks about *Rear Window*. I shall consider two (interconnected) themes of the film that now appear crucial to an understanding of it.

1. Castration. Most critical accounts of *Rear Window* have centered on its status as "artistic testament": it is a film about the experience of film viewing, with Jefferies (James Stewart) as spectator, the apartments he watches as the screen. This reading is certainly supported by much of the film's detail and, more generally, by its central tension: the events in the apartments reflect the spectator's fantasies, yet the spectator has no control over them, so that dream can turn to nightmare at any moment. However, such an account requires careful definition. First, it seems quite misguided to see the film as an allegory about "the cinema": insofar as it works, it is an allegory about *Hitchcock's* cinema, which is highly idiosyncratic. Second, the spectatorship inscribed in the film is by no means neutral: it is unambiguously male. Far more important (it seems to me) than the "artistic testament" dimension of the film is its dramatization of fundamental male sexual anxieties. Clearly, those anxieties are rooted in the fear of castration and, equally clearly (from a psychoanalytic viewpoint), "castration" is represented by Jefferies' broken leg.

The term "castration" has caused certain problems and confusions: is it meant literally or symbolically? The confusions disappear if one recognizes it as both. Within patriarchal culture, the phallus is the supreme symbol of power; conversely, power is "phallic." Loss of power on any level (money, prestige, social status, authority over women, domination of children, etc.) is therefore symbolic castration. At the same time, this is seen as reactivating the *literal* castration fears of childhood. Language acknowledges such a connection quite clearly: the word "impotence" (often used to mean "powerlessness") invariably carries sexual overtones.

"Castration," then, at the beginning of *Rear Window,* is signified not

only by the broken leg but also by the smashed camera—Jefferies'
potency as male expressing itself as much in his role as news photographer as in anything directly sexual, his recklessness and initiative taken
as the guarantee of "masculinity." It is the fear of castration and the
drive to reaffirm "potency" with which the male spectator is invited to
identify. As the film develops, Jefferies attempts to assert his "possession
of the phallus" through the power of the look, a substitute for both the
smashed camera and the broken leg (the latter explicitly associated with
the deprivation of sexual activity). Hence the significance (and the comedy) of the *growth* of "the look" as the film progresses: first the eyes,
then binoculars, finally a huge erect telescope. But Jefferies' pursuit of
power through the look only confirms, repeatedly, his impotence, a point
brought home to him (and to us) in the two major climactic scenes:
Lisa's search of Thorwald's apartment, and the culminating Jefferies/
Thorwald confrontation, where the "potency" of Jefferies' flashbulbs
proves insufficient to save him.

2. Marriage. *Rear Window* is crucially "about" marriage, and its radicalism lies in the connection it makes between that and the castration
theme. Marriage as the castration of the male: stated like that, the film
appears brazenly misogynist, and in many ways it is capable of sustaining such a reading. Only, however, if one ignores other elements. What
it is really about is the impossibility of successful human relations within
an ideological system that constructs men and women in hopelessly
incompatible roles: it relates quite fascinatingly to the "wandering vs.
settling" antinomy which Peter Wollen sees as central to Ford and to the
Western. At its center are Jefferies, the ideal American male (the "wanderer-adventurer," even if at second-hand: he photographs the adventures of others), and Lisa, the ideal American female (settled, eminently
civilized, constantly pressuring Jefferies to "settle down" with her, the
perfected "object for the gaze"). They are macabrely reflected in the
Thorwalds (the wanderer-adventurer reduced to traveling salesman, his
wife "settled" to the extreme of being bedridden). All the other apartment dwellers relate to this theme (with marvelous precision and economy—there is neither redundancy nor irrelevance): they variously embody the twin hells of marriage and singleness, in a civilization that
demands the former while rendering its success impossible. What the
emphasis on castration and impotence ultimately achieves is the calling

into question of our culture's concept of "potency" (masculinity), with the insupportable demands it makes on men and women alike.

VERTIGO REVISITED

With *Vertigo*, I want to examine the first four sequences (culminating in the introduction of Madeleine) in some detail, as the basis for a psychoanalytical (and political) reading of the film which I shall subsequently develop.

The opening sequence (the chase, the fall) is among the most succinct and abstract Hitchcock has given us; it is also characteristically fragmented in editing, requiring twenty-five shots. The abstractness is established in the first image: a metal bar against an out-of-focus background, which a hand suddenly clutches. Then the camera pulls back, the background becomes a San Francisco cityscape, and three men clamber over the top rung in a rooftop pursuit. We are given only the most minimal narrative information: the second man is a policeman, so the first must be a criminal; the third is James Stewart, clearly the male protagonist. He is connected to the cop by being a pursuer, but connected to the criminal by being in plain clothes (nothing tells us at this point that he is also a policeman: he might be a reporter, or merely a conscientious citizen). The first three shots strongly emphasize the three-character structure: 1. Each in turn climbs over the bar. 2. An extreme long shot contains all three within the frame simultaneously. 3. Each in turn leaps to another roof (Hitchcock cuts before we see Stewart fall and clutch the gutter, an action given us in shots 4 and 5).

At this point begins an alternating pattern—a favorite structural method of the mature Hitchcock, first of many in the film—that continues almost uninterrupted to the end of the sequence: a series of nine shots, all medium close-up, taken from an identical camera position, of Stewart hanging (Nos. 6, 8, 10, 12, 14, 16; then 21, 23, 25); an alternating series, slightly less consistent, of six shots showing Stewart's point of view (Nos. 9, 13, 15, 17, then 22, 24: though 15—the policeman reaching down—is ambiguous, the position of the camera being inexact). This second series includes, of course, the famous "vertigo" shot (No. 9) with the simultaneous track-out/zoom/in, an effect repeated later in the two "tower" sequences at the middle and end of the film. The interruption, on which the sequence pivots, gives us the policeman's attempts to save Stewart (with the scene's only dialogue—"Give me your hand") and the start of his fall (Nos. 18, 19, 20), at which point the alternation, thrown temporarily out of rhythm, is resumed.

The sequence represents perhaps the most extreme and abrupt instance of enforced audience identification in all of Hitchcock—an effect to which the technical means (point of view, alternation, "vertigo" shot, even the jarring rhythmic lurch at the policeman's fall) all contribute. Usually, however, he is far more circumspect, building identification gradually through a complicated process of curiosity, sympathy, emotional involvement (see, for instance, the opening of *Psycho*, where the first clearcut POV shot—the street-crossing seen through Marion's windshield—does not occur until about fifteen minutes into the film). What makes possible this drastic and brutal assault? Most obviously, the extreme physical danger (the simplest and most basic of the conditions that encourage spectator identification).

The most obvious factor, but perhaps not the most important. The sequence carries very strong and potent psychoanalytical resonances with as much claim to "universality" as the fear of heights. One such resonance arises from "the fall" itself: one common explanation of dreams of falling (and the sequence's abstraction makes it very dreamlike) is that they reproduce, or at least *refer to*, the birth trauma (from which viewpoint it is interesting that we never see Stewart "let go"). Another, more substantiated by the text, arises from the insistence on *three* characters and their interconnection: they can be taken to represent the fundamental Freudian triumvirate id/ego/superego. The id is associated with unrestrained libido, pursuit of pleasure, hence (in our surplus repressive culture) commonly with criminality. The superego is conscience, the law, the internalized authority of the father—our psychic police officer, in fact. At the opening of *Vertigo*, then, the symbolic father is killed (and the "son," if not the actual agent of his death, is responsible for it), and the id escapes to wander freely in the darkness (reflected, at the end of the film, in the fact that Gavin Elster is never caught). Stewart is left hanging (we never see, or are told, how he gets down): metaphorically, he is suspended for the remainder of the film.

The second sequence (Midge's apartment) offers an even more extreme example of the Hitchcockian principles of fragmentation and alternation: more extreme, because the "action " (mainly an extended conversation) could easily have been filmed in a single take (with the exception of a single "subjective insert"). Hitchcock breaks it down into 62 shots, in only 5 of which the two characters are in frame together. The entire scene is constructed in alternating series broken only at certain privileged moments: Midge/Scottie, female space/male space, each space defined by the framing and by its own significant object (the model brassiere, Scottie's cane) prominent throughout each series.

Apart from the opening establishing shot (whose function, although both characters are in frame, is to stress the distance that separates them), Midge and Scottie are shown together at three points in the action:

a. Shot 31, the exact midpoint and pivot shot of the scene, privileged as its only long take. This covers the conversation about the new brassiere with its "revolutionary uplift": Midge remarks to Scottie, "You know about such things—you're a big boy now," as she initiates him into its secrets.
b. Shots 47 and 48: Scottie suggests a method of overcoming his acrophobia, and Midge promptly takes over as organizer, fetching the set of steps. In the ensuing shots (in which the alternation is resumed), she will "push" Scottie (verbally) to the point where he collapses with an attack of vertigo.
c. Shot 62 (final shot of the sequence): Midge comforts the distraught Scottie in her arms, holding his head to her bosom.

All of these moments have a common theme: the presentation of Midge as mother figure, also made explicit in the dialogue ("Don't be so motherly"; later, in the scene in the nursing home, Midge will say "Mother's here"). The two come together only in the mother-child relationship; otherwise (and crucially in their discussion of their brief engagement and the possibility that it might be renewed) they are kept rigorously separated.

Of the two, only Midge is permitted close-ups (shots 36 and 38), and they are used to comment on Scottie, to call him into question. They occur during the discussion of the engagement ("Good old college days" —Midge), which lasted "three whole weeks" and was called off by Midge herself (despite the fact that "You know there's only one man in the world for me, Johnny-O"). The close-ups emphasize the troubled and enigmatic nature of her glances at Scottie: they suggest an inadequacy in him, an impossibility of a mature relationship, whose nature is left unformulated.

Other components of the film's thematic are introduced during the scene, centered on certain key words or concepts: "free," "available," "wander." a. Scottie is about to become "free" of the corset he has worn since his fall (if it is valid to relate the fall to birth trauma, the corset logically becomes swaddling clothes). The word "freedom" will recur throughout the film, connected to the word "power" and consistently associated with male prerogative, the freedom and power of domination. Gavin Elster, in the next sequence, refers nostalgically to the "power" and "freedom" of the old San Francisco. The bookstore owner, describing the casting aside of Carlotta Valdes, remarks "Men could do that in those days—they had the freedom, they had the power." And Scottie, unmasking Judy/Madeleine at the end of the film, asks her contemptuously if, "with all that freedom and all that power," Elster just "ditched" her. "Freedom," then, is freedom to dominate women, or to throw them over (even murder them) when they become inconvenient. It is associated with the past, when "men could do that"—the past to which "Madeleine" belongs and Midge emphatically does not. b. Scottie is still "available" for marriage ("That's me—Available Ferguson"); but the film, in a brilliant ellipse, instantly connects this sexual "availability" to Gavin Elster (as the old adage has it, "The devil finds work for idle hands"). c. Inherent in Scottie's situation is the notion of "wandering" (though the word itself will not occur until the next scene). With the "father" dead and the "id" at large, Scottie's immediate step has been to leave the police force (the "law"); Midge asks what he intends to do now. He will "Do nothing for a while": he is free to follow desire wherever it leads, to wander. The "freedom," the "availability," the wandering, however, also associate logically with the metaphorical suspension: with the abyss into which Scottie may fall, vividly evoked in what is, remarkably, the sequence's only point-of-view shot, Scottie's hallucinatory vision from the top of Midge's steps. Also relevant here is the question of identity, the fluidity, the lack of definition, of Scottie's being suggested by the range of names he accumulates in the course of the film. He will tell Madeleine "Acquaintances call me Scottie, friends call me John"; he presents himself as "Available Ferguson"; Elster calls him "Scottie"; Midge uses the boy-like "Johnny-O" (at one point "John-O"); Madeleine says "I prefer John," but Judy calls him "Scottie."

The third sequence (divided from the second by Hitchcock's personal appearance and two dissolves, as if to mark it as a decisive new beginning) is also built on alternation patterns, but the series are interrupted much more frequently by two shots. The main purpose of these is to underline (with the additional emphasis of low angle) Elster's growing domination of Scottie as he imposes his story on him. Scottie sits, he stands; when Scottie rises, Elster moves to the room's higher level, dominating even in long shot. Though Elster was Scottie's schoolmate we register him as significantly older (partly because we habitually think of James Stewart as young, even in middle age, "boyishness" being one of the basic components of his star persona). He becomes, in fact, a new father figure, but a father "outside the law" (the dialogue stresses Scottie's withdrawal from the police force): in terms of the traces of Catholic mythology that linger on in Hitchcock's work, he is the Devil, his function being essentially that of tempter. He knows Scottie's weaknesses, and in effect offers him his own wife, Madeleine (the film never invites us to take any interest in his plot to murder his *real* wife). Madeleine's fascination for Scottie is set up before she appears: Elster presents her as a feminine mirror image. She "wanders" (from this point on the word will weave through the film, repeatedly linking Scottie and Madeleine); and there is also the question of *her* identity (Madeleine Elster, Carlotta Valdes?—though the name itself is not introduced until later). Above all, Elster tempts Scottie with "power" and "freedom," marked by a striking cut on dialogue: 1. Back view, Scottie looking at the print of old San Francisco; Elster speaks of ". . . color, excitement, power . . ." 2. Cut to medium shot of Elster against a window through which we can see the cranes of his shipbuilding yard; he completes the sentence: ". . . freedom." The image associates the term with wealth, industry, and the possibility of escape (abroad, or into the past), after which the conversation shifts to Scottie's task: the surveillance of Madeleine.

The fourth sequence (Ernie's) offers us (and Scottie) Madeleine: indeed, it is important that she appears to *offer herself*, at least to the gaze. The fascination is conveyed in the sequence's first shot: starting from Scottie at the bar, and as if taking its impetus from his look, the camera draws back over the restaurant, turns, cranes, then moves slowly in toward Madeleine's back, her shoulders exposed above an emerald green dress (the green with which, both as Madeleine and as Judy, she will be associated throughout the film, and which links her ironically to the *sequoia semper-virens*, "always green, ever-living"). It is not (cannot possibly be) a point-of-view shot, yet it has the effect of linking us intimately to the movement of Scottie's consciousness. The camera movement is utterly unlike anything in the film up to that point, introducing a completely new tone, the grace and tenderness underlined by Bernard Herrmann's music. Madeleine is presented in terms of the "work of art" (which is precisely what she is): her movement through the doorway suggests a portrait coming to life, or a gliding statue; when she pauses, turns her head into profile, the suggestion is of a "cameo" or silhouette, an image that will recur throughout the film. As "work of art" Madeleine is at once totally accessible (a painting is completely passive, offering itself to the gaze) and totally *in*accessible (you can't make love to a picture).

At this point it becomes possible to draw all the threads together; but to do so it is necessary to digress again briefly into psychoanalytical theory, to consider the nature of desire and how it is constituted within patriarchal culture. The first love object, prototype of all subsequent love objects, is the mother's breast, to which the infant, traditionally, is put immediately after birth. The infant is born totally under the sway of of the pleasure principle (which Freud associates with the id): the infant has no sense of otherness, no sense of the mother as an autonomous person; the expectation is of instant, total, always available gratification. This innate "original desire" (I mean the term at once to evoke and oppose the familiar Catholic interpretation of Hitchcock in relation to original sin) immediately comes into conflict with the reality principle and has to learn to modify itself to accommodate the facts of existence, but it remains the basis upon which adult desire is built. It is also, of course, what adult desire must *transcend* if any equality in relationship is to be achieved, though it will still be ultimately dependent upon it for its energy. It is essential to the logic of patriarchy that "original desire" be repressed in women (it would promote bisexuality and sexual activeness, what Freud termed the woman's "masculinity") and encouraged in men. The heterosexual male—our ideological lord of the universe—is taught from infancy to believe in his superiority, his inherited rights: the right, essentially, to power and freedom. The possibility of regression to the infantile state, the unconditional demand for the "lost breast," is therefore much stronger in men than in women. The most obvious manifestation of this regression is the phenomenon called "romantic love," with its demand for perfect union and its tendency to construct the loved person as an idealized fantasy figure: the necessary condition for "perfect union" being the denial of otherness and autonomy. It is this regression that *Vertigo* so incomparably dramatizes: I know of no other film that so ruthlessly analyzes the basis of male desire and exposes its mechanisms.

Around this, everything falls into place: the reactivation of the birth trauma actually accompanied by the death of the father; the urge for freedom and "wandering"; the rejection of Midge; the appearance of Gavin Elster as tempter; the gift of Madeleine. One may ask why Midge, who so clearly offers herself as a mother, is impossible for Scottie; there are a number of answers. For one thing, she is too *explicitly* the mother: as such, she is a reminder to Scottie of his dependence. More important, the "lost breast" is not to be identified with an actual mother: on the contrary, the crucial characteristic of the object of original desire is that it be capable of being totally dominated, with no autonomous existence or desire of its own. As "mother," Midge is dominating and active, a defined ego, with her own drives and demands, the chief of which is that Scottie learn to grow up: what she wants is a relationship of equals. Further, she demystifies sexuality (specifically in relation to the breast, explaining the mechanics of the brassiere), and for the romantic lover sex must always remain mystified. She is finally disqualified by her accessibility.

It is obvious that "original desire" can never be fulfilled: the "lost breast" cannot be refound because it never existed. The fantasy of fulfillment depends, paradoxically, on the inaccessibility of the object. "Madeleine" dies (both times) at the moments when she threatens to become a real person. It will be clear that, as a construct, a "work of art," she perfectly satisfies every condition for the lover's fantasy. When she dies, she has to be re-created; when she is Judy, Scottie can't bear to touch her. One of the cinema's most perverse (and most "romantic") love scenes—so perverse it couldn't possibly be filmed—is the scene implied after Scottie brings Madeleine back from her plunge into San Francisco Bay: he undresses the woman he loves believing her to be unconscious, while in reality she is *pretending* to be unconscious. It is the nearest the romantic lover can come to physical union without sacrificing something of his fantasy. Judy's unforgivable crime is not accessory to murder, or even duplicity: it is that she isn't "really" Madeleine.

Madeleine's ultimate fascination lies in her association with death (as Carlotta she is already dead). As "original desire" can never be fulfilled in life, to surrender to it is to give oneself over to the death drive: hence the "Romantic" obsession with unions in death, of which Wagner's *Tristan und Isolde* is the supreme expression in Western culture (it can be no accident that the *Liebestod* is repeatedly evoked, though never actually quoted, in Herrmann's score).

Whatever the conscious motivation, the importance of Hitchcock's decision to divulge the solution of the mystery two-thirds of the way through the film cannot be underestimated. Until that point the spectator is locked almost exclusively into Scottie's consciousness (the only exceptions are three brief moments involving Midge, which hint at the possibility of critical distance but are not strong enough to offset the dominant identification pattern): the fascination Scottie feels for Madeleine is also his. (I use the masculine deliberately—the spectator constructed by the film is clearly male.) The shock we experience at the revelation goes far beyond anything that can be accounted for merely in terms of premature disclosure, testifying to the power and "universality" (within our culture) of the desire drive the film dramatizes: we also, at first, can't forgive Judy for not being Madeleine, in whose reality we have been seduced into investing so much.

The revelation immediately exposes the entire "romantic love" project of the first two-thirds as a fantasy and a fraud; thus it turns us back, quite ruthlessly, on to Scottie and on to ourselves. It also gives us access to Judy, who is not a "work of art" but a human being, thus exposing the monstrousness of a project built upon the "infantile" demands of the regressed male ego and its denial of the woman's human reality. Judy never becomes the film's central consciousness. She is permitted only six point-of-view shots during the entire film (as against the number given to Scottie, which must run into three figures). Four of these (two pairs, precisely symmetrical) are simply shots of trees through the car windshield during the two drives to San Juan Baptista. A fifth is ambiguous: the shot of the broken petals on the water just before Judy/Madeleine's false attempted suicide, a shot enclosed within an elaborate structure of Scottie's point of view and equally readable as *his* empathic image of what Madeleine sees. Only one shot from Judy's point of view actually excludes Scottie and comments on him: the shot of lovers on the grass as they walk by the lake and the "Portals of the Past" (it stands out the more for being an example of that privileged Hitchcock fingerprint the subjective forward tracking shot).

Scottie's remains the central consciousness; what changes is our relationship to him. Identification is not so much annihilated as severely disturbed, made problematic. We now know far more than *he* does, and what we know reflects critically on him, on our own prior identification with him, and on the whole concept of romantic love on which our culture has placed such high ideological value. Throughout the scenes with Judy-as-Judy, the film's dominant system of alternating series based on Scottie's point of view partly breaks down: point-of-view shots are not absent (Judy seen in the upper window of the Empire Hotel, as "Madeleine" was in the McKittrick Hotel; notably the "cameo" shot of Judy in silhouette/profile when Scottie brings her home from Ernie's after their first date), but their number greatly decreases, to be built up again strongly as Scottie reconstructs Judy as Madeleine. That the film's efforts to reinvolve us in Scottie's consciousness and the project of reconstructing what we know to be a fantasy are *partly* successful testifies again to the immense power of "original desire" and its derivative, romantic love, within our culture. (Like the film, I am assuming that the spectator is male; one looks forward eagerly, now that *Vertigo* is once again accessible, to articles on it by women.) It takes the final, agonizing scenes, and Madeleine's second death, to exorcise this decisively, but of course the total and unquestioning identification invited by the first part of the film is no longer possible: we are now too aware that the fantasy *is* fantasy, and too aware of it as imposition on the woman. The last third of *Vertigo* is among the most disturbing and painful experiences the cinema has to offer.

19
YOU FREUD, ME HITCHCOCK: *MARNIE* REVISITED

DOES MARK CURE MARNIE?

I am indebted, for the above heading (as for much else), to V. F. Perkins.[1] I understand that he made it an exam question at the British university where he teaches Film Studies, and it remains, in its casual succinctness, remarkably suggestive as a stimulus to thinking about the film. It is probable, today, that no one will wish to respond with an unequivocal "Yes": we have lived with *Marnie* (1964) for nearly forty years now, and its complexities and perplexities ("There. There now"), its enigmas and its contradictions—its richness, in short—have gradually revealed themselves, making simple answers impossible. As with all great works of art, everyone will have his or her own *Marnie*. There will of course be plenty of common ground (or discussion would become impossible), but there will be many differences of emphasis. What follows is *my Marnie*, as of today; I cannot promise that I shan't be offering a different, modified and qualified, version ten years from now. My new account effectively supersedes the old, but I am glad to have them both within the same book: they represent steps toward an understanding of the film which is still incomplete. With *Vertigo, Marnie* (while remaining somewhat precariously within the field of "popular entertainment") is Hitchcock's nearest approach to an art house movie, confirming the now not uncommon view of Hitchcock as a "modernist," in many respects to be placed with Antonioni and Bergman as much as with other "commercial" Hollywood filmmakers. It is surely his most difficult film, its demands upon the spectator becoming more apparent the more one sees it.

1. A hastily written (and much shorter) version of this chapter appeared in *CineAction* 50 (1999): 80–85, the Hitchcock/Cukor Centenary issue. It was Victor Perkins who persuaded me that my argument required a fuller and more analytical treatment to be convincing.

One major difference between what I write today and what I wrote in the original *Hitchcock's Films* (very shortly after the film's first release) will be immediately plain: at that time it was necessary to defend the film, received by the majority of journalist critics, like *Vertigo* before it, as yet more evidence of Hitchcock's decline (which for certain diehards had begun when he left Britain for Hollywood). Today, those of us who value Hitchcock highly are likely to place it only a little below *Vertigo* in our valuation of his work, on a level with, say, *Rear Window*, *Notorious*, and the first half of *Psycho*. Yet if the film's glaring antirealist devices (the red suffusions, traveling mattes, painted backdrops, melodramatically motivated thunderstorms), all of which it obviously flaunts rather than seeks to disguise, no longer require defense, they do I think require some definition, some rationale, and for this one need turn only to Hitchcock's own frequently reiterated definition of his art as the achievement of "pure cinema," of which *Vertigo* and *Marnie* are the most extreme manifestations.

"Pure cinema" was, for Hitchcock, the art of putting pieces of film together to create effects. The formula (an instance of Hitchcock's characteristic offhand modesty, his refusal to make any claims for himself beyond the technical/aesthetic, carefully screening himself from any necessity to delve into the painfully personal obsessions that are the films' ultimate motivating force) is far too simple to describe what he actually achieved: he makes it sound like an elementary exercise in editing more appropriate to a film school student than a major artist. Much more than editing is involved, and what finally matters is the *kind* and *quality* of the effects achieved, their nature, their value, their complexity, their intensity. We know that much of the work preceded the actual shooting: collaboration with the writers, control over the finished screenplay, the choice of actors, the meticulous shot-by-shot storyboarding to the extent that he could claim (though it is a claim we should always take with several pinches of salt) that he knew exactly what every shot would be before the first call of "Action!" *Marnie* can stand as the supreme manifestation of this particular concept of cinema: from shot to shot, gesture to gesture, line to line, expression to expression, reaction to reaction, frame to frame, composition to composition, the film exemplifies the summation of Hitchcock's virtuosity. Any of the great set-pieces would demonstrate this: the opening ten minutes, the first robbery at Rutland's, the honeymoon, the hunt and its culmination in the shooting of the horse Forio, the climactic scene of reclaimed memory. But the same goes for the lengthy and apparently static dialogue sequences—for example, the central Mark/Marnie duologue (car/Howard Johnson's/car): yes, it's just two people talking, but every exchange is perfectly judged, in emphasis and tempo, and the buildup of tension is as much a matter of editing as of acting. This kind of perfection can come only from an artist working at the highest pitch of sustained imaginative-emotional involvement, and *Marnie* is clearly among Hitchcock's most intensely personal films.

Obviously, this form of "pure cinema" represents a totally artificial concept of film; in lesser hands, without the artist's full engagement, it could easily degenerate into an intellectual exercise, mere "cleverness" (which is why Hitchcock cannot be successfully imitated). To talk of "artificiality" is by no means to denigrate the actors: everyone in the film is flawless, from Tippi Hedren and Sean Connery down to Cousin Bob, or Bruce Dern's sailor, or the gauche young office assistant who tries to interest Marnie in a Danish, or even the Howard Johnson's waitress who, totally unaware of the tension, the undercurrents of suppressed rage, the possible eruption of panic, tells the warring couple to "Be sure to come back now" to this utterly mundane and impersonal drive-in off the freeway. Yet ultimately everything depends upon the meticulous assemblage of (usually) brief shots: we are very far removed from the actor-centered cinema of a Renoir or a McCarey, from all that we call "Realist" cinema. The artifice is so transparent, our long-habituated commitment to "the realistic" so hard to overcome, that what is most remarkable is that, even while we are aware of it, awed by the sheer virtuosity, we never lose our emotional involvement (it is almost the only Hitchcock film that invariably, even after repeated viewings, reduces me to uncontrollable sobs at two climactic points). The creative intensity is never a matter of skill alone.

It is this concept of cinema (rooted, however distantly, in Hitchcock's earliest influence, his exposure to the German expressionist cinema of the 1920s), its effects achieved not by representing "reality" but by assembling little scraps of celluloid, that easily allows for the most obvious artifice: the backdrops, the traveling matte for Marnie's horseback-riding, the red suffusions for her moments of traumatic threat, the thunderstorms occurring at emotional highpoints. Once one accepts the principle nothing is barred. But the artifice serves a function beyond this. At the beginning of *Rebecca* the second Mrs. De Winter (Joan Fontaine) "dreamed that I went to Manderley again," and in *Spellbound* (a film in obvious ways superficially related to *Marnie*) John Ballantine (Gregory Peck) narrates his dream to Constance (Ingrid Bergman). But I believe I am right in saying that *Vertigo* and *Marnie* are the only two Hitchcock films in which we actually see the protagonist dream (both Jimmy Stewart's Scottie and Tippi Hedren's Marnie, in fact, awaken screaming from nightmares), and these are surely Hitchcock's two most dreamlike films; it is no coincidence that they are the two in which the artifice of "pure cinema" is most pronounced. In both films the protagonist (with whom we are invited to identify) is largely helpless (Scottie trapped in his obsession, his "wandering," Marnie in her neurotic compulsions), the helplessness having certain affinities with the dream-state. The oneiric effect (for the spectator) is created primarily through the surface unreality of "pure cinema," giving us access to the deeper "reality" of dreams. It is more pervasive (more fully and consistently realized) in *Vertigo*, a triumph made possible by the extreme logic of the narrative, in which every step necessitates the next with dreamlike inevitability until the rude awakening of Judy's (Kim Novak) confession. *Marnie*'s narrative is more cumbersome, its complicated plot demanding digressions, hiatuses, its identification demands less rigorous (as announced in the first two scenes, which switch us abruptly from Marnie to Mark). Yet the oneiric quality is there, very strongly if more intermittently, in the horseback-riding sequences (dreams of escape and transcendence), in the thunderstorm episodes and the moments of returning trauma when Marnie literally "sees red" (nightmares of dread and panic), in the painted backdrop of the huge ship at the end of Bernice's road, that seems to block any possibility of exit, and in the hunt (where dream turns into nightmare with the accident and the shooting of Forio), culminating in the nightmarish terrors of memory regained. Even the little girls who seem permanently at play outside Bernice's house, forever chanting "Mother, Mother, I am ill . . . ," seem like figures from a recurring dream, a reminder to Marnie of her own childhood.

The appropriateness of this dream quality should be clear by the film's end. Marnie, since the trauma (together with what we are led to infer of its before and after—her childhood with Bernice), has lost contact with external reality: her "reality" is almost entirely subjective. Hence her whole life is a kind of dream, descending at times of stress into nightmare. This partly answers one possible objection to the film, that Marnie is too extreme a case to have universal meaning: she can be read as an exaggeration of all of us. Who can claim to view reality with complete objectivity? We are born as "subjects," and the development of our subjectivity is determined by our childhood environment, Freud's "first five years."

Today, for many, the problem—the challenge—of *Marnie*, the cause of varying degrees of uneasiness, is not the obvious artifice but Mark Rutland (Sean Connery) and Hitchcock's largely sympathetic (though by no means uncritical) presentation of him. Before I tackle Victor Perkins's question of whether Mark cures Marnie (and whether she *is* in fact cured, and of what exactly, and is Mark cured as well?), it seems necessary today to raise another. Hitchcock made the film just at the time when the women's movement was beginning to sensitize us to those major problems of sex and gender that assumed such prominence during the following decade (unnoticed in my original account, written before I had ever heard the term "sexual politics")—problems that have tended to place Mark rather than Marnie at the center of debate. One crucial, notorious sequence brings the problem into focus, demanding a subsidiary question: Does Mark *rape* Marnie? Hitchcock himself expressed a certain uneasiness or uncertainty about Mark in his characteristically jokey trailer for the film (Mark is tender and caring but also dark and menacing, combining characteristics of hero and villain), and the attitude deducible from the film itself is markedly ambivalent. (Victor Perkins once said to me that it is a great film about Marnie but less than satisfactory as a film about Mark; I shall argue subsequently that Hitchcock's presentation of Mark is in fact very satisfying, the twin aspects of the ambivalence very precisely realized.) The problem is that Mark offends many of our most preciously guarded beliefs in political correctness, yet appears to emerge as the film's hero. Hence the tendency I have noted in recent years to demonize him, treating him as a monster of male chauvinism, with pro- and anti-Hitchcock variants according to whether the presentation is seen as critical or sympathetic. We may find this tempting (alighting at whatever point within the offered range), but it does the film great violence, especially to its final sequences: it demands that we see the ending as worse than ambiguous or hesitant, that we read Marnie as simply choosing one prison over another, and perhaps even making the wrong choice. Finding the presentation of Mark *both* critical *and* sympathetic, I hope to set the record straight, grounding my (partial) defense of Mark (despite my mistrust of the species Great White Heterosexual Male, aka Lord of the Earth) so securely in the film's detail that it will prove incontrovertible. Those who can't accept Mark on any terms will, I'm afraid, have to abandon the film on the grounds of its sexual politics.

The problem of the (alleged) "rape" scene did not begin with the completed film: it was responsible for Hitchcock's dismissal of Evan Hunter as screenwriter and his replacement with Jay Presson Allen. Hunter had written the screenplay for *The Birds,* and the occasional weaknesses of that film are (it seems to me) directly attributable to the occasionally awkward dialogue (the lengthy Melanie/Annie conversation about Mitch) and schematicism (the debate in the Tides Restaurant). While working on *Marnie* he tried to convince Hitchcock that the "rape" would irreparably alienate audiences from Mark and the film would consequently fail. When Hitchcock persisted in his original demands, Hunter sent him a version of the sequence that, in its extremeness ("the struggle on her face, her clawing hands, her twisting head, her terrified eyes . . ."), would obviously be unacceptable, together with a version in which Mark, seeing Marnie's terror, gives in and forgoes intercourse altogether. Clearly, Hitchcock was meant to see his error and accept the latter version.[2] He didn't, and Hunter left the film.

It was left to Jay Presson Allen to solve the problem, which she managed with elegance, producing a compromise rich in suggestion. The scene, like so many in the film, invites detailed examination. It is preceded by the brief scene at dinner on the ship in which Mark (who has already promised not to impose himself on Marnie sexually) tells her about a beautiful tropical flower that is in fact composed of thousands of tiny insects, disguised as a defense against birds. Marnie is at her most artificial, her hair swept up in an unbecoming pseudo-aristocratic style,

2. At least, this is what I deduce from the section devoted to the *Marnie* screenplay in Dan Auiler's indispensable but maddeningly confusing *Hitchcock's Notebooks.* The section is, as printed, incomprehensible. It begins (p. 244) with what purports to be "how Hunter preferred the scene," but what we are given is clearly Presson Allen's final version; it continues (p. 259) with "how the finished screenplay reads," opening with two characters ("Christopher" and "Terry") who don't appear in the film anywhere, then moving into dialogue that is barely recognizable. Hopefully, all copies containing these blunders have long since been withdrawn and replaced with corrected copies, but readers are warned to be careful when they shop.

her face frigid. Mark's story refers us back to Hitchcock's previous film and to Tippi Hedren's role in it, drawing attention to the similarities between her two characters, their common use of façades for protection. What follows represents the first decisive step in the erosion of Marnie's. Mark is reading a book on marine life, a large tumbler of whiskey, still about two-thirds full, beside him. Marnie appears in the bedroom door-way: "I'll close the door if you don't mind. The light bothers me." She speaks politely and the request is natural enough, but we may perhaps ask why she couldn't simply close the door herself, quietly, rather than interrupting his reading and giving him the opportunity (which he seizes) to begin a conversation. He tells her, with loaded irony, that he is anxious to find a subject they could talk about. She now seizes *her* opportunity to provoke ("How long? How long do we have to stay on this boat, this trip?"), and when this unleashes further sarcasm ("Are you suggesting . . . that these halcyon days and nights, just the two of us, should ever end?") she slams the door, presumably disturbed by the sexual connotations of his remark. But slamming the door is of course exactly the way to provoke him further, and he leaps up.

The bedroom: Marnie in her nightdress, Mark confronting her. She tells him, "If you don't want to go to bed, please get out." Again, the remark has superficial reasonableness, yet the reference to "going to bed" has its own sexual connotations, which he immediately takes up ("But I *do* want to go to bed, Marnie. I very much want to go to bed"). His response to her suddenly frantic "No!" is to tear off her nightdress, and it is at this point that Marnie's reactions seem, at least, surprising, and no longer carry any obvious logic. She remains absolutely still, naked, making no attempt to turn away or cover herself.

Mark is immediately penitent and ashamed ("I'm sorry, Marnie"). He removes his dressing-gown and places it gently around her shoulders, concealing her nakedness. But she still doesn't move, and it is clearly because of this that he takes her head in his hands, kisses her with great tenderness (Hitchcock cutting into extreme close-up to emphasize this), using no force whatever. We can if we wish read Marnie's immobility in terms of trauma; Mark clearly reads it as acquiescence, and I don't think anything in the staging or acting proves him necessarily wrong. She must realize (from his ashamed reaction to his brutal gesture and her nudity) that she has only to say "No," or merely turn away, to end the encounter. Marnie lies back on the bed, still completely passive; from her point of view we see Mark, in close-up, lower himself upon her, his eyes staring into hers, his face dark and frightening.

So, does Mark rape Marnie? My own answer is that Marnie may experience it as rape, but Mark does not know—and cannot know—that he is raping her.

The ambiguity of Marnie's behavior is clarified in the immediate sequel. The camera pans away from Marnie's face to a porthole, the sea dark beyond. Fade to black, fade in to same view. It is now the first light of morning. The camera pans back, precisely reversing its trajectory, across Marnie's now-empty bed to Mark. At almost the same second, we hear a door close and see him stir. There follows his discovery of the attempted suicide: Marnie face down in the pool, arms outstretched. We scarcely need his question as to why she didn't just jump overboard to alert us to the sense that this is a highly suspect suicide attempt: Marnie has waited until dawn (we can't imagine her sleeping, after her experience)—waited, perhaps, for the first signs that Mark is about to wake up. Her position in the pool summons up another instance of intertextual reference: it is exactly the position of *Vertigo*'s Judy/Madeleine in San Francisco Bay, a "suicide attempt" we know (in retrospect) to be faked. Marnie's slick, smart response to Mark's question ("The idea was to kill myself, not feed the damn fish") sounds very much like something she has prepared beforehand.

But what I am offering here is by no means a suggestion that Marnie has merely been playacting: her sexual terror is plainly genuine, the suicide attempt close enough to success to suggest that on one level she *wanted* to die. What interests me here is precisely this suggestion of different levels operating simultaneously, yet in a remarkably audacious reworking of Freud, entailing a reversal of his teaching. According to Freud, during the typical analysis the patient has a conscious desire for cure which is continuously impeded by an unconscious resistance. What Hitchcock seems to be postulating in *Marnie* is that there might be a very strong conscious resistance (obvious enough in Marnie's case), with an *unconscious* desire for cure constantly pulling against it. At every step in the (so-called) rape sequence and its aftermath one can read Marnie as unconsciously provoking Mark's actions, but the conscious/unconscious duality can be read most clearly in the meticulously planned (by Hitchcock as much as by Marnie) suicide attempt. On the level of full consciousness Marnie believes she is trying to kill herself because the "horror" of male sexuality, together with its constant threat in the person of Mark, now her legal husband (and blackmailer) from whom she has no means of escape, is intolerable. But just below this level, the attempt (like most such attempts) is a cry for help: she has waited for daybreak, perhaps seen Mark stirring in his sleep, allowed the closing of the door to be audible, perhaps even prepared a "witty" line "just in case" he rescues her. I find much confirmation of this reading in subsequent sequences.

"YOU FREUD, ME JANE?"

The mock-psychoanalysis sequence has been the occasion for a certain amount of ribaldry among the film's (and Hitchcock's) detractors: How stupid (they say) of the filmmaker to take seriously Mark's belief that he can cure Marnie by reading a few books. The filmmaker, of course, doesn't, and the laugh is on the laughers (or on Mark). In fact, the tone of the whole sequence (complex, inextricably combining irony, comedy, intense drama) is perfectly judged. Certainly, we are not supposed to find Mark stupid: in an extremely painful domestic situation characterized primarily by sexual and emotional frustration, he is doing his best, even if his best is none too good. Why shouldn't he (married to Marnie) read books about psychoanalysis, criminality, and *Frigidity in Women* (one of the titles we are offered, along with the remarkable *Sexual Aberrations of the Criminal Female*)? My point is that the sequence does not anywhere suggest that Mark has gained any particularly useful insights from them, or that they give him any right to believe that he can actually help Marnie by applying their teachings. Mark is not unintelligent; his weakness is male presumption, not stupidity. Marnie treats the presumption ironically and, although she is not altogether an easy identification-figure, I think we must share her position here, as Hitchcock clearly does. (That Marnie, apparently such a "special case" with an extremely detailed and specific case history, can become our center of identification to the extent she obviously does, is an issue I shall return to later. Suffice it to say for the moment, with Freud, that, as the bases of neurosis are all present in so-called "normal" life, "We are all ill.")

The sequence is introduced by a recurrence of Marnie's nightmare; we witnessed an earlier one in her bedroom in Bernice's house in Baltimore.

There, we were allowed to see only Marnie tossing on the bed; this one is more elaborate, offering us more clues (the hand, with a white sleeve, tapping at the window; Marnie's reluctance to get out of bed), as if the threat of memory were becoming stronger, closer. Hitchcock stages it in a way that recalls the extraordinary moment in *Vertigo* where Scottie and the reconstructed Madeleine embrace and the background (Judy's apartment) shifts, without a cut, to the stable of the Catholic mission. There, disturbing the moment's willed ecstasy, we saw Scottie's expression change to bewilderment, doubt, fear, as if he sensed that his reconstruction of Madeleine were too perfect to be true. With Marnie's nightmare, we first see her lying (inexplicably) on a cheap sofa on which is a cushion with "Aloha" printed on it (we can assume, the rest of the film familiar to us, that it was a gift from one of Bernice's sailor-customers). The level of reality is difficult to read: if Marnie is dreaming this, she must be dreaming of herself as a child, but what we see is the adult Marnie; the sofa (unlike the one we see in the memory flashback) is against a wall; at this stage of the trauma-scene the child Marnie would still be in her bed. Such complexities (or contradictions) underline the film's sophistication: in so many films where a dream has been used to explain the past, the dream has been much too literal. We *never* simply recover the past, as it happened, in our dreams, there is always the kind of disturbing confusion that is registered here. From Marnie's tossing and moaning on the sofa the camera pans across to show, first, the hand tapping on the window, and then (as in *Vertigo*, without a visible cut) the Rutland bedroom, with Marnie tossing and moaning in her four-poster. The two scenes, so far apart in the dramatized situation, have in common their fundamental quandary: the desire to know set against the dread of knowing. In both films the protagonist will reach full knowledge, but with almost diametrically opposed results: *Vertigo* ends in night, darkness, and irreplaceable loss; *Marnie* in the light of morning and tentative affirmation. Marnie's earlier nightmare was interrupted by Bernice (alias Mrs. Bates: the overtones of the shot of her in silhouette on the stairs, with the stick that will be a crux of the film's climax, will not be lost on anyone who knows their Hitchcock); the later one is interrupted by Mark. The opposition is exact: the woman who wants, above all, to *conceal* Marnie's past contrasted with the man, who wants, above all, to reveal it to her. The recurrent nightmare, with its increasing explicitness, can be read as the impetus behind Marnie's (unconscious) decision to take control of the ensuing psychoanalysis sequence and force herself to the point of breakdown.

It is Mark who initiates the standard psychoanalytic procedure, first by staging the "correct" setting (doctor upright on chair, patient lying on couch, in this case a fourposter), then by introducing the favorite cliché (not quite "Tell me your dreams," but "That dream. You've had it before . . . It's about your mother. She wants you to get up"). But Marnie immediately contributes, offering what clues her consciousness possesses (crucially the "three taps," which will provide Mark with the information he needs in the "reclaimed memory" sequence, but also "If I get up I'll be cold and they'll hurt her . . . I'll be cold and I'll hear the noises"—presumably the noises of sexual intercourse). It is Mark's "doctor"-like prompting ("What noises? Who makes them?") that brings her to full awareness of what is going on ("You Freud, me Jane?"), from which point she, rather than Mark, virtually controls the "session," teasing, taunting, transposing their "correct" positions so that for a moment *she* becomes the analyst ("Talk about dreamworlds, you've got a pathological fix on a woman who's not only a criminal but who screams if you come near her. So what about *your* dreams, Daddy dear?").

But having thoroughly undermined his position of dominance, she ironically reinstates it, knowing that she is now in control yet needing him to push her on to what her unconscious knows is the necessary step ("You're really dying to play doctor, aren't you?"): she introduces the "free association" technique ("Are you ready?"). Mark sits in silence, looking defeated, as if "ready" to get up and leave. So she goads him on: "Well come *on*. I thought you wanted to play doctor, so let's play"—it's become a command. The free association leads inevitably (as Marnie somehow knows it must) to the color red, and her breakdown ("Oh help me. Oh God, won't somebody help me"—first apparently a plea to Mark, then transferred to the more generalized "somebody"). Enter Mr. Strutt (Martin Gabel), at the end of the next shot (the party, with its *Notorious*-style crane down from panorama to detail), as if, praying for a friend, Marnie had inadvertently summoned up her worst enemy. But Strutt is necessary to the process of disintegration, and before Marnie's constructed façade crumbles there can be no new beginning; the grub cannot emerge from its cocoon.

So, "Does Mark cure Marnie?" No, essentially she brings about her own cure. But Mark is necessary: she uses him as her primary instrument.

"I BELIEVE WE'VE MET BEFORE"

In the analysis scene the implicit, unconscious cry for help of the attempted suicide has become fully conscious and explicit; we want Marnie to go on from there. The immediate effect of Strutt's appearance is blockage, our desire thwarted or at least delayed: we are only incidentally interested in whether Marnie will have to go to prison, our primary interest now being the truth about the childhood trauma. In Hitchcock's greatest films, where his emotional involvement is strongest, the root of all evil (as well as the route toward potential salvation) is always sex, not money (see, for example, the transference of interest in *Psycho* from the stolen $40,000 to "Mrs. Bates"). The next major step in Marnie's journey back to memory will be the hunt and its aftermath, with which Strutt has no direct connection.

But, besides the irony—Marnie's desperate plea for help "answered" by the intrusion into her home of the man who can do her the most harm—Strutt's reappearance in the film at this precise moment has its immediate significance. At the party, Marnie, and the way in which she relates to her husband, have undergone a transformation (which we can only see as the result of her breakdown, the scene following straight on). Playing society hostess (her hair up again, a return to the "artificial" mode of the honeymoon), she appears relaxed, confident of her role, superficially happy, and she treats Mark as a friend. What this suggests is the possibility of reaching a workable *modus vivendi* without the pain of cure: a life (presumably sexless) in which the couple settle for the comfortable, at the expense of all emotional depth. Strutt's reappearance shatters this possibility, replacing it with a new crisis.

"ARE YOU STILL IN THE MOOD FOR KILLING?"

From the beginning of the hunt there are no further hiatuses in the narrative; it moves forward inexorably to its climax and beyond to the final shot, every event leading directly to the next in logical steps.

Perhaps one also needs Strutt's destruction of the "society hostess" façade to prepare for Marnie's breakdown during the hunt—though the horror of the "kill," combined with the scarlet hunting jackets, is so great as to render it almost superfluous. Oscar Wilde's marvelous definition ("The unspeakable in pursuit of the uneatable") scarcely conveys the loathesomeness of the mutually congratulating participants whose smug laughter seems to upset Marnie more, even, than the pervasive brutality. The death of the fox, with its essential innocence, brings memory closer, adding a further component of the traumatic experience: the fox, like Bernice's sailor, was only pursuing its natural needs, and if both were in a strict sense predators (whether in search of chickens or prostitutes), neither thought of it quite in that way.

Marnie's flight, with its aggregation of unashamedly nonrealist "effects" (traveling matte, rapid editing of densely patterned, stylized close-ups, combined with agonizingly suspended time stretching the sensation of panic and terror) is the culmination of the film's oneiric quality, a nightmare shared by the spectator. It is a flight not only from the hunt but from the buried memory, yet its immediate sequel brings the memory closer than ever before through reenactment. We cannot say here, I think, that Marnie unconsciously wills the accident. Yet she rides a long way (not knowing that Lil [Diane Baker], Mark's former sister-in-law, is following), across fields and over fences, before she grasps (on seeing the brick wall) that there is real danger, and struggles, too late, to rein in. What is most significant here is her insistence that *she* be the one to kill Forio. The film goes out of its way to suggest that she has other options. Lil's offer to do it for her provokes Marnie's "Are you still in the mood for killing?," referring immediately to Lil's participation in the hunt, but beyond that, less literally, to the fact that it was Lil who sent the invitation to Strutt; and Lil's subsequent offer to fetch "one of the men" is ignored, Marnie now standing over Forio as if in a trance, gun pointed. Marnie's question, in fact, can also be read as referring ironically to herself: it is she who is "still" (i.e., since the traumatic event) "in the mood for killing," her unconscious driving her to reenact the past in order to restore it to her, making it at last accessible to consciousness.

But her immediate reaction is to deny it, by going to the Rutland office to steal the money from the safe, thereby insisting upon her fabricated persona. The simultaneous zoom-in/track-out (another borrowing from *Vertigo*), potentially the most alienating, in its primitive violence, of all Hitchcock's devices, is in fact the perfect visualization of Marnie's internal conflict: the desire to take the money (zoom-in), her conscious resistance to cure, now in direct and jarring conflict with the unconscious (track-out) striving toward it.

"THERE. THERE NOW."

Through her dreams and symbolic reenactments, Marnie has now reassembled most of the major components of the traumatic experience. It remains for Mark to take the initiative, forcing her to face the actual event, discover the facts behind it, and confront not merely what happened but her own active participation. Only then will she be able to speak (to herself as much as to the murdered sailor) the words she spoke when she killed Forio, the words of "laying to rest." Yet Hitchcock seems determined, right to the end, that nothing in this remarkable film shall be simple. The "reclaimed memory" sequence, if we read it carefully, casts some doubt on whether Marnie *ever* remembers everything correctly. If she doesn't, then can the cure be complete?.

The crux of this lies in the discrepancies between text and image. The most obvious is Marnie's "I hit him. I hit him with a *stick*" (the stress is Marnie's—or Hitchcock's—not mine), when what we see is her hitting the sailor with a large fire-iron, a hooked poker. But there is also her assertion (again in her child voice) that the sailor was hitting her mother, when what we are shown is the mother hitting *him*. We have, surely, to trust the images, not the verbal commentary: in other words, only the spectator has access to the whole truth, while Marnie's account of it is subject to distortions and inaccuracies. But if this is the case, how much of that account *can* we trust? The discrepancies force us to look at the details of the images and reinterpret Marnie's words in relation to them.

"I hit him with a *stick*": it is Bernice who carries a stick-cane (because of her damaged leg) throughout the film. Marnie's words imply that she is identifying with Bernice, doing what Bernice wanted done. Similarly with the hands: for Marnie, Bernice cannot be hitting the sailor, it has to be the other way round; Bernice has to be pure victim. This must, I think, lead us to see that Marnie misreads the sailor's actions and motivation throughout the scene.

"He came *out*. He came out to *me*." Marnie knows (from her mother) that terrible and disgusting things happen in that back room whenever she is taken out of her bed and dumped on the living-room sofa; not only do they "happen," they are done to Bernice by men. Marnie doesn't know quite what these things are (she hears "noises"), but now she believes they are going to be done to *her*. Perhaps the film's most terrible irony is that the sailor is the most blameless male in the film, the only one who is not (at least as far as Marnie is concerned) a predator of some kind (even at work, the young man with the Danish has designs on her). What we see is the sailor, concerned about a crying, frightened child, attempting to pacify and comfort her; I see no suggestion that he has the least sexual interest in her. It is clearly Bernice who puts such an idea into Marnie's head, by telling him to take his hands off her (he is stroking Marnie's hair, a typical method of soothing someone); his indignant response ("There's nothing wrong with my hands") is perfectly reasonable. The ensuing struggle is brought on entirely by Bernice (with whom we are identifying if we believe, as some seem to, that the sailor was going to molest Marnie); it results in her broken leg (the twisted, intertwined legs, with Bernice's "noises," becoming Marnie's image for adult sexual intercourse) and the sailor's death.

The image/text discrepancy is resolvable; arguably it is resolved in "There. There now," the words that Marnie spoke to the dead Forio and now addresses to her memories, and to herself. When the images begin (with another *Vertigo*-like zoom-in/track-out), we are given the impression that Marnie is watching them, as we are. Does she learn from them what really happened, and understand at last with whom the real cause of her condition lies? Her benediction (which belongs to the adult Marnie, not the child—she couldn't have spoken it in the past, the memory culminating in the frantic screams of mother and child) suggests that this is at least a possibility.

"WELL, I NEVER SAID I WAS PERFECT"

Before I pass to the film's final scene it behooves me to play fair and do some kind of justice to its male protagonist. Marnie's problem requires a whole movie to bring to light; Mark's disease is evident from his first appearance, in his initial summing up of Marnie ("the brunette with the legs"): the sexist presumption of the Great White Male, especially when it is backed by wealth. Marnie both benefits from his self-assurance and progressively undermines it, though it is left to Bernice to deliver the final blow ("You don't know everything, Mister," at the very moment when he is convinced he does). I described him earlier as Marnie's "instrument," but he is clearly more than that, his initiative necessary to most of the steps toward her cure.

His attitude to Marnie undergoes a thorough transformation as the film progresses. Initially, it is the fascination of a new challenge to a man who believes he can win every battle: Marnie is linked to Sophie, the jaguarundi he has "taught to trust" him, a wild animal he must tame and subjugate to his will. The recurrent imagery underlines this: Marnie, during the honeymoon, cowering on the couch, a beast trapped yet dangerous, as Mark towers over her like a lion tamer; Marnie, after Strutt's reappearance, dressed "like a *cat* burglar," pacing the bedroom in anger, panic, and frustration, the bedposts suggesting the bars of her cage as the camera tracks with her. But, as Marnie undermines his sense of omniscience, turning the psychoanalysis session against him, using him to lead her for the first time to breakdown, and as the depth of her pain and the extremeness of her condition become progressively exposed to him, his attitude changes, deepening to one of genuine caring. Mark is no "pure" saint, the "caring" is never free from desire, but the obsession with control has become greatly modified by the film's end, and we are left to feel that, if Marnie and Mark have a future together, it will be as the partnership of two very strong human beings.

"THERE WAS THIS BOY, BILLY . . ."

Only one character in the film is clearly *in*curable: Bernice. She belongs in the quite considerable gallery of Hitchcock's guilty mothers, though in this case she at least hasn't nurtured a serial killer (think of Uncle Charlie, Norman Bates, Bob Rusk, and arguably Bruno Anthony, who as far as we know has only murdered one woman but has clearly enjoyed it; and even Alex Sebastian smiles into his coffee as he watches his wife drink hers). This should, I think, be the starting point for anyone presumptuous enough to attempt to psychoanalyze Hitchcock. Bernice at least is treated with a certain compassion, as more than just a gargoyle— as, in fact, a person even more in need of help than Marnie but who would never dream of asking for it, incapable of recognizing her sickness beneath its cloak of religiosity. The film places the full responsibility for Marnie's problems on Bernice's shoulders.

We learn little about Marnie's father, Billy, for whom the sailor is some kind of symbolic replacement. Bernice goes all sentimental over Billy and his sweater, as if she feels some tenderness for the boy who initiated her not only into sex but into her career as prostitute. The tenderness seems (if it is not entirely self-delusion) nostalgia for innocence lost; she has tried (quite ineffectually) to preserve Marnie's innocence, denying her the "facts of life" while exposing her ears to the "noises" in the bedroom from which the child has been exiled. By way of education for life she has managed to pass on to Marnie her sense that sex is something disgusting and horrifying, but which Bernice is forced, for reasons that remain mysterious, to perform. The child we see in the flashback is already sick, needing only the trauma of the killing to seal the sickness inside her.

"MOTHER, MOTHER, I AM ILL ..."

It would have been easy for Hitchcock, after the overwhelming effect of the film's climax/catharsis, to fob off the audience with the traditional, easy "happy ending": that favorite Hollywood last line "I'll take you home now," or its variant "We can go home now," almost invariably spoken by the man to the woman. Instead, we are given a perfectly judged assessment of the potentialities. Marnie has confronted and to an extent transcended her trauma, but "cure"?

She remains too deeply disturbed, too damaged, ever to find "cure" beyond a certain point: perhaps an uneasy equilibrium. A terror of sexual intercourse is not got over in a flashback. And Mark, for his part, has not entirely jettisoned his sense of male privilege, the assumption of the right to control that comes as much from his class as his gender. Hence Marnie's less-than-clearly-affirmative but by no means wholly ironic last line: "Oh, Mark, I don't want to go to prison. I'd rather come home with you." Hence also the reiterated refrain of the young girls (who are about the age of Marnie when she killed the sailor), who always seem to be waiting on Bernice's doorstep. And the gender gulf is still present: as the girls chant, the boys are turned away, their backs to them.

On the other hand, Marnie has (back in the house) allowed Mark to smooth her hair, as Bernice cannot bring herself to do, but which the sailor was doing when he tried to soothe Marnie as a child before Bernice told him to take his hands off her. It is, I think, the moment toward which the whole film has been reaching, prepared for in the early scene of Marnie's visit to Bernice; it is the moment that suggests that Mark and Marnie do indeed have a future together (or that successful male/female relations are actually possible within our civilization?). Surely that is why, in the film's last shot, the huge blocking ship has disappeared from the end of the road, and Mark and Marnie can turn off down a side street we didn't know existed. It is arguably the nearest thing to a convincing and *earned* happy ending in any Hitchcock film.

CAN WE IDENTIFY WITH MARNIE?

Freud claimed (correctly, in my opinion) that our entire basic character is formed during the first five years of our lives, the period to which we have least access via memory. It is a truly terrifying perception, which is perhaps why *Marnie* is Hitchcock's most deeply disturbing film. The child Marnie is of course somewhat more than five years old, but the trauma (with its oblivion) places her in much the same situation as the rest of us, the adult Marnie formed by events of which she has no clear or coherent memory. Marnie is on one level a "special case" (not all of us have beaten sailors' heads in with pokers), yet she can also be read as an extreme case of ourselves, living our lives ("A blind man battering blind men") with only the very vaguest notion of how we, as human beings, have been formed, vaguely aware that our behavior is ultimately determined (hard as we may struggle toward full consciousness) by events, relationships, circumstances which we may never be able to drag out from the confusion of our early memories. Is any of us ever "cured"?

Personally, I have never had the least difficulty in identifying with Marnie; I knew, the first time I saw the film, that I *am* Marnie. And so the end of this book, as with every good classical narrative, answers the beginning . . .

BIBLIOGRAPHY

The following books and articles are referred to in the text:

Barr, Charles. *"Blackmail:* Silent and Sound." *Sight and Sound* (spring 1983).
Barthes, Roland. *Mythologies.* London: Jonathan Cape, 1972.
—— *S/Z: An Essay.* New York: Hill and Wang, 1974.
Bellour, Raymond. "Hitchcock the Enunciator." *Camera Obscura* (Fall 1977), no. 2.
—— "Psychosis, Neurosis, Perversion." *Camera Obscura* (1978), no. 3/4.
Britton, Andrew. "Cary Grant: The Comedy of Male Desire." *CineAction!* 7 (1987).
—— *Katharine Hepburn: The Thirties and After.* Tyneside Cinema, 1984.
—— *"Spellbound:* Text and Subtext." *CineAction!* 3/4 (1985).
Brown, Norman O. *Life Against Death.* Middletown, Conn.: Wesleyan University Press, 1959.
Cahiers du Cinéma (editorial collective). *Young Mr. Lincoln:* Available in *Movies and Methods.* Bill Nichols ed., Berkeley: University of California Press, 1976.
Cameron, Ian. *The Man Who Knew Too Much.* Movie 3 and 6. Reprinted in the *Movie Reader,* 1972.
Douchet, Jean. "La Troisième Clef d'Hitchcock." *Cahiers du Cinéma,* no. 113.
Dyer, Richard. *Heavenly Bodies.* New York: St. Martin's Press, 1986.
—— *Stars.* London: British Film Institute, 1979.
Eliot, T. S. "William Blake." In *Selected Essays.* London: Faber and Faber, 1932.
Freud, Sigmund. *Case Histories II,* vol. 9. Pelican Freud Library, 1979.
Greenspun, Roger. "On *Family Plot." Film Comment* (May/June 1976).
Heath, Stephen. "TOUCH OF EVIL." *Screen* (1975), vol. 16, no. 1.
Houston, Penelope. "The Figure in the Carpet." *Sight and Sound* (autumn 1963).
Lawrence, D. H. "Song of a Man Who Has Come Through." *Collected Poems.* Harmondsworth: Penguin, 1977.
Leavis, F. R. *English Literature in Our Time and the University.* London: Chatto and Windus, 1969.
Lippe, Richard. "Kim Novak: A Resistance to Definition." *CineAction!* 7. 1987.

Metz, Christian. *Film Language*. New York: Oxford University Press, 1974.

Modleski, Tania. *The Women Who Knew Too Much: Hitchcock and Feminist Theory*. New York: Methuen, 1988.

Mulvey, Laura. "Visual Pleasure and Narrative Cinema." *Screen* (autumn 1975).

Perkins, V. F. *"ROPE." Movie*, no. 7. Reprinted in *The Movie Reader*. 1972.

Renov, Michael. "From Identification to Ideology: The Male System of *Notorious." Wide Angle* (1980), vol. 4, no. 1.

Rohmer, Eric and Claude Chabrol. *Hitchcock*. New York: Frederick Ungar, 1979.

Rossiter, A. P. *Angel with Horns*. Graham Storey, ed. London: Longmans, 1961.

Rothman, Williams. *The Murderous Gaze*. Cambridge: Harvard University Press, 1982.

Spoto, Donald. *The Art of Alfred Hitchcock*. New York: Dolphin Books, Doubleday, 1979.

—— *The Dark Side of Genius: The Life of Alfred Hitchcock*. New York: Ballantine, 1983.

Trotsky, Leon. *Literature and Revolution*. Ann Arbor: University of Michigan Press, 1960.

Truffaut, François. *Hitchcock*. New York: Simon and Schuster, 1984.

Wollen, Peter. *Signs and Meaning in the Cinema*. London: Secker and Warburg, 1969.

Wood, Robin. *Hollywood from Vietnam to Reagan*. New York: Columbia University Press, 1985.

INDEX